The Great Game in Cuba

Also by Joan Mellen

Our Man in Haiti: George de Mohrenschildt and the CIA in the Nightmare Republic
A Farewell to Justice: Jim Garrison, JFK's Assassination, and the Case That Should Have Changed History
Jim Garrison: His Life and Times, The Early Years
Hellman and Hammett; The Legendary Passion of Lillian Hellman and Dashiell Hammett
Kay Boyle: Author of Herself
"Modern Times"
"In the Realm of the Senses"
"Seven Samurai"
Literary Masterpieces: One Hundred Years of Solitude
Literary Masters: Gabriel García Márquez
Literary Topics: Magic Realism
Bob Knight: His Own Man
Natural Tendencies: A Novel
Privilege: The Enigma of Sasha Bruce
ed. *The World of Luis Buñuel*
Big Bad Wolves: Masculinity in the American Film
The Waves at Genji's Door: Japan Through Its Cinema
Women and Their Sexuality in the New Film
Marilyn Monroe
Filmguide to the Battle of Algiers

The Great Game in Cuba

How the CIA Sabotaged Its Own Plot to Unseat Fidel Castro

By

JOAN MELLEN

Skyhorse Publishing

Skyhorse Publishing books may be purchased in bulk at special discounts for sales promotion, corporate gifts, fund-raising, or educational purposes. Special editions can also be created to specifications. For details, contact the Special Sales Department, Skyhorse Publishing, 307 West 36th Street, 11th Floor, New York, NY 10018 or info@skyhorsepublishing.com.

Skyhorse® and Skyhorse Publishing® are registered trademarks of Skyhorse Publishing, Inc. ®, a Delaware corporation.

www.skyhorsepublishing.com

10 9 8 7 6 5 4 3 2 1

Mellen, Joan.
    The great game in Cuba : how the CIA sabotaged its own plot to unseat Fidel Castro / by Joan Mellen.
        pages cm
    ISBN 978-1-62087-467-7 (hardcover : alk. paper) 1. United States-Relations-Cuba. 2. Cuba-Relations-United States. 3. United States-Foreign relations-1961-1963. 4. United States. Central Intelligence Agency-History-20th century. 5. Espionage, American-Cuba. 6. Subversive activities-Cuba-History-20th century. 7. Castro, Fidel, 1926-Assassination attempts. I. Title.
    E183.8.C9M387 2013
    327.7307291-dc23

                        2012043698

For Malcolm Blunt

TABLE OF CONTENTS

A NOTE ON AN unusual usage: "CIA" is referred to throughout this text without the definite article "the." This stylistic choice is in keeping with the Agency's own practice in referring to itself, both in written and spoken form. No one with more than a passing acquaintance with CIA is likely to affix the definite article "the" before "CIA."

ACKNOWLEDGMENTS

THE GREAT GAME IN CUBA is a work of historical exploration. The sources are either government documents or personal interviews that I conducted. That I was able to document CIA's history in Cuba was largely owing to Congress passing the JFK Assassination Records Collection Act of 1992. Under this mandate, several intelligence agencies were compelled to release tens of thousands of documents, many bearing no relation to the assassination of President Kennedy.

I owe a debt of gratitude to Malcolm Blunt, a connoisseur of documents who shared with me generously the fruits of his research. I can't think of anyone with a more profound acquaintance with the collections at the National Archives or with a stronger understanding of the U.S. intelligence community. It was from Malcolm Blunt that I first heard the names "Czarnikow-Rionda," "Robert J. Kleberg, Jr. (RJK)," and "Michael J. P. Malone."

I am deeply grateful as well to Ralph Schoenman for his support, suggestions, and encouragement throughout the years of this project. His extraordinary generosity knows no parallel.

It has been difficult to penetrate the inner workings of the Central Intelligence Agency because the Agency has so guarded its history. That includes shredding documents and creating others out of whole cloth for the "record." After Allen Dulles' death in 1969, his filing cabinets fell into the hands of former DD/P Richard Helms. Only a fraction of these files is available in the Dulles collection at the Selwyn Mudd Library at Princeton University.

CIA invaded other collections as well. George A. Braga, who presided over the Czarnikow-Rionda sugar brokerage, willed his personal papers to the University of Florida at Gainesville. Braga's papers had not yet been transferred to the library when "two men in suits," as Braga's widow described them, arrived at her door. Believing they had been sent by the University of Florida, Mrs. Braga let them in. Soon they had walked off with five boxes of papers.

"Oh, you're back!" Mrs. Braga said when Carl Van Ness, curator of the University of Florida's Special Collections, arrived. When Van Ness examined the collection, he discovered that the personal letters and correspondence between Braga and Robert J. Kleberg, Jr., his partner at *Becerra,* King Ranch in Cuba, had vanished. Van Ness and Braga's son are convinced that the "men in suits" had been sent by CIA.

Other collections have also been sanitized. Holland McCombs, who worked as Kleberg's speechwriter and was the researcher for Tom Lea's biography of King Ranch, deposited his papers at the University of Tennessee at Martin. McCombs told a librarian there that he had himself been with CIA. When two FBI men arrived at the library to look over the McCombs papers, identifying themselves to curator Richard Saunders, they left empty-handed. McCombs had been scrupulous in sanitizing his own papers.

The Bruce-Lovett Report, a 1956 scathing assessment of CIA's clandestine services commissioned by President Eisenhower, was nowhere to be found. No copy resides at the National Archives. Nor can the Bruce-Lovett Report be found either among the papers of President Eisenhower or its authors, Ambassador David K. E. Bruce and Robert Lovett. Despite his being a government insider, Mr. Bruce was no apologist for the malfeasances of the clandestine services. He should be among the heroes of any historical study of CIA.

For helping me to unravel the double game CIA played with respect to Cuba, I am deeply grateful to Alberto Fernández de Hechavarría, who shared his life story with me, speaking on the

ACKNOWLEDGMENTS xiii

record for the first time. Alberto described the trajectory of his
relationship with CIA, one that reveals the Agency's actual motives
in involving itself in Cuban operations. I am grateful as well to
Alberto's sister Gladys Smithies, a shrewd observer of Cuban history, and to his wife, Joséfina Garcia, and to his nephews Eduardo
Sánchez Rionda and John Smithies.

Dionisio Pastrana, who worked with Alberto Fernández in those
years, shared with me his unique experiences in Cuba. I would also
like to thank Gustavo de los Reyes for recounting his life story as
well as his relationship with Robert J. Kleberg, Jr., and with CIA.
Don Carlson deserves special thanks for his assistance.

I would also like especially to thank Gordon Winslow for introducing me to the Cuban community in Miami, to Jorge Navarro
Custín, and to the late Gaeton Fonzi, who generously offered me
access to his files.

Others who contributed to this narrative include Billie Sol Estes
and his daughter Pamela Estes Padgett; John Quirk and Congressman Ron Paul, along with his assistants Tracee Tolett and Jennifer
Bailey.

Jim Lesar was always available to lend his gracious assistance.
I am grateful as well to John Barbour; Tim Bowden; Lou Wolf;
Dick Russell; Larry Hancock; Rex Bradford; the late Gaeton
Fonzi; Burton Hersh; John Simkin; Greg Wagner; Barry Ford; Ed
Sherry; Jim Hougan; John Tarver; Nathaniel Heidenheimer; Profes-
sor James Cypher; Edward Rynearson; Anne Gentry; Jim Johnson;
Ed Tatro; John Loftus; Peter Lemkin; and Dawn Meredith.

The story of Czarnikow-Rionda could not have been written
without the assistance of Carl Van Ness, the curator of special collections at the University of Florida at Gainesville. Of equal help to me
was Richard Saunders, curator of special collections at the University
of Tennessee at Martin, and his colleague Karen Elmore. I would
like to thank these other librarians: Hope Sudlow, Andrea Merrick
and Diane Miller at Mercer County Library; Michael D. Greco at
Scripps Library of the Miller Center for Public Affairs, the University

of Virginia; Kim Rice at the Dallas World Affairs Council of Dallas/ Fort Worth; Edward Gaynor and Regina Rush at the Albert and Shirley Small Special Collections Library, University of Virginia. At the National Archives, I turned to Martha Wagner Murphy and her assistant, Mary Kay Schmidt.

I am grateful to Temple University for providing me with a research grant to complete this project.

Friends lent their support. I owe a debt in particular to Mya Shone, for her always-lucid critical eye; and to Dan Alcorn, a supportive colleague and friend. I would also like to acknowledge Donald Deeley; Julia Chang; Tiffany Kelly; Ken Mazur; Les Robinson; Joanne Daume; Valery Rafalsky; and Daniel S. Moore, for his militancy of caring. Special thanks and appreciation go to my cousins Judge Gerald Harris and Granny leader, Barbara Harris.

At Skyhorse, I would like to thank my shrewd and unflappable editor, Cory Allyn, and Tony Lyons for the courage to publish books that stray from received wisdom.

INTRODUCTION

A FRIEND SPECIALIZING IN the document collections scattered throughout the National Archives in College Park, Maryland, one day in 2006, shortly after the publication of *A Farewell to Justice* —my study of Jim Garrison's investigation of the Kennedy assassination—intoned the words (apropos of nothing in particular) "Czarnikow-Rionda." I looked at him blankly. He added nothing further, and neither, at that moment, did I.

After he left, intrigued, I went straight to Google. I soon discovered that Czarnikow-Rionda was a major sugar brokerage located in Cuba and boasting a venerable history dating to the early nineteenth century. Prosperous and powerful, with offices on Wall Street in New York City, as well as a controlling lineage of interconnected family members, Czarnikow was a company of which I might well have heard. Yet how, I asked myself, did this sugar conglomerate bear upon my current research and interests that included Japanese cinema, literary biography, and the Kennedy case, if also Latin America?

There the subject remained, moored in a vacuum, until my friend visited again. This time he uttered, in a similar random and seemingly unmotivated manner, the name "Kleberg." He spoke the name with resonance, then waited for my response. Again I drew a blank.

Relenting, my friend smiled and added, "Kleberg was so powerful that he could make a call any time at his own discretion and have Allen Dulles, the Director of Central Intelligence, do his bidding. The same applied to FBI Director J. Edgar Hoover."

xvi THE GREAT GAME IN CUBA

The Kleberg he was referring to was Robert J. Kleberg, Jr., president of King Ranch, the largest in the U.S. and, with nine satellites, the most expansive and powerful in the world. If Kleberg had remained below the radar of history, it was by choice. But by itself, a Texan cattle rancher didn't appear to be a promising subject. I knew nothing about cattle, their raising, or their central role in the development of economies, let alone the empowerment of their grandiose promoters.

Kleberg, as I discovered, was the model for Edna Ferber's crudely racist Bick Benedict in her best-selling potboiler, *Giant*. This certainly did not draw me closer to the man or his history.

I pursued neither "Czarnikow-Rionda" nor "Kleberg" in the course of my research until my friend added a third name, this time with a telephone number. It was that of "Alberto Fernández." Fernández, it soon emerged, was a figure who loomed large in the political struggles of the mid-twentieth century. He was a Cuban who, like Kleberg, did not court notoriety, but who emerged, discretion notwithstanding, as no less significant a personage. And I had not only a telephone number, but a home address in Key Biscayne, Florida. I telephoned Alberto Fernández, expecting to be rebuffed. For the first, if not the last time, Alberto Fernández surprised me.

They were all connected: Robert J. Kleberg, Jr. and George A. Braga, president of Czarnikow-Rionda, were partners in King Ranch's Cuban satellite, known as *Compañía Ganadera Becerra*. This ranch was managed by a long-time CIA asset, a vice-president of Czarnikow named Michael J. P. Malone. Until he was summoned by Kleberg (a summons no player in the world of Cuban wealth and politics in the years before the revolution could ignore), Malone was perched on Wall Street, absorbed in the volatility of the global market for sugar. He already possessed a number of high-level CIA officers as contacts, along with J. Edgar Hoover and the leading figure at the FBI's New York field office.

Alberto Fernández was married to a beautiful and elegant daughter of the Riondas. He commanded five cattle ranches in Cuba, along with a huge sugar mill. The forebears of Alberto Fernández had migrated from Spain; his grandfathers, no less than his father, were all far richer than he. Before long, Alberto Fernández would address Kleberg as "uncle" and communicate with Malone on a regular basis. For George A. Braga, however, and the methods through which he operated Czarnikow, Alberto Fernández felt only disdain.

The interlocking story of these men of privilege and power reveals the history and dynamics of the Cuban Revolution from an unexpected vantage: their ambiguous internal war with CIA on which they relied, while challenging the Cuban Revolution and the government of Fidel Castro. This life and death conflict encompassed a struggle about which you will not read either in anti-Castro or pro-Castro histories. *The Great Game in Cuba* is that story.

TIMELINE OF EVENTS IN THIS STORY

July 10, 1824: Birth of Richard King in New York City.

April 21, 1836: Sam Houston is victorious at the Battle of San Jacinto and the Republic of Texas is born.

December 5, 1853: Birth of Robert Justus Kleberg II, father of Robert J. Kleberg, Jr.

April 14, 1885: Death of Captain Richard King.

November 18, 1887: Birth of Richard M. Kleberg.

October 23, 1888: Death of Robert Justus Kleberg.

March 29, 1896: Birth of Robert J. Kleberg, Jr.

1925: Robert J. Kleberg, Jr. is appointed "General Manager" of King Ranch.

March 31, 1925: Death of Henrietta King.

March 2, 1926: Robert J. Kleberg, Jr. marries Helen Campbell.

November 24, 1931: Richard Kleberg is elected to the U.S. Congress.

October 10, 1932: Death of Robert Justus Kleberg II, father of Robert J. Kleberg, Jr.

1933: Robert J. Kleberg, Jr. grants Humble Oil leases to drill for oil on King Ranch to pay his inheritance taxes.

1933: As part of a coup against Gerardo Machado, Batista rises to power.

1939: The wells come in at King Ranch.

1940-1944: Batista rules as President of Cuba.

June 1941: Edna Ferber visits King Ranch.

December 18, 1944: Richard Kleberg loses his congressional seat to John E. Lyle, Jr.

September 18, 1947: Founding of CIA.

June 18, 1948: George Kennan authors National Security Council Directive 10/2, granting CIA unlimited paramilitary powers.

1950: Robert J. Kleberg, Jr. meets George A. Braga in Havana.

November 26, 1950: Robert J. Kleberg, Jr. meets Michael J. P. Malone.

May 1951: Kleberg returns to Cuba.

March 10, 1952–December 31, 1958: Batista rules as dictator of Cuba.

1952: Publication of Edna Ferber's potboiler, *Giant.*

1952: Robert J. Kleberg, Jr. meets Alberto Fernández in Cuba.

February 26, 1953: Allen Dulles becomes Director of Central Intelligence.

October 20, 1953: Centennial Conference at King Ranch.

May 8, 1955: Death of Richard Kleberg.

December 1955: First Santa Gertrudis cattle from King Ranch arrive in Cuba.

November 25, 1958: Alberto Fernández accused by the FBI of violating the Neutrality Act for his actions on behalf of the 26th of July Movement; Kleberg and Dulles come to his rescue.

January 1, 1959: Victory of the 26th of July Movement; Fidel Castro takes power in Cuba.

January 3, 1959: Alberto Fernández returns to Cuba from exile.

January 5, 1959: Alberto Fernández enlisted by the new Castro government to run the sugar industry.

February 1959: Friendship between Alberto Fernández and Humberto Sorí Marín begins.

June 12, 1959: Humberto Sorí Marín resigns as Castro's Minister of Agriculture.

June 1959: Kleberg and Malone in New York visit Cardinal Spellman and the *New York Times*, and, in Washington, J. Edgar Hoover and the State Department.

August 1959: Arrest of Gustavo de los Reyes by the Castro regime.

October 1, 1959: Fidel Castro confiscates *Becerra*.

October 28, 1959: Death of Camilo Cienfuegos.

May 1, 1960: Taking down of the U-2 over the Soviet Union.

July 14, 1960: Alberto Fernández de Hechavarría leaves Cuba and enters into permanent exile in the United States.

September 10, 1960: Alberto Fernández makes his first maritime foray into Castro's Cuba.

March 1961: Alberto and the *Tejana* infiltrate 19,000 pounds of ammunition into Cuba.

March 1, 1961: Humberto Sorí Marín arrives in the United States to present his "Plan" for an invasion of Cuba to CIA. The "Plan" presented to the Agency is dated March 4, 1961.

March 12, 1961: Humberto Sorí Marín infiltrated back into Cuba.

March 18, 1961: Capture of Humberto Sorí Marín.

April 17, 1961: CIA invades Cuba at the Bay of Pigs.

April 20, 1961: Execution of Humberto Sorí Marín.

April 24, 1961: Alberto Fernández meets with Bernard Reichhardt, Acting Chief of Western Hemisphere 4 Operations (WH/4).

November 29, 1961: Allen Dulles fired by President Kennedy.

May 20, 1963: Dionisio Pastrana infiltrates Cuba and heads for Nipe Bay.

June 12, 1963: Death of Helen Kleberg.

November 22, 1963: Assassination of President John F. Kennedy in Dallas, Texas.

February 25, 1964: Gustavo de los Reyes is released from prison and leaves Cuba on his special mission, ostensibly for Fidel Castro.

February 1965: Final meeting of Alberto Fernández with his CIA handler Robert Wall.

October 1967: CIA's David Atlee Phillips orders that JMWAVE sever all contact with Alberto Fernández.

January 29, 1968: Termination document of CIA's relationship with Alberto Fernández.

March 12, 1971: Death of Michael J. P. Malone.

October 13, 1974: Death of Robert J. Kleberg, Jr.

October 14, 2012: Death of Alberto Fernández.

CAST OF CHARACTERS

Artime, Manuel: Born in Cuba in 1932, Artime joined the Cuban Revolution only at the penultimate moment, in late December 1958. Immediately he joined the anti-Communist opposition, forming the Movement for the Recovery of the Revolution Party (MRP). On CIA's payroll, he influenced the staging of the Bay of Pigs invasion at *Playa Girón*. Over the years, Artime remained on the Agency payroll.

Baggs, William ("Bill"): Editor of the *Miami News* from 1957 to his death in 1969. Baggs was a participant in CIA's Operation Mockingbird, an effort begun by Frank Wisner to penetrate and influence the American media to adopt CIA policies. Among the journalists who signed on to Operation Mockingbird, in addition to Baggs, were Stuart Alsop, James Reston, and Ben Bradlee. Baggs remained close to CIA. He was strongly anti-Communist and anti-Castro.

Bancroft, Mary: Born in 1903, Mary Bancroft is known for her love affair with Allen Dulles in Bern during his time with OSS. Dulles hired Bancroft to translate the work of Hans Bernd Gisevius, who had been part of a plot to assassinate Adolf Hitler. Among Bancroft's Bern acquaintances was the psychiatrist Carl Jung, to whom she introduced Dulles. Jung was not impressed. Dulles was a "tough nut," Jung thought.

Bayo, Eddie: Member of the crew of the *Tejana*. Bayo fought with Castro against Batista, only later to join the anti-Castro movement. Bayo died inside Cuba, having been captured during William Paley's ill-fated expedition.

Betancourt, Rómulo: Served two terms as president of Venezuela, from 1945–1948 and again from 1959–1964. Betancourt reformed the oil industry of Venezuela and was a strong opponent of Dominican Republic dictator, Rafael Trujillo.

Bissell, Richard: Bissell joined CIA in 1954 and quickly rose in the ranks. In 1956, as head of the clandestine services (DD/P), he was in charge of the top secret U-2 spy plane project. Bissell's next assignment was the Bay of Pigs invasion; its failure led to his immediate resignation from the Agency.

Bonsal, Philip: United States ambassador to Cuba following the victory of Fidel Castro in 1959.

Braga, George A., and B. Rionda ("Ronny"): Cuban directors of the Czarnikow-Rionda Company sugar brokerage. Czarnikow-Rionda was actually a consortium of sugar companies that included Cuban Trading, which acted as a middleman for the Braga enterprises. George Braga was a long-time associate of Allen Dulles.

Browder, Edward: Soldier of fortune and CIA asset involved in Latin American adventures.

Brown, Herman and George: Proprietors of global construction company Brown & Root; CIA assets from the early 1950s on; and patrons of Texas politician Lyndon Baines Johnson. Johnson secured for the Browns the contract for the Marshall Ford Dam in 1937 and the Corpus Christi Naval Station in 1940, among other projects.

Brown, Robert K.: Editor of *Soldier of Fortune* magazine and, as an anti-Castro adventurer, an associate of Martin Xavier Casey and Gerald Patrick Hemming.

Bruce, David K. E.: Born in Baltimore in 1898, Bruce served in World War I. In 1926, he married the daughter of Andrew Mellon. During World War II, Bruce was in charge of the London branch of the Office of Strategic Services. Bruce went on to become the pre-mier American diplomat of the twentieth century, serving as United States Ambassador to France; to West Germany; and to the Court of St. James's (Great Britain). He also served as Ambassador to NATO and opened China for President Nixon. According to Tim Weiner, author of *Legacy of Ashes*, the Bruce-Lovett Report, commissioned by President Eisenhower as an examination of CIA's clandestine ser-vices, "would have destroyed the agency." Today CIA denies that the Bruce-Lovett Report ever existed.

Bush, George H. W.: Long-time Central Intelligence Agency asset, Bush served as vice president of the United States from 1981 to 1989 and president from 1989 to 1993. In the wake of the Church Committee hearings, Bush served as Director of Central Intelligence in 1976, a position he held for a year.

Bush, George W.: President of the United States from 2000 to 2008.

Cardona, Miró: Cardona was another of the anti-Castro politicians at CIA's feeding trough. Cardona fled Cuba in late 1960, and soon became the leader of the CIA-created-and-controlled Cuban Revo-lutionary Council (CRC).

Castro, Fidel: Following years leading the 26th of July Movement against the dictator Fulgencia Batista, Castro took power on Janu-ary 1, 1959. At once Castro provided dramatic improvements in the lives of the Cuban people: medical care, literacy, and universal education. The American embargo of Cuba, and the deprivation it occasioned, played a role in the rapid deterioration of civil liberties in Cuba. Several of the figures in this story, like Alberto Fernández and Gustavo de los Reyes, both dedicated opponents of the dictator Fulgencio Batista, were taken by surprise by the excesses of the Castro government.

Casey, Martin Xavier: CIA-connected soldier of fortune born in Philadelphia. Casey participated in a CIA-financed invasion of Haiti in the late 1960s.

Cienfuegos, Camilo: By 1954, Cienfuegos had become part of the revolutionary movement against President Fulgencio Batista. He joined Fidel Castro's 26th of July Movement in Mexico and became a leading figure and among the most popular of the *comandantes*. Cienfuegos perished in late October 1959 under circumstances that were not explained satisfactorily.

Colby, William: Colby joined OSS during World War II and CIA in 1951. He worked as chief of station in Saigon from 1959 to 1962 and in the Far East Division from 1962 to 1967. A Princeton classmate of Alberto Fernández, Colby directed the Phoenix Program in Vietnam from 1968 to 1971. He disappeared during a solitary canoe trip on April 28, 1996.

Collins, Edward: Collins was a gunrunner and purveyor of arms and explosives to Cuban exiles. He was a cohort of Gerald Patrick Hemming, who was with him when he drowned. A CIA asset, Collins listed his profession as "Marine Surveyor."

Cuesta, Tony: Anti-Castro activist and member of the crew of the *Tejana*. Cuesta was an intelligence officer for Castro before he defected in 1960. He went on to establish two groups, Alpha 66 and Commandos Liberty (Commandos L). Cuesta was captured during a raid into Cuba on May 29, 1960. Attempting to commit suicide, he set off a grenade, blinding himself and blowing off his right hand. Cuesta was released from a Cuban jail in 1978 when he returned to Miami.

Custín, Jorge Navarro: Naval historian, former Cuban army captain, and anti-Castro activist in Miami.

Davidson, Isadore Irving: Davidson began his career working for the War Production Board in Washington, D.C., in 1941. He became a licensed arms dealer and lobbyist for such dictators as Somoza in Nicaragua and Duvalier in Haiti. When Batista was overthrown, Davidson began working for the anti-Castro movement even as he attempted to secure for Batista residence in the United States, distributing the appropriate bribes. Davidson was close to both J. Edgar Hoover at the FBI and to CIA, for whom he supplied arms.

Díaz, Eugenio de Sosa: Son-in-law of the owner of *El Diario de la Marina*, Ignacio Rivera. Eugenio went to Choate with Alberto Fernández.

Díaz Lanz, Pedro: Díaz Lanz joined the 26th of July Movement in 1957. He became chief of the revolutionary Air Force of Cuba and Fidel Castro's personal pilot. Castro fired him on June 29, 1959, after which Díaz Lanz left Cuba with Frank Sturgis. By October 21st, he was dropping anti-Communist leaflets over Havana with his brother, Marcos Díaz Lanz. CIA recruited him as a member of Operation 40. Díaz Lanz committed suicide in 2008 at the age of eighty-one, after years of poverty and depression.

Dodd, Thomas J: United States senator from Connecticut, 1959–1971. Previously Dodd had been a special agent for the FBI and participated in the Nuremberg Trials. He was a lobbyist for the Guatemalan dictator Carlos Castillo Armas and was later censured by the Senate for misappropriation of campaign funds, having used these funds for his personal use.

Dorticós Torrado, Osvalado: President of Cuba from July 17, 1959, to December 2, 1976.

Dulles, Allen: By 1922, Dulles was at the state department as chief of the Division of Near Eastern Affairs. Dulles practiced law through the 1930s for Sullivan & Cromwell, where he represented many Nazi and pro-Nazi clients. Dulles assumed a leading role, behind the scenes, in the creation of CIA in 1947. He was employed officially by the Agency only in 1951, as Deputy Director. Two years later, Dulles became Director of Central Intelligence. He ran CIA until he was fired by President John F. Kennedy after the fiasco of the Bay of Pigs invasion. Even as Dulles "resigned," he continued to influence Agency operations until his death in 1969.

Eisenhower, Dwight David: Supreme Commander of the Allied Expeditionary Force for Operation Overlord, the invasion of France, during World War II. Eisenhower went on to serve two terms as president of the United States, from 1953 to 1961. He was known for downsizing the military and ending the Korean conflict. CIA destroyed his presidency with its insistence upon sending out one last U-2, the one manned by Francis Gary Powers and taken down by the Soviets.

Ellender, Allen J.: United States senator from Louisiana from January 3, 1937, to July 27, 1972. Ellender, a Democrat, supported Huey P. Long and came to oppose the Vietnam War. While he was, predictably, an opponent of civil rights, Ellender was also an opponent of Senator Joseph McCarthy.

Escalante, Fabián: Security chief for Fidel Castro at the time of the Cuban Revolution.

Estes, Billie Sol: King of the wheeler-dealers and intimately connected to Lyndon Johnson, who enjoyed the profits of Estes' cotton allotment, grain storage, and fertilizer scams. Billie Sol Estes served eight years in prison.

Fanjul, Alfonso: Head of Cuban Trading and collaborator of George A. Braga and B. Rionda Braga.

Ferber, Edna: Best-selling author of *Cimarron, Showboat,* and *Giant,* an attack on Robert J. Kleberg, Jr. and King Ranch that went on to sell three million copies. *Giant* was adapted into a major film directed by George Stevens and starring Rock Hudson as a racist Kleberg; Elizabeth Taylor; and James Dean in his final film role as Glenn McCarthy, a vulgar Texas oilman. In the millennium, *Giant* was adapted into a musical.

Fernández Casas, Federico: Father of Alberto Fernández and former member of the Cuban Senate.

Fernández de Hechavarría, Alberto: Son of a prominent politician and rancher, Alberto Fernández became a leading figure in the opposition to Fidel Castro, having run Cuba's sugar industry for one crop after Castro's victory. In July 1960, Fernández left Cuba for good. His efforts on behalf of an opposition movement inside Cuba, called *Unidad Revolucionaria,* were facilitated in part by Robert J. Kleberg, Jr. and his right-hand man, Michael J. P. Malone. Fernández came to be known as "the man of the boats" for his extraordinary efforts at sea.

Fitzgerald, Desmond: Fitzgerald worked for OSS during World War II. In 1962, he was named CIA's chief of the Cuban Task Force and supervised a Castro official named Rolando Cubela in his failed assassination attempt on Castro's life. In 1965, Fitzgerald was promoted to Deputy Director for Plans (DD/P). During the events of this narrative, Fitzgerald was part of CIA's SAS, Special Affairs Staff.

Forrestal, James: A Wall Street investor, Forrestal was called to testify before a Senate subcommittee in 1933 regarding accusations that he had taken part in investment practices that contributed to the Great Depression. Having worked with Allen Dulles and his Nazi clients in the 1930s, Forrestal was appointed Secretary of the Navy under President Roosevelt. As Truman's secretary of defense, Forrestal opposed the recognition of Israel, for which Truman fired him. Forrestal's suicide followed.

Franqui, Carlos: Member of the 26th of July Movement, journalist and poet, editor of the movement newspaper *Revolución*, and head of the station *Radio Rebelde.* Franqui broke with Castro and left Cuba in 1968. His searing account of the deterioration of the revolution, *Family Portrait with Fidel* (1984), is his major work.

Frondizi, Arturo: Lawyer and president of Argentina from 1958 to 1961. Frondizi had been an activist against the dictatorship of Juan Perón. His party was the "Intransigent Radical Civic Union." At one point, Frondizi met with Fidel Castro and Che Guevara in the hope of mediating their dispute with the United States.

Garrison, Jim: District Attorney of Orleans Parish who devoted himself to an investigation of the assassination of President John F. Kennedy. Garrison indicted Clay Shaw, a "highly paid" CIA contract employee and the director of the International Trade Mart, for participation in a conspiracy to murder President Kennedy.

Geddes, Robert: Pepsi-Cola executive and long-time CIA contact.

Gilmore, Ken: *Reader's Digest* editor and long-time CIA contact.

Goldberg, Arthur: Lawyer, aide to President Franklin Delano Roosevelt, and later Justice on the United States Supreme Court.

Gould, Jay: Nineteenth-century robber baron, anti-union, cutthroat railroad developer, and speculator. Among his holdings were the Erie Railroad and, later, the Union Pacific. He participated in the completion of the First Transcontinental Railroad and the Missouri Pacific.

Halliburton, Erle: While working in the oil industry, Halliburton learned the techniques for cementing the inner walls of oil wells. He was fired from his first job for implementing his techniques without authorization. In 1919, stealing the patents of his previous employers, Halliburton started the New Method Oil Well Cementing Company. Having bought out most of his competitors, by 1957 Halliburton had become among the richest men in America. In 1961, the New Method Oil Well Cementing Company changed its name to Halliburton.

Hanscomb, Rafael Díaz: One of the three major leaders of the *Unidad* movement, Hanscomb was executed in Havana, along with Humberto Sorí Marín.

Harvey, William K.: FBI officer who resigned after a Hoover reprimand and joined CIA. Harvey worked with Ted Shackley at the Berlin station, and for the Special Group Augmented (which was responsible for Operation Mongoose) for President Kennedy, devoted to sabotage against Cuba. He recruited Mafia leaders to kill Castro. After the Cuban Missile Crisis, when Operation Mongoose was canceled, Harvey became CIA station chief in Rome. He was known for having developed CIA's Executive Action (murder) program.

Helms, Richard: After the departure of Richard Bissell following the Bay of Pigs defeat, Helms became head of the clandestine services. In 1966, he was promoted to Director of Central Intelligence, a position he held until 1973. Helms' departure from CIA was accompanied by a perjury conviction in federal court involving CIA's illegal activities in Chile.

Hemming, Gerald Patrick: Former self-proclaimed U.S. Marine and long-time CIA-connected soldier of fortune participating in efforts against the regime of Fidel Castro, particularly at No Name

Key in Florida. A note by Colonel James Patchell to Colonel Edward Lansdale, dated August 1962, clearly demonstrates Hemming's CIA connections: Patchell's note is a recommendation for the use of Hemming and his group, Interpen, by the Agency. Hemming boasted that his assets inside Cuba were the first to reveal the presence of Soviet offensive nuclear weapons in Cuba.

Herbert, Raford: After first working for the FBI, Herbert joined CIA in 1947 and served until 1965. During his time with the Agency, Herbert was chief of station at various Latin American venues including Argentina, Uruguay, Brazil, and Chile.

Hogan, Donald: Employee at the Sugar Institute in Cuba and intelligence-connected associate of Alberto Fernández. Hogan's brother, Tony, headed a big sugar brokerage based out of New York.

Hoover, J. Edgar: Under pressure to quell anarchist and Marxist activity, Attorney General A. Mitchell Palmer put Hoover in charge of its suppression. Executing the "Palmer Raids" (1919–1920), Hoover sealed his reputation for ferocity. In 1924, Hoover was named Director of the Bureau of Investigation, later renamed the FBI, a position he held until his death in 1972. In 1976, Frank Church's senate investigative committee concluded that Hoover's tactics were in frequent violation of the U.S. Constitution.

Houston, Lawrence: Having graduated from the University of Virginia law school, Houston served with OSS in the Middle East. He joined the Agency in 1947. Houston was CIA's general counsel from 1947 to 1973. Among his efforts was keeping evidence of CIA's having hired Mafia hit men to assassinate Fidel Castro. Houston participated in CIA's 1954 overthrow of Guatemalan president Jacobo Árbenz Guzmán.

Houston, Sam: A disciple of Andrew Jackson, Houston moved to Texas having already served as Governor of Tennessee. He signed the

Texas Declaration of Independence on March 2, 1836, on his 43rd birthday. Two days later, Houston was named commander-in-chief of the Texas Army. Houston's victory at the Battle of San Jacinto on April 21, 1836, led to the creation of the Republic of Texas as a separate commonwealth. Houston was elected the first president of the Republic of Texas on September 5, 1836; he was elected a second time on December 13, 1841. After the annexation of Texas to the United States, Houston served in the U.S. Senate from 1846 to 1859 and as governor of Texas from 1859 to 1861. He opposed the secession of Texas from the union. Having refused to sign the Articles of Confederation, Houston stepped down as governor.

Hunt, H. L.: Born Haroldson Lafayette Hunt, Hunt had 900 wells in East Texas by 1932 and had become among the richest men in the world. Hunt was also known for his right-wing political beliefs, which he promoted on two radio programs and in an endless stream of pamphlets and letters to politicians in high office.

Hunt, Ray L.: Youngest son of H. L. Hunt, from his "second family," Ray Hunt inherited Hunt Oil when his father died in 1974. In 1984, Hunt discovered massive oil reserves in Yemen, which turned out to be the largest component of his fortune. Prior to the Yemen discovery, Hunt had been worth $200 million; in 2006, his fortune was estimated at $4.6 billion.

Hurwitch, Robert: Foreign service officer and deputy assistant secretary of state for Inter-American affairs. From 1962 to 1963, Hurwitch was the special assistant for Cuban affairs, where he negotiated the release of Bay of Pigs prisoners and served as part of the team discussing the Cuban Missile Crisis. He was a CIA asset, and served as ambassador to the Dominican Republic in the 1970s.

Johnson, Belton Kleberg: Son of Sarah Spohn Kleberg, younger sister of Robert J. Kleberg, Jr. and, as Kleberg's nephew, aspirant to the presidency of King Ranch.

Johnson, Lyndon Baines: Johnson began as secretary to Congressman Richard Kleberg in 1932. Thanks to the efforts of Brown & Root lawyer Alvin Wirtz, Johnson gained a seat in Congress in 1937 following the untimely death of a Texas congressman. Johnson became a United States senator having "stolen" the election of 1948; he was known by the sobriquet "The Senator from Brown & Root." Johnson became vice president of the United States in 1961 and president following the murder of President John F. Kennedy in 1963. Having defeated Barry Goldwater for the presidency in 1964, Johnson earned the wrath of a majority of the population for his pursuit of a war in Vietnam. Unable to appear in public without attracting protesters, Johnson retired in 1968, choosing not to seek re-election.

Kendall, Don: Pepsi-Cola executive with strong ties to the Central Intelligence Agency.

Kennan, George: Kennan served the state department in various posts in Eastern Europe and at the embassy in Moscow during World War II. He stood for the policy of containment of Communism and was enlisted by Allen Dulles to author National Security Council Directive 10/2, granting the Office of Policy Coordination (CIA) free reign over paramilitary, covert, and assassination capabilities. In later years, as a scholar at the Institute for Advanced Studies at Princeton University, Kennan called 10/2 the "greatest mistake" of his life.

Kennedy, John F.: The thirty-fifth president of the United States, Kennedy was assassinated in Dallas, Texas, on November 22, 1963. John F. Kennedy was the first and last president to stand up to CIA in its continuous attempt to gain power and retain its independence from the scrutiny of elected officials and the public.

Khrushchev, Nikita: First secretary of the Communist Party of the Soviet Union from 1953 to 1964, and premier from 1958 to 1964. Khrushchev's history includes carrying out a "Great Purge" in the Ukraine in 1938, where Stalin ordered him to execute any officers of the Red Army suspected of planning to restore capitalism in the region. After World War II, Khrushchev remained the overseer of the Ukraine. In 1956, Premier Khrushchev denounced Stalin and the Great Purge and called for change in Communist Party policy. After taking down Francis Gary Powers' U-2 spy plane in Soviet airspace, Khrushchev refused to meet with President Eisenhower at the 1960 Paris summit conference. His efforts at détente with President Kennedy were interrupted by the placement of offensive nuclear weapons in Cuba. Two years after the Cuban Missile Crisis, Khrushchev was forced to resign.

King, Henrietta: Wife of Captain Richard King, mother of Alice King Kleberg, and grandmother of Robert J. Kleberg, Jr.

King, Richard: Richard King, founder of King Ranch, which was to become the largest ranch in the United States, was born in New York City in 1824. He was the grandfather of Robert J. Kleberg, Jr. From a boy runaway, King became a riverboat captain, then a rancher, on the advice of his friend General Robert E. Lee, who presided over the defeat of the Confederacy at Appomattox. By the time of his death, Richard King owned more than 600,000 acres of land in southern Texas.

Kleberg, Alice King: Youngest daughter of Captain Richard King and Henrietta King and mother of Robert J. Kleberg, Jr.

Kleberg, Caesar: Cousin of Robert J. Kleberg, Jr. and his mentor at King Ranch. Caesar Kleberg was active in conservation and the preservation of animal species.

Kleberg, Helen Campbell: Wife of Robert J. Kleberg, Jr., daughter of a Kansas congressman, and a superb horsewoman.

Kleberg, Helenita: Only child of Robert J. Kleberg, Jr. and Helen Kleberg.

Kleberg, Robert Justus: Robert Justus Kleberg, the paternal grandfather of Robert J. Kleberg, Jr., fought at the Battle of San Jacinto under General Sam Houston. Later, a figure of distinction in the legal community, he served as a judge in the Republic of Texas.

Kleberg, Robert Justus, II: Born in 1853, Kleberg practiced law in Corpus Christi. In 1881, he served as counsel in a case on the side opposing Richard King. King was so impressed that he hired Kleberg as his own lawyer. Kleberg married Richard and Henrietta King's youngest daughter, Alice, in 1886. They had two sons and three daughters. Their eldest son, Richard Mifflin Kleberg, became a U.S. congressman and served from 1932 to 1944. Robert Justus Kleberg continued to acquire land to add to King Ranch. By the time of his death in 1932, King Ranch had grown to more than one million acres.

Kleberg, Robert Justus, Jr.: Grandson of Richard King and Robert Justus Kleberg, "Mr. Bob" was born to Robert Justus Kleberg II and Alice King Kleberg in 1896. He took over managing King Ranch in 1919 when his father's health began to decline. In 1934, Alice Kleberg consolidated King Ranch into a corporation with her children as stockholders. Richard became chairman of the board and Bob Kleberg became CEO, the position he held until his death fifty years later. Among Bob Kleberg's achievements was the creation of the first new breed of cattle certified in the Americas, the "Santa Gertrudis," named for the original land grant of King Ranch. Kleberg died in 1974 at the age of seventy-eight.

Laborde, Lawrence: New Orleans native and long-time CIA contact. Laborde served as the American captain on Alberto Fernández's boat, the *Tejana*, as it moved in and out of Cuba exfiltrating and infiltrating people and delivering arms and explosives.

Laborde, Michael: Son of Lawrence Laborde.

Lansdale, General Edward: As a member of the Office of Strategic Services, Lansdale worked in the Philippines during World War II. Under military cover, Lansdale served most of his career with CIA. Allen Dulles arranged the funding for Lansdale to return to the Philippines in 1950 to suppress a Communist uprising. When Dulles became DCI, Lansdale was sent to Vietnam to deal with the Vietminh. Lansdale was instrumental in putting the corrupt Diem government into power in South Vietnam and coordinating the annual $250 million contribution from the United States. In 1957, Lansdale began working for the secretary of defense under President Eisenhower and soon became involved in the plots to overthrow Fidel Castro. On November 1, 1963, Lansdale "retired" from the Air Force as a Major General, which rank was advanced to Brigadier General.

Lanuza, José: Mayor of Havana and friend of Alberto Fernández in Cuba.

Lee, Robert E.: U.S. Army officer and general who participated in the surrender of the Confederacy at Appomattox. Lee was a friend and advisor of Captain Richard King.

Lobo, Julio: The most powerful sugar broker in the world before the Cuban Revolution, Lobo was born of Jewish parents in Venezuela, but grew up in Havana. He had offices in Havana, New York, London, Madrid, and Manila. Lobo left Cuba in 1960.

Lovett, Robert: Secretary of defense under President Harry S. Truman. As deputy secretary of defense, Lovett was instrumental in the creation of CIA. Co-author with David K. E. Bruce of the Bruce-Lovett Report, a study of the clandestine services of CIA commissioned by President Eisenhower.

Mallon, Henry Neil: While attending Yale, Mallon became close friends with Prescott Bush. Working for the investment firm W. A. Harriman and Company, Bush secured the accounts for Dresser Industries when they went public in 1928. Neil Mallon was named president of Dresser Industries. Mallon returned the favor by employing Prescott's son, George Herbert Walker Bush, in his first job at a division of Dresser Industries. Mallon founded the Dallas Council on World Affairs, a sister organization of New York's Council on Foreign Relations, dedicated to furthering the political perspective of the Central Intelligence Agency.

Malone, Michael J. P.: "Jack" Malone was vice president of the Czarnikow-Rionda sugar brokerage and the right-hand man to its chief, George A. Braga. Previously, Jack had served as the secretary and aide to Francis, Cardinal Spellman, the archbishop of New York. When George Braga and B. Rionda Braga needed to solve the squatter problem on their Cuban land, they turned to Malone.

Manrara, Luis V.: Executive director of "The Truth About Cuba Committee" and recipient of assistance from Robert J. Kleberg, Jr.

Martino, John: Worked in the Havana casino owned by Santos Trafficante. In July 1959, Martino was arrested for having made critical remarks about Fidel Castro and for helping *Batistianos* escape from the island. Martino served three years in prison in Cuba.

Masferrer Rojas, Rolando: Masferrer fought in the Spanish Civil War on the Republican side. In 1938, he was injured when he was shot in the foot. He joined the Communist Party before moving back to

Cuba. Masferrer was elected to the Cuban legislature in 1949 where he was a strong supporter of President Carlos Prío Socarrás. When Batista overthrew Socarrás in 1952, Masferrer supported Batista. He formed an army called "El Tigres" and used it to quell the opposition to Batista. Masferrer fled to Miami after Castro overthrew Batista.

Matos, Huber: Former *comandante* in the 26th of July Movement, Matos was jailed by Fidel Castro in October 1959 and served two decades in Castro's *La Cabaña* prison.

Matt, Charles W.: CIA paramilitary officer and intermediary for Gustavo de los Reyes in his dealings with *Reader's Digest* magazine.

Matthews, Herbert: *New York Times* reporter who interviewed Fidel Castro in the *Sierra Maestra* in early 1957. In January 1958, Che Guevara was reported to have said, "When the world had given us up for dead, the interview with Matthews put the lie to our disappearance."

McCombs, Holland: *Time-Life* employee and factotum and speech-writer for Robert J. Kleberg, Jr.

McCone, John: By 1933, McCone was an executive vice president of Consolidated Steel. Together with a classmate named Stephen Bechtel, McCone formed the Bechtel-McCone Corporation in 1937. After the war, President Truman appointed McCone to the Air Policy Commission. McCone served in 1948 as special advisor to James Forrestal and was appointed undersecretary at the Air Force in 1950. In 1961, McCone replaced Allen Dulles as director of central intelligence. McCone retired from CIA in April 1965.

Meany, George: President of the American Federation of Labor, 1952–1955. Meany proposed the merger of the AFL with the Congress of Industrial Organizations and served as president of the AFL-CIO from 1955 to 1979. He was a strong anti-Communist.

Montgomery, Field Marshal Bernard: The most famous British army officer of World War II, commander of the Eighth Army in the Western Desert. Montgomery ("Monty") was the victor against the Italians at the Battle of El Alamein, considered by Winston Churchill to be the turning point of the war.

Moscoso Mora, José Teodoro: Puerto Rican politician and head of "Operation Bootstrap" to increase employment in Puerto Rico by furthering industrialization. In 1961, John F. Kennedy named Moscoso coordinator of the Alliance for Progress. From 1961 to 1963, Moscoso served as U.S. ambassador to Venezuela.

Murchison, Clint, Jr.: Like his father, Clint Murchison, Jr. was known for taking risks in business. The mirror opposite of his father's success, it is estimated that Murchison, Jr. was $500 million in debt at the time of his death in 1987. Among his successful enterprises was establishing the NFL football franchise, the Dallas Cowboys.

Murchison, Clint, Sr.: Murchison found oil on land in Wichita Falls, Texas, which he sold at a huge profit. In 1928 he founded Murchison Oil, and in 1929 established the Southwest Drilling Company and the Southern Union Gas Company. Like many Texas oilmen, Murchison was opposed to government restrictions on oil production, called pro-rationing. Murchison ignored these laws and amassed vast wealth, producing "hot oil," a term used to describe the oil which surpassed the pro-rationing limits. By the time Murchison retired in 1964, his net worth was more than $500 million.

Northway, Dr. J. K.: Veterinarian at King Ranch.

O'Brien, Frank: FBI special agent in the Bureau's New York field office and contact of Michael J. P. Malone.

Ochsner, Dr. Alton: Medical doctor, long-time CIA asset, and friend of Clay Shaw in New Orleans.

Parr, George and Parr, Archer: Corrupt South Texas politicians, both of whom served jail time. A long-time ally of Lyndon Johnson, George Parr was known as the "Duke of Duval." Eventually his evil doings caught up with him and he committed suicide.

Pastrana, Dionisio (Dennis): Anti-Castro activist and CIA asset of extraordinary bravery, Dionisio later headed Goodwill Industries of South Florida.

Pawley, William: Pawley grew up, in part, in Cuba. He became president of *Nacional Cubana de Aviación Curtiss* and was instrumental in the Flying Tigers' war against Japan. In 1948, Pawley became U.S. ambassador to Brazil. He was a supporter of Rafael Trujillo and Fulgencio Batista, was an FBI informant, and was close to CIA, participating in its 1954 overthrow of Guatemalan president Jacobo Árbenz Guzmán. Pawley is notorious for a June 1963 exploit when he attempted to infiltrate into Cuba to bring out Soviet officers. The scheme ended with the capture of Eddie Bayo, who perished inside Cuba.

Phillips, David Atlee: Long-time CIA operative based at the time of the Castro revolution in Havana as a public relations man. Phillips was instrumental in CIA's 1954 overthrow of President Jacobo Árbenz Guzmán and worked for CIA in various capacities of Western Hemisphere operations during the time period of this narrative. Dubbed "Chivas Regal" by Michael J. P. Malone, he was among Malone's highly placed CIA contacts.

Powell, Joaquín: Crew member of the *Tejana*.

Prado Ugarteche, Manuel: Served as president of Peru from 1939 to 1945 and again from 1956 to1962 with the support of the left-wing *Alianza Popular Revolucionaria Americana* party.

Quadros, Janio da Silva: Populist political leader in Brazil who resigned the presidency after serving seven months, from January to

August 1961. Quadros had been a lawyer and teacher of Portuguese history and literature before he entered politics.

Quinn, Wallace: Yacht broker and friend of Alberto Fernández.

Racoosin, Theodore: New York financier and supporter of John F. Kennedy, with high contacts in the Kennedy administration. Racoosin was also involved in the expedition by William Pawley to exfiltrate Soviet officers.

Rebozo, Bebe: Cuban exile and long-time cohort of Richard Nixon in Key Biscayne, Florida.

Reichhardt, Bernard: Long-time CIA officer and acting chief of Western Hemisphere Operations.

Reyes, Gustavo de los: A prominent Cuban rancher. By August 1959, de los Reyes had joined a movement of cattlemen opposed to the Castro regime. Imprisoned at *La Cabaña* fortress, and then on the Isle of Pines, de los Reyes was incarcerated for four years. With the aid of Swiss Ambassador Emil Stadelhofer, he persuaded Castro to utilize him as an emissary to Washington. For twenty years, Gustavo de los Reyes managed King Ranch, Venezuela, for Robert J. Kleberg, Jr.

Rionda, Salvador: Relative of B. Rionda Braga and George A. Braga and an employee in Cuba of the Czarnikow-Rionda sugar brokerage. Rionda was also the father-in-law of Alberto Fernández de Hechavarría.

Roa, Raúl: Foreign minister of Cuba under Castro.

Rodemeyer, Al: CIA officer and among the CIA contacts of Michael J. P. Malone.

Rodríguez Alonso, Armando: Cuban captain of the *Tejana*.

Romualdi, Serafino: As editor of the Italian labor paper *Il Progresso* in 1922, Romualdi was forced to leave Italy because of the rise of fascism. He was involved in labor activities in New York until he joined OSS. After the war, Romualdi became involved with the American Federation of Labor and in 1948 was appointed the Latin American representative for the AFL. After the AFL merged with the Congress of Industrial Organizations (CIO) in 1955, Romualdi was named the Inter-American representative. Through the post-war years, Romualdi worked closely with CIA.

Rorke, Alexander: Soldier of fortune in anti-Castro activities and son-in-law of Sherman Billingsley, owner of New York's Stork Club. Rorke perished during a never-explained mission with cohort Geoffrey Sullivan close to the time of the Kennedy assassination.

Rubottom, Roy R., Jr.: Assistant secretary of state for Latin American Affairs at the time of the Cuban Revolution.

Sánchez Rionda, Eduardo: Nephew of Alberto Fernández, son of his sister, Cecile.

Santa Anna, Antonio López de: Santa Anna held the presidency of Mexico on eleven separate occasions, beginning in May 1833. As a military leader, he was essential to Mexico's fight for independence from Spain. Santa Anna's notable defeat was at the hands of General Sam Houston at the Battle of San Jacinto on April 21, 1836, which led to the founding of a separate commonwealth, the Republic of Texas.

Schlesinger, Arthur: Harvard professor, professional historian, and aide to John F. Kennedy during his administration.

Shackley, Theodore: Shackley joined CIA in 1953 and began working in Black Operations, an executive action program developed to eliminate unfriendly heads of state. In the early 1960s he served as station chief at JMWAVE, the CIA outpost in Miami. Shackley was involved in the planning of several assassination attempts on the life of Fidel Castro. In 1966, Shackley was placed in charge of secret operations in Laos. He headed an operation that killed thousands (28,978) of civilians suspected of being sympathizers of the National Liberation Front in South Vietnam. While in Laos, Shackley formed a group that came to be known as the "Secret Team" and became involved with the drug trade through General Vang Pao. Over the course of the Vietnam War, the members of the Secret Team amassed a fortune through drug and arms trafficking, laundering money at the Nugan Hand Bank in Sydney, Australia.

Shelton, Bobby: Nephew of Robert J. Kleberg, Jr. and a son of his sister, Sarah Spohn Kleberg.

Shriver, Sargent: Brother-in-law of John F. Kennedy and husband of his sister, Eunice, Shriver was the first head of the Peace Corps.

Slick, Thomas: Oil heir, adventurer, and friend of Robert J. Kleberg, Jr. Slick served on the board of Dresser Industries and was intelligence-connected. He perished in an airplane accident when he was forty-nine years old.

Smathers, George: United States senator from Florida, 1951–1969. Smathers was a Democrat who denounced Brown v. Board of Education. He was the closest friend in the Senate of John F. Kennedy.

Smith, Earl E. T.: As United States ambassador to Cuba, 1957–1959, Smith remained in Cuba until the last days of the Batista regime, despite speaking no Spanish. He resigned on January 20, 1959.

Smithies, Gladys: Older sister of Alberto Fernández.

Smithies, John: Husband of Gladys, brother-in-law of Alberto Fernández, and friend of Lyman Kirkpatrick, the CIA inspector general.

Socorrás, Carlos Prío: President of Cuba from 1948, Socorrás was deposed by Batista on March 10, 1952, three months prior to scheduled elections.

Sorí Marín, Humberto: Humberto Sorí Marín was the first intellectual in Castro's 26th of July Movement. A lawyer, he was the author of the rebel army's penal code. After Castro took power, he appointed Sorí to be Minister of Agriculture. At the same time, Castro compelled Sorí to preside over tribunals leading to the executions of Batista's officers. Sorí began to organize a mass movement in opposition to Castro called *Unidad Revolucionaria.* Pleading with CIA to postpone its invasion until the movement was ready, and to locate it at a more propitious site, Sorí returned to Cuba where he was captured by Castro's militia. He was executed shortly after the Bay of Pigs invasion.

St. George, Andrew: Hungarian-born journalist, photographer, and CIA asset. St. George reportedly met with Fidel Castro in the *Sierra Maestra* in 1958 when Castro requested that he arrange a meeting for him with CIA officers. Over the years St. George filtered money to anti-Castro operations.

Stevenson, Adlai: Democratic Party candidate in 1952 and 1956, defeated twice by Dwight David Eisenhower. Stevenson was the U.N. ambassador from the United States during the Kennedy administration.

Sturgis, Frank (a.k.a. Frank Fiorini): Anti-Castro soldier of fortune and, later, Watergate burglar, Sturgis was a paid CIA operative in Cuba before the revolution with Mafia connections.

Taaffe, Catherine: An intelligence-connected "Mata Hari" who appeared in Cuba during the early days of the revolution and for a time worked at the Sugar Institute in Havana after the victory of Fidel Castro.

Tash, Lowell: Foreman of *Becerra,* King Ranch in Cuba.

Trujillo, Rafael: Dictator of the Dominican Republic, Trujillo was assassinated in 1962 with the help of CIA-supplied weapons in an operation kept secret from President Kennedy.

Truman, Harry S.: Elected to the U.S. Senate in 1934, Truman became vice president in 1945. After President Roosevelt's sudden death, Truman became president on April 12, 1945. He was re-elected in 1948 and would serve in the presidency until January 20, 1953, when he was replaced by General Dwight David Eisenhower. Truman's most challenging decision was to drop an atomic bomb on Hiroshima on August 6, 1945, and another on Nagasaki on August 9th. Truman's anti-Communist stance, the "Truman Doctrine," called for the United States to support any country that was trying to avoid Soviet influence.

Urrutia, Dr. Manuel: Provisional president of Cuba following the 1959 revolution.

Varona, Manuel Antonio (Tony): A lawyer and senator, Varona served as Cuba's prime minister from 1948 to 1950. Opposed to the dictatorship of Fulgencio Batista, he founded the Student Revolutionary Directorate. Later, in exile, he served as a director of Brigade 2506, which landed at the Bay of Pigs.

Wall, Robert (Bob): CIA officer operating out of the JMWAVE CIA station, and a handler for Alberto Fernández.

Wells, Bob: Tax specialist employed by Robert J. Kleberg, Jr. at King Ranch.

Williams, Langbourne M.: Chief executive officer of the Freeport Sulphur Company.

Wisner, Frank: Wisner, a lawyer, served with the Office of Strategic Services during World War II, based in Romania. He joined CIA in 1947. As enthusiastic a proponent of covert action as Allen Dulles, Wisner was placed in charge of the Office of Policy Coordination, forerunner of the Deputy Director for Plans, the clandestine services. In 1949, Wisner masterminded a failed coup in Albania. When Dulles became Director of Central Intelligence in 1953, Wisner was his Deputy Director for Plans. He requested President Eisenhower's permission to assist the Hungarian freedom fighters in the 1956 uprising, but was denied. Wisner's last years were marked by alcoholism and erratic behavior. He committed suicide in 1965.

Wortham, Gus: Gus Wortham was a Texas entrepreneur who joined forces with Jesse Jones, James Elkins, and John Linke to found the American General Insurance Company. Wortham became part of the Suite 8-F group at the Lamar Hotel in Houston, presided over by Herman Brown. Wortham was chairman of the board and CEO of American General from its founding until shortly before his death in 1976.

Yeagley, J. Walter: Assistant attorney general and director of the internal security division in 1959. Friendly to CIA, Yeagley later served as an aide to J. Edgar Hoover. Yeagley was close, in particular, to Lawrence Houston, the long-time general counsel for CIA.

CIA GLOSSARY

201 files: personnel files created by CIA for its assets and employees as well as for persons of interest.

AM: prefix to cryptonyms having to do with Cuba.

AMBIDDY: cryptonym for Manuel Artime.

AMBUD-1: Miró Cardona's cryptonym.

AMCHEER and AMFAST: Operations enlisting exiled Cuban businessmen and lawyers in anti-Castro operations.

AMCLATTER-1: Bernard Barker.

AMDENIM-1: Alberto Fernández's CIA cryptonym.

AMPATRIN: Michael J. P. Malone's cryptonym.

AMSWIRL-1: cryptonym for Cesario Diosdado, a U.S. Customs officer seconded to CIA, his salary paid by the Agency.

AMTHUG-1: cryptonym for Fidel Castro.

CRC: Cuban Revolutionary Council, an organization of Cuban exiles entirely under the control of CIA.

DD/P: Deputy Director for Plans, refers both to the clandestine services themselves and to the chief of the clandestine services during the period covered in this narrative.

DCI: Director of Central Intelligence.

DDCI: Deputy Director, Central Intelligence.

DRE: *Directorio Revolucionario Estudiantil*, revolutionary student directorate, militant group of young Cuban exiles.

GPIDEAL: cryptonym for John F. Kennedy.

JMARC: CIA cryptonym for Cuban operations in general.

JMBAR: CIA's maritime operations base in the Florida Keys.

JMWAVE: Mammoth CIA station in Miami where operations against Castro were launched.

KUBARK: CIA cryptonym referring to itself.

LCFLUTTER: CIA cryptonym for its polygraph tests.

ODACID: CIA cryptonym for the State Department.

ODENVY: CIA cryptonym for the FBI.

ODYOKE: CIA cryptonym for the U.S. government.

OSS: Office of Strategic Services during World War II, predecessor agency to CIA.

PBPRIME: CIA cryptonym for the United States.

PBRUMEN: CIA cryptonym designating Cuba.

SAS: Special Affairs Staff, led during this period by Desmond Fitzgerald out of Headquarters at Langley.

WH: Western Hemisphere.

CHAPTER 1

MR. BOB IN HIS ASCENDANCY

"Who is to give Texas character?"

Sam Houston

Texas and CIA: Two Cultures of Like Mind

CIA and Texas: You might as well be comparing a lion to a fish. Yet this former Republic and the ever-expanding spy agency have much in common beyond size. Both demand of their citizens absolute loyalty. With CIA, the Agency comes before the nation. CIA uses "United States" and "CIA" interchangeably. Denizens of Texas "remember the Alamo" still; the history of Texas is their abiding history. Each lives by its own rules and protocols, shunning unwelcome outsiders who are banished should they venture near.

In the Republic of Texas, 1836–1846, the rule of law was an exception. Texas drew its first inhabitants from a mob of outlaws, people from the United States in flight from creditors or the law. Hastily they scrawled on their abandoned hovels "GTT": "Gone To Texas." Foreign travelers to the Republic were dismayed by the moral anarchy and the lawlessness. Restrained by no code of justice, vigilantism was a way of life. Vigilantes even earned themselves a name: "filibusters."

In 1842, an Englishman named N. Doran Maillard published *The History of the Republic of Texas*. Texas, he wrote, was "a country filled with habitual liars, drunkards, blasphemers and slanderers; sanguinary gamesters and cold-blooded assassins." Maillard, a land surveyor working during the time of the Republic, observed, "Being beyond the jurisdiction of the United States . . . has served as a . . . convenient sanctuary for those who have fled from the pursuit of the law."

By 1892, leading Texas historian John Henry Brown had to concede that the Republic had been plagued by "the avarice of selfish and dishonest men and unscrupulous swindlers and forgers." No less a commentator than Rhinehart ("Riney") Brown, the father of Herman and George Brown—the future proprietors of Brown & Root—voiced his dismay at the contempt for the law he discovered when he moved to Texas:

> [There are] more deceitful people in Texas than anywhere I've been—every man for himself, and everybody trying to steal from or cheat his neighbor. It was always about getting ahead, no matter what.

What better environment could there be for an intelligence agency that, from its first moment, violated the law and stirred up murder and mayhem? CIA's first illegality was to violate its own charter. As Brown & Root, with CIA encouragement, roamed the planet in quest of profit, aided and abetted by CIA's military arm, Texas appealed to those infected by a taste for empire. So Aaron Burr revealed when he moved to Texas where he hoped to reign as an absolute monarch, creating a mini-empire for himself. Before he made it to Texas, alas, Burr was apprehended by federal officers and charged with treason. The year was 1807.

In Texas, Sam Houston's opposition notwithstanding, empire building was the order of the day. If the United States flexed its muscles and demanded its "manifest destiny," its ambitions took second place to the expansionist schemes of Mirabeau Buonaparte Lamar, the second president of the Republic of Texas. It was a quick leap to Texas contractors becoming components of the U.S. military, as when Navy personnel worked side by side with Brown & Root to build a military infrastructure in Vietnam. During the Iraq War, nearly forty years later, Brown & Root barges were leased to the U.S. Navy as helicopter bases.

Violence was a component of everyday life in Texas far more than in other territories, which succumbed to the blandishments of civilization. During the time of the Republic, it was unsafe to walk the streets of any town unless you were armed with the weapon of choice, the Bowie butcher knife. During America's foreign wars, Texas has boasted more recruits to the military than any other state.

As it would be to CIA, the military was a welcome friend in Texas. Their cultures were so similar that it becomes clear why so many Texans were ready to embrace CIA and sign on as its assets. Certainly it suited CIA that Texas had long believed that its unique identity rendered Texans immune to federal authority and all laws promulgated by "the fed."

An early Texan historian asserted this view of Texan exceptionalism, declaring that Texas was a "unique" state whose history was "unlike that of any other member of the Union." Texas had defeated a foreign power to become a separate country. Upon annexation to the United States in 1845, Texas did what no other territory seeking to join the Union dared propose: It decreed that it would assign none of its territory to the federal government— and got away with it. The U.S. even retired the sizable debt Texas had accumulated.

The loyalty of Texans ever after would be not to elected officials, let alone to politicians at the national level, but to their own credo: They remained citizens of Texas, stalwart inhabitants still of that independent commonwealth that joined the union with so many reservations. It was a view Robert J. Kleberg, Jr. epitomized without ever having to articulate it.

Not surprisingly, Texas became the home of a particular breed of robber baron, the defense contractor. These concerns would discover a welcome ally in CIA as, with the help of the military, the Agency, substituting itself for the legally elected government, became addicted to permanent, pre-emptive wars.

By 1948, CIA had rendered into law in the form of a National Security Council directive, as if the two were identical, its freedom to commit acts of murder, terrorism, and sabotage, crimes that CIA had already embraced in the year of its birth, 1947. From the first, assassination on foreign territory was an indispensable string to CIA's bow. It wasn't long before CIA began its alliance with business, most particularly in Texas.

An early example of CIA's collaboration with Texas business may be found in a letter of May 28, 1951, to Allen Dulles from oilman Charles B. Wrightsman, whose father had engineered the oil depletion allowance, granting Texans 27.5 percent off their taxes because they wanted it that way.

To pull himself out of debt, Wrightsman was considering the sale of some oil-producing leases he had received in a liquidation by Standard Oil of Kansas. Wrightsman had paid a 25 percent tax on that liquidation, which amounted to several million dollars.

Could Dulles, could CIA, advise him, Wrightsman asks in his letter, on whether he should hold or sell those leases? "If we are not going to have more trouble with Russia, and if the Middle East oil is safe for England and America," Wrightsman wants to know, "I believe that I should sell these producing properties at once. . . . If trouble with Russia looms and the Middle Eastern oil fields are nationalized, producing oil properties in Texas will materially increase in value and should be temporarily held," Wrightsman figures. "Timing is so important . . . " What Wrightsman is asking Dulles is whether the British and the Americans will continue to have access to Middle Eastern Oil.

Wrightsman knew that consulting Dulles, consulting CIA, came at a price. He promised Dulles that he would "cooperate . . . in every way." Whatever CIA required in return for advance intelligence, Wrightsman would provide. Allen Dulles in 1951, officially only a deputy director, was already working on behalf of his Texas friends while they were acknowledging that they would provide CIA with any covers it desired.

Nor was CIA upset by the violations of the law common in Texas. Mega-entrepreneur D. H. Byrd pocketed the funds of investors whom he had lured on false pretenses. Openly he glorified Texas as a place where there were no "schemes to equalize the wealth," adding that "there weren't many states other than Texas where this could have happened."

CIA saw to it that its corporate clients were protected as this end justified the means of murder and violent upheaval. When Iranian president Mohammed Mossadegh threatened to nationalize the oil industry in 1953, CIA sponsored a coup with no assistance in its decision-making from a president or a congress. Among the Texans doing business in Iran in 1953 were El Paso Natural Gas; Electronic Data Systems (Ross Perot); Bell Helicopter; Texas Instruments; Halliburton; and the ubiquitous Brown & Root.

CIA used these businesses for cover and protected them from governments not inclined to allow them to operate unimpeded. The Texans knew they could do as they pleased. If there were laws in the new millennium against doing business in Iran, Halliburton, having broken those laws, found a solution by moving its headquarters from Houston to Dubai. Who would stop them? Their legacy was the culture of Texas where U.S. law was unlikely to catch up with you.

CIA's relationship with the corporations was kept secret, as a CIA post-Watergate document entitled "DCD Response to the Agency-Watergate File Review" reveals. The Agency was concerned that its relationship with Hughes Aircraft might be exposed: "It is difficult [illegible] with certainty that one surfacing of the substance of a given action would not cause congressional and/or media interest."

By the millennium, CIA would render itself immune to both congressional inquiries and to media scrutiny, at least that originating from the mainstream. CIA's pretext, that its "sources and methods" might be jeopardized, was enough to hold any challengers at bay.

In a letter dated November 8, 1954, to his brother Edgar, President Eisenhower had already voiced his concern about how certain businessmen, most of them Texas-based, were exerting an unwholesome influence on domestic policy:

> Should any political party attempt to abolish social security, unemployment insurance, and eliminate labor laws and farm programs, you would not hear of that party again in our political history . . . there is a tiny splinter group, of course, that believes you can do these things. Among them are H.L. Hunt . . . a few other Texas millionaires, and an occasional politician or business man from other areas. Their number is negligible and they are stupid.

It was already too late, as was Eisenhower's later warning against a "military-industrial complex" and "the disastrous rise of misplaced power."

A 1967 *Wall Street Journal* article, "CIA & Business: Intelligence Agency's Requests Pose Problems for Some Global Firms," revealed that some companies, aware that CIA's mandate forbade its operating domestically, hesitated. The vice president of International Harvester was quoted as hoping he would never be approached by CIA, an event, however, that he anticipated.

A "Southwest-based" president of an oil well drilling company began to chat with the *Journal* reporter about CIA only suddenly to change his mind and demand that the reporter tear up his notes. Another businessman, who also chose to remain nameless, suggested that his company issue a "well-publicized statement that 'International Widget' will not allow its employees to cooperate in any manner with the CIA." The company then could do as it pleased.

Agency-think is already apparent: All you have to do is lie. At a 1975 Yale University conference, journalist Kirkpatrick Sale remarked that "The CIA, wanting to use legitimate organizations with worldwide interests as its cover, likes to have the multinationals through which to work." So it has done, from its inception.

By the mid-1970s, according to the Director of Central Intelligence, William Colby, "five hundred agents were using corporate covers." Domestically, CIA set up fronts like the Research Institute of America, serving companies that ranged from Dillon Read to EXXON, Gulf Oil, Hughes Tool, the *Houston Chronicle,* and Pan American Airways.

Nor was it, of course, only Texas companies that allied themselves with CIA. CIA favorites were the Bechtel Corporation and the Hughes companies, both doing business in California. It was Allen Dulles' personal friendship with Steve Bechtel that allowed the company to provide CIA generously with cover relationships for its employees over the years. It was Bechtel that opened its doors in Libya to CIA employees when Nelson Bunker Hunt dared to defy CIA and deny the Agency access to his business.

As *Time* magazine would report, the upper ranks of Hughes Aircraft were "studded with former ranking military and CIA officers." The alphabet of companies connected to CIA began with A: "Aero Systems, Inc. of Miami; Arrow Air; Aero Systems Pvt Ltd. of Singapore; Air America . . . " and proceeded through the alphabet. The list is long. The model of CIA's symbiotic relationship with defense contractors and other corporations is as old as the Agency itself.

But in Texas in particular there was an abundance of companies and foundations eager to enter into a symbiotic relationship with CIA. As *San Francisco Chronicle* reporter Terry Leonard noted in 1982, "Nowhere but in Texas is the relationship between government and business so purposely close." Herman and George Brown were long-time CIA assets, not only of the Domestic Contact Service, as might be expected, but of the clandestine services. In 1967, CIA released a document emanating from its Office of Security listing not only the dates of CIA service of Herman and George Brown, but of the CIA relationships with a long list of Brown & Root executives who were also Agency assets.

These Texans began from the premise that war was the price of the free pursuit of profit. In this respect, they resembled the robber barons of a century earlier, like Judge Thomas Mellon's son, who said that he hoped that the Civil War would go on forever. If

John F. Kennedy did not support this policy, he was the last president actively to oppose a ground war anywhere.

His successor, Lyndon Johnson, at once accelerated the war in Vietnam, a war from which Texas mega-company Halliburton, now the owners of Brown & Root, the Ur-construction company founded by Herman Brown, profited vastly. If you were a Texan friendly to CIA, you understood the necessity of the United States' plunge into full-scale war so that Southeast Asia—and, by extension, everywhere else—would remain amenable to U.S. corporate investment.

CIA's policy, as voiced by CIA friend McGeorge Bundy, security advisor to both Presidents Kennedy and Johnson, was clear: "support for military action [was] uncorrelated to military outcomes." War was about profit, not politics, which suited the defense contractors clustered in Texas. Wars of duration were preferable. The longer the war persisted, the greater the financial gain for the contractor.

One day President Lyndon Johnson confided to his old acquaintance Robert J. Kleberg, Jr., the unsung protagonist of the first part of this story, that he was "worn out, troubled to death trying not to get run out of Vietnam and letting the Communists take over." Kleberg at once dealt Johnson a cutting and sharp rebuke.

"Don't do that!" Kleberg said quickly. Whatever remained of their old-boy camaraderie, vestiges of the Kleberg family's long history with Lyndon Johnson, had suddenly vanished.

Allen Dulles made certain to cultivate personal ties to Texans like Robert J. Kleberg, Jr. The curtain of CIA secrecy—how the Agency did business with its friends, assets, and contacts—may be penetrated by an exposé of the Agency's relationships with men like Kleberg, Lyndon Johnson, Herman and George Brown, and George H. W. Bush, who had been a CIA asset for years before he was singled out to be director of central intelligence at a moment when the Agency was under siege by the Church Committee.

They were all connected. Of H. L. Hunt's "second family," Ray L. Hunt was appointed in 2001 to be a member of George W. Bush's

Foreign Intelligence Advisory Board; after Bob Kleberg's time, Ray Hunt joined the Board of Directors of King Ranch, as well as of Halliburton. Yet another CIA-connected board on which Ray Hunt would serve was PepsiCo, whose close relationship with CIA will emerge in this narrative.

So it should not be surprising that Robert J. Kleberg, Jr., president of King Ranch, the largest privately owned ranch in the country, was close to the highest levels of CIA leadership. When Fidel Castro expropriated *Becerra,* the King Ranch satellite in Cuba, Kleberg traveled from Texas to Washington, D.C., to find out what CIA, what the U.S. government, was going to do about it. Robert J. Kleberg, Jr. was the quintessential Texan, the prototypic "cowboy," and an intimate friend of Allen Dulles. There is no record of how their friendship first came to pass, even as there is ample evidence that the two consulted on numerous occasions. When Kleberg wanted an issue resolved, he turned easily and without hesitation to the Director of Central Intelligence. The specifics of CIA's involvement in Kleberg's life provide a window into how the Agency interacted with the most powerful corporate figures in the country.

Not all of CIA's Texan friends were greed-driven predatory robber barons. Kleberg's particular purpose transcended personal profit. For the first thirty years that he ran King Ranch, global outreach in the service of greater profit was not on Kleberg's mind. Nor was Kleberg seeking specific favor from CIA. For domestic matters, Kleberg had been on close terms for decades with J. Edgar Hoover, their relationship dating from the 1920s. At first glance, Robert J. Kleberg was too rich, too powerful, and too contented to have any need for the assistance of CIA.

Until the turn of the 1950s, Kleberg lived and worked content to raise cattle on the land of his maternal grandfather, Richard King, and his father, Robert Justus Kleberg II. Kleberg was a paradox: a worldly man who preferred to remain on the ranch where the closest metropolis was Corpus Christi.

Yet at the end of that decade, Kleberg enlisted CIA to overthrow a foreign government, much as Bechtel had done in 1949 in the matter of an oil pipeline they needed in Syria. It was Cuba that brought Kleberg to CIA's door, battered white Stetson in hand. This is not merely a narrative of Kleberg and King Ranch. It is also the delineation of Kleberg's ties to Cuba, and the emergence of two unusual Cubans, both of whom placed themselves under Kleberg's and CIA's protection.

Kleberg's story begins in Orange County, New York, with the birth of Richard King in 1824. In New York City, King, a twelve-year-old Irish boy with dark, curly hair, was living in thralldom, indentured to a Manhattan jeweler since the age of ten. Now King escaped, stowing away on a ship called the *Desdemona* bound for Mobile, Alabama. The captain who discovered the stowaway saw to it that he got some schooling ashore. From cabin boy, by the time he was eighteen King had his pilot's license and was plying the Mississippi and the Ohio rivers.

Riverboat Captain King plunged into the history of his time. By 1846, now age twenty-two, King was operating two steamboats with his partner, a Pennsylvania Quaker named Mifflin B. Kenedy. Foremost among their assignments was carrying supplies up and down the Rio Grande for General Zachary Taylor, bent on wresting from Mexico as much land as he could. After the Mexican War, King bought the steamboat he had captained, the *Colonel Cross*, for $750. In 1850, King and Kenedy formed a company, M. Kenedy & Co., later renamed King, Kenedy & Co.

A soldier named Robert Edward Lee advised young Captain King. The tip of Texas would make fine cattle country, Robert E. Lee thought. Even as King and Kenedy continued to pursue the steamboat trade, they purchased a 54,000-acre tract of land near the Santa Gertrudis Creek. They named it "Rancho Santa Gertrudis." Richard King began to raise cattle in 1851 on open country populated by wild mustangs. They bought Longhorn cattle from Mexico and shipped them on their steamboats. They bred the mustangs with stallions.

In 1853, King married the daughter of a Presbyterian minister, the first to preach in this border country. Henrietta Chamberlain was mild, blonde, and yet spunky, as well as ascetic and self-denying; their first home was an adobe house on the Santa Gertrudis Creek.

The following year, King acquired 15,500 more acres of land, paying Texan residents who had fled from the area $300 each. In 1853, King bought another 53,000 acres.

In 1852, Richard King had met a former journalist named Gideon K. "Legs" Lewis at the Lone Star Fair in Corpus Christi. Lewis had been imprisoned by Antonio López de Santa Anna when, as a nineteen-year-old firebrand, he had participated in a raid into Mexico. Lewis joined the Texas Rangers and was a captain when King took him on as a partner for $2,000 and a half-interest in King Ranch.

Tall, thin, and long-legged, Lewis was a ladies' man. In 1855, he was deep in an affair with the wife of Dr. Jacob Tier Yarrington of Corpus Christi. When Lewis decided to run for Congress, he went to the Yarrington home where he demanded the return of his love letters. Lewis was rebuffed and Dr. Yarrington ordered him never to return. Lewis ignored him and returned once more to request his letters.

On April 14, 1855, Dr. Yarrington shot and killed Lewis with a shotgun. The community sided with the wronged doctor and he was never tried for the murder. It was Texas living up to its anarchic reputation, suffering only its own peculiar brand of justice.

With no heirs, Lewis' half-interest in King Ranch was put up for auction. Richard King asked a friend, Major W. W. Chapman, to bid for Lewis' share of the ranch in his absence. Chapman signed a promissory note for $1,575, which King paid, and all seemed in order according to King Ranch legend. In 1883, Chapman's widow, Helen, claimed that *she* owned half of King Ranch. King lost, paying $5,811.75 to retain possession of his ranch. In 1903 the case arrived on appeal to the Texas Supreme Court. King Ranch remained intact.

During these years, bandits habitually invaded from across the border. One hundred years later, Captain King's grandson Robert J. Kleberg, Jr., speaking at the centennial of King Ranch, would say that the first problem confronting his grandfather was the "very personal, but also the very practical problem of staying alive."

During the Civil War, as fierce supporters of the South, King and Kenedy supplied cattle and horses to the Confederate Army. By the end of the war, they owned twenty-six steamboats and monopolized shipping up and down the Rio Grande.

"Buy land and never sell," Robert E. Lee advised. King continued to acquire land. By 1867, he owned more than 600,000 acres of land and 40,000 head of cattle. Only in 1872, squeezed by competition from the railroads and the first generation of robber barons, did King and Kenedy disband their shipping business.

Richard King was a coarse-looking, heavy-set man, strong of will and a heavy drinker. Restlessly ambitious, never idle, he built the first dam in South Texas. He created the Corpus Christi, San Diego & Rio Grande railroads that stretched from Corpus Christi to Laredo.

Always on the lookout to increase his holdings, King bought or finagled thousands more acres of land from Mexicans, sometimes paying with land scrip issued by the no-longer existing Republic of Texas, or paying less than two cents an acre. He had a taste for empire building that would reappear in his grandson Robert J. Kleberg, Jr., "third of the name."

Richard King's ambitions resembled those of Mirabeau Buonaparte Lamar, who hoped to secure for Texas not only New Mexico, but a border that would end at the Pacific Ocean, a caricature of fantasies of manifest destiny. Richard King hoped to own all the land between the Nueces River and the Rio Grande. He wanted grazing land that would be three miles wide and would stretch from the Rio Grande to Kansas, where cattle were sold.

King lived well and had bushels of live oysters sent to the ranch from New Orleans by wagon train. Rose whiskey (Old Rosebud) was transported to the ranch in barrels. He carried large sums of money and gave the appearance of being careless with it because he was generous in the making of loans.

Richard King moved in a rarefied realm now, as would his grandson. The outlaw Jesse James sent King a gray stallion, establishing a King Ranch tradition, an act of homage not so different from Allen Dulles paying a call on Robert J. Kleberg, Jr., on his way home in 1953 from addressing the Dallas Council on World Affairs shortly after he was appointed Director of Central Intelligence.

In one of his many lawsuits, this one in 1881, Captain King had been so impressed by the lawyer for his adversary that the next day King put him on retainer as his own personal lawyer for $5,000 a year ($65,000 in today's money). His name was Robert Justus Kleberg II.

It was the Chapman suit, and, before it was over, Kleberg was representing both the widow Chapman and Richard King. Representing first the widow Helen Chapman, Kleberg argued that Chapman had owned one-half of Legs Lewis' title. The settlement— in favor of King—cost the Chapman heirs dearly.

King was unrelenting in his accumulation of land. "Young man," he told one of his lawyers, famously, "the only thing I want to hear from you is when I can move my fences."

Kleberg's father, also named Robert Kleberg, had fought beside General Sam Houston in the Battle of San Jacinto: Such were the Kleberg bona fides.

"I wished to live under a republican form of government with unrestricted personal, religious, and political freedom," said the first Robert Justus Kleberg. In Texas he hoped to find "the blessed land of my burning hopes." A grateful Sam Houston appointed Kleberg as one of three guards to ensure that the wily Antonio López de Santa Anna, victor at the Alamo, neither escape nor be murdered by an angry Texan. Although Andrew Jackson and his protégé Sam Houston received the credit, it was Kleberg's idea that Santa Anna remain alive as a hostage until the Mexican Army had left Texas. The frying pan that Robert Justus Kleberg used at San Jacinto became a family heirloom.

President Sam Houston appointed Robert Justus Kleberg in 1837 to be President of Land Commissions for the new Republic of Texas. From the start, the Klebergs were above partisan politics. Houston's successor and archenemy, Mirabeau Buonaparte Lamar, appointed Kleberg Chief Justice of Austin County in 1841.

Kleberg knew Latin and Greek and three modern languages, and was both a Democrat and a strong believer in states' rights and local self-government. He died in 1888. On the base of his monument were the words, "Remember the Alamo!," the rallying cry at San Jacinto. On the reverse side was the parallel war chant, "Remember Goliad!"

Kleberg's lawyer son Robert Justus, serving as Richard King's lawyer, frequented, inevitably, King Ranch. He went on to marry King's youngest daughter, Alice, a tall, plump, straight-laced woman, who apparently fell in love with him at first sight, commenting on his "beautiful blond beard." They would be the parents of the protagonist of this portion of the narrative, Robert J. Kleberg, Jr. Henrietta King accompanied Alice and Robert Justus Kleberg on their honeymoon, an event much gossiped about at the time.

Alice Kleberg refused to have a toilet in the house; she thought it was unhealthy. She subscribed to *The Saturday Evening Post* and *Fortune* magazine; among her favorite mottos was "Forget each slight." Her hair was pulled back in a bun away from her face and neck, and she served sugar cookies and buttermilk to visiting bankers and dignitaries.

When Richard King died in 1885 in the Menger Hotel in San Antonio at the age of sixty, he left his widow a half-million acres and a half-million dollar debt. His lawyer son-in-law went to Brownsville and called for claims. When they were listed, he produced Captain King's records and the claimants vanished. "They scattered," Robert Justus Kleberg said, "like cockroaches when the light is turned on."

With the strong approval of King's widow, his mother-in-law Henrietta King, Robert Justus Kleberg took over the management of King Ranch. R. J. Kleberg's last law case was in 1903; he defended a Mexican without charge. Henrietta King paid her son-in-law $5,000 a year, a salary she never raised. This was the same salary that Kleberg had received from Captain King as his lawyer.

Henrietta King was the boss, but in the forty years R. J. Kleberg ran King Ranch, he said, the only instruction she ever gave him was "to do what I ought to do and tell her what she ought to do."

"You know best," she would say.

Ever reflecting that she was the daughter of a Presbyterian minister, Henrietta was straight-laced. There was a ranch rule, if one honored in the breach, against the use of intoxicants and gambling. On Sundays, Henrietta King compelled everyone to attend the Presbyterian Church in Kingsville in a procession of vehicles and horse-drawn carriages. She would enter the church first, followed by twenty members of the family and friends. She expected her granddaughters to wash out their own personal things and dry them before the fire in her Corpus Christi home, and never rode a horse.

Robert Justus Kleberg, known at King Ranch as "*El Abogado*," as Richard King was "Old Captain," was a stout, blue-eyed man with curly blond hair and a blond beard who resembled Teddy Roosevelt. The young architect who designed the Santa Gertrudis House remembered him as "a large, handsome gentleman, definitely of the German type, whose kindly, keen eyes and forceful mouth and chin at once bespoke power and the ability to carry the responsibilities of the empire he controlled." He was a little below medium height.

R. J. Kleberg did not drink or gamble or swear, in deference to his mother-in-law. He was a man easily moved, and despite his authority no one was afraid of him. He was a great raconteur and loved music and opera.

"To survive, I must make myself more valuable alive than dead in this country," Kleberg said. He began by prosecuting every thief that was caught. He worked with the Missouri Pacific Railroad and they built a railroad through the ranch while he donated 40,000 acres for the building of a town that would be called Kingsville. The year was 1903.

His five children, two sons and three daughters, were taken on frequent trips to places like Colorado Springs and San Antonio. R. J. Kleberg went along, and he expected that his children learn something. "Don't be a pig in a poke," he told them as they traveled by railroad. "Look out the window!"

Mild in demeanor, as his son Robert would not be, Robert Justus Kleberg, known as R. J., modernized and improved King Ranch. He located scientists, who eradicated the cattle tick and cultivated new grasses, such as the golden beard blue stem. Luther Burbank wrote him, "I will do my best to make a better cactus for Texas. You certainly ought to know something about cactus if you feed one hundred and fifty tons of cattle a day."

He discovered that buzzards carry anthrax. He was burning carcasses, so the buzzards couldn't get them, before the proof came out of the test tube; in 1900 he conquered the perennial King Ranch droughts with artesian wells. A sentimental man, Robert Kleberg wept when the first artesian well came in.

He passed his credo down to his younger son, Bob: "Those who possess property, or influence, hold it in trust for the use of their fellow men," hardly a philosophy with which Allen Dulles and his typical corporate clients sympathized. The ethos of the Klebergs was different from that espoused by the robber barons of the gilded age, or of CIA's corporate clients of later generations, including the Bragas in Cuba with whom Bob Kleberg entered into partnership.

Robert Justus Kleberg added to King Ranch in 1900, buying the Laureless Ranch from the British company to whom Mifflin Kenedy had sold it. King Ranch was now approaching the million-acre mark, and it was increased when, around 1922, a Kleberg daughter, Alice, married Tom East, who owned 75,000 acres southwest of Santa Gertrudis, which were added to the King Ranch domain.

"Land [isn't] worth anything unless you did something with it for the good of humanity," Robert Justus Kleberg instructed his children. Cattle meant food, which meant energy, which meant progress. "Civilization came and remained because of King Ranch," his son Bob came to believe.

Robert J. Kleberg, Jr. was born on March 29, 1896, in his grandmother Henrietta King's house in Corpus Christi. On his fourth birthday, he could have been observed seated firmly on his birthday present, his first horse. When the horse sent him flying headlong over its head, he suffered his first humiliation, being put back on the "check rein." One hand remarked that all five children "would ride horses I wouldn't begin to ride."

By age six he had graduated to being a member of a *corrida* or cattle-working outfit, and he rode in the round-up with the men. He would ride out before daylight with his father; his elder brother, Dick; his cousin, Caesar Kleberg; and the ranch manager, Sam Ragland.

At eight, he raced Dick, nearly nine years his senior, with Bob driving a train engine and Richard on horseback. It was a tie. Swimming the Nueces River on horseback was a matter of course for both brothers.

By the time he was twelve, Bob was a crack shot, hitting coyotes while holding his rifle in one hand, as if it were a pistol, with a strong arm. Before long he could ride, rope, cut cattle, and shoot with either hand. His brother Dick could shoot rats off a wire, and, in later years, Dick's son roped game chickens.

At thirteen, Robert J. Kleberg, Jr. was commemorated in a poem composed on the occasion of his parents' twenty-third wedding anniversary: "Robert, the liveliest of all/Full of deviltry—but so capable and so kind."

When Bob was fourteen, in January 1912, the stately King Mansion caught, or was deliberately set, on fire. Permitted to rescue one possession, Bob emerged from the burning building holding his shotgun. He was only fifteen when his grandmother, Henrietta King, presented him with a Packard automobile. A natural mechanic, Bob soon had it running at the unthinkable speed of sixty miles an hour. He had grown notorious in his family for "pungent thinking."

Classically handsome, eight and a half years older than his brother, Richard Kleberg was a superb athlete. He could sing in Spanish at campfires, delighting the Mexican "*Kineños*" who worked at King Ranch. (*Kineño* means "King's Place"). He spoke Spanish before he could speak English, and employed the classic Castilian lisp with none of his younger brother's gringo accent; he was interested in boating, designing, and photography. He dominated every gathering.

Black-haired Richard was taller and more charming than Bob. On one of his not infrequent forays into Mexico, Richard met the revolutionary, Pancho Villa. He sang "Teddy de Roos" with an Italian accent. Stranded by a broken-down train, President Theodore Roosevelt had entered the auditorium and was standing at the back. Afterwards, Roosevelt stretched out his hand and pronounced himself "dee-lighted." Dick Kleberg went off to law school.

Bob went to high school in Corpus Christi, where he had what he called an "unspectacular" career. He played football and pitched for the baseball team, but his heart wasn't in it, and then he broke his arm. He also acted the part of "Hastings" in the Corpus Christi high school play of 1914: A newspaper said he "wore his clothes à la Beau Brummel in a way that made a considerable impression on some of the older ladies present."

Following in the footsteps of their grandfather King, both brothers enjoyed their spirits. Bob was a natural leader, shrewd, confident, and more focused than his brother. It was Richard who would fall under the power of Lyndon Johnson, Bob who would hold "Lyndon" at a distance. Some would describe him as part Richard King, part R. J. Kleberg, and completely *Kineño*. Experts in animal science would call him the world's "master rancher," if not to his face.

Bob had hoped to study electrical engineering at the University of Wisconsin. His father urged him to choose agriculture. Yet even as he knew he would never farm, while he was a natural inventor and mechanically gifted, Bob obeyed his father. He promised to study agriculture for one year. He went out for track, skiing, and iceboat racing and joined a fraternity, Sigma Chi.

At other moments, Bob Kleberg was less docile. He flunked freshman English, then, in his words, "slipped into" sophomore English class as if nothing untoward had occurred. He got away with it and went on to pass the course. He was a man who would live all his life by his own rules. The first surprise of this narrative will be that Robert J. Kleberg, Jr. would solicit the help of CIA; the second that they would betray him.

The story of Robert J. Kleberg, Jr. begins in 1916. Robert Justus Kleberg had suffered a stroke. War had broken out on the border.

There was no choice but to call home from Wisconsin his young son, Robert. Down with meningitis, Richard would not have been the best candidate to run King Ranch even had he been in good health. It was "Mr. Bob," who as a boy had played hooky to work the cattle, who was the historic choice. "I guess the sensible thing to have done would have been to leave the place," Kleberg said later. "But we never considered it."

Eight days after his twenty-first birthday, Bob Kleberg became, in effect, the boss of King Ranch. He took advice from his older cousin Caesar Kleberg, and from a cattleman who had been with the ranch since the time of Captain King named Sam Ragland. Wiry and slender, Bob Kleberg was at once commanding.

The following year, one of the Kleberg daughters, Alice East, now married, was kidnapped by bandits who supposedly made her cook them supper. Then they looted the East house. Texas rangers caught up with them. Other raids by bandits followed, and outlaws arrived regularly until 1920, turning King Ranch into an armed camp.

The Mexican *Kineños* who worked the land called him "Señor Bob." Mr. Bob would remain in charge of King Ranch for the next fifty years, for the remainder of his life. Those close to him concluded that "the King Ranch is his life, and to be away from it is only to exist."

At the time, King Ranch was losing money. In 1918, the deficit was $144,475.37. Drought had withered the grasses and, with impunity, bandits continued to cross the Mexican border regularly to lay siege. Just as Captain King had always traveled with an armed escort, Bob developed the habit of riding out each day armed with a revolver and a Mannlicher rifle or a shotgun or both.

In 1918, R. J. Kleberg arranged for Bob's draft deferment on the ground that he was essential to the ranch. This was true, local disapproval notwithstanding. It was to be a Kleberg family tradition, avoiding military service. Richard Kleberg's son Dick avoided serving in World War II, and their sister Alice East's son managed to get a deferment from his congressman uncle.

CHAPTER 2

EL PATRÓN

"We lived in rattlesnake country. If we
didn't get them, they'd get us."

Richard M. Kleberg, Sr.

Like Brown & Root, King Ranch from early on functioned as
a quasi-agency of the federal government. Robert J. Kleberg, Jr.
furnished thousands of horses to the United States war department
and the Mexican government after the end of World War I.

In the 1920s, J. Edgar Hoover sent as a personal gift to Mr. Bob
two Thompson submachine guns ("Tommy guns"). They were to be
used, Hoover instructed, "for defensive purposes." Loaded revolvers
in holsters hung from the posts of Robert J. Kleberg's bed.

By his twenties, he had learned to hold his tongue. Unaware that
he was thinning the herd, his formidable grandmother, Henrietta
King, chastised him for selling 250 cows.

"Young man, don't ever sell mothers if you want to stay in the
cattle business!" said Henrietta, dressed, as always, in her perennial mourning black. You might find Henrietta King now wearing,
inevitably, her customary felt hat, like a man's hat, but soft and
pulled over her eyes to shade them. Henrietta kept a picture of the
Captain engraved on a brooch and pinned to the neck of her blouse.

At special dinners, she wore black taffeta. She preferred to be in rooms presided over by large portraits of her deceased husband.

Demonstrating the proper respect, her grandson stood silent. Later he remarked, "You know, when she said something like that, you didn't argue with it."

Bob Kleberg continued to take risks. "It's like a chess game," he said of running King Ranch. "The moves must be studied, they must be right." It was a science, a matter of the quality and function of each pasture. "You've got to know every resource," Kleberg said in 1952. "You've got to have a move for every situation . . . in ranching, you have to be on the alert for any signs of change."

As soon as there were indications that the drought was ending, Kleberg put 3,400 cattle back on the range. Both his father and brother Richard disapproved: "They'll starve."

"Maybe they won't," Bob said. "They'll surely drown here . . ." The exercise of power had become second nature to him.

In 1925, when he was twenty-nine years old, Robert J. Kleberg, Jr. finally was granted a title: "General Manager." He didn't need it. That he spent virtually all his time on the ranch was no deprivation. He had never liked "town." "I don't like it now," he added. His character had been finely honed. He treated lying as an "unforgivable sin." "NO EXCUSES" was his motto.

The following year his father gave him power of attorney "to contract, bargain, lease, sell and convey any and all of said property, and to execute all such leases, contracts, bills of sale, deeds or other instruments." His mother Alice signed a similar instrument.

For a man of abiding self-confidence, Robert J. Kleberg, Jr., as he reached full maturity, was not prepossessing in appearance. At five feet ten inches, he was not as tall as a Texan should be. He had dark brown hair, a bullet-shaped head, a round face, and a wide grin.

Tone-deaf, he spoke with a thin, reedy, high-pitched, almost squeaky Texas country accent. Personal vanity was alien to him, and he dressed each day in a white shirt and khaki pants tucked into his boots, a red bandana around his neck. He went on to favor white leather chaps. A faded white Stetson completed his outfit.

Yet his flashing blue-gray eyes bore into you. Addressing people with his head thrown back, he was a dominating presence, a "whirlwind of a man." If he seemed mild-mannered, even soft-spoken, and unpretentious, few were fooled for long. *Fortune* magazine compared him to Captain Bligh, with a trace of Charles de Gaulle. He was a man who could stand up to any intelligence agency and any government official, elected or otherwise.

When he was thirty years old, on March 2, 1926, Kleberg got married. He had known Virginia-raised debutante Helen Campbell, daughter of a Kansas congressman, for all of seventeen days when he proposed. Auburn-haired and green-eyed with a throaty, engaging voice, Helen was not only beautiful and cultivated, a worldly woman, but she was horsy. At the age of twelve, she had declared that she wanted to marry someone who would give her horses. Now she had her wish. Their New York honeymoon lasted ten days.

"She's someone I will never interrupt," Bob Kleberg said. He meant that he hoped that she would never interrupt him. As the years passed, he would tell his wife, and later his daughter Helenita, "Let me tell it, let me finish." His wife later said, "He wanted somebody who'd listen." As for Helenita, she rode out onto the range beside her father, cutting out cattle as if she were just another cowhand.

When his wife criticized him for his country ways, when she attempted to "civilize him," Bob Kleberg replied with the sardonic irony of a man secure in his self-confidence. "I wish you hadn't said that," he told her once, "because now I'm going to hate you for a whole week." He laughed when she tried to change him, and retorted, "Well, you know, I like most of what you do, but the one thing that I don't like is you're always trying to change me."

Helen Kleberg smiled. "I'm not trying to change you," she said. "I'm just trying to shape you up enough to be able to live with you." Eventually he did forego the boots and Stetson for trips outside Texas.

On a typical day, Helen Kleberg, who rode the ranch with her husband, might wear jodhpur pants and a fringed buckskin jacket, buckskin chaps with fringes down the sides, and riding boots. She wore a large Western hat made of felt with a wide brim with pheasant and turkey feathers on the side, held safely against the wind with a leather chinstrap.

Kleberg's nephew Belton Kleberg Johnson came to live at King Ranch after the death in an automobile accident of his mother, Bob's favorite sister, Sarah. Belton found Helen Kleberg "cold, distant and dispassionate." One day he drew a horse, only for her to remark, "Oh, that's not a horse. It looks like a dog. You can do better than that." The motherless boy was to remember those words for the rest of his life.

Belton took a long, hard look at the relationship of his uncle and his wife. "There was little actual warmth in their relationship," he would conclude. "They were simply not people for whom love was a criterion." He thought that for the Klebergs "an exhibition of affection was tantamount to a display of weakness," and to his uncle, "affection was a failing in a man." Belton concluded that both Kleberg and his wife were "authoritarian." He grew to fear Helen Kleberg's "piercing green eyes."

His aunt wore penny loafers at home, and "from her step, you could tell her mood . . . the slow clicking of her heels on the wooden floors of the main house." Belton thought she believed that Bob "had a place on a bigger stage than the King Ranch," and seemed overly fond of the English nobility. She sent their daughter Helenita to the exclusive Foxcroft School where Ambassador David K. E. Bruce's daughter, Audrey, went. Helenita so enjoyed growing up on the ranch that she said, remembering the pleasures of her childhood, it was "like baseball every day."

Belton's analysis of his relatives could have been skewed by resentment: His "Uncle Bob" held the ranch stock of his nephews until they were twenty-one, which "gave him considerable power over the other shareholders."

A Modest Cottage Behind the Garage

King Ranch, rebuilt in 1913 after the fire, was now a twenty-five-room hacienda-style castle with turrets and battlements and a sixty-foot watchtower. Almost a square block in size, it was built of brick, white stucco, and red tile. Everywhere you could find the Running W, the King Ranch brand. There were gaily colored awnings, with the whole, as *The Producer* magazine put it in October 1930, "set in a sea of trees and flowers of every kind, from palms to pines" so that it seemed "like a vision from some tale out of the *Arabian Nights*."

Tiffany Studio stained-glass windows gave way to vast rooms filled with oil paintings. One, depicting the siege at the Alamo, occupied pride of place. The dining room seated fifty. In the grand salon were paintings of Captain King, Mrs. King, Robert Kleberg, Sr., Mrs. Kleberg, Sr., Augustin Quintanilla, and Eugenio Garcia, a famous King Ranch Caporal. The rug in the living room was patterned after the Lone Star flag of Texas.

Italian bronze balustrades graced the marble grand staircase. On the walls of the other rooms were paintings of horses, dogs, game cocks, and ranch scenes; on the floors were cowskins and woven rugs. There were mounted heads of animals, as might be expected; a friend contributed the mounted head of a water buffalo. The dining room had a bluestone floor, designed according to the requirement of Robert Justus Kleberg: "I want a dining room that looks alright for a man to get off his horse in the mud and come right in and feel at home."

The bathrooms offered huge tubs, the soap imprinted with the letters "S.G." for "Santa Gertrudis." There was a telephone in every room and an elevator. And there was a "Lee Room," in honor of that soldier who had encouraged Captain King on his path to greatness.

A "commissary" included a kitchen and dining room for visitors, job hunters, and travelers. "Mr. Kleberg always told me if I didn't have a job for a man," the foreman explained, "I must feed and send him on his way with a full stomach." Frontier hospitality was the rule. There was a ten-car garage. This marriage of a crenellated castle and a Spanish mission had cost $350,000. Guests over the years included William Jennings Bryan, Dean Elliott of Harvard, and the ubiquitous King Ranch visitor and would-be cowboy, the humorist, Will Rogers.

As Tom Lea described it in his commissioned biography of King Ranch, meals were preceded by three signal bells. The first directed you to "clean up" because ladies were expected to change their dress and men to wear a coat to table. A British nobleman who arrived in a riding habit was requested to change.

At the second signal bell, you gathered in the big parlor prefatory to moving into the dining room. At the sound of the third bell, Mrs. King led the procession of guests and family to table. "Squire her in," R. J. asked his older son, Richard Kleberg, and so Dick would offer his arm to his grandmother and lead her to the head of the table. R. J. sat at the opposite end and carved the meat. Dinner was followed by singing at the piano. Henrietta King's favorite song was "Rock of Ages."

Robert J. Kleberg, Jr. never lived as an adult in the grand, new Kleberg mansion house. Instead, he and his bride settled into a modest, one-story, three-bedroom, seven-room cottage behind the garage that had served previously as the quarters of a ranch foreman, and had been Bob Kleberg's bachelor quarters. Even when Kleberg was drenched in oil money and had more cash than he could spend, he retained a relatively simple style of life.

Mesquite logs burned in the fireplace. On the bathroom wall were Molina Campos caricatures of pampa life. "Mr. Bob" made his calls from one of several thirty-foot long-wired telephones. His favorite song would be "On the Street Where You Live" from *My Fair Lady*, although, as his assistant John Cypher would note, he had never lived on a "street."

Kleberg's style of life stood in sharp contrast to the entrepreneurs of the Gilded Age. Jay Cooke wandered restlessly around a fifty-room fresco-splashed mansion. Among the Texans of Kleberg's own generation, D. H. Byrd rattled around a house so packed with treasure that it might have served as the mise-en-scène of *Citizen Kane*, depicting the plunder newspaper tycoon William Randolph Hearst collected on his travels. Byrd was proudest of his "Trophy Room," filled with the embalmed animals he had shot on safari—or their heads. (Bob Kleberg did also hang deer and cattle heads in his lodge-like house.)

This is not to say that, as the years passed, Kleberg did not live well. He had a valet named Adán Muñoz, nicknamed "*Gamuza*," (chamois cloth) who polished Kleberg's green, black, and white automobiles. A zebra skin adorned Kleberg's specially outfitted hunting car, which was designed for him by a General Motors executive. A remarkably good shot, Kleberg hunted not only game in season, but armadillos, hawks, coyotes, and other predators. He liked to hunt quail.

For nearly sixty years, Kings and Klebergs had run King Ranch without becoming oilmen like Erle P. Halliburton, D. H. Byrd, and the Hunts. But when his grandmother died in March 1925, Kleberg lacked the cash to pay federal inheritance taxes that amounted to over a million dollars. Witnesses testified to the relatively low value of King Ranch what with its black mesquite, sandy land, and the absence of water. The tax bill remained.

Robert J. Kleberg, Jr. spent months in Washington in the late 1920s compiling a presentation of the estate's case to the Treasury Department. He managed to have the government apply the lower rate of the Revenue Act of 1921, rather than the higher rates that became law in 1926, and paid death taxes of $604,033.76 in installments. It was to help pay this debt that Kleberg turned to Humble Oil and Refining Company of Houston, Texas.

Cash poor as they were, Henrietta King had left an estate of $5 million, the largest estate in Texas up to that time. There were 61,792 head of cattle on King Ranch, plus their calves. Her will had been drawn up in 1918 and left her daughter Alice King Kleberg 30,000 acres of land. The descendants of her deceased daughter Henrietta, the Atwoods sued the estate, challenging the will. The Atwood heirs had been left 112,421 acres, which did not satisfy them.

The Atwood case would drag on for thirty years, a regular Jarndyce v. Jarndyce as Henrietta King's Atwood descendants sued Humble Oil and Refining Company, the King Ranch, and various members of the King and Kleberg families, so furious were they over what Henrietta King had left them in her will. They wanted an accounting; they wanted mineral rights distributed more in their favor. They demanded damages.

"It's easier to lose a big property than a small property," Kleberg said in response to questions about how big King Ranch was. Because it was big didn't mean you could ease off in any way. "The bigger a thing is, the easier it is to lose," he said.

On October 10, 1932, having been bedridden for years, Robert Justus Kleberg died. He was seventy-nine years old. His wife wore black for the rest of her life, as her mother had done before her. That year, Alice King Kleberg received a letter quoting an acquaintance: "I never heard a human being say a harsh word against Bob Kleberg."

In 1933, to settle finally the inheritance taxes on Henrietta King's estate, Kleberg borrowed $3,223,645 from Humble Oil, a long-time ally of Brown & Root, in exchange for granting them a lease to drill for oil and gas on King Ranch land. It was in keeping with Bob Kleberg's approach to King Ranch: "This is a special thing. What we do here is for this kind of an operation under our special and sometimes peculiar set of conditions." He was following his own credo, and there were no rules that applied.

The King Ranch Corporation was formed in 1934. King Ranch, Inc. operated as a trust with each Kleberg child having received 20 percent of the stock. Robert and Richard Kleberg were the trustees. Bob Kleberg was now made "President and General Manager." He was also given a twenty-year trusteeship. It should be noted as well, however, that while he may have owned only one-fifth of King Ranch, Bob Kleberg ruled over all of it.

Henrietta King had refused to grant anyone an oil lease, but times had changed. At that moment, Robert J. Kleberg, Jr. created the "biggest single individual oil and gas lease in history" on 971,000 acres. Dry holes resulted.

Kleberg was nonplussed. "You do not know of any million acres of land between New Orleans and Tampico that does not have oil," Kleberg told Humble, which was the largest oil company in Texas and would later merge with Standard Oil of New Jersey (EXXON).

Humble made the deal without doing any geophysical work on the ranch. The lease was for twenty years, later to be extended. The biggest increase in holdings that the Standard Oil Corporation ever had was on the King Ranch lease. For the moment, it seemed like a very bad investment.

Henrietta King's will granted the Klebergs 400,000 acres of King Ranch. Bob Kleberg took the opportunity when the land was divided according to his grandmother's will to buy land willed to some of the others, bringing the Kleberg-owned portion to 914,000 acres. It was now that the Atwood heirs, the children of his sister Henrietta, sued, contending they had an "undivided mineral interest in the lands of the other heirs as well as their own." Before long the lawyer for the Atwoods owned a 35 percent interest in their holdings.

Lyndon

It was owing to Dick Kleberg that Lyndon Johnson moved to Washington, D.C., to cast his eyes greedily on national office.

In 1931, to Bob Kleberg's relief and, as Bob put it, "encouraged by his friends," Richard Kleberg ran for the U.S. Congress for the Fourteenth District, a seat that had been left vacant following the death of Republican Harry M. Wurzbach. It was a seat that would be occupied in the twenty-first century by that avowed opponent of CIA, Ron Paul.

"Mr. Dick" ran as a Democrat. His campaign manager was Roy Miller, a lobbyist for Texas Gulf Sulphur Corporation. Whether it was Miller who urged Mr. Dick to seek national office, or his brother Bob, Richard Kleberg, a lawyer unsuited to the practice of law, decided to run.

During the campaign, a group based in San Antonio, calling itself the Citizens League, offered its support to both Kleberg and his opponent, Carl Wright Johnson of San Antonio, who was pushed by the Bexar County political organization. Whoever would contribute $4,000 to the League, along with a promise that they could control the position of postmaster, a very important job in provincial Texas, would have its support. Dick Kleberg's opponent turned down the deal outright.

Richard Kleberg agreed to pay the $4,000. He was an extravagant man, the other side of Bob Kleberg's frugality and disdain for money. When Richard Kleberg died on May 10, 1955, he would be $1 million in debt to King Ranch. His children were compelled to pay off the sum.

Will Rogers assisted in the campaign. An old family friend, Rogers liked to work cattle with Bob, Dick, and "Cousin Caesar," roping and riding. One day Rogers was about to take off after doing some roping when Bob Kleberg rode up to him.

"Hey, what kind of cowboy are you?" Bob said. "We haven't finished. The rest of the herd is over there."

Rogers remained on the job. Asked whether he knew of any cowgirls, he replied that he had known only one. This was Sarah Kleberg, Bob's youngest sister, who once shot a hawk from an airplane.

According to Texas historian J. Evetts Haley, in an explosive book called *A Texan Looks at Lyndon*, often quoted but too infrequently cited by Johnson biographers, the individual representing the Citizens League who arrived to collect Kleberg's $4,000 was Lyndon Baines Johnson, a restless high school teacher with outsized ambitions. When Richard Kleberg was elected to Congress, winning by 5,000 votes, he brought Johnson to Washington, D.C., as his "Secretary."

Belton Kleberg Johnson has said that Bob was glad to see his brother go. Dick Kleberg's seat in Congress also granted the ranch respectability and a seat at the table of power. And Bob did not relish sharing power at the ranch with his popular, gregarious, handsome brother. During his first campaign, Dick Kleberg, who liked his bourbon, made a speech against prohibition. He was not a hypocrite. Rather, it was that Texas culture embraced contradiction, and few gave it a second thought. So, although he was a hunter, Richard Kleberg would go on to introduce several bills for game protection, inspired, no doubt, by his cousin Caesar Kleberg.

Alongside Miller, until 1935 Johnson ran Kleberg's office. "Kleberg didn't do anything," said Luther Jones, who ran Kleberg's Corpus Christi office. One effort Congressman Kleberg would make was to shepherd through the bureaucracy the certification for Santa Gertrudis as a new breed. Otherwise, Lyndon Johnson mailed letters signed by Kleberg—without first showing them to the congressman.

Johnson even wrote letters to Alice King Kleberg, signing her son Dick's name without his knowledge. An aide to Congressman Robert Jackson, who shared a bath at the Dodge Hotel with Lyndon Johnson, would later remark, according to Johnson biographer Ronnie Dugger, that Kleberg "was not very smart, and his interests were not in any drudgery."

"This is Dick Kleberg," Johnson said to whomever happened to be telephoning. They always thought it was. While Johnson decided on policy in his name, Kleberg was more often than not on the golf course. Only on New Deal–related issues did Kleberg take sufficient interest to oppose Roosevelt's projects as "socialism, very dangerous."

Kleberg threatened to vote against the Agricultural Adjustment Act as "socialistic." Kleberg wanted to vote against social security for the same reasons; it was also "socialistic," he thought, a law that would "destroy this country." The Klebergs were a land-owning aristocracy, and remained so.

This was going too far and, considering the populist persona he planned himself to affect, Lyndon Johnson threatened to quit. Not wanting to lose this energetic apparatchik on whom he had come to depend, Kleberg voted "aye" on both the agriculture bill and on social security. Mostly Johnson simply did as he pleased, including campaigning for liberal Maury Maverick—with Dick Kleberg's permission.

In 1938, after being elected to Congress himself, Johnson lobbied hard to have the Corpus Christi Naval Station awarded to his supporters Herman and George Brown, although Brown & Root had never built a military base. Congressman Johnson sat on the Naval Affairs Committee. He was aided in securing the lion's share of the Corpus Christi Naval Station for Brown & Root by Congressman Richard Kleberg, who "actively collaborated," according to the Brown & Root biographies.

The chaos Lyndon Johnson visited upon Dick Kleberg's congressional office was revisited by his brother Sam Houston Johnson, whom Lyndon persuaded Kleberg to hire when Johnson moved on. As Robert Caro describes the feckless Sam Houston Johnson in *Master of the Senate*, Sam Houston misused funds, even as Kleberg had put him on the King Ranch payroll as a "public relations consultant."

Sam Houston Johnson threw Kleberg's office bills away and a school board back in Kleberg County had to file suit to force the congressman to pay unpaid school taxes. Kleberg was compelled to pay a tailor's bill for $200 for one of Sam Houston's suits; there was a sexual liaison in the office, and more.

In the early 1940s, George Parr, famously nicknamed "the Duke of Duval County," along with his equally perfidious father Archer Parr, were among the most corrupt men in the history of Texas politics. Years earlier Robert J. Kleberg, Jr. had told his father he would not vote for Parr; there were too many points on which they disagreed.

"You vote as your conscience dictates," R. J. Kleberg told his son. "But I will support Parr."

"Why?" Bob said.

"He is my friend," R. J. said. Later Bob Kleberg said of his father, "Friendship was the biggest thing with him."

In 1933, Archer Parr was accused of receiving $100,000 from one W. L. Pearson, a Houston road contractor, for assistance in obtaining road contracts in Duval County. The federal government filed income tax liens of $101,407.31 against Archer Parr and $25,344.97 against his wife.

In the election of 1934, Archer Parr was opposed by a rancher named Jim Neal, who ran on the slogan, "Archer can't make it over the hill with that last $100,000."

Archer Parr then had a brainstorm. In the southernmost part of his senatorial district there was a concrete road, completed in 1929, designated as Texas-US 77. It ran from Raymondville north to the barbed-wire fence of King Ranch. All efforts to extend the highway through King Ranch to Kingsville had proven fruitless.

Archer decided that if he could persuade Robert J. Kleberg, Jr. to extend the highway to Kingsville, he might still be re-elected. Taking his son George with him, Archer paid a call at King Ranch. The Parrs tried to explain. The re-election of Archer Parr to the Texas state senate depended on Robert J. Kleberg, Jr.'s facilitating the extension of Highway 77, connecting Corpus Christi to Brownsville in Kleberg County south of Corpus Christi. It would run fifteen miles through the Norias division of King Ranch.

"I don't want a road through my pasture," Kleberg said.

Archer turned away, tears of frustration in his eyes.

"You're crucifying my father!" Parr erupted in anger as he headed for the door. "I'll gut you for this if it's the last thing I do!" George was a chip off the old block, and he would exact his revenge on Dick Kleberg, with the ready assistance of Lyndon Johnson. It didn't matter that neighbors also opposed the right of way; George Parr blamed Bob Kleberg.

Kleberg did attempt to pacify the phlegmatic George Parr by calling his friend Nelson Rockefeller. The two had been introduced by his brother-in-law and best friend Major Tom Armstrong, the legal counsel to Standard Oil. Armstrong had a 50,000-acre ranch between the Kenedy and King ranches. He had married Bob's widowed sister Henrietta in 1949. (Another of Bob's cronies was former Texan Howard Hughes, to whom he introduced his nephew Belton one day in Las Vegas.)

A further barometer of the Kleberg circle was that Major Tom's nephew, Tobin, had in 1949 married Anne Legendre of New Orleans. As "Anne Armstrong," she would later sit simultaneously on the board of Halliburton and on Ronald Reagan's Foreign Intelligence Advisory Board—and serve as the Ambassador to the Court of St. James's.

Rockefeller requested of city planner Robert Moses that he come up with an alternate route. By now half of Highway 77 had been completed. Moses' suggestion of a seashore diversion of the road was impractical. The newspapers sided with the Duke of Duval on the matter of the road.

During this time, George B. Parr had gotten himself indicted by a federal jury in San Antonio for income tax evasion. On May 21, 1934, he pleaded guilty and was sentenced to two years and a $5,000 fine. His probation was revoked on June 3, 1936, and George Parr was committed to El Reno, an Oklahoma Reformatory where he served until April 9, 1937. On August 7, 1943, he applied for a presidential pardon.

As if the matter of the road weren't enough, Representative Richard M. Kleberg was less than enthusiastic about George Parr's application for a presidential pardon. The request for the pardon was denied on January 22, 1944, and that was all it took. Kleberg had served seven terms in Congress, running unopposed on several occasions when in 1944 he suddenly found himself facing a primary.

Now a congressman himself, Lyndon Johnson made a point of not taking sides. He did not support the man who had brought him to Washington and set him firmly on the path to power. There was no question but that he did nothing to help Dick Kleberg.

Publicly, Johnson seemed indifferent to Kleberg's opponent, a Washington lobbyist named John E. Lyle. Lyle was a state representative, but also an active Washington lobbyist specializing in military construction contracts for the Bechtel Corporation and the Transport Company of Texas. He was now a more useful commodity for the future LBJ than the Klebergs.

Without delivering a single speech or shaking a single hand, Lyle won, 29,152 to 17,608. On February 20, 1946, President Truman granted George Parr a full and unconditional presidential pardon, with the enthusiastic support of John Lyle. Looking back on Dick Kleberg's defeat, former Johnson crony Billie Sol Estes would remark that in Texas if Lyndon Johnson didn't want you to be elected, you wouldn't be elected.

Dick Kleberg departed from the Democratic Party, arguing, "The Party left me. I didn't leave it." He returned to King Ranch only to learn that his brother had no intention of sharing power with him. Before long, Dick suffered a heart attack.

In later years Bob Kleberg was defensive on the subject of the highway. The ranch had donated a right of way to the railroad, he said. "We have donated rights of way for several roads, notably on Highway 66, the new road from Kingsville west intersecting with roads north and south through Kingsville in Jim Hogg County."

"It is a matter of record," Kleberg said, "that we have given more than 150 miles of highway right of way, which I believe is more than has been given by any individual ranch or estate in the United States." He contributed emergency landing fields for the airlines. The incident with George Parr remained a very sore point.

Red Cattle

In 1937 you might locate Robert J. Kleberg, Jr. out in the blazing sun calling out which pasture each animal was to be transferred to, while *vaqueros* opened the gates to the pens.

As time went on, at least on his travels, Bob Kleberg lived less simply. In New York, having put up at the Ambassador Hotel and then at the St. Regis, Kleberg bought an apartment on the thirty-seventh floor of the Pierre Hotel on Fifth Avenue. After some years of flying around in borrowed Humble Oil aircraft, he bought his own plane.

Helen encouraged him to pursue thoroughbred racing, and in 1946 a King Ranch horse, Assault, won the Triple Crown. (Two Kleberg horses would win the Kentucky Derby: Assault and Bold Venture.) It was only at this point that Robert J. Kleberg met the press and the public.

Yet, as President of King Ranch, Bob Kleberg collected a salary of only $500 a month. At one point, his mother, Alice Kleberg, wrote a letter to the Santa Gertrudis Board of Directors: "I wish to enter a protest against the salaries paid by the ranch to: Caesar Kleberg, Richard Kleberg, Robert Kleberg & Mr. Finnegan." Addressed to "Bob," and signed "Mother," she protests in her covering note that their salaries are too low, even while acknowledging that "all of the 4 would work for Mother if they could for nothing." "Mother" in this context is Henrietta King.

Asked, years later, how he presided over the multifarious global affairs of King Ranch, Bob Kleberg had a ready answer. "You do things with and through people," he said. "The world works and runs on human energy and we aim to supply that human energy in underdeveloped nations. Some of the countries we are in have perennially been short on protein. We supply protein through meat and thereby supply human energy which is what the world runs on." This had been his credo from the start.

Always Bob Kleberg's heart belonged to King Ranch, which to him was neither Texas, nor Mexico, nor the United States. It was another country. Kleberg referred to the ranch as "this institution." Over the years, his ruling passion remained the same: to breed his Santa Gertrudis cattle in the hope of feeding the world.

One day at Norias, the southernmost of the four divisions of King Ranch, the great game haven of the ranch presided over by Caesar Kleberg, he stooped down and picked up some grains of sand. Then he rubbed them between his fingers. "Colloidal film," he said, "through grass and red cattle," is the way to "keep human beings alive." Grass and roots was the key, Kleberg said. Without roots, the colloidal film "becomes inert, barren, like cement." All the while, "red cattle [were] the best way to purvey food from colloidal film."

He regarded these "red cattle" as his great achievement. Through genetic experimentation, Kleberg produced the first new breed of cattle born and certified in the Americas (in 1940). It had been a particularly bad year. Many of the ranch's cattle had developed worms and more than half of the *vaqueros'* time was spent in doctoring cattle. Bob Kleberg wondered if he could create a breed less susceptible to worms and disease. With that goal in mind, he had gone to work.

Kleberg named his muscular, dark cherry-red creation "Santa Gertrudis" after the original land lease on which King Ranch had been founded. The Santa Gertrudis animal was a cross between a Brahma bull originating in India and the British Shorthorn.

As a consequence of its Brahma bull heritage, Santa Gertrudis turned out to be particularly well suited to tropical or semi-tropical climates, perfect for Texas (and later, Cuba). Cattle experts scoffed and thought Kleberg was crazy, breeding the "dew-lapped, cantankerous muley-eared Brahmans on the refined British breeds." He didn't care.

Later a geneticist said of Kleberg, "He works in the medium of heredity with the steady hand and eye of a man at a lathe turning out a part of a machine." This applied to grass, to quarter horses, and especially to cattle.

The original sire of all the Santa Gertrudis animals was called "Monkey." This was a creature granted considerable reverence at King Ranch. Monkey was mentioned in dinner table conversations as if he were a family member, and there were family debates disputing the year of his birth. (It was 1920.)

Monkey was seven-eighths Brahma bull on his father's side and a lowly milk cow on his mother's, one-sixteenth Brahma and fifteen-sixteenths Shorthorn. Captain King had only tough and rangy Longhorns, brought to the New World by the Spanish. This was an animal entirely different.

From the moment of his birth, Monkey's value was esteemed. This first Santa Gertrudis was considered "a new creature, something that never walked the earth before." He was bred to his daughters and granddaughters, and his best sons were bred to his best daughters, their sisters. Monkey lived until 1930.

Only in 1950 did King Ranch begin to sell bulls on a regular basis. Two thousand ranchers turned out for the first auction and the twenty-nine bulls offered sold at once. One brought $10,000. (The average price of a bull was $3,413.) Every buyer of Santa Gertrudis was given a five-year breeding program and all the scientific data available. When he was asked when he became interested in Santa Gertrudis cattle by someone not knowing that he had invented the breed, Kleberg, not suffering fools gladly, said, "I got interested in these cattle when I found out they could make money."

Someone asked Kleberg how he would define a "new breed"; he offered a ready reply: "It's putting together combinations of genes that heretofore had not existed and concentrating the desirable new combinations into a uniform breeding population." He defined his grass program as "having the world by the tail on a downhill pull."

"Mr. Bob," a ranch hand said one day after the Santa Gertrudis herd had multiplied, "these cattle are outlasting the country. I am worried about the country." Robert J. Kleberg, Jr. smiled.

Since 1931, Bob Kleberg had been shipping calves to New Orleans to serve as veal in the fine restaurants. But Santa Gertrudis beef was so tender, Kleberg claimed, that you could cut it with a fork. Before long, other Texans were raising Santa Gertrudis cattle, among them Houston insurance magnate Gus Wortham, who joined the Santa Gertrudis Association. That ubiquitous entrepreneur D. H. Byrd named his ranch "Byrd Santa Gertrudis Farm, Ltd."

Life on King Ranch

Aided by legendary powers of concentration, there was no ranch problem Kleberg couldn't solve. As his father had done before him, he invented new strains of grass. Battling fever ticks, drought, and mesquite, using his mechanical and engineering skills, he created machinery to clear the land, machinery he would eventually send to Cuba. One day, Kleberg said, respectfully, of the mesquite, *"Está habiéndose su ropa."* The mesquite was *putting on its clothes*, sprouting feathery green leaves.

He invented saddles; tree dozers; a widget-shaped root plow ("Rooter-Plow") that bore its way underground at twelve inches without disturbing the turf in any way; gate latches; a new type of tractor; and methods for getting minerals into cattle. "We build everything to last the life of the material," he once said. His fences boasted neither a nail nor a staple. He was considered a progressive in his field.

Kleberg also bred a new strain of quarter horse that ranked among the finest in the world. Just as Monkey was the progenitor of all Santa Gertrudis cattle, all King Ranch horses descended from Old Sorrel. One enterprise that was anathema to Kleberg was growing agricultural commodities. Kleberg abolished cotton farming on King Ranch land, even when cotton was selling high and cattle were cheap.

"When it runs, it loses money," Bob Kleberg told his cousin Richard King III, referring to King's cotton gin, "and when it stops, it loses more." Kleberg obsessively viewed cattle ranching as a superior force and a branch of agriculture. "I never wanted to do anything else," he once said. For most of his life, he did not belong to that class of empire builders whose interests CIA would serve.

Every morning Kleberg rose between 5 and 6 AM. He ate heartily in his younger years: oatmeal, bacon and eggs, orange juice, and black coffee, so as not to waste time on lunch. Only later in life did his morning fare consist of milk laced with bourbon (*leche colorado*, literally "red milk"). He was fond of beef and black beans and barbecued ribs, as might be expected, and was addicted to chilipiquins—green, berry-size chili peppers, red hot and either eaten alone or mashed into duck, goose, venison, or turkey.

Dinner at camp might be lamb lungs and liver cooked in their own blood from an animal slaughtered that morning, then salted and hung up to dry. If he had his choice, he said, he would rather have *carne asada* roasted over a camp grill than a sirloin or a filet. Kidneys were broiled in a wrapping of intestines. There was always skillet or camp bread cooked in Dutch ovens over wood coals.

Dinner at home began with Old Fashioneds concocted out of Bonds Mill Old-Time barrel bourbon, imported from Kentucky. It might be venison, wild duck, goose, or turkey. The desserts were Spanish-Mexican as often as American.

Both the Kleberg women painted and sketched. Conversation ranged from cattle, horses, dogs, hunting, and industry to politics and world affairs, and the way the government should run things. Or Kleberg might debate how high the hawk flies.

Down the decades, Bob Kleberg shared with Herman Brown a work ethic reflective of the century in which they were born, although Herman Brown was born into poverty and Kleberg to a feudal landed family. Mr. Bob defined "rest" as "hard physical exercise, mostly in the saddle."

Riding the herd, he gave orders from the saddle, calling them "horseback decisions." Or Kleberg might say, "No work is nearly so important as hard work. No question about it. I'm right as a fox." Work was fun, better than baseball. Kleberg had initiated baseball games on the ranch only for interest to be scant. "Cow punching is baseball," he concluded. "We combine work and play and have the greatest sport in the world."

In his presence, everyone had to stand up straight and no one dared advance an opinion unless asked. If you worked for Bob Kleberg, you didn't stop for a drink of water until a task was completed, the cattle safely in the pen. No one was permitted to ask a *Kineño* to do a job he could do himself.

"Executives? Bookkeepers?" he once said. "Hell, you can get them anywhere. But a top cowhand has to start when he's a baby." Hierarchy was bred into him, and it was a foreman's son who was first in line to receive a foreman's job. People who belonged to the old families of the ranch, who dated back to the "Old Captain's" time, were most likely to be promoted to become foreman or caporals (straw bosses). You worked on Sundays and holidays, because meat was a perishable commodity.

By 1951, King Ranch was not only the largest private ranch in the United States, but also the biggest beef-producing enterprise in the world. From 85,000 acres in 1870, the ranch now consisted of 920,000 acres of land and hosted 85,000 head of cattle.

The *Kineños* were paid little in cash, and a *vaquero* might earn only $85 a month. In Kleberg's anachronistic feudal style, they were afforded free housing, free schools, doctors, food, utilities, and clothes as well as a modest house for life. The clothes included spurs, chaps, shirts, pants, and raincoats. Free food consisted of milk and butter, meat, meal, flour, beans, sugar, and coffee. There were public schools on the ranch and Dick Kleberg, Mr. Bob's nephew, attended the ranch school so he could learn to live and get along with the Mexicans.

Almost no one was ever fired. "Any damned fool can fire somebody," Kleberg told one of his managers. "It takes management to find a place where he can be of best service. You must have had some reason for hiring him in the first place. So go and try to find the right place for him." The widow of a foreman who died retained her home and allowance on the ranch, as did her children, as if they, like Kleberg himself, enjoyed an inalienable right.

"They are of the institution," Kleberg said. "We retire them and take care of them as long as they live." When an employee who had worked for only two months came down with tuberculosis, the ranch maintained her in a private sanatorium for two years, took care of her children, and continued to pay her salary. When she came home and was still unable to work, she was given a living allowance.

If someone stole, Kleberg did not call in the Texas Rangers. "Oh, I let him go," the senior Kleberg had remarked of a thief. "I guess he was hungry." In 1951, someone remarked, "I never saw a man wearing a pistol on any part of the ranch." Kleberg taught his children to work with a kind manner. A King Ranch carpenter remembered once in 1903 having tried to borrow $200 from the elder Kleberg. Kleberg gave him yard work to do until he had earned the money.

You left King Ranch only in wartime. When his orphaned nephew, Belton, was hired at King Ranch, he chafed at his uncle's autocratic manner, at the way he second-guessed decisions not his own. Angry and frustrated that his uncle had questioned his judgment, Belton quit. The year was 1956. His uncle was unmoved.

"Nobody's ever left King Ranch," Kleberg said. "You'll be back."

This time he was wrong. When Belton bought his own ranch, his uncle gave him 3,000 steers to fatten. But he never trusted Belton again. "Belton's gone to do whatever," Kleberg told someone who asked.

Belton, in turn, found his uncle "at times petulant, opinionated, short-tempered, charismatic, domineering and, to some, arrogant." He was "highly strung and did not often relax or let his guard down." Yet Belton had to grant that Uncle Bob "could just as readily be kind, generous, humane, interesting, fun to be with, fair and open-minded."

He was a man to whom it was important to think well of himself, which included dispensing justice to those who worked for him, so long as they contributed their energy and loyalty to the enterprise. Still, his unpredictability could be disconcerting. Bob Kleberg, Belton knew, could "be as mean as a junkyard dog."

Richard Kleberg's son, Dick, Jr., had made himself indispensable at King Ranch, and he fared better than his cousin Belton. "My job is to do what Uncle Bob is too busy to do," Dick, Jr. said.

The dark side of Robert J. Kleberg's paternalism was that he was hostile to the autonomy of others, not only of Belton, but of the residents of the town of Kingsville. When the school board tried to levy a tax for improvements to the education buildings, he "fought it tooth and claw."

Yet, always, as *"el patrón,"* Kleberg made sure the *Kineños* understood that he, like them, worked for King Ranch. "Do you work for Mr. Richard and Mr. Robert Kleberg?" a Mexican was asked.

"I work for the King Ranch. Mr. Dick and Mr. Bob, they work for the King Ranch, too" was the tutored reply.

When a visiting British official asked a ranch hand what he did, the reply was not subservient. "I don't do anything," this *Kineño* said. "I live here."

If the manner was feudalistic, the atmosphere was one of shared obligation, if based upon knowing one's "place." The terms "high hat" and "exclusive" applied to other Kings and Klebergs, but not to Robert J. Kleberg, Jr.

He may have proclaimed that surpluses be used "for the common good," but he was determined always to secure "attractive prices."

He opposed the government's regulation of anything to do with the ranch, and was, in fact, opposed to all regulation. Countries like Argentina, which had a long history of government controls in the cattle business, found themselves confronted by a black market. A free economy and a free market were necessary, Kleberg believed.

He had emerged out of an America that believed that if you worked hard, you would do well; the America of the century in which he was born. Still, in 1953 he urged President Eisenhower to purchase half a billion pounds of dressed beef and make it available to countries with shortages. During the summer of 1952, Kleberg had devoted "a lot of last-minute attention" to ensuring Eisenhower's victory. "I really believe he is going to win," he said.

In the last year of his life, he was talking about how it might be possible for the ships that brought oil and gas to take agricultural produce back to the "Arabian" countries and, for that matter, to Europe and Russia. By now, he did think globally. He also thought minutely, pondered how all meat might be made tender, and talked about a project with Texas A&M on the subject.

Always his prodigious self-confidence fueled him. "Every time he tries," his lawyer Leroy Denman noted, "he is completely confident and he's always trying." If an animal did not gain 300 pounds a year, "out he goes," Kleberg granted. First and foremost he was a producer of food. He noticed in the 1950s that the population had increased 16 percent, while meat production went up only by 9 percent. He saw himself as charged with feeding not only the country, but the entire world.

You did things Mr. Bob's way. At times Bob Kleberg seemed as "tough as his boot leather," even as he could be "supple when the occasion required it." He might be "dictatorial," his wife, Helen, remarked, "but he was never petty and he was not grandiose." He let people have their say, Helen Kleberg observed.

Holland McCombs, that reporter who came to work for him, said he never knew Bob to "exert unpleasant pressure." With his natural attitude he could dominate any room, scene, or group, "even when he was not trying to do so." Told that he was having lunch with a group from the Department of Agriculture in Washington and some agricultural ministers from other countries, Kleberg assumed immediate command of the situation with a force of concentration that made you think he had been thinking about the event for months rather than minutes.

He could also be daring and reckless, and it was said that on one occasion when he stayed at the Gunter Hotel on West Houston Street in San Antonio he shot pigeons off the roof of the adjacent building with a Colt .45.

"My, Mr. Kleberg, but this is a fabulous place," a visitor to King Ranch said.

"Fabulous, my eye," Kleberg said then. "This is just a beef factory." There was a variation on the theme. "This is a big meat store down here," he might say. As the years passed, he remained interested in increasing production, which he did by soil conservation, improvement of grasses, supplementary feeding to supply grass deficiencies, and constantly improving the animal by breeding and increased fertilization.

Always there had to be clearing and reclearing of brush. His approach was as a scientist; science was the subject he had hoped to study when he went to college. Obsessed by the problem of hoof and mouth disease, and the effect it would have on the meat supply, he suddenly one day barked at a room full of people, "Not only me! It's YOU, too."

He claimed that he preserved King Ranch traditions because they were "the BEST way." Bob Kleberg added, "Tradition must be something or they wouldn't have paid so much attention to it. They would not have remembered it so long."

His self-confidence prevented him from being paralyzed by the fear of being wrong, and in this Herman Brown joined him. "The road to progress is paved with mistakes," Kleberg said, embroidering on his father's less graceful "The road to success is paved with failures which have been corrected." Neither father nor son was afraid of failing.

Robert J. Kleberg, Jr. was not a book reader. "I want no educated man in camp, R. J.!" Captain King had told his son-in-law, Kleberg's father. Finding himself once at Harriman House in New York, listening impatiently to an academic babble on, Bob Kleberg remained silent. Finally he offered his opinion: "Well, I don't agree with ANYTHING he said."

"Maybe Mr. Kleberg has got something there," said a sycophantic Henry Luce of the *Time-Life* empire. Luce's reaction was similar to Allen Dulles'. Kleberg was a man to be heeded. "You should goddamn well know I never listen to anybody!" Kleberg told his assistant, John Cypher. The habit of command became him. If his father had promoted for farms and towns, Bob considered the country as range country.

Tact was not high on the agenda of this man. He gave a radio address in Australia and after counting down the country's virtues, he told them not only their faults but, in his estimation, how they should cure them. His lawyer told him he should have waited until he got home to be so frank, but that was not his style. Just as Robert J. Kleberg, Jr. disliked movie cowboys, he abhorred pretense. He didn't like corrals because they bruised the cattle, which smashed themselves against the gates. If he was a hard driver of men, he was relentless with himself.

Six years passed and no oil had been discovered on King Ranch. In 1939, the wells came in and never stopped.

Kleberg affected disinterest. "I have no business except King Ranch business," he said. He put the cash into "the thing we knew. The thing we had used our lives doing. The thing that interested us most. Ranching." He never discussed exactly how much was earned by the oil and gas deposits.

The presence of oil wells and derricks on his land irritated him. If firearms were ever discovered in a Humble Oil truck, that driver was banned from King Ranch forever. Oil company refuse left on the property awakened Kleberg's anger. "When we made the contract with Humble," he explained, "we knew who we were dealing with. They keep their places tidy."

By the turn of the 1950s there were 650 producing oil and gas wells on King Ranch. In 1960, to cite one year, the Humble revenue amounted to $20 million.

Although it was the biggest individual oil and gas lease in existence, and King Ranch oil revenues far exceeded those from ranching, Kleberg disabused anyone who dared call him an "oilman." Nor, as some gossiped, had the oil had anything to do with his racehorse stables. These were set up before the oil wells came in. "We operated the ranch for eighty-five years without oil and did well," he said. "With oil we do better." Later Kleberg would boast of having known seven Humble chairmen.

Accumulating money was neither his passion nor his talent. Once he did a real estate deal with Gus Wortham. Kleberg quickly sold his half-interest to EXXON, losing big. The land became the most valuable in Texas.

In December 1947, the year that marked the creation of CIA, Robert J. Kleberg, Jr. made the cover of *Time* magazine. *Time* described him as "lean-faced, gimlet eyed, wearing a Stetson, and high-heeled boots." He commanded his *vaqueros* with "swift gestures."

As Kleberg situated himself under the radar of notoriety, despite those *Time* and *Fortune* stories about him, King Ranch became an American institution. Presidents, British royalty, and movie stars coveted invitations. The Queen Mother became besotted with Bob Kleberg. In earlier times Tom Mix was a favored guest. Mix arrived dressed all in white, behind the wheel of a white Packard and pulling a trailer with a white horse (who was not Tony the Wonder Horse; Tony was black).

You could not ask to be invited to King Ranch. When Bing Crosby solicited an invitation to go hunting on King Ranch, Kleberg drove him out onto the range and demanded that he sing. Crosby began, with his pipe between his teeth.

"You can't sing with that in your mouth!" Kleberg said. Then he reached over and removed the pipe. There was no hunting that day.

In 1948, when Lyndon Johnson ran for the second time for the United States Senate, the Klebergs supported Governor Coke Stevenson, his opponent. Johnson complained that there had been a "bloc vote behind the locked gates of the King Ranch." Not a single vote from anyone working at King Ranch went to Lyndon Johnson.

Kleberg marked the 1953 centenary of King Ranch not with a self-congratulatory orgy, but with a scientific conference on "Breeding Beef Cattle in Unfavorable Environments." "If you cannot improve the breed, you might as well stop" was another of Kleberg's maxims.

Kleberg paid tribute to his grandfather Captain King for his "permanent occupation," which was "the beginning of permanent civilization in this area. For that once at least, civilization came and remained because of a ranch." He invoked his father, Robert Justus

Kleberg II, who had told him often that "in order to survive in this country he must make himself more valuable alive than dead."

As for himself, Kleberg humbly described his own responsibility as following the examples of his grandfather and his father. "We've been trying to do it ever since," he added. His own goal had to do with feeding the increased world population. "Today food is important *in* and *to* human affairs," he said. "Food has become an effective instrument of diplomacy. More than ever before FOOD has become a weapon for *peace!*" King Ranch has produced surpluses that "can be used for the common good. They can be used to a better advantage than bullets . . . they can be used *instead* of bullets." He believed he was contributing to "the world peace effort."

Not surprisingly, he contrasted the United States with Iron Curtain countries unable to feed themselves. But he urged the government to make food surpluses available to those "in real need of food." He was an idealist, as quixotic as his future Cuban friend Alberto Fernández de Hechavarría. He wanted "to help the free world to make *all* of the world free! And to be free from hunger." In the service of these ideals, he was celebrating the centennial "not by a big parade or pageant—or a blow-out," but to give recognition to the cattle industry and the animal sciences. The master of ceremonies was Dick Kleberg's son, Dick, Jr.; Robert J. Kleberg, Jr. appeared on the centennial conference program as if he were just another speaker. Behind the scenes, of course, Bob Kleberg orchestrated everything.

The keynote speaker at the centennial was a freewheeling adventurer and oil heir named Tom Slick, for whom Neil Mallon would attempt to secure a job at CIA by enlisting the help of Allen Dulles. At the time, Slick was president of the "Southwest Foundation for Research and Education." Before he delivered his speech, Slick, who sat on the Dresser board of directors, showed the text to Dresser CEO Mallon.

In his speech, titled "Past and Future in Animal Breeding," Slick called its foreign expansion a part of King Ranch's "private point four program" and "perhaps the outstanding achievement of the last administration." (Tom Slick would perish in a crash of his twin-engine plane in the Montana Mountains in 1962; he was forty-six years old.)

When President Eisenhower chose centennial day to visit King Ranch, Kleberg declined the privilege. It was yet another indication that Kleberg moved in realms of power above that of mere presidents and elected officials. The centennial was an emotional moment, and Kleberg was not about to allow anyone to interrupt. His conference of scientists meant far more to him than hobnobbing with a president.

Kleberg was only a 20 percent owner of King Ranch, and ostensibly he ran King Ranch for the Klebergs. Still, Kleberg used King Ranch's oil revenues not to make his relatives rich, as they would have preferred, but to develop King Ranch satellites in foreign countries. He was notorious for paying as low a dividend as he could. The King Ranch letterhead now named Robt. J. Kleberg, Jr., Pres; J. H. Clement, Sec'y; and Richard M. Kleberg, Jr., Vice Pres. Kleberg decided that "for some time to come I must say that I think we should stay out of print." He remained comfortable only with King Ranch being far from the public spotlight.

Global politics interested him, party politics scarcely at all. Governor Shivers was plain Allen Shivers to him and President Johnson would always be "Lyndon." When there was talk in 1959 of Nikita Khrushchev visiting King Ranch, it seemed a desirable idea, if one that never happened.

Later, when John F. Kennedy made the error of sending left-leaning President João Goulart of Brazil to visit King Ranch, Bob Kleberg made certain to absent himself that day. He couldn't refuse Kennedy's request outright. Kleberg's King Ranch satellite in Brazil might suffer consequences. Brazil was but one of nine satellites, even as it made the radio news when, in January 1954, King Ranch shipped 200 Santa Gertrudis heifers and some bulls to that country.

Kleberg's political approach requires some context. His perspective transcended narrow party politics, and he could be classified neither as a Democrat nor a Republican. When President Lyndon Johnson ran for re-election in 1964, Bob Kleberg offered his enthusiastic support to Republican Barry Goldwater. Kleberg had already voted Republican—for Dwight Eisenhower. Yet there is a snapshot dating from 1968 of Bob Kleberg in the company of Lyndon Johnson, and there was continued sporadic contact between the two despite the falling out attendant upon Johnson's betrayal of Richard Kleberg. Kleberg visited the Johnson ranch on the occasion of a visit by German chancellor Konrad Adenauer and Kleberg was seated at the table with the guest of honor.

Kleberg also attended Johnson White House dinners, including one for the king of Morocco, with whom Kleberg was to do business as he established a King Ranch Moroccan satellite. Still, Bob Kleberg would forever treat the treacherous former secretary of his brother with irony, and the locution "Mr. President" was alien to him when it came to Johnson. The true feeling of the Klebergs toward Johnson is epitomized by a moment in 1970 when Ronnie Dugger, writing his biography of Johnson, requested an interview with Richard M. Kleberg's widow, Mamie.

"I don't think you'd be interested in my opinion of Mr. Johnson," Mamie said.

CIA-connected Texans like Kleberg were loyal neither to Democrats nor Republicans, and behaved as if there was no appreciable or principled difference between them. In this, they resembled the robber barons of the Gilded Age.

Jay Gould attempted to put to rest the myth that there was any appreciable distinction. "In a Republican district, I was a Republican," Gould admitted. "In a Democratic district, I was a Democrat. In a doubtful district, I was doubtful; but I was always for Erie." Erie was Gould's railroad. Robert J. Kleberg, Jr. might have uttered the same sentence, substituting "King Ranch" for Erie.

Gould was not unique among late-nineteenth-century robber barons in this view. "No politics of any kind," said H. O. Havemeyer, who headed the American Sugar Refining Company, "only the politics of business." A popular volume of the day, *The Passing of the Idle Rich,* summarized the prevailing view:

> It matters not one iota what political party is in power or what President holds the reins of office. We are not politicians or public thinkers; we are the rich; we own America; we got it, God knows how; but we intend to keep it if we can.

It was not only how they could keep what they had, but also how they might expand their wealth that brought CIA into the picture.

For corporate leaders in a symbiotic relationship with CIA, party politics had to be irrelevant. CIA's long-time General Counsel Lawrence ("Larry") Houston admitted to the Church committee in 1975 that CIA "put officers in both the Republican and the Democratic Committees." The Agency knew well enough that it must transcend the myth that Democrats and Republicans did not serve one system.

Giant

In the years before Kleberg's foray into Cuba, and the advent of Fidel Castro disturbed his tranquility, one particular incident left Kleberg in defeat. In March 1940, the thorniest visitor of all began her siege on King Ranch. It was author Edna Ferber, a prolific middlebrow novelist and a transplanted easterner who resided at fashionable 812 Park Avenue in New York City. Ferber enjoyed some notoriety by now. She had won a Pulitzer for *So Big* (1924) and had also written *Showboat* (1926), which became a Broadway hit in 1927, and *Cimarron* (1929), a film adapation of which won the Academy Award for Best Picture in 1931.

Ferber approached the former republic with humility. She admitted that "to write a book about Texas would be an impertinence, since it was such a large state, with so many varied interests, climates, meanings and peoples." She granted, "Only a minute part of Texas could be used at a time."

Ferber opened her siege on Bob Kleberg by writing to King Ranch factotum and sometime Kleberg speechwriter Holland McCombs, who was also a journalist with *Time* magazine. McCombs at once perceived the danger. He tried to steer Ferber away from King Ranch as the subject of her next novel.

"The thing has been done to pieces by too many people," McCombs told Ferber.

The following November, Ferber wrote to McCombs again, this time requesting that he locate some other ranches for her to visit. Relieved, McCombs promised to fix her up with "a couple of the really new rich Houston oil boys and girls and maybe a power politician like J. Frank Dobie." Texas ranchers "are a bit gruff-like," McCombs warned Ferber.

Ferber met with Dobie. She needed to live on a ranch and observe a roundup to write her book, Ferber explained. Dobie thought: For her purposes, any kind of cowboy would do. He didn't know of any ranches that might accommodate her, Dobie said.

It was June 1941 when Ferber got herself invited to lunch at King Ranch. She is frumpish and bookish, thought Belton Kleberg, who was at that time still living at King Ranch. She was also "feisty and very, very smart."

Helenita, Bob and Helen's only child, was present to observe the event.

Professing to have taken too long a walk in the hot sun, Helen Kleberg pleaded that she was not up to appearing for lunch and escaped to her room.

Conversation was not Edna Ferber's strong suit. "I once had a cow," she said. Kleberg looked at her then with what Ferber would later call a "steely" gaze. She perceived that he was "on his guard" and that he didn't much like her.

Ferber was right. For Kleberg, she was a "lady writer," someone not to be taken seriously and in a category somewhere below the male intellectuals he scorned.

"I want to write about a typical Texas ranch," Ferber said, her foot planted firmly in her mouth.

"King Ranch is far from typical," Kleberg said mildly. He added that there would, someday, be an accurate history of King Ranch that she might reference, but he didn't have time right now to devote himself to one. He certainly didn't want an inaccurate book written. In Kleberg's mind, that closed the subject.

"I'm going to write the book anyway," Ferber said, "with or without your consent."

This was going too far. Coffee hadn't yet been served when Kleberg asked Helenita to call for Ferber's driver, who had been sitting in the kitchen eating his lunch. Then Kleberg rose, took Ferber's arm and escorted her to the door. Her parting remark was to the effect that she was not yet finished with him.

When Kleberg returned, Belton observed a "black scowl" on his face. As for Edna Ferber, she concluded that Robert J. Kleberg, Jr. was every bit as difficult a man as she had been led to believe.

September 1948 found Edna Ferber as enthused as ever about her Texas novel. "During all these years the Texas idea has taunted me and deviled me," Ferber wrote to McCombs. She now had a list of what she needed: "to visit two or three or four cattle ranches, in particular the main house; the dwellings of the employees, an autumn roundup . . . the lay of the land."

She wanted to "talk to Mexicans who have worked or are working on ranches"; she wanted to meet Texas "old-timers," Texans "born and bred, and who have lived there fifty—sixty—seventy—eighty years. If possible." And, she said, echoing McCombs, she would "love to meet a couple of the really new rich Houston oil boys and girls. And maybe a power-politician." Edna Ferber was nothing if not thorough.

Undeterred, tone-deaf as far as Robert J. Kleberg, Jr. was concerned, Ferber bided her time. In October 1948, she asked McCombs to arrange for her to make a return visit to King Ranch. This request was handled by Kleberg's secretary, Lee Gillette, who wrote to McCombs: "At the present time, Mr. Kleberg is out of the state and is not expected to return for quite some time. However, I wish to advise that Miss Ferber was here in June of this year for a short visit and as far as I know nothing was worked out for a return visit."

"I see that I made rather a mess of it," Ferber writes to McCombs in a December 1948 letter. She recalls that Kleberg had been "hot!" and "on guard." She adds, "Oklahoma didn't like me immediately after *Cimarron*," but "the years have mellowed them." Still, Ferber confides to McCombs, "I'm frantic to get a couple of good bites of ranch stuff." Her interest in Texas had been revived, and Holland McCombs was once more enlisted to help her. He would tell people that she was a personal friend, and he even invited her to his own little ranch in the Pedernales country.

Ferber's enthusiasm for Texas flowed unabated: "I think Texas is wonderful and unbelievable and exhilarating and different and very American—with a strong dash of Latin for color," she gushes in her letter. What she would lack in subtlety she made up in energy and warmth for her subject.

Still, few in Texas wanted anything to do with her. Lewis Nordyke, *Amarillo Globe-News* reporter and author of a book about Texas called *Cattle Empire* (1949), wrote that she could learn the routine of running a ranch in one afternoon. She rejected visiting the Panhandle area because of the winter rainy seasons. Having returned to Texas, she wrote on April 18, 1949, that she had a "fine time!"

McCombs remained a Kleberg vassal and was invited to his daughter, Helenita's, wedding in 1949.

Edna Ferber never again set foot on King Ranch, a place she attempts to depict, with Robert J. Kleberg, Jr. as the thinly veiled inspiration for the protagonist, in her 1952 novel *Giant*.

In *Giant*, Ferber exacts her full revenge on Bob Kleberg. The hero, Bick Benedict, the cruelest of *latifundistas*, is harsh, stubborn, and a racist. His wife, Leslie, arrives at King Ranch, as did Helen Kleberg, from Virginia. Their lifetime of marital dissension focuses on Bick's ill treatment of the impoverished Mexican *vaqueros*, who are relegated to a ghetto of dilapidated shacks on a vast property that boasts its own private railroad, as did King Ranch. The Mexicans in *Giant* are desperate and suffer from lack of medical care.

The climax of *Giant* is a real-life incident that took place in 1949. It's the vulgar, even grotesque, grand opening of oilman Glenn McCarthy's Shamrock Hotel, a three-day-long orgy attended by the Klebergs, although Helen left early, leaving Bob and Belton to fend for themselves. Edna Ferber also attended the event. In George Stevens' 1956 film adaptation, McCarthy appears as Jed Rink, played by James Dean. Bick Benedict is played by Rock Hudson, and his wife, Leslie, by Elizabeth Taylor.

Despised by everyone who called themselves "Kleberg," *Giant* went on to sell three million copies. Later, Edna Ferber was lunching at a Beverly Hills restaurant when one of the Klebergs walked in. Ferber hid behind her menu. "He didn't want me around, nor any of my kind," Ferber said, her final word on the subject of Robert J. Kleberg, Jr.

Kleberg never attacked Edna Ferber publicly, although he told a Cuban friend that Edna Ferber was "the only woman I ever called a son-of-a-bitch!" *Giant* rankled Kleberg and the publicity compelled him to introduce King Ranch to the general public. He commissioned Texas artist and writer Tom Lea to write an authorized history. He hoped, Kleberg said, that "truth, rather than fiction, will prevail."

"Let me say right here and now that I don't give a damn what you write, just as long as it is the truth," Kleberg told Lea. "I can't help but believe that when you stay very close to the truth in anything you do in life or in print you are better off." Kleberg insisted that he wanted a "bare knuckles" approach to the story.

Still, Helen Kleberg, finding the text "overly critical" of her husband, applied a hagiographic blue pencil to Lea's manuscript, according to the project researcher Holland McCombs. (McCombs received a scant $12,000 for more than five years of work on the book.) The censored two-volume history of King Ranch was swept clean of Robert J. Kleberg's political views. You won't find them there.

CHAPTER 3

KING RANCH GOES GLOBAL

> "I'll take care of the cattle. You take care of
> everything else."
>
> Robert J. Kleberg, Jr. to
> Michael J. P. Malone

Satellite King Ranches, more often than not joint ventures, proliferated in Latin America, Australia, and Europe. His fellow King Ranch owners, Kleberg relatives, whined that Bob Kleberg was creating an "overseas empire." His nephew Belton remarked, sarcastically, that his uncle was doing "his bit to alleviate Third World poverty and famine." Belton complained that Kleberg "had little time for the board unless it operated to rubber stamp what he wanted."

Mr. Bob ignored his protesting relatives and went ahead. Before he settled on a country in which to develop an outpost of King Ranch, Kleberg corresponded with people there. He requested books on the history of the country, its current economic condition, the social dimensions of the society, and the political currents. He wanted a dossier on the leading politicians and who was most influential in the government.

He also studied the geography and the topology of the country; he studied the variations of soil, the nature of the vegetation, and the amount of annual rainfall. He sought local partners with whom to structure joint ventures. In 1951, he began in Australia with Sir Rupert Clarke, an Oxford-educated lawyer. Among his partners in

Australia was Swift and Company, then one of the largest meat-production outfits in the world. By 1951, there were 500 Santa Gertrudis breeders in the world, including one E. J. Barker in Cuba, who had 4,500 head, plus 3,000 more very close to registry quality.

By the 1950s, Robert J. Kleberg, Jr. was a figure of planetary power—without portfolio—forging alliances with foreign entrepreneurs like General Maximino Ávila Camacho, ex-president of Mexico. Kleberg sent Camacho a foundation herd of Santa Gertrudis not only as a "gesture of personal friendship, but of international good will." Allen Dulles' visit to King Ranch after his talk at the Dallas Council on World Affairs should be placed in this context.

At King Ranch, Kleberg entertained the Moroccan royal family where the King, spotting a pigskin chair in his room, collected his entourage and searched for more appropriate quarters. There would be King Ranches in Spain and Morocco. Government officials in Morocco held Czarnikow-Rionda, Kleberg's Cuban partners, at a distance, but they were much taken with Robert J. Kleberg, Jr.

The satellite ranch closest to Kleberg's heart was *Becerra,* King Ranch in Cuba. It was the fate of *Becerra* that brought Kleberg back in touch with Allen Dulles and in direct connection with the Central Intelligence Agency. There had been Santa Gertrudis bulls in Cuba since 1936, and so the climate had been tested. Grass grew all year long. "Cuba has some of the best grazing land on earth," Kleberg discovered.

"What are you trying to do, Bob?" the editor of *The Kingsville Record* asked him, referring to the King Ranches in Australia and Cuba. "Find some place in the world where it rains?" Kleberg estimated that it would take five years or more for them to see "substantial beef production from our foreign operations."

In Cuba there was little beef available for public consumption, and government manipulation of beef prices had been catastrophic. In 1945, there were 3,800,000 cattle grazing. Kleberg figured that Cuba's vast pastureland could support a herd of seven million.

What Kleberg envisioned for Cuba was beef for the whole population at cheap prices.

In his speech that closed the centennial conference at King Ranch, Tom Slick talked about King Ranch's "foreign expansions" as a "technical aid program." Kleberg's goal for all King Ranches was messianic: to bring the best beef to the world's hungry at fair prices. Cuba needed desperately "an improved and increased beef supply." Who better to make that happen?

For expansion, Kleberg looked to the "tropical belt of the world" where the largest undeveloped areas were to be found, along with cheap land.

One day in 1950, Bob and Helen Kleberg were in Havana attending a dinner given in honor of the Duke and Duchess of Windsor, people more to Helen's taste than to Bob's. Kleberg loved the Havana Yacht Club and the daiquiris he dubbed "Cuban lemonade."

On that trip, Kleberg made the acquaintance of sugar broker George A. Braga, whose company, Czarnikow-Rionda, was based on Wall Street. With its confederation of small sugar companies, Czarnikow attempted obsessively to corner the sugar market. The Bragas functioned as middlemen, buying up sugar from mills and then selling it on the open market. They controlled hundreds of miles of railroads. Manati, among their companies, owned vast forests. The Bragas managed in the process to exploit both the cane growers and their laborers. Manati stretched over 200,000 acres of land and extended from the northwest corner of Cuba's Oriente Province into Camagüey. Of those 200,000 acres, only 30,000 were under cultivation.

The Braga brothers, George and Ronny (B. Rionda Braga), exhibited few altruistic impulses. In the company files, there are no stories about how average Cubans were faring. They were suitable targets for the cries of "Yankee Go Home" that would greet American businessmen in Cuba by the last years of the Batista dictatorship.

The Bragas held a great deal of land in scrub, unsuitable for sugar cultivation. Yet when they discovered poor Cuban squatters on this unoccupied ground, they ejected them forcibly. Their enforcer was a relative, Salvador Rionda.

Salvador was compelled to leave the tranquility of his home and was charged with making the long journey to Santiago de Cuba where he appeared in court before a *Tribunal de Urgencia* on behalf of the Bragas. The squatter was forced to prove uninterrupted occupancy of the land with tax records. Of course, there were none.

The Bragas bribed judges in the service of disenfranchising the poor from their land. When necessary, the Bragas hired vigilantes, bands of armed men who roamed the fallow land. In 1948, employees of Manati Sugar attacked a community, killing the *precarista*, the squatter leader.

Casting a cold eye on all this was Salvador Rionda's son-in-law, Alberto Fernández de Hechavarría, and he will be the hero of this section of the story. It is through Alberto's life history that CIA's methods and motives in relation to Cuba come glaringly to light. When Alberto enters the narrative, he is a sugar grower and cattle rancher, and among the most influential men in Cuba.

Furious at the Bragas' cruelty to fellow farmers, Alberto telephoned the main office of Manati Sugar in New York to complain. The land was just sitting there, fallow, and the squatters were doing no harm, he argued.

Alberto's approach, then, as later, was direct. This has to stop, Alberto said. He would engage his uncles, who were lawyers, and take measures in defense of his father-in-law, Alberto threatened. "There is a duty for a citizen to help," he thought. Not wanting his own father, Federico Fernández Casas, to be touched in any way by this unsavory business with the Bragas and the squatters, Alberto did not involve him.

Alberto viewed the Bragas' business practices as devious and dishonest. They juggled numbers and bought what they needed not from Cuban-owned companies, but from their own subsidiaries, freezing the Cubans out. They contributed nothing to enriching the community.

The Bragas controlled hundreds of miles of Cuban railroads, and even their railroad ties were purchased not from Cubans, but from a Braga-controlled company called Cuban Trading. The Bragas also bought and sold petroleum through their own companies. They cared nothing about the Cuban people and what might benefit them. The Bragas and Czarnikow-Rionda were the paradigm of what was wrong with the Batista-nourished imperial presence of American business in Cuba. Alberto saw himself as a Cuban patriot as he experienced the last years of the Batista government.

Facing checkmate, unwilling to cross Alberto Fernández, the Bragas devised a new plan to solve their squatter problem. If they could discover someone with sufficient ready cash, they could raise cattle on their barren land, and so eliminate the squatters that way. They would put up 1,000 *caballerías* of pastureland (a *caballería* is about 33.1 acres), and their partner would finance the rest. In 1950, in Havana, George Braga met the very person able and willing to provide the cattle and the cash: Robert J. Kleberg, Jr.

"One thing is Kleberg, the other is these people," Alberto Fernández told me, his final word on the Bragas.

The Virgin Mary

On November 26, 1950, Robert J. Kleberg, Jr. entertained a charming, roguish visitor at King Ranch. His name was Michael John Patrick Malone, although everyone called him "Jack." Malone had been dispatched to Kingsville by George A. Braga, his employer. Situated at his office at 106 Wall Street in New York City, Jack Malone was a vice president of Czarnikow-Rionda and Braga's trusted right-hand man.

A devout Catholic—one of his brothers was a priest—Jack was a 1936 graduate of Fordham University. On bumpy airplane trips in the South American jungles, Jack invariably drew out his rosary beads. He was on friendly terms with the presidents of

Georgetown and Fordham universities and was a member of the Knights of Malta, to which many CIA assets, like himself, were connected.

(The Knights of Malta—Hospitallers of St. John of Jerusalem—originated as a medieval order in about 1050 to provide hospice care for poor and ailing pilgrims to the Holy Land. By 1099, they had become a military order on behalf of the Crusades, its members recruited from the nobility. The Knights fought on behalf of Christianity, claiming sovereignty under international law. The motto of the Knights of Malta is "*Tuitio Fidei et Obsequium Pauperum*"—Defense of the faith and assistance to the poor.

More recently the Knights of Malta has functioned as a secret society with the flavor of the intelligence community. Among their members have been John McCone, William F. Buckley, Jr., Alexander Haig, Bill Casey—and, of course, Michael J. P. Malone. CIA enjoys a symbiotic relationship with the Knights of Malta, CIA veteran John Quirk told me.)

Malone's previous employer was the Archbishop of New York, Francis, Cardinal Spellman. Malone had been Cardinal Spellman's most favored aide, his personal assistant, but you won't find Malone's name in John Cooney's biography of Cardinal Spellman, *The American Pope*.

Jack Malone could claim to be among the most important CIA assets of his era, although he would never himself make such a claim. His CIA relationships predated his service to Cardinal Spellman, who also made himself available to the Agency. During World War II, Malone and George Braga came to know Allen Dulles, and Braga would serve on the board of directors of J. Henry Schroder Bank & Trust Company, alongside Dulles; Czarnikow-Rionda was represented by Dulles' law firm, Sullivan & Cromwell. Jack Malone had interacted with Cardinal Spellman's intelligence contacts. On behalf of the FBI, Spellman had enlisted priests throughout Latin America as spies. As his biographer put it, he worked "as an agent of the United States Government."

Spellman's relationship with CIA came to light after Jack Malone had left him. In 1954, CIA requested of Cardinal Spellman that he author "Epistles," which would be read out in Guatemalan churches to reconcile the peasant population to CIA's coup overthrowing President Jacobo Árbenz Guzmán. These letters were designed with one objective in mind: to invoke fear of Communism.

When the Agency requested that Spellman arrange a meeting between a CIA officer and Archbishop Mariano Rossell y Arellano, the Cardinal obliged. According to Belton Kleberg Johnson, Malone "had played the part of his Holiness' bag-man, delivering the lavish gifts" for which Cardinal Spellman was notorious.

Jack Malone was married and lived in Bronxville, New York. He was the father of two sons and two daughters. The first thing you noticed about him was that he walked with a noticeable limp, the vestige of a childhood struggle with polio. Stocky and weighing over 200 pounds, he did not cut a fine figure. He was a plain-looking man who resembled everyone's favorite uncle.

Yet Jack won you over at once. This was a wonderful fellow, a gentleman, a man brimming with wit, a twinkle in his eye. Jack Malone was a delightful companion, and great fun. At any moment, he could transform himself into a fine Irish tenor and burst into his favorite song, "Strangers in the Night."

If you worked with Jack, you discovered that he was not only competent, but fair. You would be wise to trust his judgment. And he was unflappable. If you found yourself in trouble, you could do worse than turn to Michael J. P. Malone with his many CIA contacts and allies. "Best employee I ever had," George Braga declared. No mean judge of human beings (as of horseflesh), Bob Kleberg took to Jack Malone at once.

"You are the new president," Kleberg told Malone when the joint-venture agreement between King Ranch and Czarnikow-Rionda was sealed on March 12, 1951, creating *Compañía Ganadera Becerra* in Camagüey Province, Cuba. Kleberg began the operation on Manati land, Manati having sold the new King Ranch "the least desirable land" it had.

Manati Sugar Company would be the major stockholder, owning 75 percent of the shares of *Becerra* with King Ranch Corporation
the minor one, owning 25 percent. Beginning with 30,360 acres,
Becerra would grow to 40,000 acres. It would produce the finest beef
on the island of Cuba.

"I know nothing about cattle," Jack said.

"I'll take care of the cattle," Kleberg said. "You take care of everything else."

Kleberg appreciated people who were honest, and responded to
them in kind. Once Malone persuaded Kleberg to attend a Catholic
mass in Kingsville. Kleberg wondered what it would cost him.

"I think we have a Protestant among us," the priest said. Kleberg
had placed $1,000 in the collection plate.

From the moment they met, Kleberg talked to Jack Malone on
the telephone every day of his life. Some Cubans underestimated
Michael J. P. Malone's effectiveness because he couldn't ride a horse.
But to the anti-Castro Cuban exiles, he came to be a "saintly figure."
One Cuban rancher called him "one of the best men I ever met—
courageous and honest."

Some close to Kleberg called Jack Malone "the Virgin Mary"
because he was the saint to whom you prayed when you wanted
money or a favor from Kleberg. Others called Jack "Mr. Fix-It," a
man who would travel anywhere in the world at a moment's notice
when needed.

Jack could spirit you out of prison, provide a forged passport,
and plunk you down on an airplane headed for safe haven. He is the
Rasputin of Kleberg adventures with CIA, a master of intrigue and
a Dickensian conniver. He remains a shadowy figure, one deserving
of his own place in history.

Malone accomplished these feats with the assistance of his multifarious CIA (and FBI) contacts. As far as the FBI was concerned,
when Jack didn't deal directly with J. Edgar Hoover, he met with
Frank O'Brien, a well-liked, highly connected and respected special agent out of the New York field office. Malone was O'Brien's
informant "NY T-2."

Malone was particularly gifted in the range of his CIA contacts. He boasted not one, but two 201 files, one perhaps a "covert," the other an "overt" file. These were two distinct files, even if CIA's system read them as one. A "201" file was a "personality" file. The subject could be anyone in whom there was sufficient intelligence interest. The individual need not necessarily be an asset or employee of CIA. Influential critics of the Agency immediately earned "201" files.

CIA awarded Jack his own cryptonym, AMPATRIN. The "AM" stood for matters pertaining to Cuba; the "PATRIN" was a seeming riff on "patriot" or "patron."

Not to be outdone by CIA, Jack created code names and cryptonyms of his own. Robert J. Kleberg, Jr. was "Uncle" or "Patron." Fidel Castro would be "Giant." Allen Dulles was "the man with the pipe." Malone also awarded U.S. government agencies their own codes. Numerical codes accompanied business transactions: AID was (001), high on the list; Foreign Assets Control was (025); the U.S. Government itself was (074); the Chase Manhattan Bank was (012).

David Atlee Phillips, a CIA officer who would be forever obliged to Malone for saving his life, spiriting him out of Castro's Cuba, was Jack's "Chivas Regal friend." (It was "Chivas Regal" who was named by one of Phillips' operatives, Antonio Veciana, as having been observed in the company of Lee Harvey Oswald in Dallas.) With his endless resources, in this case, a lawyer friend, Malone found out that Castro had targeted Phillips, and CIA then moved him out of the country—fast. Phillips subsequently returned, and had to escape again.

David Atlee Phillips was close enough to Robert J. Kleberg, Jr. to refer to him as "Bob."

The most highly placed of Malone's CIA contacts was Raford Herbert, Deputy Chief of the Western Hemisphere Division, who worked directly under Colonel J. C. King. Next came Phillips, whom Jack addressed as "Dave." For more mundane matters, Malone turned to Paul Manson, Charlie Mechen (whose real name was Charles W. Matt, a figure who will turn up frequently in this narrative), or James K. Pekich, whose task was to instruct CIA assets prior to their infiltration into Cuba for sabotage operations. Mechen was an "alias in the field," and was supposedly a deskman. As Charles W. Matt, he was chief of paramilitary operations for William Harvey's Task Force W, which was devoted to black operations inside Cuba.

Pekich, in turn, introduced Malone to his associate Walter P. Kuzmuk. For the record, CIA created a document declaring that Malone was "not a CIA employee, but has been a contact and a source of information."

Among Michael J. P. Malone's social friends was Dean Rusk, John F. Kennedy's Secretary of State.

Brushing aside a researcher's question about the Klebergs, Billie Sol Estes said, "They didn't know anything about anything." Nothing could have been further from the truth. Deeply embedded in the intelligence community, Malone was for Robert J. Kleberg, Jr. a bottomless fount of information.

In particular, Malone served as Kleberg's intermediary with CIA and the FBI, and also with those whom Kleberg elected to assist in their struggle against Fidel Castro. By the time King Ranch Cuba was operational, Malone was as close to Kleberg as Kleberg's long-time lawyer, Leroy Denman, and his chief assistant John Cypher, who would work as a King Ranch employee over forty years, from 1948 to 1988.

"You will do what I ask you to do!" Kleberg told all three. They were to help him "accomplish the things I want to accomplish." Of course there would be "no excuses!"

One evening Malone raced all over Washington to find little brass buttons to fasten Kleberg's collar so that he could appear in appropriate style at a White House dinner hosted by Richard Nixon. In the morning, the first person to arrive at Kleberg's bedroom was Malone, eager to hash over the previous evening's revelations. Robert J. Kleberg, Jr. was to contribute $100,000 to Richard Nixon's 1972 re-election campaign.

Compañía Ganadera Becerra

In May 1951, you might have run into fifty-five-year-old Robert J. Kleberg, Jr. galloping through the Cuban jungles and amazing the Cubans with his horsemanship and his prodigious energy. "He came down here and out-gunned us, out-rode us, and out-rummed us!" said one Cuban observer. "He'd keep us drinking rum all night and have us in the saddle at dawn and ride us ragged all day long. *¡Qué hombre!*" There was no doubt but that he had the energy of a thirty-year-old.

Requiring a horse one day, Kleberg stopped at *La Caridad,* the ranch closest to *Becerra.* Its owner was Gustavo de los Reyes, who had studied medicine at the University of Havana only to become an agronomist. His family had been in Cuba since the Spanish conquest, his first ancestor a poor Castilian farmer who had distinguished himself in the defense of Havana when it was attacked and burned by a French corsair, Jacques de Sores.

From the 1500s on, the de los Reyeses grew sugar. They raised cattle to feed the labor on their plantations. De los Reyes grew up amid what he grants was an "anachronistic" colonial style of life: When he reached the age of seven, his father took him to the fencing master. They used sabers.

Returning home that day, de los Reyes decided to catch up with the Kleberg group. He requested his favorite horse, Carmelo.

"One of the Texans liked your horse and took it," a ranch hand said. "There was no way of avoiding it except by shooting the man!"

Carmelo returned, carrying a rider wearing an old, battered hat. There was a stubborn look on his face.

"That's my horse, you know," de los Reyes said in his quiet, self-contained way.

"And a damned good one, too!" the man in the hat said, stretching out his hand. "I'm Bob Kleberg." So began their friendship. De los Reyes invited Kleberg's half-Cherokee foreman, Lowell Tash, and his family, to reside with him while a house was being built for them at *Becerra.*

"How much do I owe you?" Kleberg said after the projected two-month Tash family visit had stretched into six.

"It means so much your coming to Cuba," de los Reyes said. "You owe me nothing." Kleberg then bestowed on de los Reyes his first Santa Gertrudis animal. A yearling named Babar, he went on to win first prize at the 1954 *Feria Nacional de Ganadería*.

"There I go!" Kleberg said, "Making mistakes again!"

It was a time when investing in Cuba was as safe as investing in the United States. Article 90 of the Cuban Constitution proscribed "large landholdings," stating that the "acquisition and possession of land by foreign persons and companies shall be restrictively limited." But this restriction had never been enforced.

Kleberg met with George A. Braga at Manati. He amazed Braga by being as knowledgeable about grass as he was about cattle and referred to the "meek grass." Then he quoted from a speech by Senator Ingalls: "Grass is the forgiveness of nature, her constant benediction . . . forests decay, harvests perish, flowers vanish, but grass is immortal . . . Should its harvest fail for a single year, famine would depopulate the world." Braga found Kleberg "as sentimental about his business as a Rionda about his."

The next morning, all business, Kleberg asked to see the Czarnikow-Rionda maps. There were none.

After Kleberg inspected the Cuban cattle, comprised primarily of Brahmas, he arranged to send Santa Gertrudis animals from Texas to Cuba to grade up the herds. He found restrictive governmental regulations in Cuba that had resulted in overproduction of sugar and under-production of beef, and he wanted to play a role in changing that. He was attempting to make the cattle industry as significant in Cuba as it was in the United States. "In Cuba now they eat mostly bulls," Kleberg said. Then he added, "I'm going to be bull-headed and produce something they don't want—something good!"

On the 30,000 acres on which they began, about half was virgin forest. Kleberg looked ahead to Cuba becoming a source of supply of beef—for the United States.

He chartered a ship at a cost of $50,000 to establish *Becerra* and equipped it with stalls, pens, bins, and all the equipment necessary. On April 11, 1952, "Operation Noah's Ark," as Helen Kleberg named it, set sail from Houston on the cargo ship *Nancy Lykes*. It carried 140 heifers, 100 bulls, and 40 horses. They loaded at Houston. In Cuba, the cattle scattered and had to be rounded up. Other journeys followed. Roads had to be built, and King Ranch sent its own road builder to Cuba.

Sparing no expense, Kleberg shipped the first mechanical brush-clearing machines to Cuba. He had invented them himself for King Ranch. Now they would clear the Camagüey jungles of the pesky *marabou*, which was more difficult to root out than Texas mesquite. Kleberg sent fencing materials, well-digging tools, windmills, cars, trucks, and chemicals, along with small items like ropes and saddles. The operation was overseen by Michael J. P. Malone.

There were still squatters on the land when King Ranch took over; in 1947 they occupied thirty *caballerías* of Manati land. Lowell Tash, the ranch manager, negotiated directly with *precarista* leaders, according to James Cypher in his study of the squatter issue. One pocket of *precaristas* was given $1,000 to abandon their *colonia*. Three *precarista* families requested a total of $650. Cypher writes that another group refused King Ranch's offer and were fenced out.

The situation wasn't simple to resolve. *Precaristas* and local farmers appealed to a peasant league, *La Asociación Campesina de Adelaida*, as they sought redress. The *precaristas* also fought back by covering King Ranch roads with *marabou* storks. Cypher relates that in 1954 they staged a demonstration, marching into the city of Camagüey with signs that read: "Campesinos from the Adelaida farm threatened by the King Ranch demand an end to the evictions from their land." These peasants had been cultivating and harvesting sugar cane, which King Ranch now fed to its cattle. A Manati sugar worker remarked, with no shortage of irony, "Mr. Kleberg's idea of converting cane into meat appears to be a very profitable one."

On behalf of Kleberg, Tash accused the squatters of depleting the soil and thinning the forests for charcoal. Tash went on to argue after Castro was victorious that INRA, the *Instituto Nacional de la Reforma Agraria,* was itself committing these offenses, overgrazing the pastures.

It took three years, but King Ranch solved its squatter problem. Cypher goes on to argue that King Ranch's and Manati's treatment of the local squatters created support for the 26th of July so that King Ranch inadvertently contributed to the success of the Cuban Revolution.

Compañía Ganadera Becerra was soon producing the highest quality of beef in Cuba. Jack Malone flew to Havana to persuade the Batista government to pay more for this beef, since they now no longer had to rely on imports for the lucrative tourist trade. *Becerra* hired only Cuban cowboys. They were treated so well that when Castro finally confiscated *Becerra,* Lowell Tash did not fear violence from his ranch hands.

Freeport Sulphur, another Texas-based company and the largest producer of sulphur in the U.S., mined nickel ore at the Moa Bay Mining Company. Despite generous tax concessions from Batista, Freeport was not generous toward its Cuban workers. Jack Malone learned that Freeport had decided to grant a 17 percent salary increase for its Cuban employees on its contracting jobs—but this occurred only in March 1959, after 26th of July had taken power. Braga's Fanjul partners were notoriously unsympathetic to their workers, as an article in *The Wall Street Journal* would note.

It took three years to establish *Compañía Ganadera Becerra.* First came the clearing and plowing of the land, then the seeding of grass. "*El agua es la semilla del zocate*" ("Water is the seed of the grass") was a favorite Kleberg line.

In December 1955, after much jungle had been converted to grass using seed developed in Brazil, a herd of purebred Santa

Gertrudis was flown down to Cuba: forty-nine heifers and three bulls. One pilot complained. He had agreed to haul cattle, he said, but "these are elephants with their tusks pulled out." Santa Gertrudis were gigantic.

Fifty horses were unloaded one midnight to avoid the crowds that customarily gathered on the wharf to welcome the ships carrying Kleberg's animals.

There were risks. On one occasion, recounted by Belton Kleberg, a plane was tested on a watery runway. On the test run, the water held the plane down and prevented it from taking off. Had it gone with a full load, it would have crashed and everyone would have been killed. "We're not flying today," Kleberg said. "Let's go have a drink."

By 1956, there were 4,500 head of King Ranch cattle in Cuba, of which 1,500 were pure Santa Gertrudis. Kleberg had converted 20,000 acres of jungle into a productive ranch. He was elated. He had "produced and created things which have bettered the living and lives of the people of the country as a whole." The yearlings would be fattened and shipped to Miami, where they would be slaughtered and sold as fresh beef.

Becerra suffered only a 2 percent death loss of its cattle. All the profits were plowed back into the operation; King Ranch did not extract any money from Cuba. Profit would derive ultimately from breeding Santa Gertrudis in Cuba. The new cattle would then be sent down to other King Ranches in Latin America.

Alberto Fernández de Hechavarría

Robert J. Kleberg, Jr.'s complex relationship with CIA began in earnest only following Fidel Castro's overthrow of the dictator Fulgencio Batista. It was activated after Kleberg's loss of *Becerra*, and inspired by the struggle of Alberto Fernández de Hechavarría, in whom Kleberg came to take an avuncular interest. Neither would have preferred to subject himself to collaboration with CIA. History made it inevitable. Kleberg was to accept CIA's treason quietly, but he was a worldly man and he had not lost his country.

Alberto Fernández was born in *Santiago de Cuba* on August 7, 1918. His ancestry combined the Spanish aristocracy with generations that had grown up in Cuba. Alberto's paternal grandfather, Federico Fernández Rosillo, had married a Cuban woman and become a cattleman in Oriente Province. From his Spanish aristocratic ancestors, Alberto inherited a naturally gracious bearing and formidable pride. He grew up amid servants and privilege. It was not unusual for his parents to entertain such visitors as Bishop Fulton Sheen.

His mother's family had arrived in Cuba in the 1590s, settling in *Santiago de Cuba*, then the center of the Spanish empire in the Americas. From being a Cuban, Alberto says, he inherited a down-to-earth quality and a humility that allowed him, despite his family's great wealth, to appreciate what he would call "the humblest of the humble people." If CIA would entertain the belief that Alberto's first loyalty would ever be to them, and not to the people of Cuba, they would be sorely mistaken.

I learned the story of Alberto Fernández in a series of interviews over a five-year period both in person in Key Biscayne, Florida, and on the telephone. Alberto savored ranching. "My people were better cattlemen than Kleberg," he said, with some irony. He would never have left the family property (this he had in common with Kleberg), had his mother, Dolores de Hechavarría de Fernández, nicknamed "Lolita," not decreed that from the time he was twelve years old he must spend one month of his school vacation every year in Europe. This was so that he wouldn't be stuck culturally "in the bush," as he put it. It was the Fernández version of R. J. Kleberg's invocation to his children that they not be "a pig in a poke." At his grandfather's summer home in *San Sebastián*, Spain, Alberto developed a life-long code of ethics.

They were being driven late one afternoon by the family chauffeur to the *Plaza de Toros*, although Alberto already hated the bullfights, despising in particular the spectacle of the goring of the horses. He much preferred those days when he and his grandfather and the chauffeur would attend *jai alai* matches at the *frontón*.

"*Noi,*" his grandfather said, using the familiar term of endearment. "I'm going to tell you something. *Acuérdate, no hacen falta papeles. Con tú palabra tiene que bastar.*" (Papers are not necessary. Your word has to be enough.) The code of the Cuban cattleman was a handshake. The check would come later. When years later some sugar mill owners told Alberto that he had to open a letter of credit under certain conditions before they could do business, he walked away from the deal.

Bob Kleberg operated from the same principle. As Kleberg assistant John Cypher explains, at King Ranch, "a verbal agreement was usually binding on both parties, leaving a scant written record of the decision-making process."

Another of Alberto's childhood lessons came from Luis Hechavarría, his maternal grandfather. Luis was a very rich man who, during the sugar crash of the 1920s, insisted on fulfilling his written word, refusing a mortgage consolidation. In the process, he lost everything. Luis returned to the practice of law, later becoming Chief Magistrate of Oriente Province.

"Don't be impressed by anyone," Luis told Alberto. All his life, Alberto Fernández would embody this lesson. He was never intimidated or impressed by the rich and the powerful, Cuban or North American.

Then his grandfather pointed to a spot on a long line of law books. "From here to here says you're right," Luis Hechavarría said. Then he pointed to another spot. "From here says otherwise." The notion of absolute truth was a myth. There was one more element to this lesson. "*Cumplir el deber no es una virtud.*" (To do your duty is not a virtue.)

Between the ages of six and eight, Alberto studied with the LaSalle Brothers, never with the Jesuits, whom he would later view as adversaries. For the rest of his life he would maintain his Catholicism.

It was customary for Cubans of Alberto's social class to be educated abroad. His father had completed his secondary education in France, and his mother hers at the Pierce School in New York City.

Dolores was fluent in English, French, and German, as well as, of course, Spanish. Alberto went to Choate, the exclusive Connecticut boarding school, class of 1936. The practiced religion was High Episcopalian and you had to attend chapel seven days a week.

All his life, Alberto would remember an incident that occurred during his sophomore year at Choate. One day he was summoned by the headmaster, Reverend George St. John. It was eleven o'clock in the morning. *What have I done?* Alberto wondered. There were six hundred boys at the school. "I almost shit in my pants," he said, remembering more than half a century later. *Why did he want to see me? Why me?*

St. John had noticed that when Alberto signed his name, he made the "o" almost invisible. St. John urged him to retain his identity as a Latin American. He was not "Albert," but "Alberto." It was a lesson not lost on the pupil.

Among Alberto's Choate classmates was John Fitzgerald Kennedy. When Alberto was a junior and Kennedy a senior, they resided in the same house. Alberto saw Kennedy every day, but they were not friends. Kennedy would visit Alberto's room often because he was determined to seduce a cousin of Alberto's roommate. Her name was Olive Cawley, and she did not succumb to Kennedy's advances. Olive went on to marry the CEO of IBM.

Kennedy was "shallow," Alberto concluded of the man he would later view as his adversary. "All he was interested in was one thing, and that was sex." At Choate, Alberto says, Kennedy was "as he was later."

When it came time for university, Alberto first visited New Haven where, with distaste, he saw a city choked by automobiles. He didn't like "town" any more than Bob Kleberg did. Instead of Yale, he chose Princeton, which was in the luxuriant central New Jersey countryside. Alberto was a member of the class of 1940. His classmates included future Director of Central Intelligence William Colby, who did become a friend. Alberto majored in mechanical engineering.

After graduation from Princeton, Alberto returned to Cuba with an addiction to American slang. "I'm fed up!" he would say. Huber Matos, the former schoolteacher who, following service to the 26th of July Movement as a *comandante*, had been imprisoned by Castro, "came out of the woodwork." Or: "Fidel yakked." Or: "I almost shit in my pants."

Back in Cuba, Alberto worked alongside his rancher father, Federico Fernández Casas. A political career was an option, but not one to Alberto's taste owing to his father's experience. Persuaded that the future of Cuba depended upon people becoming involved in the electoral process, Federico had served as a senator in the Cuban legislature. He had received more votes in the elections of 1944 and 1948 than any other senator in the history of Cuba.

With a group of friends, Federico Fernández Casas founded the *Partido del Pueblo Cubano (Ortodoxos)*, which stood for the same principles as the *Auténticos*. The difference, Alberto explained to me, was that the *Ortodoxos* lived by their beliefs. They were anti-Batista from the start. All his life, Alberto Fernández would blame President Truman for not listening to his own ambassador to Cuba, Willard L. Beaulac, who urged him not to recognize Batista.

One day, Alberto suggested to his father that they visit a heavily forested area adjacent to their property. Alberto had horses ready. Federico rode with an English saddle, Alberto with an American cowboy saddle.

"We're going to take a ride across the river," Alberto said. Alberto had seen this property when he was a boy and he and his cousins tried to catch crocodiles on the Cauto River. He had entrapped his father, who believed they were visiting part of his own property.

When they arrived, Federico was overwhelmed by the beauty of the landscape. "Whose property is this?" he said. Then Alberto requested a loan from his father to purchase this forestland.

"Done!" his father said.

Situated at the confluence of two rivers, at the very spot where Cuban patriot José Martí had died in combat with the Spanish,

Hacienda Algodones belonged to an American company. They were willing to sell. There, in homage to that liberating moment in Cuban history, Alberto built his own home.

On *Hacienda Algodones,* Alberto raised cattle and grew sugar, building his own sugar mill. If he seems a *"latifundista,"* (literally, owner of a large estate with the connotation of a rich landowner presiding over the lives of farm workers), in his case the feudal designation is anachronistic. At one point he would employ more than a thousand women and children on an unprofitable tomato crop just to provide them with an income. These were women who needed to free themselves from abusive husbands.

Like Bob Kleberg—in many ways his American counterpart—Alberto Fernández made his own rules. His humility precluded authoritarian practices or expressions of superiority. He ignored with disdain those who termed his family *"billetuda,"* a slang word for the rich, people with "bills" or disposable currency.

Alberto told me that his family could have been far richer had his paternal grandfather accepted the offer to buy his firm tendered to him by the founder of Bacardi rum, who was suffering hard times. "I'll lend you the money, but I won't buy you," Alberto's grandfather told *Señor* Bacardi.

Alberto had grown up to be a man who was tough, yet soft-spoken. Sardonic irony masked his seriousness of purpose. Like Kleberg, he could not abide fools. He matched Kleberg's devotion to Texas as well as the traditions of King Ranch established by his grandfather, Richard King, and his father, Robert Justus Kleberg II, with Cuban patriotism and his own unique heritage. Alberto and Bob Kleberg were kindred spirits.

On the Sunday in 1952 that he met Robert J. Kleberg, Jr. for the first time, Alberto Fernández was thirty-four years old and Kleberg was fifty-six. Alberto was now a muscular man with black hair and piercing hazel eyes, a man pious in his Catholicism. He owned five ranches. The "big one," *Vega Beaaca,* was next to the *Río Cauto,* which begins in the *Sierra Maestra* and winds down into Oriente Province. "I was a *latifundista* in Cuba," Alberto acknowledged to me.

Bob Kleberg

Robert J. Kleberg, Jr.: "The road to progress is paved with mistakes."

Michael J. P. Malone: CIA awarded Jack his own cryptonym, AMPATRIN.

Babar: Kleberg bestowed on Gustavo de los Reyes his first Santa Gertrudis animal. *Courtesy of Gustavo de los Reyes.*

Robert J. Kleberg, Jr. with Michael J. P. Malone: "I'll take care of the cattle. You take care of everything else."

At left, Michael J. P. Malone, with Lowell Tash: "The Virgin Mary."

A Santa Gertrudis bull at *Becerra*, the King Ranch in Camagüey: "I'm going to be bull-headed and produce something they don't want—something good."

Federico Fernández Casas: He received more votes in the elections of 1944 and 1948 than any other senator in the history of Cuba.

Left: John Smithies, with Federico Fernández Casas, 1946. *Courtesy of Gladys Smithies.*

Dolores de Hechavarría de Fernández, nicknamed "Lolita."
Mother of Alberto Fernández de Hechavarría.

Dolores in Seville, Spain: "He must spend one month of his school
vacation in Europe." *Courtesy of Gladys Smithies.*

Gathering at the Habana Country Club. Federico Fernández Casas is second from left. *Courtesy of Gladys Smithies.*

Dolores de Hechavarría de Fernández with baby Alberto Fernández and his sister, Gladys. *Courtesy of Gladys Smithies.*

Alberto Fernández de Hechavarría as a student at Princeton University. His classmates included William Colby, a future Director of Central Intelligence. *Courtesy of John Smithies.*

The marriage of Ofelia Rionda y del Monte and Alberto Fernández de Hechavarría. *Courtesy of Gladys Smithies.*

On one of Alberto Fernández's ranches, Oriente Province: "My people were better cattlemen than Kleberg." *Courtesy of Gladys Smithies.*

Gladys Smithies with her daughter and one of her sons.
Courtesy of Gladys Smithies.

Christmas gathering of Federico Fernández Casas with his grandchildren.
Alberto's two daughters, Marianne and Ileanne, are dressed alike. The
beautiful woman on the left is Gladys Smithies' daughter Dolores. Her arms
are around her brother Michael. *Courtesy of Gladys Smithies.*

The *Tejana:* "We weren't sailors. That became our profession." *Courtesy of Alberto Fernández.*

Unsung heroes of the Underground, all members of *Unidad Revolucionaria*, on board the *Tejana.* Left to right: Ramon Corona; Juan Fajardo; Alberto Fernández; Hilda Barrios, who was in a relationship with Humberto Sorí Marin; Humberto Sorí Marin; Emilio Posada. Rear: Joaquin Powell; Tony Cuesta Pae. *Courtesy of Alberto Fernández.*

Lawrence Laborde, the American captain, on the *Tejana*: "A Louisiana bayou pirate."
Courtesy of Alberto Fernández.

Humberto Sorí Marín: "I'll be all right. Don't worry."

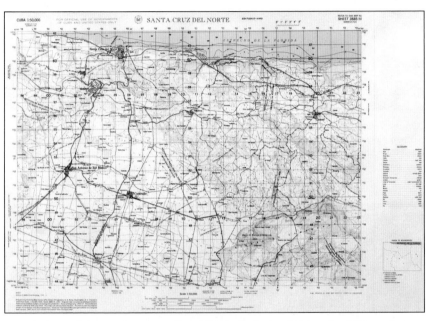

Detail of one of the maps given to Alberto Fernández by his CIA handler "Clarence" upon Clarence's departure for the Congo. *Courtesy of Alberto Fernández.*

On the *Tejana:* At left is the Cuban captain, Armando Rodríquez Alonso, a veteran of the Cuban navy. Armando is holding a piece of inferior-quality rope that was used in lieu of a heavy anchor so that the *Tejana* might make a quick getaway. At center is Humberto Sorí Marín; at right is Alberto Fernández. *Courtesy of Alberto Fernández.*

Ernesto (Che) Guevara with Camilo Cienfuegos: Camilo's plane landed safely at a small airfield on the outskirts of Havana.

Fidel Castro: "You're a *cabrón!*"

Bob Kleberg's lawyer, Fausto Iturria, and a secretary from the Mexican embassy pleading for our lives before the all-powerful. Havannah, 1959.

Robert J. Kleberg's lawyer, Fausto Yturria, with a secretary from the Mexican Embassy, pleading for the life of Gustavo de los Reyes before an all-powerful Havannah, 1959: "If I save one, I have to save all." *Courtesy of Gustavo de los Reyes.*

Gustavo de los Reyes: "That's my horse, you know." *Courtesy of Gustavo de los Reyes.*

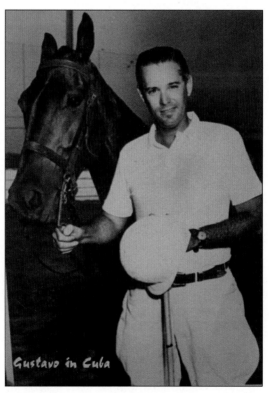

Gustavo de los Reyes: "We fear, therefore we exist."
Courtesy of Gustavo de los Reyes.

It had been Alberto's solitary defense of Salvador Rionda (his wife, Ofelia Rionda de Monte's father) that had precipitated the Bragas' enlisting Bob Kleberg to come to Cuba. Now Bob Kleberg arrived to look over the land and study cattle ranching, Cuban style.

Salvador requested that Alberto meet Kleberg at Bayamo Airport and drive him to the future site of King Ranch Cuba. Alberto would introduce Kleberg to the cattle business. Alberto chuckled to himself. He had started the trouble and now the problem had been dropped into his lap.

Earlier that morning, Kleberg had breakfasted at *Varadero* with President Fulgencio Batista, an event George Braga had no difficulty in arranging. Kleberg wore his customary white shirt and khakis. He couldn't have known, but he had chosen a costume permitted only to members of Batista's army. An officious army captain at once moved to arrest him.

Laughing, Alberto intervened. "You'll be arresting a man who had breakfast this morning with President Batista," he said. The captain backed off, and Alberto carried Kleberg off to *Vega Beaaca,* where proudly he displayed the four breeds of cattle that he raised: Brown Swiss; Brahma; *Criollos,* who were native to Cuba; and Alberto's prized Charolais, brought to Cuba originally by his paternal grandfather and great uncles. "Our breeding herds," Alberto told me, "were far superior to Santa Gertrudis. Even the *Criollos* were more beautiful."

Kleberg professed himself to be "enchanted with Cuba." When they rode out onto the land, to Alberto's astonishment, Kleberg suddenly in his enthusiasm took a swan dive off his horse, sailing into a pasture of guinea grass. Kleberg's jaw dropped when he spotted Alberto's Charolais. Immediately he asked if he could choose ten of them to purchase.

"I have never sold one in my life," Alberto said. "And I don't intend to for a while."

Then Alberto smiled. He would not "sell" any of his cattle, but Kleberg could choose the ones he wanted and have them as a gift. Meeting a man with a character that so matched his own, Kleberg liked Alberto at once. Alberto, in turn, appreciated Kleberg, who

was so different from his Braga partners. Close relatives and partners of the Bragas in Cuba, the Fanjuls, were *Batistianos*. The senior
Alfonso Fanjul sat on Batista's Consultative Council.

Alberto did not inquire about what Kleberg had discussed with
Batista; there were no conversations about politics.

The grass had not yet grown high enough on *Becerra*. Alberto's
foreman, Rosario, took charge of Kleberg's herd until the grass grew
tall enough on the King Ranch land. Kleberg entrusted Rosario to
select females for his Santa Gertrudis bulls, and they were placed
on one of Federico Fernández Casas' properties, the cattle company
called *Ganadera Las Piedras*.

Later the head cattleman working for Federico purchased heifers
to be bred with Kleberg's Santa Gertrudis bulls. Kleberg's goal was
to breed the native cattle of Cuba, originally from Spain, with his
Santa Gertrudis.

To Alberto Fernández, Kleberg seemed down-to-earth, unpretentious, and supremely self-confident. He had no need to prove
anything to anyone, and seemed like an ordinary man. There was
no showing off. He was what he was and there was no flaunting the
power he could summon should it be necessary.

Kleberg was in love with nature, with the soil, and, above all,
with cattle. Alberto believed that Kleberg's concept of the importance of beef for Cuba was exceptional and welcome. Beef should be
cheap and you shouldn't persecute those who produce it. Beef was
sacred.

Soon Kleberg went to work ridding the King Ranch land of the
marabou with machinery he transported from the United States.

Later Kleberg offered to buy all the Fernández family ranches,
with their forests covered with ninety-foot-tall hardwood trees.
Fernando Fernández Casas put it up to the three children since all
that land would ultimately be theirs. It was what their grandfather
and father had built up.

Alberto and his two sisters voted. Alberto's worldly older sister,
Gladys, agreed to sell, but Alberto and his younger sister, Cecile,

refused, so attached were they to the land. Captain Richard King's credo, adopted from Robert E. Lee, "Buy land and never sell," was theirs as well.

Gladys did sell Kleberg 7,000 acres of virgin hardwood forests. Later, needing the lumber, Castro brought in bulldozers, but he could not budge those trees. He then sent in army sappers, who blew the giant trees out of the earth so that not one remained.

"He destroyed to survive," Alberto told me.

After Gladys and her husband, John Smithies, moved to New York, Helen Kleberg tried to get Gladys a job with David Rockefeller at the Chase Manhattan Bank and went so far as to make the introduction. Gladys did meet face to face with David Rockefeller, although ultimately she did not get the job.

John T. Smithies remained in touch with Michael J. P. Malone, whom he continued to consult on matters relating to Cuba, as a Malone memorandum to Smithies dated December 16, 1963, reveals.

The Final Days of Batista

In 1958, perched high in the *Sierra Maestra* with his band of 26th of July rebels, Fidel Castro was already casting his eyes on *Compañía Ganadera Becerra*. Unaware, Bob Kleberg, declaring himself "very bullish" on King Ranch Cuba, was in search of more land to purchase in Cuba. In January, Malone consulted George Braga on sponsoring a survey at Manati "concerning the potential of growing winter vegetables." Malone had in hand a circular published by the U.S. Department of Agriculture about tomatoes and cucumbers as well as eggplant, okra, peppers, watermelons, and even cantaloupe.

In August 1958 at *Becerra,* 3,000 heifers were being bred. Within the previous few weeks, 1,000 calves had been branded. The Czarnikow-Rionda Insurance Department had added 2,222 bulls to their policy.

Malone decided to go ahead and secure a credit line of $60,000 from King Ranch for the purchase of a D-8 Tractor with auxiliary equipment for the land clearing program at *Becerra.* Three fine quarter horses were chosen to be shipped down to Cuba, too. Kleberg also asked Malone to begin negotiations for a *finca* (estate) near Havana and for between fifty and seventy-five "cabs" (*caballerías*) adjoining the back end of *Becerra monte* (mountain land).

Throughout the fifties, improvements had persistently been made, grasses planted, wells and dykes added, canals cleaned, old buildings taken down, dirt reservoirs constructed, and camp houses built. February 1956 witnessed the construction of four bridges. At Tash's house on *Becerra,* a Running W was embedded in the tile floor. Around his house they planted mango trees along with palms, cedar, and big algarrobo trees used as fences. A King Ranch stallion, named *Chamaco,* won the grand championship twice at Havana.

Building at *Becerra* proceeded throughout 1958. A watermill was erected; the corrals were painted; a new dipping vat was constructed; new fences went up; repair was completed on two houses; roads were repaired; and bridges damaged by a flood were also restored. Kleberg kept watch over it all, with Malone and B. Rionda Braga focusing on the creation of the King Ranch satellite in Morocco.

Money was no object: Humble was building a new gas plant on the Santa Gertrudis division of King Ranch and planned within the next year or two to uncap the fifty gas wells on the property. In the summer of 1958, American investors had not yet cooled on Cuba, and even the people who owned the majority interest in the Fontainebleau Hotel in Miami Beach were selling their interest in order to invest $4.5 million in a new hotel in Havana located beyond the Havana Riviera on the *Malecón.*

Malone assessed the economy of Cuba. "Barring a big step-up in rebel activity," he wrote to the Braga brothers, "Cuba would have another good year in 1958, although not as good as 1957."

"Over the longer term," Malone added, "Cuba will need to diversify further to decrease her dependence on sugar." He remained confident that "Cuba will continue to offer an attractive climate for private United States investment." (Alberto Fernández saw through Malone at once: He didn't know Cuba any more than George Braga did.)

Malone remained a "fixer" for the Bragas in their personal lives as well. In May 1958, Bernardo Braga, the father of George and B. Rionda Braga, died in New York. "Jack Malone is to handle everything pertaining to the Church," George Braga decreed. Every aspect of the funeral, including arrangements at the church, was entrusted to Malone.

On a daily basis Michael J. P. Malone reported to George Braga on the progress of Fidel Castro in the *Sierra Maestra.* In July, Malone clipped an article from *Business Week* titled: "Business In Cuba Still Not Recovered As Castro Rebels Continue Fighting." Malone reported that the rebels might "gain recruits from laid-off workers during the present 'dead season' in the sugar industry." Commerce in the main cities was at a near standstill. Elections were scheduled for November 3rd, even as the rebels were "stepping up their operations in an attempt to prevent the elections."

During the summer of 1958, the Klebergs traveled for six weeks in South America, visiting Brazil and Argentina. Accompanying Bob were Helen Kleberg, his lawyer Leroy Denman, and his nephew Bobby Shelton, Belton Kleberg's half-brother. At the same time, Kleberg was negotiating for another large tract of land in Australia. Bob Kleberg was now a stocky man nearing sixty, his eyebrows descending toward his eyes. He still tucked his trousers into his boots.

He eyed the world political situation with skepticism. The Middle East, Kleberg thought, was at a stalemate. Neither the United States nor Russia would become fully committed, Kleberg believed, and "this would probably turn out to be another Korea."

That August some rebels "got into the reserve forest area" of *Becerra* only for the Batista Army to come in with a plane and drop a bomb or two "which flushed the rebels out and so far that is the last we have heard of them," Malone wrote George Braga. In Havana that August, Malone found more Cubans going out at night. The city appeared to be returning to a more normal life, he thought. On August 5th, Malone reported to Braga that things in Cuba were "fairly quiet."

Less sanguine, Alfonso Fanjul wrote to his cousin and partner George A. Braga on August 7th, "The liquidation of the armed revolt continues to be Cuba's number one problem."

By the fall of 1958, foreman Lowell Tash was ready to classify 100 head of Santa Gertrudis with the Santa Gertrudis Breeding International. With little thought to the war raging between the rebels and Batista, they were constructing the new dipping vat to thwart the robust tick population. Tash had urged the King Ranch official veterinarian Dr. J. K. Northway to visit *Becerra*. They were looking forward to the arrival of a breeding age bull to be sent from King Ranch to Cuba. (When Dr. Northway needed a double hernia operation, he went to the Ochsner Clinic in New Orleans, the facility of Kleberg's fellow CIA asset Alton Ochsner.)

By September 4, 1958, Kleberg had bought a property of 49,000 acres in Argentina. It would be a showcase for a purebred Santa Gertrudis herd. His eggs were never in one basket, even if he had not entirely registered what might be the consequences for *Becerra* of a 26th of July victory.

Despite the rumbling of political upheaval in Cuba, Michael J. P. Malone encouraged Kleberg. "The dependence of Cuba on the United States as a market for sugar would militate strongly against any action directed at American capital in Cuba," Malone believed. Cuba was still receiving $370 million in annual income from the U.S. sugar quota. Cuba was sugar, Alberto told me. Surely *Becerra* was safe. Malone would be visiting Cuba shortly to attend to all these matters.

Malone reassured his other boss, George Braga, as well. "The government will not take lands that are being worked or are producing," Malone was certain.

Alberto Fernández and his father had long been fierce opponents of Batista, beginning with Batista's advent to power in 1933.

Alberto mocked Batista's alliance with the Communist Party, despising both. He abhorred Batista's practice of torturing his opponents and sympathized profoundly with Eugenio de Sosa, the son-in-law of Ignacio Rivera, owner of the anti-Batista newspaper *El Diario de la Marina* and among Batista's victims. Eugenio had attended Choate for two years; they had that in common as well.

Eugenio had told Batista's emissary that he would not ask his father-in-law to back Batista unless Batista cut all his ties with the Communist Party. Batista not only refused, but he had Eugenio de Sosa imprisoned. Eugenio de Sosa was subjected to electric shock treatments in an insane asylum.

One day in 1958 Batista's soldiers swooped down on Alberto. In a Bayamo compound, they tied him to a chair. For six hours, bayonets were held at his throat. The soldiers had found a box of cartridges at his house and concluded that he must be supporting the rebels. Alberto explained that the cartridges were used to frighten sparrows, which could eat an entire rice field in a couple of hours.

"Look at the newspapers in which the box is wrapped. They're three years old," Alberto said. Only the intervention of the mayor of Bayamo saved his life.

That year, Alberto went into exile in Bal Harbour, Florida, escaping from Batista's gangster colonels. His distaste for the Batista regime led him to feel so "bitter" that, according to Michael J. P. Malone, he was "looking for financial backing for the other people."

Shortly after Alberto arrived, he received a call from a sugar mill owner's son. What he wanted was to see if Alberto and his father would each contribute $10,000. They had contacted spiritualists who would use voodoo to get rid of Batista, although they were *Batistianos*. This was the atmosphere of the days just before the revolution: irrationality, despair, and confusion. This cultural moment in Cuba resembled the mood in Japan in 1868 just prior to the fall of the Shogunate. People believed that amulets were falling from heaven. In fact, they were planted by agents provocateurs.

When Castro was victorious, the man gave up voodoo and became a Communist.

To finance his army, Batista had begun to extort money from American businesses in Cuba. He claimed that he needed this money so that the army could protect them from the rebels. Meanwhile, Castro's rebel army demanded that the sugar companies pay a tribute of fifteen cents per bag of sugar or else "steps would be taken to stop all operations of these mills."

In April 1958, the rebels had burned a warehouse of raw sugar, for a loss of $2,757,000. The mill owners turned to Alberto Fernández. Batista had requested that the Sugar Institute (*Instituto Cubano de Estabilización del Azúcar*) collect money to increase his garrisons in Oriente Province, where all the trouble was. The American sugar mill owners complained to Alberto because they knew he opposed the Batista regime.

It was Alberto who suggested that they help the enemy of Batista. That was Fidel Castro and his 26th of July Movement. As far as Alberto and most Cubans knew, the rebel army was mostly anti-Communist.

From his base in the United States, Alberto sent out word to Cuba to those who were "fed up to the teeth with Batista," as he collected money for 26th of July. Manati Sugar contributed $151,927 and Francisco Sugar, $160,929. Even Freeport Sulphur had offered to help 26th of July because it was so imperative to rid Cuba of Batista.

The financial picture was chaotic. Raúl Chibás, former treasurer of 26th of July, later told the FBI that Alberto had turned $2.5 million over to the Castro movement. The Chase Manhattan Bank questioned Alberto's endorsement on checks. J. S. Levene, the vice president of Francisco Sugar, was called to the bank; upon arriving, Levene noted that the Francisco checks were endorsed by Alberto Fernández de Hechavarría and Marcelino García Beltrán.

Questioned by the FBI, García Beltrán said that the money was to be used to buy medicines and possibly armaments for Fidel Castro. When asked how the purchase would be sent to Cuba, García said, "They have an airlift." The Bureau learned that García Beltrán was in fact handling transactions for Czarnikow-Rionda.

Speaking for Alberto, Jack Malone told the Bragas that the correct figure Alberto had collected was $361,039.97. Malone had to tell the FBI that his companies in Cuba and the United States paid Fidel Castro that money, which represented taxes levied on their properties: the Céspedes, Manati, and Francisco Sugar Mills.

Alberto Fernández himself placed the figure he collected at $1.5 million. When Alberto explained to the FBI that he was raising money "on behalf of the anti-Batista movement, and not specifically for Fidel Castro," the fall of Batista was less than a month away. Unsure of what to do with the "hot potato" of all this money, Alberto endorsed the checks over to Manuel Urrutia, who would be the first President of Cuba under Fidel Castro.

Late in October 1958, George Braga went to Washington, D.C., to solicit help from the U.S. government to protect his properties in Cuba. He claimed that he "did not take sides," and referred to Alberto Fernández as the "contact man" for the rebels. In the memo traffic between the Department of Justice's Internal Security Division and the Department of State's Bureau of Security and Consular Affairs, Alberto Fernández, not for the last time, was confused with his father and was misidentified as "Alberto Casas."

Complaining to Roy R. Rubottom, Jr., the Acting Assistant Secretary of State for Inter-American Affairs, Braga reported that the rebels had removed people from a car at the Francisco Sugar plant entrance. Then they cut the tracks so that three railway cars slid into the water.

Rubottom was evasive. He said he hoped logic would prevail to deter the actual destruction of property. He noted, "The rebels are getting a lot of money from employees of American companies and Nicaro."

Offering Braga no satisfaction, Rubottom told him that the American position was "not to pay tribute" to the rebels. Braga replied, "The matter is being watched very closely and the President is following it personally." Yet even after Braga revealed that he had made contact with President Eisenhower, and that Eisenhower had conveyed, "Mr. Braga's report is much appreciated," the State Department offered no assistance.

The Bragas were furious about Alberto's collecting of money for the rebels. There was a great difference, Alberto told me, between the Bragas and Julio Lobo, who were sugar mill owners and wanted to control everything, and *hacendados*, native sugar people like himself and his father. (Among Lobo's partners in his sugar business in Cuba was Joseph P. Kennedy.)

The Bragas and Julio Lobo were opposed to reform and social change, and were not interested or concerned with alleviating the poverty, illiteracy, and disease that plagued the Cuban population. They would have been perfectly content for Batista to remain in power. Alberto Fernández and Federico Fernández Casas recognized the urgency of addressing these issues. For them, the first step to solving the problem of the chronic suffering of the Cuban people was to remove Batista from power. In that spirit, Alberto undertook to raise money for the 26th of July Movement.

During that last week of October 1958, another meeting was held at the State Department on the "Cuban Political Situation and Possible Effects on American Interests in Eastern Cuba." Along with executives from Lone Star Cement, Freeport Sulphur, and the United Fruit Company, Kleberg and Malone were in attendance. (As yet another example of the symbiotic relationship of many Texas companies and CIA, Lone Star Cement's Uruguayan subsidiary provided cover for the CIA operations officer in Montevideo.)

As late as October 1958, Freeport was planning a $119 million nickel-cobalt project, the bulk of the funds to be expended at Moa Bay on the north coast of Oriente Province. Kleberg wrote to Langbourne M. Williams, the president of the Freeport Sulphur Company, requesting his assessment of the political situation in Cuba. Freeport had been engaged in mining in Cuba since 1932, and wanted to believe that its presence in Cuba would continue forever. "All in all," Williams replied to Robert J. Kleberg, Jr., "we have a great deal of confidence in Cuba as a place for American investment."

The corporations with interests in Cuba who met with the FBI during the late fall of 1958 offer a cross section of how deeply American business had penetrated Cuba. They included: United Fruit Company; Lone Star Cement Company; Francisco Sugar Company; Manati Sugar Company; Freeport Sulphur Company; Czarnikow-Rionda Company; The Texas Company; Punta Alegre Sugar Corporation; Chase Manhattan Bank; West Indies Sugar Corporation; King Ranch; First National City Bank of New York; *Compañía Cubana Primaderas S.A.*; Cuban American Sugar Company; American Sugar Refining Company; Carl M. Loeb Rhodes and Company; Hilton Hotels Corporation; Standard Oil Company of New Jersey; and International Harvester.

To the October 1958 meeting in Washington, D.C., Kleberg had brought along "before" and "after" photographs revealing how beneficial *Becerra* had been for Cuba.

"When you invested abroad you did so with the knowledge that you would have to incur certain risks," Kleberg was told.

At the close of the meeting, Kleberg raised the question of "Communism in the Castro movement." The State Department affected no concern. They "had no conclusive evidence that the movement was Communist-inspired or Communist-dominated."

Kleberg and Malone had proceeded lawfully, addressing the highest reaches of government to seek relief. It was clear that they would have to look elsewhere for support. As Jorge Navarro Custín, a Cuban familiar with that moment, pointed out to me, CIA was ready to move against Castro, but the State Department was not. Or so it seemed.

Feelings ran high and B. Rionda Braga found his way to the FBI to report angrily that on December 4, 1958, Alberto Fernández Hechavarría presented himself at the company office in New York to shake him down for funds. He had been commissioned by Fidel Castro, Alberto supposedly told "Ronny" Braga, to collect money due on the 1958 production of sugar at the Francisco, Manati, and Céspedes mills.

Alberto Fernández was someone of whom Ronny Braga did not approve. Alberto was, Braga told the FBI, "a playboy who never worked and always had too much money to spend." According to Braga, since Alberto "had joined up with Fidel Castro he had become an exile from Havana, but felt that he was doing his country a service in assisting the Castro forces in any way that he could." What emerges from this highly distorted picture of Alberto Fernández, who had fled from Cuba after being threatened by Batista's forces, was that those for whom Cuba had for years been a cash cow, like the Bragas, did not trust him and seized any opportunity to undermine his credibility. The Bragas quickly discovered that Alberto Fernández would not enlist his authority, position, and wealth to serve the imperative of the economic exploitation of Cuba. He had little sympathy for those who took from Cuba, but gave little if nothing back to improve its infrastructure and further the development of its business. That these companies, from Czarnikow-Rionda to Freeport Sulphur, wished for nothing more than to continue doing business as usual was of little concern to him.

B. Rionda Braga then turned over his records to the FBI. One was signed by Haydée Santamaría, treasurer of the 26th of July Movement in exile, and dated December 7, 1958, from Miami, under the heading: "TO THE REVOLUTIONARY AUTHORITIES OF THE FREE TERRITORY OF CUBA." Braga told the Bureau that the total contributed by Francisco Sugar Company, Manati Sugar Company, and Céspedes Sugar Company was $361,039.97.

On November 25, 1958, the FBI accused Alberto Fernández of violations under the "Registration Act." The charge was that he had been "working very closely with Fidel Castro" (which was not true) and "collecting money for his organization" (which was). Learning of this development, Bob Kleberg exercised his power by writing a stinging personal letter to his friend Allen Dulles. Kleberg demanded redress.

He had discovered that a "U.S. agency" was investigating Alberto Fernández and that he "might be in trouble," Kleberg wrote Dulles. "The United States Government should bear in mind that a prosecution of Alberto Fernández at this time could have a pertinent bearing on relations between the United States and the new Castro government."

It is unlikely that figures like Texas oil moguls Clint Murchison, Sid Richardson, or Herman Brown could have rung up Allen Dulles and demanded and received such quick action. Kleberg could pick up the phone and make people at CIA jump, and Dulles jumped. Kleberg may have operated behind the shadows, leaving no footprint, but that only further demonstrated his power.

Dulles did not hesitate. Through CIA liaison Sam Papich, Dulles contacted the FBI. He requested copies of all reports having to do with Alberto Fernández. CIA requested that the FBI not disseminate the result of any conversations they had with the State Department. By now it was January 9, 1959, and Castro was at the helm in Cuba.

"No purpose would be served by further investigation," Dulles decided, insisting nonetheless that the matter be "expedited." The Internal Security Division of the FBI at once complied. There would be no legal action against Alberto Fernández.

CIA's predominance in the affair, and its control of information regarding Kleberg and Alberto Fernández, is spelled out in an FBI memorandum: "On January 13, 1959, Jack Earman, Executive Assistant to Allen Dulles, advised the Liaison Agent [Sam Papich] that CIA did not want the Bureau to disseminate to State the results of the conversation between the Director of CIA and the Liaison Agent. Earman explained that CIA representatives were conferring with the State Department concerning the Cuban political situation and that CIA would inform the State Department concerning the Kleberg letter."

In the last days of the Batista dictatorship, the King Ranch airstrip in Cuba had hosted a twin-engine Cessna loaded with weapons and men. On board was Manuel Antonio ("Tony") Varona, who had served in the government of the corrupt ex-president Carlos Prío Socarrás. They hoped to halt the advance of the rebels only for the plane to lack sufficient fuel to return to the United States to retrieve the remainder of the group.

Resting up at *Becerra,* Varona attempted to contact a Batista army captain who had agreed to join his effort. Then the rebel army arrived and confiscated Varona's ten rifles. The local militia surrendered to the rebels, and Varona managed to escape to the United States and into the arms of the CIA benefactors who had been financing his effort. The moment, inconsequential for the history of the Cuban Revolution, marks the first instance of King Ranch's involvement in the opposition to Fidel Castro.

CHAPTER 4

ALBERTO FERNÁNDEZ RETURNS TO CUBA

"You mind the Treasury and keep your mouth
shut about sugar."

Alberto Fernández

When Fidel Castro took power on January 1, 1959, he had already decided that "land reform" was to be the "fundamental law" of the revolution. Two days later, on January 3rd, Alberto Fernández returned to Cuba, ready to support the new regime. On January 5th, he was having supper at his house in the Miramar section of Havana with several anti-Batista friends, two of whom would die at the Bay of Pigs, all of whom would perish in the combat of the 1960s.

At the stroke of midnight, there was a hard knock at the door. The butler answered. Three truckloads of rebels were outside with orders to carry Alberto off to the presidential palace.

There, Dr. Manuel Urrutia, provisional president of Cuba, greeted Alberto with the news that he would now be running Cuba's sugar industry. As Alberto Fernández put it, Urrutia had stuck a metaphoric gun into his chest.

"No," Alberto said.

"You have to," Urrutia said.

Urrutia had been made president by virtue of his having been the judge at the "Urgency Court" in *Santiago de Cuba* who cast his vote to acquit Fidel Castro for his role in the July 26, 1953, attack on the Moncada Barracks. The eloquence of Castro's speech, "History Will Absolve Me," had greatly impressed liberal jurist Urrutia. As the *New York Times* pointed out in an editorial, "A Drama Is Played in Cuba," Dr. Urrutia had "risked his freedom to proclaim that Cuba had a legal right to take up arms against tyranny." His part in the founding of the 26th of July Movement had not been forgotten.

"For one month," Alberto said. Thirty days stretched into the whole crop. Alberto would run Cuba's sugar industry for one crop, a crop that would produce 6,000 tons of sugar, nearly double the average at the time. Alberto's appointment would be reported in the *New York Times* of January 9, 1959, two days after the United States recognized the new regime.

That night, in the office of Batista's wife, Alberto and Urrutia discovered hundreds of checks made out by the elite of Cuba, people like the Braga partners, the Fanjuls, to *Señora* Batista's "charities." Alberto gathered up the checks, put them in a pillowcase, and took them to his Guanabo ranch where he set them on fire.

Executions by firing squad of *Batistiano* "war criminals" began on January 12th.

Himself part of the Castro government still, Miró Cardona ran into Alberto one day at a restaurant called the *Zaragoza*, four or five blocks from the Sugar Institute. When Cardona realized that Alberto went to the *Zaragoza* every day for lunch, Cardona stopped going there so as not to run into him.

One day, Alberto was seated at his usual table with his back to the wall, when all conversation in the room ceased. A deadly silence ensued. Alberto looked up to find rebel soldiers moving from table to table, Tommy guns at the ready. They stopped at his table, and then came back, escorted by one of the Sugar Institute executives.

Alberto remained to have his coffee. When he returned to the Sugar Institute, his fellow executive asked him if he knew someone knowledgeable about ships. The rebels had been looking for him so that he might recommend someone in the United States to buy a boat, which they planned to take on an expedition to Santo Domingo to get rid of the dictator Rafael Trujillo.

Alberto called his friend Wallace Quinn, a yacht broker, and he put them together. They bought a ship out of New Orleans only for Trujillo to discover the plan. Meanwhile, Alberto dealt with Michael J. P. Malone on the matter of "making available certain quantities of molasses at a varying price scale for the manufacture of high-quality and low-grade alcohol for export to both Europe and the United States."

Business was proceeding as usual. In a letter of July 20, 1959, to Alberto Fernández , Malone refers to "the interest that we had from one of our chemical friends." Czarnikow-Rionda did considerable business with the Sugar Institute on behalf of American corporations such as Merck & Company of Rahway, New Jersey, Charles Pfizer & Co., and Brown & Williamson of Kentucky, who were buying "invert molasses."

In a memorandum to: RECORD, dated April 21, 1959, Malone had noted: "On next trip to Cuba talk with Alberto Fernández re the fact that he has a friend in the lumber business in Oriente, whom he referred to in a phone conversation of April 20th, stating that this man was the largest distributor of wood in Oriente and that he wanted to buy directly from Francisco [Sugar]."

During this time, Alberto and his wife, Ofelia, had dinner with CIA-connected journalist Andrew St. George at the Hotel *Nacional*. Alberto viewed St. George with suspicion. He was there "to pump me," Alberto suspected.

One day the future mayor of Havana, José Lanuza, invited Alberto to accompany him on a dawn flight to meet Fidel Castro in Santa Clara. It would be their first encounter. For the occasion, deliberately looking more American than Cuban, Alberto wore a blue seersucker suit. Mistaking him for an American journalist, or so he pretended, Castro began "yakking in bad English," as Alberto would describe the incident to me.

"We will talk further when I'm in Havana," Castro said suddenly in Spanish. He knew perfectly well who Alberto was. Castro added that he was glad that Alberto would be running the sugar industry. Yet in the six months that Alberto was to work at the Sugar Institute, he would claim, Castro "never talked to me about sugar. He knew I was against him, that he couldn't bullshit me." Alberto concluded that Castro had decided that the sugar industry was in good hands. Castro chose Alberto for his competence and because he had done 26th of July some service.

For running Cuba's sugar industry, Alberto refused to take a salary. He had, he told me, a face that doesn't pay attention to money, *una cara que no come mierda* (literally, a face that doesn't eat shit). *"Mierda"* was what Fernández thought about money and the rich.

Alberto had assumed his position as head of Cuba's sugar industry on January 6th. He was already wary of the new regime. Ten days later, since the Pan American Airways subsidiary Cuban Aviation was no longer operating, Alberto hired a small plane and flew to Camagüey. He ordered the pilot to land at the Regimental Command in Northern Oriente.

The plane taxied up to a house at the edge of a cornfield where the Army regiment was headquartered. There Alberto met with the head of the Regimental Command who had led the anti-Batista underground in the area. After a quick coffee, the army man had the room emptied. Then he ushered Alberto into the bathroom and locked the door.

"All has been lost," he said, as he embraced Alberto. "This is a disaster. They're a bunch of Communists. It's a complete Communist takeover." Then he wept.

When Alberto returned to the Sugar Institute, he telephoned Wallace Quinn. Knowing no one at CIA, Alberto gave Quinn a plane ticket and the assignment of carrying a note to Frank O'Brien at the New York field office of the FBI to warn the U.S. about Castro's intentions. It was now January 20, 1959. Alberto had met O'Brien through Donald Hogan, whose brother Tony was a sugar broker with offices at 120 Wall Street, where Julio Lobo also had his office.

Alberto had, in turn, made Donald Hogan's acquaintance at the Sugar Institute where Hogan was working. By January 20th, Hogan had completed papers for registration as a foreign agent for the new Cuban government, submitting them to the Department of Justice. He had also tipped an FBI informant that Alberto Fernández had been appointed head of the Sugar Institute.

A few days later, Alberto met the new U.S. Ambassador to Cuba, Philip Bonsal.

"This is a Communist government," Alberto said.

"Oh, they're just young nationalists," Bonsal said. "They'll settle down."

"You're lost in the woods, Mr. Ambassador," Alberto said. "You're a boy scout lost in the woods without a compass, Mr. Ambassador."

Within the Castro government, by February 1959, Bonsal's files were reviewed dating back to the time when he was a Vice Consul at the U.S. Embassy. Among those with questions about Bonsal were Dr. Carlos Prío and Carlos Franqui, editor of the newspaper *Revolución*. A cable from LEGAT, HAVANA quotes Fidel Castro as saying that he had "Bonsal in the palm of his hand." It is noted as well that Bonsal had gone to the airport to greet Minister of State Raúl Roa.

At his Sugar Institute office, Alberto became so grouchy that people were afraid of him. He never laughed. Only irony drew a smile. Otherwise, he was preoccupied. He was forty years old, and would supervise Cuba's sugar industry from January to May 1959.

At the end of January, Alberto met Fidel Castro for the second time. Alberto was spending the day in the company of an acquaintance, the lawyer Humberto Sorí Marín, who had been a *comandante* in the Rebel Army. Considered to be the first Cuban intellectual to join Castro, in 1958 Sorí was made Judge Advocate General of the 26th of July Movement. In that capacity, Sorí had drafted the Rebel Army's penal code.

After the defeat of Batista, Castro appointed Sorí Minister of Agriculture. In a clever ploy, Castro also enlisted Sorí to serve as his chief prosecutor, meting out justice to those who had carried out Batista's most vicious policies. That way, Castro, making all decisions behind the scenes, could be as harsh as he liked. Sorí would be blamed for the executions.

As Castro's prosecutor, Sorí presided over military tribunals, sentencing Batista's highest officers to their deaths, among them the notorious killer Captain Jesús Sosa Blanco, who was consigned to *La Cabaña* prison to await his fate. After the war crimes trials that took place in December 1960, Sorí's detractors would refer to him as the "Cuban Robespierre." This was a reference to the revolutionary figure most remembered, perhaps unfairly, for his support of the "Terror." Robespierre ordered executions as a means of preserving the fragile gains of the French Republic, in defiance of those who would restore the *Ancien Régime.*

It might also be noted that Batista's police had long been discredited, as American reporter Jim Bishop, reporting for *King Features,* had written in 1959, summing up the excesses of the Batista regime: "They arrested citizens by the thousands. They ripped out fingernails, burned prisoners, raped women in the presence of their families, shot men who faced no trial and mutilated men who refused to inform."

In fact, Sorí had opposed the executions even as he was secretly planning to create an anti-Castro organization. Sorí had begun to play a dangerous game. To conceal his political activity, Sori retained his role as public prosecutor, rendering it impossible for him to reveal that it was Fidel Castro himself who had ordered the death penalty for the Batista officers.

Publicly, Sorí appeared to be responsible for the death sentences. If he lost his prestige, he would be no rival to Castro. Alberto suspected that Castro must have been informed that Sorí was creating an underground opposition. Castro, he told me, "smelled a rat" and, pre-emptively, he had discovered a means of discrediting Sorí.

Humberto Sorí Marín was a thin, wiry man, only five feet two inches tall. His demeanor was intense behind oversize dark-rimmed eyeglasses. He was even a bit pinch-faced. You would not know from his appearance that Sorí was a warrior, fiercely principled, courageous, determined, and a man of honor.

The Agriculture Ministry was short of cash, and Sorí had come to request a favor of Alberto. Would Alberto pay out of Sugar Institute funds for a reception in honor of a commercial mission from Japan? The Japanese had long bought Cuban sugar, selling the Cubans textiles in exchange. At Batista's invitation, a big textile company had muscled in on the Japanese business. In retaliation, the Japanese were about to suspend their order of Cuban sugar. Alberto provided the funds for the party. Fidel Castro attended the party for the Japanese. He never appeared at the Sugar Institute during Alberto's tenure there.

It was on this February 1959 afternoon that the friendship between Alberto and Humberto Sorí Marín began. Sorí invited Alberto to lunch at Tarara Beach to discuss the war Sorí planned to wage against Castro. Suddenly, Sorí said he needed to make a stop. They crossed the harbor tunnel and turned toward Cojimar, where Fidel was staying at a senator's beach house. In a very grand living room were gathered dozens of people eager to talk to Fidel Castro.

While Alberto remained in the car, Sorí went inside. Seated on a small, straight-backed chair in a corner of the room, Ambassador Bonsal sat awaiting his turn. The house was so crowded that Alberto and Sorí went off for lunch at Tarara. On their way home they stopped again, and there was Bonsal, still seated in the corner on his little chair, waiting for Fidel Castro to notice him.

Bonsal's predecessor, Earl E. T. Smith, had been even less effective. Smith spoke no Spanish. Once, before a group of sugar growers, he told an anti-Semitic joke, unmindful that the richest sugar grower in Cuba, Julio Lobo, was Jewish. In its dealings with Cuba in the years before Fidel Castro took power, the U.S. affected little interest in the needs of the island's people, as reflected in the choice of Smith as its envoy.

On December 31, 1958, that fateful night that is the entire temporal setting of Cuban novelist Guillermo Cabrera Infante's masterpiece, *Three Trapped Tigers,* Smith stopped at the Havana Country Club for a highball. This would be the preface to the night's revelry.

"What's new, Earl?" said Gustavo Halley, a friend of Alberto Fernández.

"Batista has just named José Pedraza as chief of police," Smith confided, proud that he was in the know. "He'll clean things up in a few weeks." Smith had been handling the Cuban investments of Senator George Smathers of Florida and other politically influential persons from Florida, including Nixon crony Bebe Rebozo, who will reappear shortly in this narrative. The FBI learned that Nixon "was also in on investments in Cuba, and had benefited financially."

Smith declined an invitation for a bridge game. He had to go home and dress for the annual New Year's Eve ball. Smith's wife was among the lovers of John F. Kennedy and was known as "among the most beautiful of the socialites with whom Kennedy was sleeping."

Four hours later, less than a mile from the Country Club, the dictator Fulgencio Batista fled from Cuba. Earl Smith resigned as Ambassador to Cuba on January 10, 1959. He was replaced by Philip Bonsal. Following Smith's departure from Cuba, Kennedy sent him to Switzerland to be ambassador there, only for the Swiss to refuse to take him.

Later in February, Sorí called Alberto. He needed a quiet place to work. Could he use the Sugar Institute? So began the organization of the popular underground anti-Castro movement inside Cuba to be known as *Unidad Revolucionaria.* That month, Manuel Urrutia invited Alberto to attend a meeting of the Council of Ministers, although Alberto was not a Minister. Alberto sat next to

Foreign Minister Roberto Agramonte, who had been a friend of his father.

"How is everything going in the sugar industry and what has been the reaction of the U.S. government to the sugar situation?" Urrutia asked Alberto.

"I don't see why the U.S. should have any say in Cuban sugar affairs," said Rufo López-Fesquet, Minister of the Treasury.

"You mind the Treasury and keep your mouth shut about sugar," Alberto said. Under the table, Agramonte patted Alberto's knee.

"Don't pay attention," he said.

"Are the Communists taking over the government?" President Urrutia found occasion to ask Alberto in a whisper later that month. Urrutia would remain in office only until spring.

Increasingly wary, Alberto obtained visas to the United States for the mayor of Bayamo, who had rescued him from Batista's marauding soldiers, and his extended family. Ambassador Bonsal delayed so long in processing the twenty-some-odd visas that Alberto paid a visit to the American Embassy on a Saturday morning to avoid Bonsal. He came away with the visas. Bonsal continued in his belief that the U.S. should "maintain our attitude of understanding and sympathy with the broad aspirations of the Cuban Revolution."

By May 1959, Castro had moved against American interests in Cuba. *The Dallas Morning News* ran an article, "Cuba Threatening King Ranch Land." The new law prohibited anyone from owning more than 3,316 acres of ranch land, although the National Institute of Agrarian Reform (INRA) seemed to contain a loophole, allowing foreigners to own land "beneficial for the development of the national economy." Was *Becerra*, then, safe? (By July, the death penalty would await those decreed to be traitors for opposing the land reform program.)

At the end of May 1959, at King Ranch in Texas, Robert J. Kleberg, Jr. began to receive what he termed "vulgar, obscene telephone calls" that were somehow connected with *Becerra*. The calls, emanating from Washington, D.C., were received on Kleberg's personal unlisted telephone number, one known only to his closest friends. There was cursing, there was noise, there were obscenities coming over the line. The woman on the other end identified herself by name. She claimed to have been "a close friend of Mr. Richard Kleberg."

The local sheriff was instructed to inform the Houston FBI field office in an effort "to stop these calls and admonish the caller." Noting that "Mr. Kleberg is a close personal friend of the director," the FBI investigated and soon identified the callers. FBI agents visited her residence, a new apartment, and discovered that the woman caller was a character so "notorious" that they would make no attempt to "admonish her."

The FBI decided to maintain its distance because of the public notoriety attached to this woman, and the danger of unpleasant publicity from her exposure. The woman had a male companion who claimed to be acquainted with Bob Kleberg. Two men in particular seemed to visit her apartment repeatedly. There were three names on the mailbox. The telephone was apparently used non stop during the daytime.

In her calls, the woman addressed Kleberg as "Bob" and then as "dear" and "darling." Richard Kleberg's name came up. There was mention of a package containing $10 million in cash that had turned up in Cuba. The woman then referred to "two disasters" affecting King Ranch. One was the death of "Black Hill," a thoroughbred horse owned by King Ranch and recently disposed of after a racing accident.

The other was "the loss of the King Ranch in Cuba," which had been expropriated by Cuban Premier Castro. Kleberg was told, "You used my money to buy this land in Cuba, and you can't get away with it. The hand is going to reach out again and the next time will be in Pennsylvania. You had better watch Pennsylvania."

The woman's male companion came on the line to claim that he knew the numbers to a safe and had a torn letter relating to the Richard Kleberg estate.

My brother's estate is closed, Kleberg said, only for the man to contradict him.

In his third call of that evening, the man told Kleberg, "I am coming to Kingsville, and I will be there in ten hours, and you better see me." An hour and a half later, at 11:30 PM, the phone rang again. Kleberg did not reply. He took the declaration that the man was coming to Kingsville as a threat and once more he notified the sheriff.

The man and woman actually flew to Corpus Christi where they registered at the Robert Driscoll Hotel. At King Ranch headquarters they met with Dick Kleberg, Jr. His father had kept "a valuable package" for her, the woman said; she had come to King Ranch to claim it. If they did not oblige, the woman threatened, she "would just have to use other means."

Supposedly the package contained $10 million, for which they had serial numbers and other evidence. It was a shakedown, even as the woman added that she had a sister who was ill with cancer and her mother was subsisting on a small pension.

Between the Kleberg attorneys and the FBI, the extortionists were chased off, although the threats did not fall under Bureau jurisdiction since there was no federal violation. Once more Robert J. Kleberg, Jr., for whom public scandal was unthinkable, had occasion to express his appreciation to J. Edgar Hoover.

The names of these people remained redacted in Robert J. Kleberg, Jr.'s FBI file into the millennium.

On June 12, 1959, Humberto Sorí Marín resigned as Fidel Castro's Minister of Agriculture.

Late in June 1959, the fate of *Becerra* hanging in the balance, Kleberg and Michael J. P. Malone flew to New York to gather political support to save King Ranch in Cuba. Castro is "insane and therefore impossible to work with," Kleberg told Cardinal Spellman on June 22nd. Kleberg brought with him a statement made by Archbishop Peréz Serrente in *Santiago de Cuba* complaining about Communist influence in the agrarian reform program.

The following day, June 23rd, Kleberg and Malone marched into the offices of the *New York Times,* where Kleberg demanded to meet with its editor, Arthur Hays Sulzberger. His purpose was to confront reporter Herbert Matthews, who had written so favorably about Fidel Castro and, in Kleberg's opinion, accomplished more than anyone else in granting Castro credibility. Without further ado, the editorial page editor Charles Merz introduced Kleberg to Matthews.

Kleberg's power was such that he could march into the *Times* on a whim and receive the attention he demanded. His closeness to Allen Dulles alone suggests the level of power at which he operated. As for CIA and the *New York Times*, a 1975 CIA document indicates that the Agency enjoyed the ability to hack into the *New York Times'* computers. "The NYT computer can be monitored," reads a document signed by Theodore C. Poling and issuing from the Counter Intelligence Research & Analysis branch of the Agency.

"Castro is immature and at times irrational," Herbert Matthews admitted to Kleberg and Malone. "The Agrarian Reform Law is quite unsound as it stands, although not necessarily beyond repair."

Matthews now had to contend with the Irish temper of Michael J. P. Malone.

"Are there Communists in the Cuban government?" Malone demanded.

"There are no first-class Communists," Matthews said.

"Is there a difference in classes of Communists?" Malone said. "Either they are or they are not."

Matthews held his ground, but so did Malone as he remarked that Castro "had Camilo Cienfuegos as Chief of Staff and he is one, so it is silly to differentiate between who is a first-class Communist and who is not."

Kleberg was a man whom all those in power, journalists included, knew enough to take seriously. The *Times* removed Herbert Matthews from the Cuba beat on the ground that he was "too subjective."

Along the way, Belton Kleberg Johnson took Herbert Matthews to dinner at The Palm steakhouse in New York in the hope of altering his perspective.

Kleberg was not yet done with Herbert Matthews. Using Malone as his intermediary, Kleberg enlisted J. Edgar Hoover. Would the FBI kindly look into Matthews' background? Kleberg proposed. People like Hoover and Dulles were hired hands, after all. As Allen Dulles had rushed to the defense of Alberto Fernández, so now J. Edgar Hoover investigated Herbert Matthews. Hoover at once turned up records indicating that Matthews had taken "a rather active part in portraying favorably the Loyalist Movement in Spain and he was in favor of the Abraham Lincoln Brigade, which was a Communist outfit."

Matthews is "very pro-Castro in tone," Hoover remarked. He noted that the idea that there were "no Communists in high positions in the government of Cuba or in the Cuban army" was "an absolute lie." Later Hoover told Malone that he placed Matthews "in the category of being an apologist for Castro's government."

"Would you call Matthews a Communist?" Malone persisted.

"I would not," Hoover said. "Sometimes I think I would rather deal with an out-and-out Communist than with a fellow like this with all his double talk." Then Hoover added, "Mr. Kleberg's suspicions are well-founded."

"Mr. Kleberg certainly appreciates the assistance given him," Malone said.

It was also during June 1959 that Kleberg enlisted Holland McCombs to persuade *Fortune* magazine to do a story about King Ranch in Cuba. It would speculate on whether "foreign investments are good or bad for Cuba, Cubans, and the Cuban economy." The focus would be on "the King Ranch operation in Cuba as a classic example of good behavior and beneficial contributions of a foreign investor." Kleberg was ready with his "before" and "after" photographs.

Kleberg knew enough to know that it was better to be on offense than on defense, in life, as in sports. When *Fortune* expressed interest, Kleberg at once instructed McCombs to get in touch with Malone.

The *Fortune* article appeared, having been vetted by Kleberg. He was not a man to allow others to write about him unimpeded.

Kleberg told the reporters who interviewed him that he was not privileged by his board of directors and stockholders to release profit figures, although he did grant that Santa Gertrudis "served enough dollar purpose to keep us in existence." He did not mention King Ranch's oil revenues.

On June 24th, the day after Kleberg and Malone had their encounter with Herbert Matthews, they flew to Washington, D.C., to meet with acting Secretary of State Christian Herter. Kleberg handed Herter three memoranda. One was of his conversation with Cardinal Spellman. This was to be treated "very confidentially." A second was of his conversation with Herbert Matthews. The third document was a translation of the statement of Archbishop Peréz Serrente.

Introducing Malone as the manager of his Cuban property, Kleberg claimed that *Becerra* was worth $3 million. Should Castro's agrarian reform program go forward, Kleberg would lose his entire investment. At the same time, the United States would find "a Communist-controlled nation close to our shores."

Kleberg explained that Castro proposed to compensate him for his land with "worthless bonds," agrarian reform bonds, they were termed, and worth less than 20 percent of the value of the property. In their defense, the Cubans argued that their bonds would be redeemable in a much shorter time than the American bonds for the agrarian reform in Japan had been after the war. The Cubans had twenty years to pay at a yearly interest of 4.5 percent.

On August 29, 1959, Castro said on television, "Private investments can feel safe and guaranteed from government intervention." Then, the next day, Minister of State Raúl Roa went on television and declared that Cuba could not pay for land expropriated from U.S. interests in cash because monetary conditions here did not make it possible." By July 1960, the bonds would bear interest of only 2 percent annually and would be redeemable in not less than *thirty* years.

The new owners of the land lacked capital, technical knowledge, equipment, and marketing arrangements to run a ranch properly. It "behooved" the U.S. government to take a very firm position against the Agrarian Reform Law, Kleberg said. Only "economic pressure" would be effective.

Kleberg then proposed that Cuba's sugar quota be slashed drastically. The Cuban sugar industry would at once suffer an abrupt decline, causing widespread unemployment. People in Cuba would be forced out of work and go hungry. Kleberg urged a total economic blockade of Cuba to bring about "the end of Castro politically." It was a strategy that ultimately would be embraced by the U.S., although it would not achieve the end, the fall of Fidel Castro, that Kleberg envisioned.

"Measures of economic warfare during wartime are one thing, whereas in peacetime they are quite another," Herter demurred, seemingly unaware that Allen Dulles had already decreed that "we" were at war with Cuba. With Herter's view, Alberto Fernández agreed: He could not imagine deliberately starving the people of Cuba even in the hope of the fall of Fidel Castro.

But Kleberg had had enough. He figuratively snapped his briefcase shut. *He* was not one to decide policy, Kleberg said as he headed for the door. He would seek assistance elsewhere.

CHAPTER 5

AWAY ALL BOATS: THE LION AND CIA

> "Without the Company, I couldn't get weapons. I couldn't
> operate."
>
> Alberto Fernández

When Fidel Castro took power on January 1, 1959, Gustavo de los Reyes, owner of the graceful Carmelo, was a former president of the Cuban Cattlemen's Association. Led by anti-Communist figures that had been part of the rebel army, like Captain Reynaldo Blanco, by the summer of 1959 the cattlemen had formed a group with the goal of building a popular movement to oust Castro. Having believed that Castro would restore democracy to Cuba, and concluding that the truth lay elsewhere, they became part of an oppositionist underground well before Castro confiscated their properties.

The leader of the group was William Morgan, nicknamed *El Americano,* a former U.S. Marine and CIA asset who was in Cuba working with the Cuban army. Advising the cattlemen was that ubiquitous CIA officer David Atlee Phillips, who had been instrumental in CIA's 1954 overthrow of Jacobo Árbenz Guzmán in Guatemala under the command of Tracy Barnes of the clandestine services. Phillips was, of course, also Jack Malone's "Chivas Regal friend." It was Malone who had introduced Phillips to de los Reyes.

Phillips was embedded in Havana with a proprietary public relations company called "VISIÓN" when Castro learned of his presence within the cattlemen's plot. It was Michael J. P. Malone who warned Phillips and pulled him out of Cuba to safety. In his highly selective memoir, *The Night Watch,* Phillips mentions neither this daring exploit nor the name of the man who saved his life.

Malone himself appeared at one of the cattlemen's meetings in the company of yet another CIA operative on the scene, "Douglas J. Freapane." Freapane's real name was David U. Groves, and he too had taken part in CIA's 1954 Guatemala coup. Groves used the Catholic Church in Mexico as his cover. With CIA's endless ability to provide covers for its employees, Freapane had become a member of the "World Conference of Bishops."

As the cattlemen's plot developed, they drew into their net the dictator of the Dominican Republic, Rafael Trujillo. Trujillo offered the cattlemen, free of charge, the assistance of members of the foreign legion who had been working for him in his efforts to control what he viewed as unwelcome Haitian immigration to his side of the island of Hispaniola. Trujillo's help, however, was far from sufficient and the cattlemen, as Bob Kleberg had done, sought the assistance of CIA in their effort to overthrow Castro. In the company of Malone and George Braga, Gustavo de los Reyes flew to Washington, D.C.

With the further assistance of Braga's partners, the Fanjuls, de los Reyes gained an audience with Allen Dulles. Alfonso Fanjul would later surface as a CIA asset with the David Sánchez Morales group operating out of JMWAVE, CIA's Miami station. Pepe and Alfie Fanjul both became part of CIA operations AMCHEER and AMFAST, which enlisted exiled Cuban businessmen and lawyers to be part of the "liberation" CIA promised it would sponsor once they had overthrown Fidel Castro. (At one point Robert J. Kleberg, Jr. named a King Ranch Quarter Horse after Alfonso Fanjul.)

De los Reyes' meeting with Allen Dulles took place on or about August 1, 1959. To the astonishment of de los Reyes, given the presence of CIA people at the cattlemen's meetings, Allen Dulles was far from hospitable.

"We don't agree with what your group is doing," Dulles said coldly. "We're on good terms with Russia. Castro is their ally. We don't want trouble with Russia and so we cannot back efforts against Castro." Then Dulles added, as de los Reyes recalls the conversation, "Besides, Morgan is a crook!"

Dulles followed all this with a seeming non sequitur.

"How much money do you need?"

"We don't need any money," de los Reyes said. "We're here to notify you of our intentions."

So de los Reyes exposed the essence of CIA's relationship with those who fled Castro's Cuba and sought to resurrect representative institutions in Cuba. Had the cattlemen's group accepted CIA money, their efforts would have fallen under CIA control. Only then would CIA have assisted them in their struggle.

For CIA, control was the highest priority, along with the health and well-being of the Agency as an institution. The price of CIA interest was the relinquishment of leadership to them. The first step for those who wanted CIA's help was to show their good faith by accepting CIA's ready, inexhaustible cash.

"We cannot back you," Dulles said. "If you don't put a stop to this, you'll end up in a Cuban jail—or a cemetery."

"I'd prefer the cemetery to doing nothing," de los Reyes said. As he was about to depart, he requested of Dulles that the meeting be held in strictest confidence. The lives of the men involved, as well as his own, were at stake. (De Los Reyes' experience is echoed in a novel by long-time Castro friend Norberto Fuentes. In *The Autobiography of Fidel Castro,* Fuentes has Castro call Allen Dulles "the first gringo to seem conciliatory and even understanding." Fuentes appends to his "novel" the following statement as to the veracity of his depiction of Castro and his policies: *"The author has avoided mention of any event of which confirmation besides his own testimony is inaccessible."*)

Having promised the cattlemen's group strict confidentiality, Dulles at once contacted the State Department. A telegram dated August 2nd went off to Ambassador Philip Bonsal in Cuba, informing him of everything that had been said at de los Reyes' meeting with Dulles, the names of the plotters included. Bonsal then sent a telegram to Castro's foreign minister, Raúl Roa. "There is a conspiracy in your Army to betray you," Bonsal writes Roa, naming William Morgan as the leader of the group.

Later de los Reyes discovered from State Department records an assertion that the information in the telegram originated in an "FBI report," preserving the secrecy of Allen Dulles' role in betraying the group to the Castro government. Mary Bancroft, Allen Dulles' wartime mistress, had not been wrong in her assessment that Dulles was as cold as he was self-interested. On August 3rd, Bonsal reported back to the State Department that he had conveyed the information about the cattlemen's conspiracy to Raúl Roa.

It wasn't long before the information traveled from Raúl Roa to President Dorticós and then to Castro himself. On August 5th, Gustavo de los Reyes returned to Havana. On August 7th, five days after Bonsal had advised Roa of the plot, the cattlemen, now with Castro's infiltrators among them, were sitting around a table at the home of Roberto Betancourt, a member of the group. The president of the cattlemen's association was now Dr. Armando Caíñas Milanés, a former member of the Cuban Senate.

Their properties still had not been confiscated by INRA. But Caíñas had already made his views known at a national assembly held in Havana, and they were in firm opposition to the new land reform law. "Cattle growers will never accept a doctrine foreign to our status as a democracy," Caíñas had said. "If it is planned by other persons to establish a Communist regime in Cuba, then cattlemen and their families will fight to the death." The land will not belong to the man who works it, but to the state, the cattlemen pointed out in opposition to INRA.

The government response appeared in the newspaper *Revolución*. It declared that the cattlemen's action was "counter-revolutionary."

A commotion at the door was followed by the thunder of invading rebel army soldiers. De los Reyes felt the cold muzzle of a submachine gun pressed to the back of his neck. The cattlemen were now driven to Camp Columbia prison, with the dreaded *La Cabaña* in their future. William Morgan was captured separately. Both he and de los Reyes were sentenced to death—in all about twenty members of the group were placed on a list of those to be executed by a firing squad.

Revealing itself to have been aware of everything going on in Cuba, CIA sent a soldier of fortune and long-time asset named Edward Browder to rescue Morgan, "crook" or not. Instead, Browder was captured. Then, in deference to the time when, with a wink from U.S. customs, Browder had run guns for the 26th of July Movement, Castro let him go.

Monitoring the fortunes of Gustavo de los Reyes was Nelson L. Raynock, CIA Chief of Station in Havana. Raynock reported to the chief of the Western Hemisphere Division that on September 16, 1959, de los Reyes was reported to be in good condition. When he was first arrested he was placed in an overcrowded cell that lacked a toilet, but then he was transferred to another cell.

On one occasion, psychological torture was applied to de los Reyes. One morning, shortly before dawn, the chief of the Revolutionary National Police visited *La Cabaña*. De los Reyes and others, including members of Batista's army, were roused out of bed and told to strip. They were marched outside and informed that they would now be shot. Then they were ordered to turn around and face the prison wall.

Defiantly, a prisoner who was an army veteran called the group to attention, military style. Then he led them in singing the national anthem. The head of the Revolutionary Police, Major Efigenio Almeiras Delgado, then announced that it had all been a joke; they were not going to be shot after all. It was only one such incident that

befell de los Reyes. It is the same form of torture depicted by Fyodor
Dostoevsky in his novel, *The Idiot,* based upon Dostoevsky's own
experience when he had been arrested by the tsar's police for having
been a member of a liberal discussion group.

CIA had its own worries. De los Reyes had a KUBARK (CIA)
contact. The chief of station reported, "There is still no reason to
assume that Reyes has disclosed his KUBARK contact."

Eventually Morgan faced a firing squad. It would be Fidel Castro
personally who ordered him to be shot to death.

"Kneel and beg for your life!" his executioners told Morgan.

"I kneel for no man!" Morgan returned. The first volley fractured
his knees.

Only then did Gustavo de los Reyes know for certain that his
suspicions of Morgan had been unfounded. It had not been Morgan
who had betrayed the cattlemen, but Allen Dulles himself.

Along with about twenty others, including the members of a
scouting party who had been captured earlier, de los Reyes was now
actually scheduled to face a firing squad. Then Bob Kleberg and Jack
Malone roared into action. To represent de los Reyes, Kleberg hired
a Mexican-American lawyer named Fausto Yturria, who operated
a cross-border law practice between Matamoros and Brownsville.

Several years earlier, a group of 26th of July revolutionaries had
been captured in a boat whose engine failed off the South Texas
coast. Their aim had been to smuggle arms from Mexico into Cuba.
Yturria had offered them free legal representation and had arranged
for their release. Now Yturria hurried to Havana to save the life of
Gustavo de los Reyes.

Accompanied by a secretary from the Mexican Embassy, Yturria
found himself before a Castro tribunal called a "*Havannah*" where
he pleaded for Gustavo de los Reyes' life. From behind a long table
of *comandantes*, Castro faced Yturria.

A big man, tall and broad and fearless, Yturria knew that he must
exhibit no weakness. He pointed his finger directly in Castro's face

and demanded that Castro remove the name "Gustavo de los Reyes" from the long list of people scheduled for immediate execution as "counter-revolutionaries."

"If I save one, I have to save all," Castro said.

He relented, in deference to Yturria's having saved those members of 26th of July caught gun-running off the South Texas coast.

Yturria then visited de los Reyes at *La Cabaña*.

"Don't worry. You are no longer on the list," Yturria said at once. "My name is Fausto Yturria. I'm Bob Kleberg's lawyer." With him was his teenage son.

Castro kept his promise and removed Gustavo de los Reyes and twenty others from the list of those awaiting execution. De los Reyes was sentenced to twenty years in prison, to be reduced at his February 1960 trial to ten years.

All the while, Gustavo de los Reyes was receiving messages from Jack Malone, facilitated by Malone's many CIA contacts still embedded in Cuba. "He almost joined me on the Isle of Pines," de los Reyes says, referring to the desolate prison where he was sent to serve his time. Malone might not have been able to ride a horse, but he was not lacking in courage or daring.

Comandante Camilo Cienfuegos

CIA continued its dance with Fidel Castro. The Agency's motives grew ever more murky to those who sought its help. On July 20, 1959, Alberto handed in his resignation, only for Castro to refuse to accept it.

In August 1959, CIA noted for the record that Alberto Fernández, still residing in Cuba, was among the leadership of a "counter-revolutionary movement against Fidel Castro."

Alberto Fernández had a private meeting with Fidel Castro on a Thursday that August. The articles by the government's economic columnist were causing considerable harm to the world market, Alberto said; for every point the market went down, Cuba lost about $1.2 million. Castro made no comment.

Alberto was not yet done. He told Castro that the low price of sugar this year, plus the exorbitant charges that had been imposed on the industry, was putting many sugar mills in the red. Some could not continue to operate. This might force the government to take them over, which would involve considerable operating expenses for INRA, Alberto said. If things did not improve, possibly further losses would occur and there would be less money to carry out the agrarian reform.

The man Michael J. P. Malone had nicknamed "Giant" replied frankly. It was very unfortunate that Russia, which has bought sugars from Cuba in previous years, had not seen fit again to buy this year, Castro remarked. He could not understand why Russia, with a large supply of gold on hand, had not come into the market.

Russia expected a large crop this year, Alberto said, and did not need to buy sugar on the world market.

Castro told Alberto that he wanted to see him again within two weeks. They would talk, Castro said, after he returned from Santiago, Chile, where he was going to attend a conference of prime ministers.

That August, Havana newspapers published lists of the properties that would be "intervened." INRA had already confiscated 25,000 acres of *Becerra*. That had taken place in June, and the government had begun to sell off the cattle. Yet King Ranch did not appear on any of the new lists of properties about to be confiscated.

Enjoying what would be the final months of his freedom, *Comandante* Huber Matos offered the Castro government's explanation. King Ranch was not on the list because "it hides its identity under many other names, the better to carry out its nefarious imperialistic practices."

On September 30th, Castro said that he was not taking over the Moa Bay Mining Company and the Nicaro nickel plant, but he might well want a bigger share of Freeport Sulphur's profits.

In October came a defining moment for the Cuban Revolution. *Comandante* Camilo Cienfuegos was among the most charismatic figures in the rebel army. Apart from the Castro brothers and Che Guevara, Camilo stood as the highest in authority in the Castro government.

Castro had dispatched Cienfuegos to Camagüey with the assignment of arresting for treason Huber Matos, a former schoolteacher and rebel army leader. Matos had been head of the rebel army in Camagüey and had talked openly against the entrenchment of Communists in the government.

Former Cuban Army Captain Jorge Navarro Custín told me that Camilo reported back to Castro that Huber Matos may have been against the Communists, but he had never acted against Fidel or Cuba. Matos admired Cienfuegos. As Robert E. Quirk notes in his biography of Castro, Matos called Cienfuegos "a man of the people, easy, *simpático,* a fine friend and an excellent comrade." The feeling was mutual.

Matos had sealed his fate by writing an inflammatory letter to Fidel Castro, which Castro received on October 19th. The angry letter accuses Castro of "burying the revolution." Matos pleades with Castro as a "comrade" to "help us save the revolution." Matos writes Castro that he is destroying his own work.

Raúl Castro and Che Guevara supposedly wanted Matos to be executed *al paredón!* ("at the wall"), according to the slogan of the time. Shrewdly, Castro decided not to make a martyr of his fellow *Comandante.*

Despite his friendship for Matos, Cienfuegos obeyed orders and had Matos arrested. Later Matos would wonder whether Castro had chosen Cienfuegos to make the arrest in the hope that followers of Matos might kill him. The source for the following account of the death of Camilo Cienfuegos is *Comandante* Humberto Sorí Marín, as told to Alberto Fernández. It is one of those many unacknowledged narratives for which there is not even one first hand source, let alone the quixotically requisite two.

On October 28th, with Matos firmly under house arrest, two planes left Camagüey to return to Havana. One, a twin-engine Cessna, carried Camilo Cienfuegos, returning from his distasteful errand. The other was an escort. The weather was fine, although official word later insisted that there had been a ferocious storm. That was false.

The escort plane crashed into the sea. Several witnesses reported that Camilo's plane landed safely at a small air field on the outskirts of Havana. It was a Friday when Camilo met alone at the palace with Fidel and Raúl Castro. Sorí learned from his inside source that suddenly Fidel pulled out his pistol and shot Camilo Cienfuegos dead.

The corpse was kept at the palace overnight. The next day, Saturday, a black-out was declared over the area. A curfew was ordered and the streets around the palace cordoned off. Camilo's body was placed in a steel tank and dropped into the sea. Shortly thereafter, Castro left the country for a visit to Venezuela. As for Matos, he would languish for two decades in La Cabaña prison. (He was released in 1979.) Within days, two of Cienfuegos' closest lieutenants died in "accidents."

In the aftermath of the disappearance of Camilo Cienfuegos, Juan Vieras, the King Ranch pilot at *Becerra,* who also flew for the Francisco Sugar Company, was accused of complicity in Camilo Cienfuegos' death. Vieras' "crime" was that he had once instructed Cienfuegos' pilot on how to fly a twin-engine Cessna. Vieras had checked out Cienfuegos' pilot on this type of plane.

Under the pretense that they were investigating the death of Camilo Cienfuegos, soldiers hauled Vieras off to jail where he languished for six days. He was being held for "interrogation," it was said.

The manager of the tiny Camagüey airport was outspoken. He called the rescue effort and ensuing "investigation" of the death of Camilo Cienfuegos perfunctory at best. Two weeks later, the airport manager was found with a bullet in his brain. His death was ruled a suicide. Not even Camilo's Cuban biographer Carlos Franqui, exiled former editor of the 26th of July newspaper *Revolución* and commentator on the rebel station *Radio Rebelde,* was satisfied with the official explanation that Cienfuegos' airplane had crashed into the sea.

And yet . . . it gives one pause that Fidel Castro, in a November 23, 1963, speech about the Kennedy assassination, trenchant in its demonstration that Lee Harvey Oswald could not have been either a Marxist or a bona fide member of the Fair Play for Cuba committee, infiltrated as indeed it was by CIA, invokes Camilo Cienfuegos. Castro closes with an invocation to the Cuban people to defend the revolution and their fatherland. "As Camilo used to say," Castro declares, the Cuban people should "be ready, alert, and vigilant as always, facing intrigues and dangers, whatever they may be."

Four years after the death of *Comandante* Camilo Cienfuegos, Castro invokes his spirit, which must have remained alive in Cuba. Castro does not bother to mention the surname—everyone knew whom he meant by "Camilo," that most popular of *comandantes.* Surely it would have taken breathtaking cynicism for Castro to summon the spirit of a man he had shot to death, even as there remains the haunting fact that on that sunny day—his plane flying close to shore, certainly not out at sea—no wreckage of a crash was discovered. Che Guevara would name one of his children "Camilo."

Losing *Becerra*

"Cuba confiscated the ranch!" Helen Kleberg records in her diary on October 1, 1959. King Ranch manager Lowell Tash attempted in early November to appeal the order that *Becerra* turn over all but 1,600 acres to the National Institute for Agrarian Reform, even as he had torn down the INRA signs that had been posted on the property. He considered the signs "propaganda," Tash said.

Castro's agents were furious when they discovered that photographers had accompanied Tash to the hearing. Tash, his lawyer, his secretary, a foreman, and two Cuban photographers who had been working with NBC were arrested, detained for eight hours, and then set free. From New York, NBC said the two photographers had been assigned to cover the takeover of the ranch property.

On October 29th, the government suspended the right of habeas corpus in Cuba, for the second time. The Constitution of 1940, a bulwark of Cuban democracy, was being steadily eviscerated, the rule of law becoming an anachronism. A group of judges had accused the Batista government of "unresponsiveness" to habeas corpus. Now under Castro habeas corpus had suffered a deathblow.

Alberto Fernández's lands were confiscated on November 4th: 700 cabs with 16,000,000 arrobas of cane, 80 cabs of rice ready to be threshed, 4,000 head of Charolais cattle, and 6 cabs of tomato plantings.

One November day a detachment of soldiers drove up to the main gate of *Becerra* and nailed a copy of a confiscation decree to the gatepost. Tash came out, read the paper, and delivered a powerful kick to the testicles of the captain in charge. Again Tash found himself in a Cuban jail.

Michael J. P. Malone enlisted the Swiss ambassador Emil Stadelhofer, who now represented U.S. interests in Cuba. Still, Malone was not about to delegate the task of saving Tash's life. Visiting Tash in prison, Malone slipped him an airplane ticket. As soon as you are released, head for the airport, Malone said.

Tash boarded a Miami-bound plane only for soldiers to rush into the cabin at the last minute and drag him off. It was all bluff. Finally, they escorted Tash back onto the plane. Tash left Cuba for good with only the khaki shirt on his back.

INRA announced that King Ranch would be converted into a cattle cooperative under the name of the late Camilo Cienfuegos upon the wishes, it was said, of the farmers working there. By now *Becerra* was comprised of 59,266 acres and 6,989 head of cattle with a declared value of $4,728,779. The changeover certificate was drawn up hastily and signed by five witnesses.

Among the U.S.-owned properties that Castro confiscated, many were, as we have seen, managed or owned by people with long-time CIA connections. Among them were Freeport Sulphur and United Fruit. Two United Fruit freighters would be enlisted as part of CIA's invasion at the Bay of Pigs. It was to CIA that these businesses turned for redress when Castro moved against them.

Along with both Braga brothers, Kleberg and Malone tried one final time to salvage *Becerra* using official channels. On November 24, 1959, Kleberg attended a Washington, D.C., luncheon hosted by Douglas Dillon, Secretary of the Treasury. Roy Rubottom represented the State Department.

"Scarcely a day goes by when I'm not called by a member of Congress to give my views on Castro," Kleberg said. He had no doubt now. Castro was "a dictator," and one who would soon infect all of Latin America.

At this meeting, Kleberg proposed that one and one-quarter cents be levied as an import tax on each pound of sugar the U.S. bought from Cuba in order to compensate property owners like himself. Alberto Fernández, whose first loyalty was to Cuba, opposed a tax on the importation of sugar.

"Must be an idea of Braga's," he thought when later he heard about Kleberg's proposal. The U.S. was accused of exploiting Cuba as it was. (At the time of Castro's seizure of Cuba, the Braga family owned 500,000 acres of land in Cuba and seven sugar mills, along with railroads, warehouses, and docks; 40,000 people lived on these plantations.)

Copies of Malone's memos of his meetings with State Department officials, CIA officers, the FBI, and anti-Castro militants went to the head of Freeport Sulphur in Cuba, to Frank O'Brien at the FBI in New York, to David Atlee Phillips, to the Bragas, and to RJK, of course, Robert J. Kleberg, Jr.

The world was Robert J. Kleberg's for the taking. By October 1960, he had sent Santa Gertrudis cattle to Jamaica for the "Reynolds people" and they were "having considerable success." There would be King Ranches wherever he could create them.

On December 18, 1959, Freeport announced that it had been "meeting with the Cuban government for the purpose of clarifying the new Cuban mining laws. It is expected that satisfactory results will come out of these conferences." That Freeport believed this message to Michael J. P. Malone seems a willful denial of reports in the Cuban press "that the revolutionary government has expressed interest in acquiring the Nicaro nickel plant in Cuba which is owned by the U.S. government." (Nicaro was the second largest nickel plant in the "free world" and had been a primary source of U.S. strategic nickel since World War II.)

The deprivations facing the Cuban people seem not to have been noticed by people like Langbourne M. Williams. Their experience had been that "where American ventures are concerned," Cuban administrations honor the obligations of their predecessors. Would Fidel Castro be any different?

In January 1960, Philip W. Bonsal delivered a note to the Minister of Foreign Relations protesting the government's denial of the "basic rights of ownership of United States' citizens in Cuba" in the name of the National Institute for Agrarian Reform. By August, the Cuban government had taken possession of the properties of Manati, Francisco, and Céspedes sugar. 700,000 tons of sugar had been sold to Russia.

In March, Nicaro would make its last shipment of ore, to the tune of 2.5 million pounds. Castro had imposed a 25 percent levy on ore exports, and Freeport closed down construction of its new facility. That month, INRA assumed provisional administration of the Moa Bay mining company properties. Robert J. Kleberg, Jr. was duly informed of all these developments.

In April 1960, there was a sale of cattle at King Ranch, which Alberto hoped to attend. "I know my uncle would be pleased to see you," Malone wrote Alberto.

Malone and the Bragas continued to monitor Fidel Castro's efforts to reach out to the wider world and influence public perception of his revolution. A letter from George Braga to Michael J. P. Malone dated May 16, 1960, refers to his brother B. Rionda Braga's having discovered that *Agencia de Prensa Latina* had opened offices to cover London, Brussels, and Rome. The agency was headed by the poet Heberto Padilla, soon to find himself in a Castro jail. In a speech on June 27, 1960, Castro referred to U.S. interests in Cuba as amounting to more than $800 million.

Unidad Revolucionaria

On July 14, 1960, celebrating a Bastille Day of his own, Alberto Fernández left Cuba for good and entered into permanent exile. He had found himself forced to witness the destruction of everything he held dear: not least the properties to which he and his family had been attached for generations. Like so many Cubans, he had concluded that his survival, and that of his family, necessitated that he leave Cuba.

In recounting his departure from Cuba into exile, Alberto did not dwell on the emotional impact of the moment. There was no sentimentality in his depiction of that turning point in his life. He talked about his departure from Cuba as having been inevitable, even delayed, and was far more interested in discussing the course of action that he took immediately upon his arrival in the United States.

It did not occur to Alberto Fernández that he would never return to Cuba. He was already a member of *Unidad Revolucionaria,* a group dedicated to enlisting ordinary Cubans in large numbers to the cause of returning freedom to Cuba. With every hope of being successful, he committed himself to a struggle conducted, at least for the present, from foreign shores.

Just before his departure, an army officer arrived at his home and presented him with "legal" papers that granted the government permanent ownership of all his properties. Then the government carted away the furniture.

Alberto took with him to Florida only $125,000 in cash. When he arrived in Key Biscayne, he purchased a house. Then, without delay, he immersed himself in the struggle.

In Texas that July, Robert J. Kleberg, Jr. was introducing Michael J. P. Malone to his friends in New Orleans at International House. "They are getting ready for you," Kleberg wrote Jack to encourage him when a letter came announcing the arrangements. "I told you this was a good place." Malone was invited down to inspect the new private dining rooms at International House and the opening of the new facility.

By August 19, 1960, the government still had not taken over the *Becerra* business office in Camagüey, although at the ranch they had been notified on August 9th. Nothing had yet happened. Alberto Fernández had requested of the King Ranch officers in Texas that they employ his foreman, who had left Cuba.

Unbeknownst to Alberto, CIA granted him a Covert Security Approval for its project JMARC, CIA's cryptonym for overall Cuban operations. On this document, the term "PROJECT JHNRC" also appears. Still, Alberto had not met with any CIA employees or agents.

Having himself long worked for CIA, Don Hogan now put Alberto in direct contact with the Agency. Using Hogan's New Haven, Connecticut, law firm contact, John Hewitt Mitchell, CIA helped Alberto create a tax-deductible entity to collect funds for the struggle on which he planned to embark. Then, fearing that too many people would talk ("yakk"), Alberto never utilized this tax instrument. Dating at least from March 1960, Don Hogan had been reporting on everything Alberto Fernández did to the FBI field office in New Haven.

The evidence of Hogan's informing came from one Catherine Taaffe, a Sugar Institute employee until she was fired in July 1959. A pint-size, brown-haired, brown-eyed woman, five feet in height, and a self-styled Mata Hari, Taaffe had acted as an informant for both the FBI (her FBI file is copious) and CIA. She was a mother of five and a veteran of several marriages.

Born on July 13, 1917, in 1959 Catherine Taaffe was forty-two years old. Her childhood was not uneventful. Her grandmother had accused her father of attempting to kill her mother. He was killed in a gunfight with sheriffs. Three months after the incident, her mother died of cancer. Taaffe's chequered history included service as an agent for the Batista regime in 1953 for the purchase of British Vampire jet fighter planes. She called herself "the only woman arms dealer registered in Washington, D.C."

"She's nuts!" New York lawyer Morris Ernst said. He met her only once, confided I. I. Davidson, registered agent for Somoza and arms dealer for Israel and for CIA, whose name the Bureau protected. One $500 check in Taaffe's possession was drawn on the account of the Sugar Institute during the year 1959.

Among the rumors swirling about Taaffe was that she had received $5,000 from the Cuban Revolutionary Government for information regarding anti-Castro activities at the Sugar Institute, which obviously refers to Alberto Fernández's providing a place where Humberto Sorí Marín might work on his organizational plans for *Unidad Revolucionaria*. Taaffe was accused of being an informant for both the Cuban National Revolutionary Police and the anti-Castro *Acción Democrática Cristiana (ADC)*.

Taaffe was known to have had several contacts with Frank O'Brien at the FBI field office in New York. O'Brien was, an FBI document indicates, "familiar with all her activities and her cooperation with the FBI." The Bureau's Miami field office also knew her well. Taaffe is among the many minor characters, among them women spies of considerable panache, who move in and out of the shadows of the Cuba story. Another is CIA's June Cobb, whom apparently Catherine Taaffe knew well.

In its correspondence with Assistant Attorney General J. Walter Yeagley, the Bureau pronounces Catherine Quinby Taaffe "of extremely doubtful reliability." Taaffe's contacts with anti-Castro oppositionists were many and included Rolando Masferrer Rojas, the former Cuban senator in exile in the United States. She knew also Joaquín Meyer, the representative of the Sugar Institute based in Washington, D.C., who held diplomatic rank. She had been introduced to Don Hogan by Alberto Fernández; her contacts in Cuba were multifarious. Not least, she communicated directly with Attorney General Robert Kennedy.

Was Catherine Taaffe a Castro agent? She claimed to have met on the night of December 7, 1959, with Raúl Castro, Minister of Defense, and two other of Castro's assistants. She claimed that Raúl told her that the Cuban treasury did not have enough money to cover the government's expenses for the month of December.

Supposedly Raúl Castro told her that the 26th of July Movement had $11,870,000 in a Swiss bank and that Czechoslovakia was offering the Cuban government Russian-built MIGs. Taaffe herself would be their intermediary; she claimed she would like to tie up the money the Cubans had in Switzerland. In February 1960, Catherine Taaffe held an option on 300 tons of sugar and had contacted Cargill, a large commodity organization in the Midwest, to sell her sugar.

No one knew for sure for whom Taaffe worked. Her FBI file remains heavily redacted.

Catherine Taaffe reported to the FBI on Alberto Fernández; on January 9th she advised them that "Fernández is a member of the cabinet in Cuba," which was not, however, the case.

The same document contains the name "Fernández" in its discussion of the Sugar Stabilization Institute, suggesting that Alberto Fernández also reported to the Bureau. The FBI attributes to Alberto Fernández, in that solitary sentence that they neglected to redact, that "they had also located records showing various figures were in business with Batista, as well as Generalissimo Trujillo of the Dominican Republic."

It was shortly after his arrival in Key Biscayne that Alberto first met Michael J. P. Malone, who had been monitoring his movements in Cuba all along. Malone at once reported on this auspicious moment to his CIA handlers, as well as to Frank O'Brien. Twelve days after Alberto's arrival in the United States, Malone told CIA he would be "happy to arrange an interview" with Fernández, "should they wish it, or should Alberto."

Malone also met with Alberto's sister-in-law Hortensia Rionda, his wife, Ofelia's sister, bringing her much-needed Czarnikow-Rionda cash. Jack Malone had "a presence," Hortensia's young son, Eduardo Sánchez Rionda, thought. He was no lightweight. Malone would provide the family with funds for about two years.

Alberto had decided that he would accept no salary from CIA, differentiating himself at once from the majority of anti-Castro militants. The DRE's (*Directorio Revolucionario Estudiantil*) monthly CIA stipend ran in the tens of thousands, with the money delivered by their CIA handler in brown-paper grocery store bags, according to former DRE militant Isidro Borja. For joining the CIA-created Cuban Revolutionary Council (CRC), Miró Cardona received $100,000 in cash. Tony Varona, too, stood in line for CIA bounty.

With the direct approval of Allen Dulles, Jack Malone paid out large sums of money to Cuban exiles in the summer and fall of 1960. Malone consulted the Agency even when Kleberg wanted to contribute his own money to someone. And always Malone reported to CIA on whatever he and Kleberg were doing. On July 20th, Malone reported on a trip to Miami where he had met with the "MRDR," which supported Tony Varona.

CIA said no to their request for $15,000. But on August 5, 1960, Malone authorized a check for $10,000 to go to Varona, courtesy of CIA's Office of Security. Our James Bond, Michael J.P. Malone, was acting on behalf of CIA's Office of Security, which had been using Czarnikow-Rionda as a conduit for funneling money to the Cubans. With CIA authorization, Malone also arranged for Lowell Tash to lease "three or four acres of land" on Andros Island for Varona's *Frente Revolucionario Democrático* (FRD). CIA records reveal that Jack, a tireless intermediary, also offered David Phillips the opportunity to meet an exile named Salvador Ferrer. At least half of the Agency's budget was being spent on covert action and para-military activity. There seemed no reason to doubt that CIA would do all in its power to rid Cuba of Castro and Communism.

CIA described Alberto Fernández at the moment they made his acquaintance. He was a handsome, well-groomed man with jet-black hair, a "heavy beard" (which he denied to me), and "no promi-nent features." He used the "term 'huh' for emphasis in speaking," CIA noted.

CIA approved of Alberto's way of life. He did not smoke, was a strong family man (he had three children, to whom he was devoted), and "never made the slightest reference to extra-marital activity." Upright and pious, he was "not known to gamble."

Among Alberto's friends, CIA listed his brother-in-law John T. Smithies, who was married to Alberto's older sister Gladys; his Princeton classmate Robert Goheen, later to become president of the university; Michael J. P. Malone; the FBI's Frank O'Brien; and Robert Hurwitch of the State Department. (Alberto says he had little to do with Hurwitch, whom the State Department would send down to Miami to keep watch over anti-Castro operations.) Despite negative remarks about Hurwitch in CIA documents, some observ-ers, like soldier of fortune Gerald Patrick Hemming, concluded that Hurwitch was a CIA asset embedded in the State Department. It was yet another instance of ambiguity: who was working for whom?

CIA noted Alberto's financial obligation to King Ranch for $20,000. He had worked at the Sugar Institute "to protect its funds from Castro." This was CIA's spin.

Alberto's political model for his revolution against Castro was the Cuban Constitution of 1940. This document granted all Cubans full democratic rights, including due process, the crowning jewel of the U.S. Constitution. All Cubans were equal under the law with the right of habeas corpus. One article prohibited discrimination on the grounds of race or ethnicity. The Cuban Constitution also respected property rights in its Article 24: *Se prohibe la confiscación de bienes.*

"It's the best of the best," Alberto told me.

Unidad Revolucionaria was founded formally in November 1960, but the seeds of the organization had been planted in their meetings in February 1959, when Alberto was heading the Sugar Institute and Sorí already had become disillusioned with Fidel Castro. All organizations that subscribed to *UR* principles were welcome.

The majority of *UR* groups were localized entities consisting of a few key leaders with personal followings. Among the groups that participated, only the *MRR* was excluded. Sharing the leadership inside Cuba with Rafael Díaz Hanscomb and others, Humberto Sorí Marín coordinated *Unidad*'s United Front. Hanscomb was the first general coordinator, Sorí the national military coordinator. CIA adds his rank as "Major."

Unidad was conceived as a mass movement of Cubans of all social classes. It did not intend that a small group of leaders substitute themselves for the majority, which may account for why the names "Humberto Sorí Marín" and "Alberto Fernández" are less known that those of other exile personalities. *Unidad* was designed as a broadly based organization with no hierarchy of leadership, even as CIA would recognize that, unlike the *Frente*, *UR*'s "only goal was to overthrow the Communist dictatorship in PBRUMEN," CIA's cryptonym for Cuba, and establish a "real democratic regime."

Along with the reinstatement of individual rights would come the cancellation of military courts and the abolition of the death penalty, with the exception of murders committed by agents of Batista or the Communists. "The past which prevailed under Batista shall never come back" was among *Unidad*'s "Declaration of Principles." The non-Communist labor unions would be reinstated. *Unidad* recognized that the "agrarian structure of our country should be entirely revised."

Another principle was that "all properties confiscated, intervened or seized by the Castro regime shall be returned to their owners." Alberto and Humberto Sorí Marín supported the Sugar Coordination Law (*Coordinación Azucarera*) which created the *Banafic*, the *Banco Agrícola Nacional y Fomento Agrícola*, charged with stimulating agricultural production and industry. No one doubted that Cuba was sorely in need of agricultural reform.

Unidad also carried a religious component. In a statement issued by Alberto Fernández, its avowed goal was "to restore Cuba to the brotherhood of free Christian nations." *Unidad's* symbol was a fish, standing for Chrisitan love and charity. Its motto was "DIOS-PATRIA-LIBERTAD," (God, Fatherland, Freedom).

"Here we have no Indian chiefs, only Indians," Alberto said, at once distinguishing *UR* from all the other anti-Castro groups. Alberto Fernández certainly had no desire to be a "leader" and was never to develop personal ambitions. "I'm not a politician," he explained to me. "I got into what I did because of principles." He talked about "the general good" and accepted the radical change in his personal circumstances with good grace.

Unidad soon established a newspaper called *Cruzada*. In February 1961, the name would be changed to *Unidad Revolucionaria*. A robbery of the Tropical Brewery netted $20,000 that aided the cause.

Cautious, CIA described *Unidad* as "one of seven major resistance movements in PBRUMEN." CIA affected no preference for one group over the others, but *Unidad's* independence would doom it to be underestimated by the Agency. CIA defined *Unidad* as "moderately liberal."

Within a month, CIA had a list of the "true names and war names" of the individuals and groups participating in *Unidad Revolucionaria*.

From the first days of what would be a long struggle, Alberto questioned the commitment to liberate Cuba of his new allies. In their meetings, Kleberg had evinced no interest in the history of Cuba, how Batista came to power, or his many malfeasances. He exhibited no feeling about the harm Batista had done to the Cuban people. It seemed to Alberto that Kleberg was interested only in cattle. Malone also didn't ask many questions about Cuba. He focused on maintaining his opportunistic role as the intermediary between Kleberg, the exiles, the FBI, and CIA.

Alberto was different. His life focused overwhelmingly on the liberation of Cuba. Years later, Alberto would reflect that he could not have operated against Castro at all had he not accepted the assistance of CIA. CIA had facilitated his obtaining visas for friends desperate to leave Cuba. CIA had helped him rescue his friend, Delio Gómez Ochoa, who had been stranded in Ciudad Trujillo. As part of what would become their symbiotic relationship, Alberto in turn alerted CIA to agents of Cuba's intelligence service (G-2) who had entered the United States.

In his operations against the Castro regime, Alberto Fernández adhered to a strict code, one that transcended his refusal to accept a salary from CIA. The groups he supported inside Cuba had to be "free from foreign influences." If he had his way, the operations CIA sent forth would originate from within the United States rather than from foreign locations, unlike the Bay of Pigs invasion that would set forth from Guatemala.

Neither Alberto nor *Unidad* would join CIA's Cuban Revolutionary Council. This position would alienate CIA from Alberto, but it reveals no less the real nature of CIA's political motivations and intent, and underlines the experience of Gustavo de los Reyes. If CIA did not control an operation, not only would it not support it, but it was likely to sabotage it.

The freedom to pursue his operations unimpeded by CIA that Alberto demanded at once awakened their distrust. Naming Alberto "AMDENIM-1," CIA acknowledged Alberto's simplicity. It was aware that he had no desire to renew the style of life he had enjoyed as a rich man in Cuba. CIA noted Alberto's "shrewdness." CIA's cable traffic describes Alberto's activities as moving steadily upward to the office of Allen Dulles. Among those reporting on Alberto to CIA was Donald Hogan who, unbeknownst to Alberto, nurtured the ambition to be employed formally by CIA. (CIA would turn him down.)

One CIA component keeping Alberto under surveillance attempted to uncover the "identity of rich American businessman said to be financing the group." As always with CIA, everything was on a need-to-know basis and one component might well not know what others were doing. This man, referred to only as "Uncle" in Jack Malone's communications with the Agency, kept his customary low profile.

CIA's surveillance of Alberto Fernández was intensified by his aloofness and the conclusion that he was not entirely reliable. The Agency thought he had set up a guerrilla organization of "four hundred of his ex-employees inside Cuba, planning to carry out acts of sabotage" with "the backing of rich American businessmen," which was far from the reality. Among CIA's tactics to ensure its power was to prevent any of the Cuban groups from becoming too powerful and to set one exile leader against the others. When Tony Varona asked Alberto to take over Oriente Province during a proposed *Frente* operation, CIA advised Alberto "not [to] take any precipitous steps."

Inside Cuba, Humberto Sorí Marín had been making great strides in organizing *Unidad Revolucionaria*. By late 1960, twenty-three grassroots organizations had joined *Unidad*. The recruits were mostly *Guajiros*, country people, whom Alberto described as strong, healthy, and bright, of a high cultural level. They were also "anti-Communist" and willing to live "like animals in holes" for the cause. The educated, Cuba's wealthy elite, were not interested.

The *Tejana*

Upon his arrival in the United States, never even considering that he should seek employment, Alberto at once became "the man of the boats." Sailing to the shores of Cuba, he infiltrated fighters, exfiltrated members of *Unidad*, and carried into Cuba quantities of ammunition, explosives, and weapons. He was never caught. Soon you could observe Marine equipment drying in his front yard. Castro had allowed him to leave Cuba when he must have known that Alberto would hit the ground running and work against him. But it might have been that the G-2, Cuban intelligence, was not as good as it became later.

His first boat was the *ILMAFE*, a twenty-two footer named for the initials of his three children Ileanne, Marianne, and Federico. With the *ILMAFE*, Alberto sailed between Key Biscayne and Key

West in search of bases from which to launch infiltration teams into
Cuba. It didn't occur to him to enlist CIA in these efforts.

A supporter named Dan Taylor, whom Alberto met through
a contact at the Manati Sugar Company railroad, granted Alberto
dock space free of charge. Taylor, deeply sympathetic, gave Alberto
the Cuban pesos that he retained, and even went on to send a pony
for Alberto's children.

As they walked to Alberto's car, Taylor handed him a set of keys.
He grabbed Alberto's hand.

"Alberto, whatever you need, let me know. You can count on
me," Taylor said.

He embraced Alberto. "But I want you to know," Taylor added,
"you're never going to go back to Cuba."

Alberto Fernández's first infiltration trip into Cuba was on
September 10, 1960. Each trip placed him and his team in enor-
mous danger. Yet he never hesitated.

The *ILMAFE* proved to be too small and not equipped for what
Alberto had in mind. On the Miami River, through a connection of
Michael J. P. Malone, Alberto found a Chris Craft, a wooden power-
boat used by "weekend sailors," virtually in ruins. He dubbed it "*El
Real*" after, he claimed, the ship of the Christians under the leadership of the Duke of Austria fighting the Turks at the 1571 Battle of
Lepanto; it was in that battle that Miguel de Cervantes Saavedra,
author of *Don Quijote*, serving on the galley *Marquesa*, had lost the
use of his left hand.

"We were going on a pilgrimage of the same nature," Alberto
says, explaining why he chose to call his boat *El Real*. He, too, was
engaged in a crusade, a quest for justice, with no concern for the
danger or the consequences.

Marathon Key would be the point of embarkation because it
provided a direct route to Varadero in Cuba (Varadero was a high-
toned resort town in Matanzas known as *Playa Azul,* "Blue Beach").

Don Hogan induced Alberto to run supplies to another militant,
Manolo Ray, who remained in Cuba. Now Hogan did request that

CIA supply Alberto. Alberto questioned Tony Varona to learn the terms on which CIA participated in operations. There were always terms and conditions, and they pertained to the advantages CIA perceived for itself.

One day Alberto and his crew were sailing back into Marathon Key after a trip to Cuba when they observed a man standing on the dock waiting for them. He was thin and lanky, not very tall, yet he cut a striking figure dressed as he was all in white: white shirt, white tie, white pants. His name, he said, when Alberto introduced himself, was "Clarence Connors." An expert in Asian operations, Clarence would be Alberto's first CIA handler. Some Asians, Clarence confided, were trained to laugh off lie detector tests, the Agency's "LCFLUTTER" (polygraph) tests, obligatory for its assets.

Under its JMATE program, infiltrating Cuba by sea, CIA was already short of boats. The Agency had contracted with one of its corporate allies, General Dynamics, for at least one high-speed boat for use in raids into Cuba, but it wasn't sufficient. Alberto proved useful. With *El Real,* he made between six and eight trips between Marathon Key and Varadero, carrying explosives to attack Castro's power plants and cripple his petroleum industry. Each trip took only four hours and forty-five minutes.

Alberto hadn't waited for his approval, but Allen Dulles seemed to have come around. On December 21, 1960, Dulles addressed a meeting of President Eisenhower's "Special Group." He had met yesterday with Americans who did business in Cuba, Dulles said, among them the head of Freeport Sulphur.

"It was time for the U.S. to get off dead center and take some action" was the prevailing view. This meant burning Cuba's sugar crop; interrupting the electric power supply; embargoing food, drugs, and spare parts; and forcing the shutdown of the Freeport nickel plant at Nicaro. (By the year 2010, nickel rather than sugar would be Cuba's largest export.)

These businessmen opposed a socialistic post-Castro government led by someone like Manolo Ray, whose movement had been dubbed *"Fidelismo sin Fidel,"* which meant the socialist programs of Castro without Castro himself. (The correlative was *"un Castrismo sin Comunismo."*) This would be as bad for business as Castro himself. DD/P Richard Bissell hoped for a major revolutionary uprising in Cuba. Eisenhower had already enlisted Arturo Frondizi of Argentina and Don Manuel Prado, the president of Peru. They wanted to remove Castro, but for the "U.S. to take the lead."

So the tone of what would become CIA's consistent policy toward Cuba was set: CIA would support no effort on the part of the exiles unless CIA had control of the group. The Agency's concern from the outset was "the possible orientation of any anti-Castro government in exile."

Michael Haider, Standard Oil of New Jersey's Vice President for Latin America, spoke for the group. He "worried that unless more positive steps were taken to force the conservative Cuban exiles into a cohesive organization, any post-Castro government would automatically be in the hands of the leftists." In July 1960, Standard Oil enjoyed a more than $75 million economic stake in Cuba.

What Dulles and the "high-level business group" with whom he met feared was that a government alternative to Castro might concern itself with the needs of the Cuban people rather than those of the group in attendance: not only Standard Oil of New Jersey, but Cuban-American Sugar Company; American Sugar Domino Refining Company; American & Foreign Power Company; Freeport Sulphur Company; Texaco; International Telephone & Telegraph, and others. CIA wanted no part of that.

Dulles was his usual self. He denied that CIA made policy: Policy planning was not his responsibility, but that of the Department of State, he insisted. Then he added that what he was interested in was getting rid of Castro as quickly as possible and in this field he had direct responsibility and would welcome any ideas or suggestions on how this might be achieved. In attendance as well was future Brigadier General Edward Lansdale, a CIA agent under long-time military cover.

It was in December 1960 that CIA listed Alberto as a "DDP contact" of its Miami station, JMWAVE, the most active component of the Agency's Directorate for Plans, as the clandestine services were then called. (A CIA document lists Alberto as having worked with JMWAVE "to at least 31 January 1966.")

Alberto was operating in uncharted territory. Few such operations had been undertaken in the western hemisphere up to this point. When even *El Real* proved unequal to the task, Alberto located a 116-foot submarine chaser that boasted a history of having engaged with German submarines in the North Sea during World War II. It was named the *Tejana* or the *Tejana III* because it had been owned by a Texan named Robert H. McCoy. Its blades were feathered so that they didn't grab water, but changed position without the intervention of a clutch.

Alberto bought the *Tejana,* which cost between $60,000 and $70,000, with his own money, along with a $38,000 contribution from "Uncle." CIA provided some equipment and talked about a formal support agreement with Alberto that never materialized. CIA contributed no money toward the purchase. The *Tejana* was registered under a front called the "Inter-Key Transportation Company" as a U.S.-documented vessel. It began operations in January 1961 delivering arms and supplies inside Cuba.

"We weren't sailors," Alberto told me. "That became our profession." He was the only member of his social and economic class to risk his life in dangerous operations into Cuba.

Situated in New Orleans by Lake Pontchartrain, the *Tejana* had arrived with its own mechanic, a long-time CIA operative named Lawrence Laborde, who had worked for the U.S. Department of Agriculture in Mexico on a project eradicating hoof and mouth disease. For Mexico, Laborde retained no love. "All they want is to take a bite out of you," Laborde told Alberto. He was a man who said everything that he thought, which, for Alberto Fernández was an endearing quality.

Alberto had no choice. "I had to buy him with the ship," he explained. Taking a stranger on would have brought its own complications. They would have to learn all about the ship. Sabotage would have been a risk.

Laborde remained on the CIA payroll; the Agency paid him $700 a month, plus bonuses. Alberto also kept him on because Laborde knew, as Alberto put it, "every screw on the boat." When there was a major problem, a U.S. Navy mechanic helped out, yet another example of the seamless connection between CIA and the military.

Alberto was amused by Laborde, whom he called a "Louisiana bayou pirate."

"Educated pansies from Harvard, Yale, and Princeton don't come down to solve these problems," Alberto remarked to me. Alberto's nephew Johnny Smithies was a student at Tulane; Alberto invited him to come and see the *Tejana*, of which he was at once very proud.

Lawrence Laborde became Alberto's loyal protector, it seemed, his shadow. Laborde wore a Greek sailor's cap rather than a fancy captain's hat, and he never hesitated to risk his life. Yet he was not beyond reporting on Alberto to CIA.

Laborde was at the helm only while the *Tejana* remained on American territory. As soon as they crossed into international waters, down came the U.S. flag and up went the Cuban. A Cuban crew now took over, piloted by Armando Rodríguez Alonso, who had been an officer in the Cuban navy. Unlike Laborde, who seemed to be laughing all the time, Armando was *serio*.

Half of the crew of the *Tejana* were young commercial fishermen. Don Hogan enlisted two young Americans, George "Mickey" Kappas and Robert Stevens, to work with Alberto.

The *Tejana* became fully operational in February 1961 when CIA requested cryptonyms, along with Provisional Security Approvals, for the members of the crew. The "captain" was "Robert Clark Stevens, Jr."; the "engineer and operations officer" was

"George Michael Kappas." Lawrence Laborde was "Port Captain," according to CIA.

Among the most courageous and competent of Alberto's operatives were Tony Cuesta and Joaquín Powell. Cuesta was large and powerful, a tower of strength. Powell was tiny and wiry. Mutt and Jeff. It was Joaquín who had introduced Alberto to Tony Cuesta.

CIA began to contribute a $600 monthly subsistence purely for the vessel itself. Alberto paid the salaries of the crew out of his own pocket—until his money ran out. The Bragas offered him no assistance.

The *Tejana's* kitchen and dining room had wood-paneled walls, which were all closets. The main cabin, a huge storeroom for war materiel, was presided over by a statue of the Virgin of Charity, the patron saint of Cuba. What had once been a master bedroom was filled to the brim with weapons and ammunition. There were no beds on board. Alberto slept on top of one of the engines; Armando slept on a bunk beside him. When they slept, no one else slept. When they were in harbor, they rented motel rooms.

The *cocinero* (cook) had been a police commander in Havana, and a cattleman. At sea, water would clog up his glasses, which he kept in a Kleenex box. Having been born in Cataluña in the north of Spain, he specialized in dour Basque cuisine, featuring beans and sausage, inspiring the sailors to head for Howard Johnson's whenever they were in port. There was always a doctor on board.

Once they set sail, there were only sandwiches and cold food because the freezers and refrigerators were filled with weapons: Browning automatics; submachine guns; M-1 Garand rifles; C-3 and C-4 plastic explosives; and grenades. On the *Tejana's* deck were mounted .50 and .30 caliber machine guns and a 75 mm lightweight recoilless rifle. The .50 caliber machine guns belonged to the cook and the doctor. Two boats and two motorized rafts were used to deliver people and weaponry ashore, a process that required eight men.

"What we did, nobody else did," Alberto told me.

The *Tejana* would set sail from Key West at nine or ten in the morning, bound for the North of Cuba. The flag they flew was an 1868 flag belonging to Cuban rebels who had risen up against Spain, people who burned their own city to the ground so that the Spanish would take possession only of ashes.

When the mountains appeared on the horizon, or on the radar, twenty miles out, the *Tejana* dropped anchor and waited until nightfall. Dropping anchor had symbolic value. Alberto wanted to give his operatives the confidence that he would be out there, not far from land, waiting to pick them up.

They sat and waited beyond the horizon, just sitting and watching to see if there was any unusual activity, cars, or trucks in the area.

The receiving party would flash its signal to let them know they were there. It was close to nine o'clock when the *Tejana* would launch its boats and motorized rafts. Reaching shore, they would quickly unload explosives and people. The weapons were hidden in bags that had once held sugar, and were made to look as if they carried charcoal. They were placed in trucks embellished with the insignia of the Cuban government. The drivers were all members of *Unidad*. Once his operatives had returned to the *Tejana*, Alberto would slash the rope connected to the anchor with a hatchet and sail back to Key West.

This was war, and the operations organized by Alberto moved swiftly without attending to the predilections of CIA. Alberto discovered the true nature of his Agency "collaborator" on the *Tejana's* first mission.

CIA let Alberto know that the Agency was contributing several crates of weapons to this inaugural effort. As "shrewd" as CIA feared that he was, Alberto hesitated before loading these crates onto the *Tejana*.

"Let's see what we're taking in," Alberto said. They had loaded up in the evening, turning off all the lights. Alberto consulted with his Cuban captain Armando Rodríguez Alonso and they decided to open a few packages.

Uncovering the weatherproofing, Alberto discovered boxes of old Springfield rifles dating from 1903. They were of the vintage used by General Pershing in his battles with Pancho Villa. The actions of these rifles were so decrepit that they rattled when you shook them.

Alberto thought: If the weapons dated from World War I, or earlier, CIA could claim deniability. CIA could argue that the weapons could not possibly have originated with the Agency. (Other groups received boxes from CIA marked "ABC Manufacturing, San Francisco, California" with the words "nuts and bolts" scrawled on the outside of the box, for the same reason.)

In the crates with the Springfield rifles, Alberto found bags full of a religious manifesto by a Catholic bishop named Eduardo Boza Masvidal. CIA had compromised his mission in more ways than one.

What would the members of *Unidad*'s Underground in Cuba have thought if Alberto had brought them not only those useless weapons, but the Bishop's irrelevant manifesto? Alberto dumped the religious pamphlets into the ocean. Whoever had this idea must have been "in cahoots with the religious hierarchy," he concluded.

Then Alberto telephoned CIA's munitions warehouse.

"When you decide to be decent people, let me hear from you!" he said.

So from the moment of his first mission, Alberto had good cause to doubt the sincerity of CIA's professed claim that it was working for the removal of Fidel Castro. "The entire incident showed CIA's contempt for us and what we were doing," he reflected. "They were either trying to destroy the movement inside or simply going through the motions. It was mind-boggling."

"I am not shrewd," Alberto insists. "I am a *no come mierda*." It was a favorite slang expression of Alberto's: "I am not someone who eats shit."

Neither Clarence, nor his successor as Alberto's CIA handler Bob Wall ("Lauriston" or "Loristan") ever set foot on the *Tejana*. If they had not ventured onto the boat, it did not exist. From the start, Alberto and the members of *Unidad* had few illusions about the honorable intentions of their CIA "benefactors." Yet they had nowhere else to turn.

Other Cubans at the time shared similar experiences with CIA. Jorge Navarro Custín, who served in the Cuban Merchant marine and whose closest contacts were with the Office of Naval Intelligence, says that his friend Sergio Carbo, piloting a ship from Cuba to Canada, had been promised asylum in the U.S. by CIA. In Montreal, CIA's man was not there to greet him as promised. Canada refused to grant Carbo asylum.

Manning a ship carrying Julio Lobo's sugar, Navarro himself was promised by Bobby Kennedy that he would be granted asylum in the U.S. Instead, President Kennedy ordered his ship sent back to Cuba. CIA betrayals of the Cubans were the rule rather than the exception, and this was true well before the self-defeating adventure at the Bay of Pigs.

Alberto had risked what remained of his fortune. He had jeopardized the well-being of his family, compromised the educations of his three children, and damaged his marriage. Yet as CIA perfidies multiplied, there seemed no other way but to play along with the Agency. Nor did political activity among *UR* members in the U.S. interest Alberto. His focus was entirely on operations into Cuba.

During these years, Alberto went twice to the Dominican Republic to try to get a friend of his out of jail. He went to see Trujillo at his palace. Trujillo wanted to know about the sugar mills he had bought from the Americans.

"Why do you have officers of the Army instead of engineers running the sugar mills?" Alberto returned. He could only succeed in getting his friend's conditions changed, so that he was no longer kept naked in his cell. The man got out only when Trujillo was assassinated. Later, Alberto rescued him from Cuba.

Eduardo Sánchez, Alberto's nephew, longed to be part of his movement, but he was only seventeen, and so *Tío* Alberto never allowed him on the *Tejana*. But Eduardo invariably would be waiting on the dock when the ship sailed back to Florida, and sometimes he would drive people Alberto had rescued from the Keys to Miami. Eduardo's father had been part of a group that had been asphyxiated in a sealed truck under the command of Osmaní Cienfuegos, the brother of Camilo. These were people who had refused to surrender. Osmaní was heard to have remarked of the suffocating prisoners locked up behind him, "It makes no difference. They're going to die anyway."

One day, driving a group of Cubans from the dock, Eduardo was stopped by a state trooper.

"Has anyone here any weapons?" the trooper demanded. The Cubans admitted they were carrying, among other guns, a .45 and an M3 machine gun. It was a federal crime to have a machine gun in the car. Alberto had told Eduardo only that the sheriff was on their side—he had not coached him otherwise.

"Call Key West," Eduardo said. After talking to the sheriff in Key West, the trooper escorted the group 100 miles to Homestead, with his lights flashing, racing along at seventy miles an hour all the way.

CIA malfeasances were matched by sheer incompetence. One day Clarence radioed that they should alter their course because of "enemy action!" Yet the *Tejana*'s radar revealed no ships in the vicinity for miles around. It turned out that Manolo Ray's group, the MRP, had faked an incident, pretending to have been involved in a fight with the Cubans by firing off their guns from the docks. They had hoped by this to impress CIA into contributing more substantial payouts.

Among CIA assets who did assist Alberto was Cesario Diosdado, a U.S. Customs officer who was co-opted into serving CIA. As CIA's AMSWIRL-1, Diosdado was on the CIA payroll. Every day Diosdado would call and ask Alberto what he needed, if he could help solve any problems that had arisen. Diosdado watched over the crew of the *Tejana* like a mother hen over baby chickens. His agents rode herd on carousing *Tejana* sailors. Not all CIA people were disingenuous.

The *Tejana*'s strongest month was March 1961 when, in four operations, Alberto infiltrated 19,000 pounds of ammunition into Cuba. Only 12,700 pounds had been infiltrated during the previous six months by all other boats combined.

One day, Alberto told me, "the Company" came moping around to see if he would take into Cuba teams of Brigade 2506 as CIA's plans for an invasion of Cuba progressed. It was a tremendous risk, but Alberto acquiesced and they took in twenty members of the brigade in groups of two or three. A few of these men would defect. One became a colonel in Castro's *Seguridad de Estado*.

"I'd be in big trouble today," Alberto laughed, referring to the terrorist dimension of his efforts to unseat Fidel Castro.

Michael J. P. Malone kept watch on the media and its handling of Castro and the Cuban Revolution. His confidante was Frank O'Brien, the special agent at the New York field office of the Bureau, from whom he requested "your reactions on an outfit called BALLANTINE BOOK CO., 101 Fifth Avenue, N.Y. I understand that they publish paper back books and our [sic] putting out the C. Wright Mills book."

This was *Listen Yankee!* (1960), a work that decidedly did not share the O'Brien-Malone-Kleberg-Braga perspective on Cuba. Cuban resentment against the United States is based on real grievances, Mills argued. The imperatives of the First Amendment did not surface in the discussions between Malone, Kleberg, and the intelligence services.

CHAPTER 6

THE AGONY OF HUMBERTO
SORÍ MARÍN

> "It was common street knowledge that the
> [Bay of Pigs] operation was to occur and that it
> would fail . . . the CIA deliberately botched the
> operation."
>
> Edward Browder, gunrunner,
> mercenary for hire, CIA asset

As Alberto sailed in and out of Cuba with impunity during the winter of 1961, high on his list of objectives was to exfiltrate Humberto Sorí Marín to the United States. Sorí alone would be able to convey to CIA *Unidad's* strategy for an effective invasion of Cuba. On March 1, 1961, after seven or eight attempts, Alberto was, at last, successful in evading Castro's security.

Sorí arrived in Key Biscayne in the company of four militants from *Unidad's* Underground. Watching, CIA termed it, melodramatically, a "black visit." In CIA's self-serving documents, with its overwrought locutions, Alberto's home is referred to as a "safe house." It was nothing of the sort. Alberto put Sorí up at the local Howard Johnson's. He did surround Sorí with bodyguards.

Sorí's strategy for this visit included his revealing to CIA *Unidad's* "Plan" for the coming invasion of Cuba. This plan depicted how CIA and *Unidad* inside Cuba could coordinate their efforts. Sorí counted on a popular uprising, a corrective to the Castro revolution that would return democracy to Cuba. Among Sorí's objectives was his disabusing

CIA of its illusions regarding the integrity of some of the exile leaders who had become CIA favorites, among them Manuel Artime.

A pupil of the Jesuits, Artime had been a latecomer to 26th of July. He joined only on December 28, 1958, three days before the fall of Batista. A man of overweening ambition, Artime had quickly forged a document, scratching out the word "Lieutenant" and granting himself the status of *Comandante*. All the while, Artime remained close to *Batistianos*.

Kleberg advised the Agency to give up on Artime, but it disagreed. For Alberto, the Jesuits and their influence had been "hiding under the rug in Cuba," in a "hidden brotherhood with the Communists."

Now, in March 1961, exerting undeserved influence over the 2506 Brigade about to invade Cuba, Artime—with the personal support of long-time CIA operative E. Howard Hunt—was advising CIA to land at a location that all but ensured defeat.

In his conversations with CIA officers, Sorí argued vehemently against the landing location at the swamp off the Zapata Peninsula known as *Playa Girón*, the Bay of Pigs, favored by Artime. It was a natural trap, a semi-deserted place populated more by alligators and cormorants than people. The mountains were too far away for survivors of the landing to retreat safely to fight another day.

Sorí went on to explain to CIA that the Underground was not yet ready to participate in an invasion, although he was confident in the growing strength of *Unidad*. At the right time, a simultaneous U.S. invasion and an uprising within Cuba could overthrow the Castro government. Sorí's goal, a democratic Cuban government, had everything to do with Cuba and nothing to do with either CIA or U.S. interests.

Dated March 4, 1961, Sorí's "Plan" was an ambitious blueprint for action. Dividing Cuba into a grid, it outlined all government military installations that should be attacked. Arms would be delivered to the struggle both by air and by truck.

Unidad refers to itself as "apolitical." It stresses unity among groups and projects a mass movement of the Cuban people. By

P L A N "URM"

A) Este plan se propone por una organización estrictamente militar nacional sin militancia política de ninguna índole dirigida por oficiales de alta jerarquía del Ejército Rebelde, del Antiguo Ejército Profesional, de la Marina de Guerra y de la Policía (activos, li
cenciados o retirados), todos de probada ejecutoria anticomunista
y reconocido prestigio personal. La coordinación nacional se en -
cuentra a cargo de dos comandantes, un coronel, un comodoro y un
civil que funge provisionalmente de ejecutivo del que suscribe. Actualmente su contacto en Miami es el Sr. A.F. y su único enlace con
los distintos grupos y sectores civiles es Rafael. Con anterioridad
y en las respectivas regiones donde hay preparadas acciones militares se obtuvo, a ese efecto, la unificación total de las organiza-
ciones civiles en la correspondiente localidad, lo que hará más fácil la labor de Rafael en el sentido de lograr de las dirigencias
nacionales de dichos grupos, en caso necesario, la aprobación expre
sa de tales operaciones.

B) Bueno es hacer notar que la "URM" está ya en situación de poner
en práctica todos sus planes sin más trámites, ya que esencialmen-
te está integrada por militares no políticos y además debido a que
el personal civil que está reclutado para los distintos alzamientos
cualquiera que haya sido su procedencia, se asimila a la disiplina
apolítica de esta organización militar y coloca en situación subal-
terna su filiación política específica. Esta es una condición inal-
terable que se le exige a los comprometidos con URM, de tal manera
que en casos en los cuales alguno de ha sectarizado o parcializado
o pretandido convertirla en un grupo político más, ha sido inmedia-
tamente separado.

C) En la organización figuran veinte mil hombre que, por haber sido militares, conocen el manejo de las armas. Diez mil civiles, jo-
venes aptos para combatir en su casi totalidad, integran además la
URM.

D) Las operaciones que se proponen han sido cuidadosamente estudia
das y su inicio no debe ser demorado debido a los constantes arres-
tos, registros, persuciones que se suceden en la Isla y por los movimientos de personal y unidades en las tropas del Gobierno, que
obligaría a consecuentes cambios en los referidos planes. Por ejem-
plo: una operación que se proyecta sobre determinado punto de la
costa ocupada por tropa del Gobierno comprometida con nosotros, e-
xigiría una alteración en el respectivo plan, si trasladan al Jefe.
Las operaciones combinadas, por consiguiente, que deben y pue-
den llevarse a cabo con éxito, escalonadamente y en el tiempo y for-
man que se señalarán, son las siguientes:

1.- Levantamientos en las zonas de MAYARI, ALTO SONGO, PALMA SORIANO y
EL COBRE, en torno a la Sierra de Nipe (centro de la Provincia de Oriente) que incluyendo ataques a poblaciones aledañas se harían fuerte en
esta cordillera y se enfrentarían a las poderosas guarniciones guberna-
mentales en la Sierra de Cristal.
Los alzamientos y concentraciones de hombres se harán en cinco pun
tos diferentes, encontrándose pendiente otro punto más correspondiente
a la costa norte (zona de Sagua de Tánamo) donde no ha sido posible
coordinar con nosotros a los jefes (Hirán y Crespo), aunque han existi
do contactos. Las armas se harían descenden por aviones, simultáneamen
te en los diferentes puntos, a partir de cuyo instante se daría comien
zo a la operación Num. UNO. Con excepción del punto seis, los restan-
tes se hallan perfectamente coordinados a traves de un responsable pro
vincial.

2.- Levantamiento en la Zona de Baracoa (Imías), especialmente para re
forzar con armas y unir a nuestra organización a los grupos que en su

Dated March 4, 1961, Sorí's "Plan" was an ambitious blueprint for action. Dividing Cuba into
a grid, it outlined all government military installations that should be attacked. Arms would be
delivered to the struggle both by air and by truck.

casi totalidad desarmados y desconectados (unos 700 hombres) se encuentran en las Cuchillas de TOA. Las armas se harán llegar por aire.

3.- Para esta operación que debe iniciarse conjuntamente o inmediatamen-
te después de la anterior, se hace preciso hacerles llegar desde ahora
y hasta completar cien toneladas de armas y parque por un lugar de la
costa ya establecido. Las armas se recibirán por camiones que las irán
trasladando a distintas zonas, donde el día señalado las tomarán las respectivas compañías al efecto organizadas. Incluye operaciones simultá
neas de ataques a poblaciones en todo el Noroeste de la Provincia de -
Oriente (Holguin, Victoria de las Tunas, Purto Padre, Gibara, Alto Ce-
dro, Etc.) La víspera del día fijado para el alzamiento, se descarga-
ría artillería por un punto ya escogido del Golfo de Guacanayabo, al
Sur, que se instalaría en la margen norte de la cuenca del Cauto, a
fin de hacerle frente a las tropas del Gobierno que desde la Sierra
Maestra, Niquero, Manzanillo, Bayamo y Palma Soriano, tratarán de a-
brirse paso hacia el Norte.

4.- El último golpe en la Provincia de Oriente, a fin de ponerla total
mente en pie de guerra, sería el ataque y apertura de frente en la
costa meridional de la Sierra Maestra, en un momento en que todos los
efectivos del Gobierno estarían ocupados en el Centro, Norte y Este
de la Provincia; eliminando así la posibilidad de que Fidel escoja
como parece (por sus recientes traslados de tropas veteranas a la
Sierra Maestra) como último refugio su antigua zona de operaciones.
Se pondría en práctica pues el plan que el que suscribe preparó para el día 15 de noviembre ppdo. y que dió lugar al arresto de todos
los oficiales que estábamos comprometidos en la operación, el ppdo.
día 29 de noviembre. Los mandos para esta operación tienen que ser
muy competentes y practicos en la región, para enfrentarse exitosa-
mente a las mejores tropas del Gobierno, actualmente acantonadas en
la misma. Para estas cuatro operaciones hay celulados y comprometidos diez mil hombres aproximadamente.

5.-

5.- Alzamientos simultáneos en Pinar del Río, la Habana y Matanzas.
En Pinar del Rio contamos con mandos rebeldes en los puntos dóonde
con base en la Sierra de Los Organos se hará un bolsón que incluye
un puerto de la costa norte y una pequeña pista para aterrizaje. Esta perfect amente programada y coordénada la acción en toda la zona,
que comprende voladura de puentes en las carreteras que circundan la
Sierra. Al Oeste de la ciudad de Matanzas, con ayuda en los primeros
momentos si es posible de comandos invasores, se establecerá un frente, como Cabeza de playa, que requerirá mucho parque y desde el cual
poder lanzarse sobre la Capital, donde al mismo tiempo, en la zona
este de la misma se tomarán diez extaciones de policias, con el pro-
pósito ademas de armar y sublevar a la población. Tenemos un servicio
de informacion permanente en la zona, que está bien estudiada a los
efectos de la estrategia a seguir y las guarniciones enemigas a ata-
car. En la ciudad de Matanzas se estará coetáneamente realizando una
operación para tomar la ciudad y el puerto. Sobre la parte oriental
de esta ciudad, con armamento que arribará por mar el mismo día se
establecerá un bolsón desde Punta de Hicacos al Río Canímar por el
Norte y por el Sur y dejando dentro la ciudad de Cardenas alcanzará
su punto más avanzado en las Lomas de San Miguel de Los Baños, tra-
tando de envolver por el oeste del bolsón a la ciudad de Matanzas
y reforzar en su caso a los que operen dentro de ella, debiendo que-
dar unidas las treze zonas en una gran cabeza de plana y con dominio
de dos pistas de aterrizaje y dos puertos, Matanzas y Cárdenas.

Se ofrecen las grandes líneas de esta operación que, como es
fácil comprender, exige un planeamiento minucioso por la multipli-
cidad de movimientos que precisa realizar; y como quiera que debe
llevarse a cabo con posterioridad a los alzamientos de Oriente y
teniendo en cuenta los despliegues de tropas hacia las Provincias

·de las Villas § Oriente, en ese momento es que en una última consulta entre los mandos de dichas tres provincias occidentales se fijarán definitivamente las operaciones.

La Marina de Guerra respaldará las distintas acciones de esta operación final. Al disponer de territorio dominado por nosotros, puertos y pistas de aterrizaje, aviones que nos faciliten podrían intervenir decisivamente, desde bases cubanas. En este caso podían efectuarse raids aéreos sobre todas o varias de las instalaciones militares del Gobierno y sus campes de aterrizaje (San Julián, Base Gramma, Quinto ─Distrito, Jaruco, Tapaste, Base San Antonio, Aeropuerto, Cuaftel de Milicias en el Horno (Guisa), El Jigüe, Las Mercedes, Pino del Agua, Posiciones de Artillería en La Maya y Mayarí Arriba, así como el Aerópuerto de Camagüey.)

Los puntos a que se hace referencia en este informe-propuesta, se encuentran cuidadosamente escogidos, tanto para hacer llegar las armas por avió p por mar, mediante sus respectivas coordenadas.

Aun cuando desde el punto de vista de las operaciones no es en modo alguno necesario, no obstante opinamos que resultaría muy vonveniente aprovechar el mecanismo apolítico de la "URM" para fortalecer la unidad en los frentes civiles radicados en Miami, labor que en estos momentos realiza en Cuba Rafael, con el respaldo nuestro y con las mejores perspectivas. Conocemos la idionsicracia del cubano y podemos asegurar que la creación de un órgano de lucha inmediata para combatir con las armas como es la "URM", es el mejor remedio contra las divisiones y pugnas que parecen minar la moral de una empresa como la de rescatar a Cuba de las garras del Comunismo Internacional.

En lo politico abrazamos el ideal democrático sin hacerle una sola concesión a radicalismos de clase alguna, ni a formas encubiertas de socialismo o estatismo. Defendemos sin reservas de ninguna clase los valores del espíritu frente a cualquier materialksmo, los derechos de la persona humana frente al control oficial policiaco que los merma y desnaturaliza, la libertad de empresa frente al dominio público de la producción ye l comercio, la reforma agraria como fué postulada en la ley que tuvimos el honor de redactar durante la Guerra, conocida por Ley Num. TRES de 10 de octubre de 1958 y sobre los principios que claramente están proclamados en los fundamentos y por cuantos de la misma; la división ¢ los pdderes frente a la Dictadura o la Oligarquía; la propiedad privada frente a la nacionalización. Tenemos fe en los principios en que se sustenta y en el destino de la Organización de Estados Americanos. Y somos, finalmente, partidarios del severo castigo a los responsables de la traición y entrega de nuestra Patria al Comunismo Internacional.

En Miami, a 4 de marzo de 1961.

now, 20,000 Cubans, people who had served in the military and were expert in the handling of weapons, had signed on with *Unidad*. One front would immediately be opened on the southern coast near the *Sierra Maestra*, anticipating that Castro's troops would fan out everywhere but there.

The goal of the Underground is spelled out: *Rescatar a Cuba de las garras del Comunismo Internacional*. Soviet-style Communism of the Stalinist variety was to have no place in Cuba.

Inside Cuba, Robert Geddes, a British national who worked as a CIA operative with cover as a Pepsi-Cola executive, had worked diligently to ready *Unidad* to participate in a mass struggle that would emerge with an invasion of the island by CIA. Geddes had penetrated twenty-seven Havana police stations with the objective of utilizing them when the revolt materialized. He was also working on a plan for the capture of northern Las Villas province, utilizing contacts among rebel army and police forces with access to arms. They would seize the G-2 and PSP *(Partido Socialista Popular)* offices in every city and town in northern Las Villas.

Geddes had been reassured by CIA that no invasion would take place until the *UR* had completed its preparatory work. *Unidad* was confident of coordinated uprisings in Pinar del Rio, Matanzas, and Oriente Provinces, with planned sabotage operations throughout the island, and had organized a rebellion in the Cuban navy. Organized strength was mounting steadily.

On the morning of March 4th, or possibly March 5th, Sorí was having breakfast at Alberto's home when the nanny answered a knock at the door. *"Dos Señores"* wished to speak with Sorí. One was CIA's AMBIDDY, Artime himself, the fair-haired boy of the Company. (Artime was the foremost Cuban betrayer of the cause, Alberto came to conclude.) Accompanying Artime was a paid CIA source named Bernard Barker, who would be one of the Watergate burglars. (The Cubans in this story were to come to the conclusion that Watergate had been a CIA operation to get rid of Nixon.)

Artime stretched out his hand. Sorí ignored him.

"Cómo se atreve?" Sorí began. "How dare a traitor like you come to see me?!" Artime and Barker turned around and stalked off.

Sorí continued his talks with CIA officers at JMWAVE on the subject of how best to manage an invasion of Cuba, among them Bob Wall. It perhaps did not further his cause when Sorí informed CIA, "Two of the top military men in charge of the encampments are homosexuals."

Alberto went to Washington, D.C., where he attended a meeting devoted to planning the organization of the Cuban government that would follow a successful CIA invasion. Exile "leaders" were flush with anticipation of which offices they would occupy. Dissension borne of the rampant ambition of everyone present was followed by the selection of a *junta executiva* that would preside over the coming post-Castro government. Alberto was dismayed to hear Humberto Sorí Marín described as a minor "military leader" of the MRP, one among many groups jockeying for position.

Back in Florida, Sorí struggled to persuade CIA officers at JMWAVE to reject DD/P Richard Bissell's Bay of Pigs scenario. Sorí advised moving the 2506 Brigade forces directly into Matanzas and Oriente Provinces where they would be met by 5,000 members of *Unidad*. CIA led Sorí to believe that it would delay the invasion.

In a compromise Sorí believed he had worked out with the Agency, Sorí agreed to include Artime's *MRR (Movimiento de Recuperación Revolucionaria)*. He promised to work closely with "Francisco" (Rogelio González, Orzo), an Artime supporter whom Sorí had employed in Cuba.

Artime's *MRR* was assigned to build roads into the *Sierra Maestra* under the discipline and leadership of *Unidad*. The *MRR* was "thrown a sop," as Alberto put it, command of Pinar del Río province. When his discussions with CIA concluded, Sorí believed they had an agreement, beginning with the abandonment of the swampy Bay of Pigs as the landing location.

"I don't know what was promised him," Alberto told me. In their youthful naïveté, neither Alberto nor Sorí could imagine that CIA would not wish to take advantage of the indigenous mass movement that they were organizing inside Cuba. It was a movement that would place the economic and political interests of Cuba before those of U.S. business.

Sorí was well on the way to organizing a bona fide Cuban revolution, an authentic challenge to Castro, but one that CIA would not be able to control. There was no Shah, no military front men waiting in the wings to serve CIA interests in Cuba as there had been in Iran and Guatemala.

That CIA and Allen Dulles had no intention of succeeding at the Bay of Pigs, that CIA was not about to risk an invasion whose outcome it could not control, is amply revealed in an incident recorded by the biographer of General Edward Lansdale. Under military cover as an Air Force colonel, Lansdale was in fact an Operations and Plans officer for CIA. An OSS veteran, by 1950 Lansdale was operating under military cover in the Philippines; between 1954 and 1956 he was Chief of Station of CIA's Saigon Military Mission. In Saigon, Lansdale's cover was a CIA front group, the International Rescue Committee.

1957 found Lansdale assigned to the Pentagon as Deputy Assistant to the Secretary of Defense for Special Operations where he developed Department of Defense Policy on matters involving certain CIA activities "of a counter-insurgency nature." The career of Edward Lansdale illustrates amply how inextricably linked CIA and the Pentagon were, with CIA higher on the chain. Publicly CIA claimed that it took a dim view of Lansdale's adventurism within its Operation Mongoose anti-Castro sabotage program. But nothing was as it seemed. Allen Dulles wrote to Curtis LeMay, who didn't know Lansdale at all, "suggesting" that Lansdale be promoted to Major General. Lansdale was duly promoted. The year was 1963.

An incident at a Kennedy administration meeting on the subject of the feasibility of the invasion of Cuba at the Bay of Pigs reveals the familial relationship between Allen Dulles and supposedly military officers like Lansdale. It took place in 1961, not distant from the time when Humberto Sorí Marín was discussing an effective strategy for the April landing at the Bay of Pigs.

Lansdale found himself at a meeting of President Kennedy's Special Group. Seated at the table was Lansdale's long-time boss Allen Dulles, the Director of Central Intelligence. By now an expert strategist in guerrilla warfare, Lansdale listened carefully to the description of CIA's plan for the invasion of Cuba at *Playa Girón,* the swampy Zapata Peninsula.

Summoning his counter-insurgency know-how, Lansdale could not remain silent.

"We're going to get clobbered," Lansdale said.

Allen Dulles then turned his cold blue eyes in Lansdale's direction.

"You're not a principal in this!" Dulles said harshly, cutting Lansdale off. Gone was the familiar Dulles persona of the pipe-smoking, tweed-clad professorial bumbler.

After the meeting had broken up, Dulles took Lansdale aside. He did not attempt to suggest that Lansdale was wrong in predicting the failure of the Bay of Pigs invasion. Instead, Dulles ordered Lansdale to be "discreet" about his assessment "as a favor for past efforts."

Rather than hang around to witness what he knew would be certain disaster, Lansdale requested an assignment to tour Vietnam and left the country. "It doesn't matter who takes Allen's place at CIA," said a friend of Dulles, who preferred to remain anonymous, at the time of the Bay of Pigs invasion. "He's given CIA his imprint. It will be a long time before CIA will be anything but Allen Dulles's baby."

La Cabaña

Confident that he had persuaded CIA of the folly of a precipitate invasion, with the Underground not yet ready and at so unpropitious a location, believing CIA's assurances that it would heed his advice, Sorí decided to return to Cuba. On March 11th, as he was ready to depart, a station wagon pulled up to the dock. Inside were two people from the *FRD (Frente Revolucionario Democrático)* talking to Havana on a shortwave radio. When Alberto raised an eyebrow, Sorí said he knew and trusted them.

CIA had requested that Alberto carry one of its radio operators, Manuel Puig Miyar (nickname: Ñongo), into Cuba with Sorí to serve as *Unidad*'s radioman. Believing that CIA had accepted his "Plan," Sorí agreed.

"In Cuba, you can overrule the Company at Sorí's orders!" Alberto told the uninvited CIA passenger.

On March 12th, Sorí prayed at a Key West church. Then he and Alberto went to the beach and the *Tejana* set sail once more for Cuba.

Sorí had requested that three *Unidad* leaders meet him on the beach in Cuba upon his arrival so that he might brief them on CIA's plans. Included was "Francisco," the Artime follower. Yet when they landed, the three men were nowhere to be found.

Instead, standing there on the beach, waiting to be exfiltrated from Cuba into the United States by Alberto, was Aldo Vera Serafin and his family. In the confusion, the baby fell into the water and everyone dove in, even Eddie Bayo, who didn't know how to swim. The *Tejana*'s doctor brought the baby miraculously back to life, but it was one more ill omen. (Later Aldo Vera Serafin would be murdered in Puerto Rico by Castro's G-2.)

Observing the chaotic scene, noting that Sorí's key operatives had not shown up but that three entirely different people awaited him, Alberto was worried. He was reluctant to abandon Sorí into Cuba now. It seemed far too dangerous. He enlisted Tony Cuesta and Joaquín Powell to help him persuade Sorí to return to Florida with him. "Tie him up and bring him back hog-tied" was what Alberto wanted to say. But he could not.

Sorí was stubborn, determined to take CIA at its word. He allowed himself to believe that CIA was planning to adopt the *Unidad* "Plan," which meant a postponement of the invasion, and a change in the landing site.

Sorí then set about rounding up the missing leaders of the Underground, including the *MRR*'s "Francisco." High on Sorí's list of tasks was to inform Artime's *MRR* members of what he had agreed upon with CIA, that they would be under the discipline of *Unidad*.

"I'll be all right. Don't worry," Sorí said. "Pick me up on Friday!"

Only later would Sorí realize that CIA had "pumped him for information" while committing itself to nothing, including changing the landing site.

On March 18, 1961, at a yellow house in Miramar on *Calle Once,* at the home of a retired engineer, Sorí presided over a meeting of *Unidad* leaders. Thirty people, including Rafael Díaz Hanscomb, whom CIA had been shadowing, discussed the merger of *UR* and *MRR* with the other groups. Four of those present were CIA employees carrying forged papers. Sorí sat apart at a refectory table covered with maps. When he heard that Fidel Castro had chosen a house in this neighborhood to stay the night, Sorí withdrew into the shadows, making himself less conspicuous.

There was a robbery in the area, and the militia was now moving from house to house in search of the thieves. Outside, a nervous woman walking in the street with her daughter panicked at the sight of the militia and ran into the engineer's house. The militia followed her. Suddenly, they were in the room.

The lieutenant of this militia group had fought in the *Sierra Maestra* with 26th of July. He recognized Humberto Sorí Marín at once.

In a desperate attempt to escape, Sorí plunged through a window. Quick on the trigger, the lieutenant shot him in the leg. Bleeding, Sorí was carried off to a naval hospital. Also shot in the fray was the CIA radio operator whom Alberto had taken to Cuba only reluctantly. Manuel Puig Miyar and Rogelio González Corso were also arrested.

From his hospital bed, Sorí faced the most unwelcome of visitors.

"You're a *cabrón!*" Fidel Castro said. (A "maximum shit" is how Alberto defined the word. Literally it means "male goat.") Castro accused Sorí of being a "traitor" who had "sold out to the Yankees." Then Fidel added: "I am going to see that you are cured so I can put you in *La Cabaña* and watch you die with my own eyes."

The official Cuban version of the incident, as outlined by former Castro security chief Fabián Escalante, insists that the G-2 had infiltrated Sorí's operation. Yet Cuba's G-2 had not infiltrated this group, as the government would claim. Sorí's arrest was a consummate example of bad luck.

Contrary to other details of Escalante's narrative, there was no plan to seize the *San Antonio de los Baños* air base near Havana, and no scheme for Sorí to assassinate Fidel Castro with a *pettaca* or plastique bomb. Sorí had not returned to Cuba to murder Fidel Castro. Sorí saw himself as a popular leader, not a terrorist.

Another radio operator, whom Sorí had chosen to trust, now disappeared. His name was Pedro Sergio Cuellar Alonso, and he was observed at the headquarters of Castro's *Seguridad de Estado*. Cuellar named a long list of *Unidad* activists as Castro began a sweep, jailing thousands of *UR* sympathizers and members.

Immediately a plan was set in motion to facilitate Sorí's escape. Some officers at the naval hospital agreed to help, provided that they would then be delivered out of Cuba by the *Tejana*. Coordinating the effort in Cuba was CIA asset Robert Geddes. (Another high-up Pepsi official, Don Kendall, spent more time on Agency operations than on soft drinks. Yet another CIA recruit working for Pepsi was named Enrique González.)

A flash forward: As CIA made policy in these years, its choices had everything to do with furthering the interests of its client corporations. Don Kendall remained into the next decade wearing two hats: He was CEO at Pepsi-Cola, and a CIA operative, close to Director of Central Intelligence Richard Helms. In the wake of the CIA-sponsored coup in Chile, Helms told reporter Bob Woodward that President Richard Nixon himself had ordered him to be certain that Salvador Allende not take office in Chile, whatever the election results might be.

"I don't want the goddamn CIA to make policy anymore," Nixon had told Helms earlier. It was President Nixon, Helms claimed, who ordered CIA to make the Chilean "economy scream!"

Helms confided to Woodward that the key to Nixon's order that CIA get rid of Salvador Allende resided in Nixon's relationship with his law firm's client, Donald Kendall, chairman and chief executive officer of PepsiCo, which had a plant in Chile. Nixon's anti-Allende operation was "a business decision": "Kendall and other U.S. firms didn't want a Marxist leader in Chile." What Helms apparently neglected to tell Woodward was that Kendall had been an important CIA asset for years.

Geddes got a message to Alberto. $300,000 was needed to rescue Sorí. The money was for bribes to high officers in the rebel army, who would also have to be brought out of Cuba with their families. There would be fifty in all.

Alberto appealed to his very rich father, who contributed most of the $300,000. CIA provided 50,000 pesos, "a few pennies," as Alberto put it. (With about ten pesos to the dollar, this would have been $5,000.) CIA brought Geddes out of Cuba to Florida where he conferred with Alberto. Geddes collected the money. Then he returned to Cuba. For safekeeping, he deposited the $300,000 in the safe of the Hotel Capri.

The treasonous radio operator Cuellar Alonso was not yet done. He remained close enough to *Unidad* to learn about the plan to spring Sorí from the hospital. Then he slipped away, headed for a telephone, and turned Geddes in. Two days after he returned from Florida, Geddes was arrested and tossed into *La Cabaña* prison. The semi-gangster owner of the Hotel Capri immediately helped himself to the $300,000. (The nineteen-story high-rise Hotel Capri had been owned by mobster Santos Trafficante, Jr.; scenes in the film *Our Man in Havana* were filmed in its rooftop swimming pool.)

CIA feared being implicated, compromised. As for Sorí Marín and Geddes, there was no Cuban, no asset who was not expendable. "We do not know at this stage of the game whether or how much GEDDES has talked," writes a CIA Western Hemisphere/4 Counter Intelligence operative to his paramilitary superior, "but every precaution should be taken to avoid picking up an already-blown group."

CIA hesitated to help those with whom Geddes was known to have contact. "It is the opinion of this Desk," the paramilitary chief of WH/4 wrote, "that before any commitments are made regarding the support of the *UR* a more detailed plan of their proposed activities together with a list of individuals they intend to use be submitted."

Rapidly now, CIA distanced itself from *Unidad*. Wondering whether one of Geddes' contacts had been a spy for Castro's G-2, as was indeed the case, CIA concluded, "A portion of the *UR* has been blown by the events in this case."

Hobbling on a crutch, too weak to dress himself, Sorí was transported from the hospital to *La Cabaña* prison.

Some of the prisoners took pity on Sorí and gave him painkillers.

John Martino, a fellow prisoner, was amazed at how Sorí was able to shave himself without a mirror. Sorí had been a "*barbudo*," as members of 26th of July were called, without a beard, and had developed this skill in the *Sierra*. Sorí told Martino that he had opposed the executions, but had been powerless to prevent them.

The Bay of Pigs
April 17, 1961, came and went, and with it that CIA operation that had been organized to fail. Of the three vessels that sailed, one was loaded with all the ammunition, and another with all the weapons, so that if either were lost, the entire Bay of Pigs operation would implode. Edward Browder, quoted above, believed that Castro had more than 300 of his own men aboard the U.S. vessels.

In Placetas, in the Escambray, four trucks with identification and markings testifying to their belonging to the agrarian reform program had been filled with hardware, weapons, and coal. All of this had been carried into Cuba by the *Tejana* and awaited collection by *UR* revolutionaries. No one arrived to pick them up.

CIA's bad faith included its enlisting a coal-burning ship that had been abandoned in Havana and was in such bad shape that

Lloyd's of London no longer included this wreck among its active records. It name was the *Santa Ana*.

Clarence had told Alberto one day, "I need your help. Let Armando [the *Tejana's* Cuban captain] go out and wait for a freighter." No ship had arrived either that day or the next. Then, Alberto's second officer, who had been doing his exercises high on the rocks adjacent to the docks, yelled out, "We have to pull that ship in with ropes!" Quickly they moved the *Tejana* out of the way to make room for the inoperable vessel.

The *Santa Ana* had no radio. The diesel engine had been put in backward. It lacked a meter to measure fathoms of water. The winches that moved the booms, designed to lower the small boats into the water, were not working. The propellers had been installed, mistakenly, in the same direction, so that the ship tended to move sideways or in a circle. It took ten men to turn the rudder, hanging on to keep the ship straight.

CIA unleashed the broken-down *Santa Ana* into the Bay of Pigs operation with 170 men aboard, along with a CIA radio operator. It was to serve as a decoy and sail to the far side of the island, away from the Bay of Pigs, on the southern coast just east of Santiago. Possessing advance knowledge, and confirming Edward Browder's assessment that Castro's agents were planted in the operation, Castro dispatched 5,000 members of his militia to this site. Now they stood waiting for the arrival of the *Santa Ana*.

On board were two of the people Alberto had brought out of Cuba when he extracted Humberto Sorí Marín.

Good fortune then smiled. Lacking a radio, the *Santa Ana* couldn't locate the landing place CIA had decreed. Wandering aimlessly at sea, it encountered two American destroyers who at first concluded that this must surely be one of Castro's dilapidated boats. They were about to blow up the *Santa Ana* only at the last minute to realize their error. Later, the surviving sailors of the *Santa Ana* were incredulous that the United States would do this to them.

CIA's decision to land at the Bay of Pigs was so obviously suicidal that it was difficult to know whom to blame. Alberto focused not only on the odious Artime, but on the older leaders Miró Cardona and Tony Varona, both of whom had urged CIA to go ahead. Miró was "flabby," and Varona "hard-headed and wanted to control everything."

Neither seemed to realize that had the landing been successful, and they had been imposed by CIA on the Cuban people, Artime, with CIA's help, would have removed them. It had been agreed. Should there have been victory at the Bay of Pigs, Artime would have staged a coup, aided by the heads of the brigade, against Miró Cardona and Tony Verona.

Yet *UR* inside Cuba had been fragile and vulnerable. Worried, Rafael Díaz Hanscomb had told the Agency back in January that were action not taken within the "next 30 to 40 days," the *UR* groups might break up.

Many groups blamed John F. Kennedy for not calling off CIA's charade. Yet Kennedy had been kept in the dark by CIA until very late in the planning. During the 1960 campaign, Richard Nixon had ordered Allen Dulles that "under no circumstances" must Kennedy be briefed about CIA's planned invasion of Cuba.

Dulles had no choice but to comply because he was in Nixon's debt. According to author John Loftus, Dulles faced a scare when after World War II he was threatened with exposure of his copious Nazi alliances in the 1930s. The records of Dulles' client, oil cartel Kontinental II A.G., came under the scrutiny of the Office of Naval Intelligence and would have exposed Dulles' Nazi connections. The incriminating records soon vanished, courtesy of a Navy man named Richard Nixon, who performed for Dulles a sizable favor.

What neither Sorí nor Kennedy perceived was that, for its own reasons, CIA had no wish to remove Castro if it meant a new government that was not under CIA's domination. CIA leadership, from Dulles on down—as Dulles' rebuke to Edward Lansdale cited earlier makes clear—knew precisely that defeat was inevitable, if only by the choice of location. "The Zapata peninsula was one of the worst parts of Cuba to make a beachhead," Alberto later told Frank O'Brien at the FBI's New York field office. He was hardly alone in that knowledge. (Alberto, and other Cubans, found O'Brien a sympathetic ally. "Cubans are the best bandits in the world," O'Brien said one day with appreciation.)

Called on the carpet by the Senate Foreign Relations Committee, Dulles talked his way out of responsibility for the disaster, even as he all but admitted that he knew about Sorí's "Plan" and his warnings. CIA had gone ahead without enlisting the Underground in Cuba, Dulles now claimed, because "it would alert Cuban forces and might lead to the assassinations of Underground members." So Dulles admitted publicly on the record that Sorí's message had gotten through to the highest of CIA authority, only for Dulles to ignore it.

In the oral history he provided to the JFK Presidential Library, Dulles lies outright about the Bay of Pigs invasion. He argues that the landing point at the Zapata Peninsula was "very largely dictated by the military," and the military thought "the Bay of Pigs . . . was better," which is not true. Dulles makes no mention of the debate within his own agency about where the landing should have been and whether at the final moment they should go ahead at all. That debate, led by the knowledgeable Miami agent Jake Esterline, was conveniently ignored.

History concludes that the self-defeating invasion at *Cochinos* had not been about overthrowing Castro. That had not been CIA's agenda. Rather, the elaborate, expensive charade had been an exercise in CIA's flexing its muscles, justifying its bloated budget and embarrassing an unreliable president with whom the Agency was at war.

Alternatively, the Agency had sought to blackmail Kennedy into authorizing a full invasion of Cuba, absolving CIA of responsibility. That a successful invasion at the right time and place might have inspired a popular uprising, one that the Agency would not be able to control, was itself motive enough for CIA to sabotage the effort.

The Death of Humberto Sorí Marín

As Sorí awaited the inevitable at *La Cabaña* prison, one of his twin brothers, Mariano, gained an audience with Fidel Castro and begged for Sorí's life "for old times' sake," if nothing else. Fidel reassured Mariano. Sending "*abrazos*" and "*besos*" to their mother, Fidel promised to spare Sorí.

"Don't worry, Mariano," Fidel said, slapping him on the back affectionately. "In the Sierra I learned to love your brother. Yes, he's in our custody, but he's completely safe from harm. Absolutely nothing will happen to him." Castro supposedly sent Sorí's parents "a big hug and big kiss from me and tell them to calm down." ("*En la sierra yo aprendí a querer a tú hermano. Si, lo dale un gran abrazo y un beso a tus padres de mi parte.*")

Alberto had long viewed the Sorí twins as "skunks." Neither had joined Sorí when he founded *Unidad*.

Sorí's mother appealed in person to Castro for her son's life.

"Don't worry," Castro repeated. "Your son will live."

On April 20, 1961, Humberto Sorí Marín, along with Rafael Díaz Hanscomb, the CIA operator, and other "counter-revolutionaries," were brought before the firing squad at *La Cabaña* prison. On this auspicious occasion, Fidel Castro himself was present as a witness, as he had threatened Sorí that he would be. Sorí's twin brothers were in attendance, wearing the uniform of Castro's militia.

Sorí wore his *comandante*'s uniform. As he stood "at the wall," an officer shot him in the head. Sorí was killed before he was executed. Only after he was dead did the firing squad begin to shoot. They aimed deliberately at his face so that it became an unrecognizable mass of pulp and blood. Humberto Sorí Marín was forty-six years old. Supposedly Mariano collapsed in shock at the sight of his brother's mutilated corpse in a grave into which all those executed that day had been tossed.

Executed with Humberto Sorí Marín were Rafael Díaz Hanscomb, Manuel Puig Miyar, and Rogelio González Corso, also known as "Francisco," chief of the *MRR*.

Alberto told me that the execution of Sorí represented "the collapse of everything," all real hope of regaining Cuba. It demonstrated that you could not sustain an underground in a police state. Almost simultaneously with his ascension to power—and providing the Cuban poor with literacy, universal medical care, and freedom from starvation—Castro had created a *Seguridad* modeled on the East German "Stasi."

Yet *Unidad* was not done. The leaders who remained turned to sabotage, disrupting public services, electric power, and the means of communication to affect a spontaneous uprising.

As for Dulles, he assumed no responsibility for the suffering occasioned by the Bay of Pigs invasion. "It was very simple; we were at war with Cuba," Dulles said, although it was CIA that was at war with Cuba, not the United States. Cynical Soviet spy Kim Philby summed up Dulles' persona wittily: "Dulles's unprofessional delight in cloak-and-dagger for its own sake was an endearing trait," Philby said. "It sank him, finally, in the Bay of Pigs."

Four days after the Bay of Pigs landing, as if nothing untoward had occurred, Michael J. P. Malone was moving on, suggesting to George Braga that he take an interest in the "People to People Program" sponsored by Joe de Celis. It called for an establishment of a University of the Americas; a 24-hour-a-day radio station broadcasting to the Spanish-speaking residents of Florida but spilling over to Cuba and the Caribbean; and a program directed at organizing overseas Chinese colonies in Latin America for the purpose of opposing Red Chinese infiltration."

Malone strategized that they should talk to Kleberg about the program. De Celis replied that he agreed: "Bob K. would be interested." The world was their arena, and whatever happened in Cuba there was, for these people, a world elsewhere.

On April 23rd, the day after Sorí died, Alberto Fernández, serving as general coordinator of *Unidad* in the United States, in the company of Michael J. P. Malone traveled to Washington, D.C., to consult with the Agency. The struggle was far from over for Alberto.

He met with an operative named in the files as "Roderick," who was apparently Bernard Reichhardt, the acting chief of Western Hemisphere 4 Operations.

CIA instructed Alberto now to "remain quiet until you receive further instructions." It did not please him to be told that "perhaps the unsuccessful invasion was a blessing in disguise because they have probably averted a civil war in Cuba," the position that Allen Dulles would espouse.

Alberto departed with "the definite impression that plans for future action in Cuba were being made." Otherwise, he met with hypocrisy, evasion, and obfuscation. The blood of the Cubans who died in the invasion is "our blood," Reichhardt said. "Our" referred to CIA.

On April 24th, Alberto met with Ambassador Bonsal. Alberto told Bonsal that he had the only effective underground group in Cuba, one far larger and more influential than Manolo Ray's. Ray had lost ground because of his "extreme pronouncements." Bonsal kept his own counsel. Alberto Fernández "takes quite literally the accusations of political and economic extremism which have been made against Ray," Bonsal thought.

On April 24th, as well, Michael J. P. Malone received an unsigned Western Union cable assessing the situation: "Main reason for defeat was underestimation of power of secret police who prevented popular support stop arrest of 50,000 means complete domination stop. Either we intervene now or lose Caribbean and alter Latin America with disastrous effects on NATO SEATO U.N. stop. This major defeat for West can be turned into great victory if we act immediately with courage stop. This morning's news indicates we gain relapsing into words and legalisms stop. If we do so we will miss the tide stop. Almighty won't go on saving us indefinitely. He eternally damns people and nations who fail to heed His warnings or seize the opportunities He offers."

Alberto next went to New York to talk with Frank O'Brien. He put up at the Carlyle Hotel. Afterward, O'Brien wrote, "Fernández was dumbfounded and confused by the decision to invade Cuba by Artime which in light of information known from inside Cuba was an inopportune time and, further, the place of the invasion was one of the worst parts of Cuba to make a beachhead." O'Brien concluded that the Cuban exiles had lost complete trust in CIA, and now believed that "the Bureau is the only government agency whom they trust."

Alberto also told the Bureau, "An Englishman, an executive of the Pepsi-Cola Corporation in Havana, Cuba, was expected to get out of Cuba soon. Upon his arrival in the U.S. he would be made available to the New York office." This was Bob Geddes, whom Alberto called "the most well-informed person on the activities of the counter-revolutionaries in Cuba." The term was not a pejorative to Alberto and his movement. "That's what we were," he told me.

Alberto said that Geddes was at the British Embassy and would be taking the first available Pan-Am flight to the United States. He was more than quixotic.

Less sanguine, the FBI decided, "If and when this Englishman gets out of Cuba and contacts the New York Office, all information furnished by him will be submitted to the Bureau in a form suitable for dissemination."

One day Alberto was told that he had 106 visitors, people who had come out of Cuba. They had been charcoal workers who were part of the Underground. He rented a house on an island on the Miami River, bought everything from mattresses to baby items, and managed to find them jobs.

In June 1961, Bob Geddes, far from being available to the New York field office of the FBI, was still languishing in *La Cabaña* prison. En route to a doctor's office, Geddes bribed the militia officer guarding him and escaped. He headed for the British Embassy to seek asylum, only for the British to deny him entry. Great Britain could not "engage in activities of an irregular nature," an Embassy functionary told Geddes.

Geddes then attempted to bribe members of the G-2, offering 15,000 pounds sterling as ransom to be guaranteed either by his wife "or Kendall of Pepsi-Cola in New York City." The ransom was paid, only for everyone involved to be arrested. The ransom agreement had been a Castro-inspired scheme to expose the identities of remaining members of the *Unidad* Underground. More members of the group were now arrested.

Late in September 1961, in Havana, Robert Morton Geddes was tried and sentenced to thirty years in prison for coordinating subversive activity while acting as a link between revolutionary groups and KUBARK (CIA). He seemed destined to live out the rest of his life in *La Cabaña* prison.

In February 1963, Geddes was set free. In its documents, CIA falsely credits Geddes' release to the U.K. embassy ("through efforts of U.K. embassy"). In fact, it took the intervention of World War II hero Field Marshal Montgomery, the legendary hero of El Alamein, to pry Geddes out of Cuba.

"Monty" was on a tour of Latin America when he learned of Geddes' plight. He did not travel to Cuba, but communicated his wishes from Mexico. Why Castro listened to Monty is unknown. CIA wrote that Geddes "arrived in PBPRIME via Mexico City." A free man, Geddes moved to Brazil where he settled and remarried. He was never to appear in anti-Castro circles again.

A cryptic note from Michael J. P. Malone to Alberto Fernández, dated December 30, 1964, states: "I checked and the English man has returned to his native shores. They do not know when he will return." The reference might well have been to Geddes.

In the aftermath of the Bay of Pigs, Bob Kleberg cooperated with the U.S. government in a "Tractors for Prisoners" program.

CIA processed reparations for the widows and orphans of the participants in its Bay of Pigs operation through the Bankers Trust Company on Wall Street in New York. On its board sat George A. Braga and B. Rionda Braga. Now in his letters when Alberto Fernández referred to CIA as the "friends," that word was set firmly between quotation marks.

The Bruce-Lovett Report

Over the years, others had been less forgiving of Dulles and his historical role. Assigned by President Franklin Delano Roosevelt to spy on Dulles during the 1930s as Dulles represented a cache of Nazi corporations and clients, future Supreme Court Justice Arthur Goldberg issued a strong denunciation. For their alliances with Nazis, Goldberg termed both Allen and his brother Foster, the managing partner at Sullivan & Cromwell, "traitors," with Allen in particular designated "a traitor to his country."

Dulles' view of a central intelligence agency was of a secret espionage agency with the power to conduct sabotage, guerrilla operations, and murder, a view that placed Dulles in opposition to that saner voice, Ambassador David K. E. Bruce, who had run OSS out of London.

In the summer of 1946, Bruce had defined the function of a central intelligence agency as the "procurement and evaluation of information of major importance," intelligence gathering. CIA would produce "jewels, the precious gems of intelligence," and that, Bruce suggested, should suffice. It had been, of course, Dulles who had carried the day.

A decade later, disturbed by the free-wheeling policy-making of CIA, President Eisenhower, a general who, famously, found war repellent, appointed a Board of Consultants on Foreign Intelligence Activities, later to be renamed the "President's Foreign Intelligence Advisory Board." The names of the members were kept secret, but one participant was David K. E. Bruce.

Eisenhower then enlisted Bruce, whose integrity could not be impeached, or his views subverted, to write a report that would supersede the Doolittle Report on the same subject that had been written with the participation of Allen Dulles. General James Doolittle, assigned by Eisenhower to write a history of the clandestine services and its methods, acknowledged that his sixty-nine-page justification of CIA's seven-year history of operations was written "with the very active support and cooperation of Allen Dulles." The Doolittle Report had also been signed by Joseph P. Kennedy, who was a member of Eisenhower's President's Foreign Intelligence Advisory Board.

Assisting Bruce would be Harry Truman's Secretary of Defense, Robert Lovett.

The Bruce-Lovett Report is devastating in its unflinching condemnation of the clandestine services. Appalled by what he termed CIA's "rogue elephant" operations, Bruce zeroed in on CIA's "increased mingling in the internal affairs of other countries," its "King-making" propensities. Bruce was too experienced not to know that the Soviet Union, which had lost 28 million people to Hitler's rampages, was not about expansion, but its own survival.

Under the guise of "frustrating the Soviets," Bruce wrote that "almost any [covert] action can and is being justified." Bruce attacked as well CIA's embrace of secrecy: "No one, other than those in the CIA immediately concerned with their day-to-day operation, has any detailed knowledge of what is going on." Bruce noted that CIA was enjoying "almost unilateral influence . . . on the actual formulation of our foreign policies."

Having already served as Truman's ambassador to France (an appointment to which Dulles ally James Forrestal had aspired), Bruce knew firsthand that CIA's activities were "sometimes completely unknown to the Ambassador or anyone." Those who endorsed George Kennan's 10/2 granting CIA what amounted to full military powers "could not possibly have foreseen the ramifications of all the operations which have resulted from it," he added. [National Security Council Directive 10/2, the cornerstone of CIA's early history, granted the Office of Policy Coordination the full operational capabilities that Dulles craved. It made it "legal" for CIA to engage in: propaganda, economic warfare, preventive direct action (including sabotage, anti-sabotage, demolitions and evaluative measures), and subversion against hostile states, including assistance to underground resistance movements, guerillas and refugee liberation groups."]

In all fairness to Kennan, by 1989 he had fully repudiated 10/2. It was "the greatest mistake I ever made," he said.

Bruce wrote in his report for President Eisenhower that the Directorate for Plans, the clandestine services, was now operating "on an autonomous and free-wheeling basis in highly critical areas," its actions "in direct conflict with the normal operations being carried out by the Department of State." Dulles had not been slow in gathering power to his agency. By 1956, CIA was running a shadow government.

Bruce lamented that America's reputation in the world had been damaged by CIA. The clandestine services were "responsible for stirring up the turmoil and raising the doubts about us that exist in many countries of the world today." The report concludes with a prescient question: "Where will we be tomorrow?"

Later Robert Lovett was to recall David Bruce's indignation as he worked on the report. "What right have we to go on barging into other countries, buying newspapers and handing money to opposition parties or supporting a candidate for this, that or the other office?" Bruce had demanded. It was "outrageous interference with friendly countries" and "beneath the dignity and principles of the United States."

Bruce and Lovett were certain that "Congress had never intended to grant a United States Intelligence Agency authority to conduct operations all over the earth." Their report recommends that CIA "confine itself to its mandate, the harder and more tedious work of collecting intelligence." It was, of course, much too late. Bruce and Lovett's final recommendation in the report would echo down the years: "We suggest, accordingly, that there should be a total reassessment of our covert action policies." On the strength of the Bruce-Lovett Report, Eisenhower was determined to fire Allen Dulles, Richard Bissell, the DD/P, and Dulles' deputy, General Charles Pearre Cabell.

Just as references to Allen Dulles' appearance at a meeting in January 1933 in Berlin attended by Adolf Hitler have vanished from newspaper archives in Berlin, so, too, the Bruce-Lovett Report has vanished from history. The above citations come from Arthur Schlesinger's biography of Robert F. Kennedy. Apparently Schlesinger discovered a copy of the Bruce-Lovett Report among the Robert Kennedy papers at the John F. Kennedy Memorial Library. It has since disappeared from that repository.

Neither the Virginia Historical Society, which houses Bruce's papers, nor President Eisenhower's papers contain copies of the Bruce-Lovett Report. No copy resides at the National Archives. David Bruce, who is another of the unsung heroes of this story, was no apologist for the malfeasance of the clandestine services; he stands in sharp moral contrast to the Dulleses and the McCones, the David Atlee Phillipses and the Lawrence Houstons, who dedicated themselves to Jesuitical justifications of CIA's most flagrant illegalities.

In 1957, the year after David Bruce wrote his devastating attack on the clandestine services, Eisenhower appointed him to be ambassador to Germany. Bruce had not forgotten his research into CIA skullduggery. As soon as he arrived in Bonn, he summoned CIA station chief John Bross, an "old DDP operator," as his CIA colleague Ray Cline would describe him.

"I don't want to hear the sound of a single CIA spade digging without my approval," Bruce warned Bross. There would be no Bay of Pigs under his watch, even as he had, at least for two years, thwarted the 1954 CIA coup against the legal government of Guatemala by persuading President Truman's Secretary of State, Dean Acheson, to scuttle the operation.

CHAPTER 7

LITTLE BOY BLUE AND OUR CHIVAS REGAL FRIEND, 1962–1967

"If Little Boy Blue was confronted with a situation,
he would act with firmness, despite Vietnam and Berlin."

Michael J. P. Malone, conveying a
message from CIA's David Atlee Phillips,
his "Chivas Regal Friend," March 1962.

Despite the death of Sorí, which would haunt him all his life, and the fracturing of *Unidad*, Alberto soldiered on. "Sucker that I am!" he exclaimed to me with sardonic irony fifty years later. "[CIA] never went into action in the way we wanted." At the time, he asked himself, "Am I going to fold my arms and not do anything?"

The *Tejana* was feeling its age. Alberto began to utilize CIA ships. It was too dangerous now for him to sail into Cuba himself, and so he directed operations from land. It had always been his ethos not to take unnecessary risks.

As Alberto was dismissing the crew of the no-longer seaworthy *Tejana*, Clarence arrived to say goodbye.

"What do you need?" Clarence said. As an individual, he was eager to be of assistance to Alberto one last time.

Alberto requested two sets of official CIA maps of Cuba, in Spanish.

Clarence complied. He wept as he said his last goodbye to Alberto. "Clarence" would soon perish, a quiet sacrifice to CIA's tangled operation chasing down Che Guevara in the Congo.

As Alberto's CIA handler, Clarence was replaced by Robert Wall, as CIA's pretense that it was interested in helping the Cubans overthrow Fidel Castro continued. Alberto's FBI file still identifies his CIA handler as "Roderick," "his contact in CIA who directs all his activities."

"You should do this!" Wall would order. Behind his back, the Cubans nicknamed him "*clavo*" or "nail," because of his habit of slamming his fist into his palm as if he were hammering a nail. He was a retired U.S. Marine colonel and seemed to be a man with tunnel vision, intelligent, focused, and practical, but cold.

Wall's title was "Assistant Chief, Operations Branch" out of JMWAVE. There he competed unsuccessfully for influence with the brutal David Sánchez Morales. Those whom Wall handled came to conclude that he didn't know anything about Cuba.

The chief of station, Theodore Shackley, preferred Morales. Still, once when Alberto had trouble re-entering the United States after a trip to Jamaica, since he possessed only a *tarjeta*, not even a green card, Wall dispatched his agents. The screech of tires outside the Miami Airport heralded CIA's rescue of its asset.

Determined to retain his independence from CIA, Alberto trained operatives in the Carolinas and Georgia as well as in Florida. Traveling down the Florida coast in search of training locations, he took along four people from the *Tejana,* none from CIA. A promising location was "Adam's Key," owned, however, by Richard Nixon's confederate, Bebe Rebozo. Rebozo confided to Alberto that one night Nixon had lost $12,000 at Havana's *Hotel Nacional,* then said haughtily that he would send them a check.

Alberto arranged to meet Rebozo at a bar on Coral Way in Miami. Rebozo had a laundromat business and Alberto claimed he had a laundromat to sell. The real subject of the meeting soon emerged. Refusing to rent, Rebozo demanded that Alberto purchase his land on Adam's Key for $177,000. (JMWAVE lists Rebozo's price at $25,000.)

They got into Rebozo's car and were driving toward Miami Beach when Alberto ordered Rebozo: "Stop at the next light! I want to make a call." They stopped at a gas station.

"I'm not going one more mile with you!" Alberto said. "*Hijo de puta*!" ("Son of a bitch!")

"Don't talk to him again," Wall said. "Leave it to us." CIA then enlisted the Internal Revenue Service, which was as much at CIA's disposal as the military or U.S. Customs. The IRS informed Rebozo that Adam's Key had been taken over by the government. They would pay him rent of one dollar a year. Alberto moved in and trained some Cubans there.

"I was a man of action," he told me. His goal remained to penetrate into Cuba, learn what was happening inside, and organize and supply guerrilla groups all over the island. The Bay of Pigs betrayal still rankled: "John Fidel Kennedy" sending those men to a swamp and abandoning them to die or be captured.

Bypassing JMWAVE, what he considered to be the corrupted Miami CIA station, Alberto aired his grievances with the Agency at headquarters in Washington, D.C. CIA's Inspector General Lyman Kirkpatrick, a friend of Alberto's brother-in-law John Smithies, was sympathetic as Alberto made the case for CIA's providing compensation for the widows of Humberto Sorí Marín and Rafael Díaz Hanscomb.

"What I asked for," Alberto told me, "they gave."

On May 16, 1961, a month after the invasion, Alberto met with CIA's Bernard Reichhardt, Don Hogan, and Michael J. P. Malone. CIA now viewed Hogan as an "undesirable hanger-on" and tolerated him only because of his "continued association with AMDENIM-1." Reichhardt agreed to the meeting only if Malone, who has "for a long time been in contact with us," would be present.

At the top of Alberto's agenda was CIA's continued assistance to *Unidad*. As if the Bay of Pigs was a minor setback, Alberto requested war materiel, funds, training facilities, and "a more professional corps of advisers," in particular people from the U.S. military. He demanded "a measure of independence" for himself and, once more, an agreement that there would be no operations emanating from outside the United States, "no Nicaragua shit."

Shortly after this meeting, Bobby Kennedy set up anti-Castro operations in Nicaragua. Spending millions, Bobby's group actually engaged in only two operations, Alberto recounted. In one, they mistakenly fired upon and hit a Spanish vessel, believing it was Cuban. In the other, pointlessly, they fired a missile on a sugar mill inside Cuba.

In his plea for CIA help, Alberto talked about Cuban exiles who were interested in their own power and influence, but lacked the ability or the inclination to fight inside Cuba. CIA's "Revolutionary Council," Alberto said, was "politically bankrupt." He wanted CIA to "junk the politicians."

Reichhardt was noncommittal, keeping to CIA's strategy of gathering all the exile leaders under the umbrella of the Cuban Revolutionary Council. Alberto's concerns fell on deaf ears. "I was not and did not wish to be concerned with this matter [of the exile leaders]," Reichhardt writes in his memorandum of the meeting with Alberto Fernández.

Alberto explained that *Unidad*'s new plan was to disrupt public services in Cuba: electric power, water, and the means of communication. Their goal remained a mass spontaneous uprising. He hoped to set "ground rules" for his relationship with CIA. He wanted greater latitude "in the command structure and greater freedom in decisions as to the type of operations to be run." He spoke as if CIA and *Unidad* were committed to the same goals. Either he was self-deceiving, or had chosen a strategy of taking no notice of CIA's recalcitrance.

CIA would not be making any "package deals," Reichhardt said coldly. CIA retained the right to work with other anti-Castro groups. Alberto would do well to work with the Cuban Revolutionary Council, Reichhardt said pointedly. Meanwhile he would not be indicating the support "we might wish to give" Alberto Fernández. In his memo of the meeting, Reichhardt is even more direct: Aid to Alberto and *Unidad* will depend upon "the establishment and maintenance of mutual objectives."

For now, CIA would offer only help in refitting the *Tejana*, pending "further discussions when the internal representatives of his group arrive from Cuba." Politely, firmly, but insistently, Alberto replied that before his people took up the struggle again, "they would want reasonable assurances as to the nature and extent of the support they could expect."

This CIA would never grant him. He had arrived, although he would not yet admit it, at checkmate. Afterward, Hogan suggested that he and Alberto visit Richard Goodwin and Bobby Kennedy and request their help. Alberto demurred. "It would have been a waste of time," he told me.

Before the meeting was over, Reichhardt had Hogan sign a Secrecy Agreement. By the next day, Reichhardt had a full biography of Hogan in his hands. He knew that Hogan had been "thrice married," had been suspended from the *New York Herald Tribune* at the time it faced a strike, and had taken on a job to write a history of Castro's 26th of July Movement.

Hogan had interviewed Fidel Castro in the *Sierra Maestra*, had met Che Guevara, whom he did not like, and knew the CIA-connected journalist Andrew St. George. (St. George had told KUBARK that Che had denied meeting Hogan.) It had been Manuel Urrutia who had asked Alberto Fernández to give Hogan a job at the Sugar Stabilization Board. It was at this time, after the invasion, that George "Mickey" Kappas and Robert Stevens went to work for CIA; immediately they refused to talk to Don Hogan.

Among Hogan's specious connections was with Isadore Irving (I. I.) Davidson, an arms dealer and registered agent of governments ranging from Somoza in Nicaragua to Duvalier in Haiti; when Davidson asked Hogan to write up his views on Cuba, Davidson distributed the piece, "CIA Data Cited Against Castro," to, among others, journalist Drew Pearson. Since mid-1960, Hogan had been an informant for CIA. Reichhardt collected a variety of assessments of Hogan, which describe him as a "bigamist [this is untrue], son-of-a-bitch, opportunist, extremely inquisitive and curious."

So began Alberto's losing game of demanding that CIA keep its promise to support his efforts against Fidel Castro. CIA, in turn, granted only small favors. In June, CIA offered Alberto $5,370.76 to repair the *Tejana*'s engine. JMWAVE and JMBAR, CIA's maritime operations base in the Keys (the latter headed by G. V. Gneitling, a pseudonym), remained reluctant to place supervision and monetary independence in "AMDENIM-1's hands." CIA agreed to finance Alberto's travel to New Orleans where the *Tejana* was docked—only if he formalized his understanding with KUBARK, which meant his joining the Cuban Revolutionary Council.

Alberto was not alone in his suspicion that CIA was abandoning the cause. On July 7, 1961, Tony Varona had complained to Robert Hurwitch at the State Department that the United States "was abandoning Cuba to its fate under Castro." The sense that CIA had no intention of liberating Cuba from Castro was also registered by Arthur Schlesinger.

On July 9, 1961, just two days later, Schlesinger authored a memo to Richard Goodwin: "Those most capable of rallying popular support against the Castro regime are going to be more independent, more principled and perhaps more radical than the compliant and manageable types which CIA would prefer for its operational purposes." It is as if Schlesinger is describing Alberto Fernández.

"It is a fallacy to suppose that clandestine activity can be carried out in a political vacuum," Schlesinger adds shrewdly.

Shortly after the Bay of Pigs invasion, a cousin bought a sugar mill in Costa Rica and invited Alberto to join him as a partner. Was there a world elsewhere? Alberto turned him down.

"I'm in something more important than that," Alberto said.

All the while, CIA kept Alberto under surveillance. Learning that he planned yet another trip to Washington, D.C, on July 13 or 14, 1961, CIA telephoned his wife, Ofelia, and inquired about "his plans or whereabouts." CIA termed her reply "evasive." Ofelia had been an alcoholic ("a drinking problem," her doctor said) back in Cuba.

Tensions arose over the financial deprivations ensuing from Alberto's commitment to his cause; his children would resent his not recreating in the United States the lifestyle they had known in Cuba. Meanwhile Alberto struggled, as he put it in a letter to Michael J. P. Malone, to "coordinate my family necessities with my other activities." Alberto noted that he had also maintained "a small organization, which I believe has prestige amongst Cubans and amongst our friends."

As of July 12, 1961, CIA had determined that the *Tejana* was deteriorating rapidly. It needed a "haul out," painting, the re-installation of its radar, and other repairs in order to be operational.

On August 15th, the *Tejana* blew all the seals on one engine during sea trials. JMWAVE contacted Headquarters, which agreed to "provide limited support AMDENIM-1 for one op." CIA admitted itself to be "reluctant to again place supervision and monetary control of these matters in AMDENIM-1's hands."

At the end of June 1962, William F. Harvey, a former FBI agent and CIA specialist in "executive action"(murder), requested Alberto's "political profile" dating back to December 1960 when Miró Cardona had recommended that Alberto be named Minister of Agriculture in a post-Castro Cuba. Harvey had asked in particular for information as to "whether there is any derogatory info on AM/DENIM-1 and whether, in fact, he was "the owner of the yacht, *Tejana.*" At this time CIA had recommended that Alberto go back into operation for the purpose of bringing certain Army and Navy personnel out of Cuba to the United States.

CIA officers at the highest level were interested in the activities of Alberto Fernández. Martha Tharpe, who prepared the memo for Harvey, added, "During 1960 WAVE and Hqs considered the

activities of subject and his side-kick and public relations man"
Donald Hogan, who was "somewhat unscrupulous and hazardous
from a security standpoint."

Investigating, CIA's Seymour Bolton could uncover "no substantive derogatory information" about Alberto Fernández. Martha
Tharpe referred to Alberto's "reported friendship with the Kennedys,"
which did not exist, but for those glancing encounters between
Alberto and John F. Kennedy at Choate.

CIA acknowledged that Alberto was "well-liked at the State Department." Yet, Tharpe warned, Alberto's wealth and contacts, "coupled
with his arrogance, shrewdness and ambition, make it impossible
for CIA to maintain something resembling an agent relationship."
Doubting, correctly, that CIA would ever succeed in persuading
Alberto to join its Cuban Revolutionary Council, Tharpe concluded
that CIA's relationship with Alberto was "rocky and will continue so."

For Alberto, the CRC remained "politically bankrupt" and was
"unable to rally any Cuban support in or out of Cuba." If only for
security reasons, he would not recommend that *Unidad* join CIA's
CRC.

From the outset, Alberto Fernández was known to operate
independently and had never been under the direction of the
Central Intelligence Agency. It was for this independence, his
reluctance to place the liberation of Cuba in the hands of CIA,
that the Agency had accused him of "arrogance, shrewdness, and
ambition."

By now, Alberto had separated himself from *Unidad Revolucionaria.* The new leadership, he believed, did not represent the original
UR principles, and he was unwilling to be involved with them.

Among Alberto's most promising recruits in the post–Bay of
Pigs period was a University of Havana student named Dionisio Pastrana. Inside Cuba, Dionisio had supported *Unidad,* along
with other groups. From Dionisio's perspective, CIA had been
sending weapons into Cuba, but they weren't reaching the people

who could make use of them. They were able to secure explosives to blow up five sub-stations, only to find that they lacked detonators.

Dionisio was twenty-two years old in July 1961 when he arrived in the United States and found himself face to face with Bob Wall. It was Wall who provided Dionisio with Alberto's address.

Dionisio trained with a CIA team that collapsed when a Castro infiltrator from the G-2 penetrated the group. He trained on the *Tejana*, awaiting the time when he could participate in paramilitary operations into Cuba. Nothing less would suffice.

Meanwhile Alberto labored on, his conflicts with CIA seemingly equal to his enmity with Fidel Castro. He located a farm on Key Largo where he could train recruits. Having raised $20,000 of the necessary $26,000, he requested of Jack Malone that he ask "Uncle" for the remaining $6,000. Kleberg "never said no, never," Alberto repeated several times to me.

Addicted to intrigue, Malone, without informing Alberto, telephoned CIA's Charles Matt on a "sterile phone." Did CIA have any objection to Kleberg's providing this money, which "he was inclined to do?" Malone asked.

Matt hesitated. Then he told Malone that he must consider the idea "in terms of his own interests, which we presume coincide with those of the Agency."

"Call back Monday morning," Matt told Malone. CIA hesitated. The "Malone group" had furnished support of this kind to the "Fernández group" in the past, the Agency knew. Still, CIA insisted that JMWAVE must be consulted to assess whether "this Fernández activity does not conflict with any of our programs."

It was certain now. CIA no longer trusted Alberto. The Agency suspected that he was "double dealing," taking money from both Malone and CIA for the same purpose. CIA unleashed more informants to spy on Alberto, among them one José Manuel Martínez. The Agency demanded "at least tacit agreement that he [Alberto] is not

acting contrary to U.S. interests." "U.S." was, as always, synony-
mous with "CIA."

Nor did CIA entirely trust Malone now. He, too, might be "acting
contrary to U.S. interests."

"Let the buyer beware," CIA decided. In this game of cat and
mouse, Malone, no more trusting of CIA than it was of him,
reported everything to J. Edgar Hoover.

The question of Kleberg's $6,000 contribution to Alberto's farm
went all the way up to Allen Dulles, who issued CIA's verdict. CIA
had no objection to the provision of the money so long as Alberto's
activity did not "conflict KUBARK programs or indication [sic]
double dealing."

Alberto moved forward. At his training facility, there were classes
in man-to-man combat; explosives and demolition; cryptography;
Communism; commando exercises; communications; frog-man
techniques; military organization; fundamentals of espionage; and
ethics. People exfiltrated from Cuba would be put through CIA lie
detector tests. Only then would CIA provide them with six months
of training and salary.

The training was grueling, and recruits often pleaded that they
were sick and begged off. Alberto had a solution. After two weeks of
training, Alberto suggested to CIA, you take them to the mangroves
and leave them there with two cans of water. Growing in the ocean,
mangroves were trees that harbored sand flies and mosquitoes. Only
a dedicated militant could last half a day there.

If they survive two weeks in the mangroves, Alberto continued,
you order the recruits to take pictures at Homestead Air Force base.
If they survive the dogs and the security, they are worthy.

Our Chivas Regal Friend

Having given up on influencing State Department policy with
respect to Cuba, Bob Kleberg turned to Jack Malone's CIA contacts
to facilitate Castro's removal. While Kleberg remained under the

radar of notoriety, Malone functioned as his intermediary, lobbying CIA officials.

Malone and Kleberg shared the view that the Kennedys were "like children" in their lack of political sophistication. In their dialogue with each other, they adopted Dwight Eisenhower's nickname for John F. Kennedy: "Little Boy Blue," a name they occasionally also bestowed on the self-serving Manuel Artime. In Malone's memos to Kleberg, however, it was John F. Kennedy who was "blowing his horn," to no avail. Alberto agreed: Nowhere more than in their losing battle with CIA were the Kennedy brothers "like children." Malone and his cohort took to applying the name "Little Boy Blue" to people who were blindly naïve and for whom they felt only contempt, whether it was the President of the United States or Artime.

In their conversations, Malone and Kleberg are not on the record as noticing John F. Kennedy's war with CIA; his attempts to transfer CIA surveillance programs to the defense department; his efforts to limit the powers of the Director of Central Intelligence and to cut the Agency's budget; or even his attempt to take over Radio Swan, CIA's Caribbean propaganda outlet run by David Atlee Phillips. (Kennedy's effort to take over Radio Swan, for which he used Richard Goodwin as his emissary, was thwarted by Gerald Patrick Hemming, a soldier of fortune loyal not to the United States, but to the Agency, to the embarrassment of his cohort Howard K. Davis.)

Kennedy had given specific orders that CIA was not to infiltrate the Peace Corps. The Agency ignored him, as Kennedy's brother-in-law, Sargent Shriver, running the Peace Corps, had to inform the president. "Some of our friends over in the Central Intelligence Agency might think they're smarter than anybody else and that they are trying to stick fellows into the Peace Corps," Shriver told Kennedy. McCone and Dulles had promised they would not do that, Shriver said, and then went ahead anyway.

So the Dictabelt recording Kennedy's presidential conversations reveals. Kennedy had refused to submit to CIA blackmail that would have saved its Bay of Pigs nightmare, as he refused to send ground troops into Vietnam, a policy Kennedy's cabinet, as well as CIA, favored. Kennedy would not be forgiven.

In February 1962, King Ranch manager and tax man Bob Wells arranged for Michael J. P. Malone to lecture at International House in New Orleans, a CIA redoubt.

Lunch would be with Dr. Alton Ochsner, a CIA asset who shared membership in the Cordell Hull Foundation with Robert J. Kleberg, Jr. With Ochsner, Malone discussed a forthcoming trip to Central America. Cuba was not his sole venue for operations.

Malone had also joined the Dallas Council on World Affairs, another component of his and Kleberg's CIA profile. Kleberg's participation in the Dallas Council was a rare instance of Kleberg personally interacting with CIA assets, although, of course, the Dallas Council, ostensibly an organ of information about foreign policy, was not openly connected to CIA. Kleberg enlisted Bob Wells to communicate with the Council on his behalf.

Kleberg also opened King Ranch to visits from speakers who came to Dallas to address the Council. On an October afternoon in 1952, Dulles intimate H. Neil Mallon, founder of the Council, had escorted Robert L. Garner, the executive vice-president of the International Bank for Reconstruction and Development, on a tour of King Ranch. It was at that moment when Kleberg had gone global.

Garner's purpose was to "study ranching conditions there so he can better advise foreign governments." Cattle ranching was not his sole interest. "We are keenly interested in the production of rubber, sugar and oil," Garner said. Yet another Dallas Council speaker fortunate enough to gain access to King Ranch was Sir Percy Spender, the Australian ambassador to the United States. Kleberg had already begun operations in Australia on a major joint venture.

In October 1961, on Kleberg's behalf, Bob Wells had requested that the Council host a panel chaired by Luis V. Manrara, the executive director of "The Truth About Cuba Committee," a Kleberg-financed entity based in Miami Beach. If the Dallas

Council would cover local expenses, Wells proposed, Kleberg would provide the airfares. To facilitate this program, Wells flew to Dallas to meet with the executive director of the Council, Philip Bethune. Wells promised also to keep Neil Mallon informed as to whether he was successful with the project, which never, in fact, came to fruition.

Malone and Kleberg more directly became involved in CIA's policy-making. In March 1962, Michael J. P. Malone met with Serafino Romualdi, the "principal CIA agent for [AFL] labor operations in Latin America." Romualdi had worked with Allen Dulles and OSS in Bern, Switzerland during the war. On behalf of OSS, Romualdi had helped Italian novelist Ignazio Silone cross two national borders to safety. During World War II, in Uruguay, Romualdi represented Nelson Rockefeller's Inter-American Affairs organization at a conference of anti-fascist exiles. (Robert J. Kleberg, Jr. would be friendly with Nelson, David, and Laurance Rockefeller.)

Romualdi headed the CIA-controlled "Free Trade Union of the American Federation of Labor," funded with AFL-CIO pension funds. Its goal was to train people to fight Communism. As part of its strategy, the group lobbied against John F. Kennedy's Alliance for Progress, which promoted local business development.

The Alliance for Progress, CIA believed, destabilized the military juntas that had been so supportive of American investment. An agreement had been drawn up between George Meany, Fowler Hamilton, and Romualdi. They planned to supervise the construction of housing projects, if only they could secure "a 100% guarantee against expropriation."

Romualdi was meeting with Malone now in the hope of obtaining money from Kleberg to set up his own "labor-management foundation." The two pondered Soviet political strategy. Along with the joint chiefs of staff, Romualdi was confident that Khrushchev would "not do anything relative to a war in Cuba in the event the U.S. were to make a move against Castro." Kleberg and Malone had not yet given up hope of removing Castro, although a year had passed since the Bay of Pigs invasion.

Romualdi and Malone shared the view that "President Kennedy was still being pushed and pulled by the intelligentsia." They despised Adlai Stevenson and Arthur Schlesinger for their "soft line relative to Cuba." Sharing Alberto's skepticism, Romualdi remarked that the Cuban Revolutionary Council headed by Dr. José Miró Cardona was "falling apart." It was "held together only by the money which is being paid to it by the U.S. Department of State," a euphemism for CIA, whose name is not mentioned in Malone's memo of the meeting.

Among those in the Kennedy administration handling policy for Latin America, Romualdi preferred Richard N. Goodwin, who he believed was "waking up to the fact that the future of President Kennedy depends upon a strong, firm policy and the elimination of Castro and Communism in Cuba immediately." Romualdi suggested that Malone and "his associates" meet with Robert Kennedy, who "has been pressuring the President to get rid of the featherheads in the present administration."

For these men close to the wellsprings of power, there were decided differences between the Kennedy brothers. When Malone met with Bobby Kennedy, the president's brother confided that he planned to persuade his brother to fire Arthur Schlesinger. Romualdi advised Malone that they might find likely allies in senators Smathers, Dodd, and Ellender.

Regarding recalcitrant Latin American leaders whom President Kennedy feared might be upset by another invasion of Cuba, Romualdi was unperturbed. "The U.S. should take the attitude of 'to hell with them,'" he told Malone. "If you do the job to clean up the mess, the Latins will applaud you, and if you fail, they will criticize you." Romualdi claimed to have himself heard President Rómulo Betancourt of Venezuela and President Manuel Prado of Peru "scream" for the U.S. to go ahead and overthrow the Castro government.

Romualdi did not go home empty-handed. The "American Institute for Free Labor Development," his project, would spend $17,438,481 between 1962 and 1967. CIA did not contribute in its own name, but, rather, in that of AID, the Agency for International Development, which gave $15,440,065. Making up the difference was, among other corporations, King Ranch.

On the same day that Malone was meeting with Romualdi, March 15, 1962, Vice President Lyndon Johnson arrived by invitation—or summons—at King Ranch. Kleberg wanted a report on John F. Kennedy's intentions with respect to Cuba. "Lyndon" scurried to King Ranch, as requested.

"Will Kennedy act against Castro and commit U.S. troops to Cuba?" Kleberg said.

Kennedy will not commit troops to Cuba, Johnson said. Kennedy's position had been set six months before he learned of the presence of Soviet missiles in Cuba. He would not invade Cuba again.

Malone next met with his CIA handlers, first Raford Herbert, and then David Atlee Phillips. With each CIA officer, Malone debated U.S. policy as if they were members of an elected government charged with making decisions on foreign policy. Malone saw Herbert on March 16th, one day after he met with Romualdi.

CIA had separated its section charged with Cuban matters, Herbert confided to Malone. It now functioned "as a separate unit, having its counterpart in the Department of Defense and in State." When Malone reported Lyndon Johnson's skepticism that Kennedy would act against Castro, Herbert said he "did not exactly agree." Johnson's view "was true as of many months past," but was no longer so.

Herbert suggested to Malone that he confer with both Bobby Kennedy and John McCone, who had succeeded Allen Dulles as Director of Central Intelligence.

If only President Kennedy would assign CIA "more authority on which to operate," Herbert mused, they could create a climate inside Cuba "which would be favorable to some activity to over-throw the Castro government." Kennedy, in fact, was moving in the opposite direction; he was attempting to strip CIA of many of its existing powers, and was not about to increase them.

Malone's conference with Herbert further exposes CIA as having been immersed in unilateral policy-making. They agreed that Chile should not receive a loan of $385 million, as proposed by José Teodoro Moscoso, Kennedy's man at the Alliance for Progress. Chile, Herbert pointed out, was not "in a position to intelligently utilize such a large sum of money." Besides, the Chileans had been "against us at Punta del Este."

This was a reference to the conference of foreign ministers of the American states that had been held in Uruguay the previous January. "We should give more encouragement to Colombia and Argentina, who have sensible plans for social reform already drawn up," Herbert believed.

Herbert promised a "build-up of military strength in the Florida area and a minor one is already taking place at Guantánamo." He stressed the necessity that operations will have to take place from an offshore area because of security.

Herbert echoed Romualdi in finding John F. Kennedy soft and Bobby a very "strong-minded individual, and if he made a decision would carry it out." The president was naïve, a "Little Boy Blue" out of his depth.

The career of Raford Watson Herbert reveals in microcosm the close connections between Robert J. Kleberg, Jr., King Ranch, Malone as Kleberg's intermediary, and CIA. Herbert served CIA beginning in 1947 at posts ranging from station chief in Buenos Aires, Montevideo, Rio Janeiro, and Santiago de Chile, to executive positions in the Western Hemisphere Division.

Upon his retirement from CIA in 1965, Herbert suddenly became president of Swift Armour Argentina, a Kleberg partner, as

Kleberg and Malone rewarded him for his service to their efforts. (Beginning in 1947, King Ranch was selling virtually all its cattle to Swift & Co. to keep prices from being driven down.)

Herbert went on to be employed by King Ranch in New York in 1971, only to move on to become managing director of Ethiopian Livestock Development Company in Addis Ababa from 1972 to 1977. It was a gentle move from CIA operative, a leader in Western Hemisphere operations at the highest level, to joining King Ranch and advancing in the cattle business. Cows, cattle, ranches: None of these subjects previously appeared on Herbert's curriculum vitae.

The parallels of CIA officers going to work for CIA-connected corporations are many. Kermit Roosevelt went to work for the Northrop Corporation when he left the Agency; Richard Helms was hired as an "international consultant" by the Bechtel Corporation.

When Malone met with David Atlee Phillips, "Dave," his "Chivas Regal friend," later that week, on March 30, 1962, he asked also for Phillips' assessment of Lyndon Johnson's statement that President Kennedy would not commit troops to another invasion of Cuba.

"If President Kennedy was confronted with a situation," Phillips said, "he would act with firmness despite possible repercussions in Berlin and Viet Nam." In his written report of the meeting, Malone renders this as, "If Little Boy Blue was confronted with a situation he would act with firmness *despite* Vietnam and Berlin." Phillips praised "the successor to Bissell" as DD/P, Deputy Director for Plans, as "a very good man." This was Richard Helms, always popular among the highest echelons of the CIA hierarchy.

"In the opinion of Chivas Regal," Malone told Kleberg, "in two or three months you could see an appropriate climate available in Cuba." Malone was actually paraphrasing Herbert, who had said, "Within the next two to three months a favorable and appropriate climate will be created inside Cuba which would be favorable to some type of activity to overthrow the Castro government." As high up in Cuban operations as Herbert and Phillips were, they apparently were not aware that in four months Soviet offensive nuclear missiles would be streaming toward Cuba.

"Bobby Kennedy is strong," Phillips said, agreeing with Herbert, "and should be worked on." Malone and Kleberg, Phillips suggested, should "cultivate senators Humphrey and McCarthy, since they are New Frontier men and if you convince them it would make a tremendous impression on Jack." Phillips offered to send Malone "some ideas relative to contacting Senator Humphrey."

Phillips had policy-making suggestions of his own. Nothing should be done for Brazil, he thought, "until they are straightened out." He was very concerned about this country, Phillips confided to Malone. The military there was divided, but CIA "hoped to get them together." Among insiders, there was no jargon about "democracy" being brought to what was then called the "third world."

"Jango [a reference to João Goulart] is a son of a gun," Phillips added, "and [Jânio] Quadros is unstable." Argentina's Frondizi was "no good," since he voted against Cuba's being excluded from the Organization of American States. But he had been replaced by José María Guido, who was backed by the military and supported armed action against Cuba. CIA appreciated Guido.

CIA was acting in its role as protector of American business and its investments in the countries of Latin America. Intelligence gathering may have been an Agency mandate, as President Harry Truman had intended when the Agency was created, but it was intelligence on behalf of the corporations whose profit-making it was CIA's purpose to ensure. Whether it was Brazil or Argentina or anywhere else, CIA's motive was apparent. It was to see that the governments of those countries, whether they were ruled by a military junta or a democratically elected president, made certain to protect American businesses and see to it that they functioned unimpeded.

Phillips had some good news to report to Malone and Kleberg. CIA would soon be exercising more authority. A military build-up "can be expected in the Florida area." Then Phillips added, echoing

Herbert, "a minor one is already taking place . . . at the U.S. Naval base at Guantánamo, Oriente Province, Cuba." Phillips stressed that "out of necessity future operations against Cuba would have to take place from an off-shore area because of security of the operation," a position to which Alberto was strongly opposed.

Both Herbert and Phillips sent messages to be conveyed to Alberto Fernández. Herbert referred to Alberto as Malone's "friend, the Lion." Phillips advised that Alberto Fernández of Key Biscayne should "be patient and that before long CIA would fully utilize his abilities and equipment."

Among those to whom Malone sent copies of his memos of these meetings was Frank O'Brien at the FBI field office in New York. When they met in person on April 10th, Malone shared his concerns about the "current tumultuous relationship" between Alberto Fernández and CIA. "They're on better terms now," Malone confided. Alberto was "going very cautiously and slowly," although they were "having another squabble about money."

In the FBI's April 5, 1962, summary of Malone's memos about his meetings with Herbert and his "Chivas Regal" friend, Herbert's name appears, but Phillips' is redacted. Malone shares with the FBI that "he and his associates were going to arrange for an interview with Robert F. Kennedy," as well as with other senators who had been recommended to them. Malone promises to keep the Bureau's New York field office "advised of developments and would continue to furnish results of their meetings with certain influential people relative to Cuban matters."

Intra-Agency rivalry played no role in the activities of Malone and Kleberg. Malone behaved as if the FBI and CIA were on the same team, a position that recalls the 1948 agreement Frank Wisner had forged between CIA and the FBI. It was an agreement of mutual cooperation, and is as old as the Agency itself.

As Malone reported to O'Brien, another supplicant at Kleberg's door was Alexander Rorke, a soldier of fortune who was involved in infiltrations of Cuba with Watergate burglar Frank Sturgis and

Chief of the Cuban Air Force Pedro Díaz Lanz, a crack aviator who had defected. The defection of Díaz Lanz was considered by the U.S. government to be "the first major break in Castro's revolutionary command, which could lead to others," according to Roy Rubottom, Jr. at the State Department.

Rorke was the son-in-law of Sherman Billingsley, a New York man-about-town who owned the "Stork Club." Malone shared this information as well with Charles Matt at CIA. Malone knew about a U.S. Coast Guard interception of a Fiorini/Díaz Lanz expedition, among other matters.

Rorke had told Malone that he hoped that Malone's "principals," by which he meant Robert J. Kleberg, Jr., might offer him monetary support. It was only after the FBI released Rorke files stating that Michael J. P. Malone was assisting Rorke with plans and funds courtesy of CIA that CIA relented and shared Malone's name with history.

The Lion

On May 9, 1962, two months after Malone's meetings with Romualdi, Herbert, and Phillips, Alberto Fernández sent a heartfelt appeal to Michael J. P. Malone. He was broke, Alberto confessed. He had "spent everything I had and have, [and] worse, still gone on to spend funds that are not mine." His father had ceased to fund his operations.

A proud man, Alberto now had no choice but to request a loan from "Uncle," "one solely for my family upkeep." He would repay this loan "in the future, upon our return home," he wrote. "Home" remained Cuba. This loan, Alberto explained, would "liquidate my debts in Key West, three thousand dollars in all," and cover motels, car-rentals, dockage, phone bills, and his debt to a hardware store. Alberto had been told that the "friends" would finance his personal travel between Key West and Miami.

Close to despair, Alberto admitted that he had found few "good trusted persons . . . in the Cuban picture." CIA continued to badger him about joining the CRC, the better to monitor his activities and control the parameters of his operations. At CRC, he knew, the "friends" were "using the old man as a smoke screen." The "old man" was Miró Cardona, CIA's AMBUD-1.

Alberto considered his options. He could demand of Cardona that he and *Unidad* assume a major role in directing the activities of the CRC. Or he could work "with the enemies or 'friends' as we call them." By May 1962, all Cuban groups, but for Alberto's *Unidad* and *Rescate,* had joined the CRC. Yet giving himself up to CIA meant Alberto would have to carry out "the plan of Boy Blue and his whole corporation." By "Boy Blue," Alberto was referring not to John F. Kennedy, but to the duplicitous Manuel Artime.

Unbeaten, unbowed, Alberto signed his letter to Malone, "THE LION."

Some Cubans, veterans of the Bay of Pigs, who had survived the fiasco of the *Santa Ana,* asked Alberto why he didn't count on them.

"You all want to be Indian chiefs," Alberto said. He repeated his mantra: "Here there are no Indian chiefs, only Indians."

"What do you mean?"

"Are you ready to put sixty pounds on your back and enter Cuba?" Alberto said. "No." Nor, Alberto thought later, were these Cubans capable of "living in a hole like the Vietnamese."

Alberto devised a new strategy, one that he believed would pit CIA against the State Department. He telephoned Robert Hurwitch and told him he planned to negotiate with Miró Cardona about Miró's joining *Unidad* instead of his joining the CRC. Alarmed, revealing that he was, indeed, a CIA asset, Hurwitch rushed to inform JMWAVE of this development.

CIA mulled over its response. To prevent Alberto from contacting Hurwitch, putting Hurwitch on the spot, would "agitate" and complicate the relationship between the State Department (ODACID) and CIA (KUBARK). In this context, CIA was viewing Alberto Fernández as one of its own. Ultimately, Hurwitch encouraged Cardona to join *Unidad,* while CIA moved to eliminate Alberto's direct contact with Hurwitch because it "limits our control." CIA planned to inform Alberto, "Such trips and contacts jeopardize his security."

Together, JMWAVE in Miami and CIA at headquarters in Washington, D.C., developed a strategy of isolating Alberto Fernández from contact with government officers outside CIA's direct purview. Alberto saw through this ploy, even as he was powerless to do anything about it. "Our friends or enemies blew a stack when they learned that I had talked to Bob H.," he wrote Malone.

Hurwitch was sent to Miami as the State Department's representative to Operation Mongoose, the latest of CIA's anti-Castro efforts. In its ongoing warfare with the Kennedys, CIA viewed Hurwitch as an enemy, or so it seemed.

To maintain Hurwitch's cover, CIA pretended to view Hurwitch as an adversary. When Edward Lansdale, on behalf of Bobby Kennedy, inaugurated his "Cuba Project," Hurwitch participated as the representative of the State Department. Hurwitch remained a double agent within the U.S. government.

Alberto had been impeccable in his dealings with CIA. CIA acknowledged that he had followed the direction of Bob Wall. He had been loyal to the Agency, reporting on a DRE raid on Havana and on Manolo Ray's meetings in Puerto Rico. He had told CIA what he knew about the plans of Alpha 66. The Agency could have no complaint.

CIA continued to attempt to co-opt Alberto. Not yet having given up its scenario of forcing Alberto more tightly under its control, the Agency enlisted Michael J. P. Malone to persuade him to join CRC as its "action coordinator" on behalf of his wing of *Unidad.* With Alberto in the room, from his New York office Malone telephoned CIA paramilitary officer Charles W. Matt. Without warning Matt, Malone, the ceaseless fixer, put Alberto on the telephone so that Matt might offer him "corroborating reassurances."

Later Matt claimed that he had been "shocked" by Malone's taking the liberty of putting Alberto on the telephone without informing him first. Malone certainly knew CIA's protocols, its deeply ingrained and nuanced compartmentalization, and the rules of its internal discourse. He was well aware that he was breaching those protocols by putting Alberto on the telephone without warning. It was an unusual action, but Malone was making a point. On behalf of Alberto Fernández, with whom he sympathized deeply, Malone was sending a message to CIA: It ought to take Alberto's struggle seriously, and state explicitly that it was with him and that their goals were identical. Malone had hoped that Matt would let Alberto know that he was not alone, that the Agency was his ally and supporter. (Matt refers to Alberto Fernández in his memorandum for the record of that "telecon" as a "KUBARK bilateral asset.") Alberto had better talk all this over with Bob Wall, Matt declared. CIA was adamant. Malone was to persuade Alberto Fernández that it would strengthen anti-Castro efforts should there be a "united front" under the umbrella of the CIA-controlled Cuban Revolutionary Council.

News of this unorthodox telephone encounter traveled from JMWAVE to such operatives as Charles Ford (a.k.a. Fiscalini), Bobby Kennedy's operative assistant, and even to William K. Harvey, who was running Mongoose.

Alberto continued as a thorn in CIA's side. He remained independent, selfless, and immune to CIA's blandishments. Time did not diminish his fierce determination to liberate Cuba. He is "a rather tricky person," one CIA officer thought. "My impression of him is one of high integrity," another CIA operative admitted.

Alberto's class background granted him "a somewhat grandiose method of doing things which tends to overawe those who are more accustomed to dealing with impecunious refugees," CIA thought. "His English and mannerisms allow him to pass as a citizen of

PBPRIME [the United States]." As "a highly educated member of the upper class of his country," Alberto Fernández de Hechavarría had to be handled differently. Unlike many other exiles, he could not be bought.

CIA was especially mindful of Alberto's influential friends. Not only was CIA's Inspector General Lyman Kirkpatrick a close friend of Alberto's brother-in-law John Smithies, but the Agency seemed obsessed by the fact that Alberto had known "GPIDEAL" himself, John F. Kennedy.

CIA decided to subject Alberto to an LCFLUTTER, one of their lie detector tests. According to CIA, Alberto had been in touch with KUBARK representatives since January 1959; these are not named, and might well refer to Don Hogan and Catherine Taaffe.

CIA determined that Alberto "has not been involved with any non-intelligence service, nor had he been involved in any Communist activities," which seems ludicrous. He told CIA he considered himself an "ally" working with the U.S. government "to bring about the end of Castro." Later the CIA operator said that the interview with Alberto "provided somewhat more of a workout for the flutter operator than he usually runs into with the Cubans." They had encountered someone who was a match for their machine. Or, unexpectedly, they had met an honest person.

Had he used KUBARK funds for anything forbidden by KUBARK? No. Had he concealed from KUBARK his relationships with other persons or groups? No. In none of Alberto's replies was there any indication of deception. Always CIA kept in mind Alberto's "gamble": that ODYOKE, the U.S. government, "will eventually make it possible to recover his country." On this, he had staked everything.

CIA remained in contact with Alberto Fernández. The Agency admitted, "His ability, stature, and stigma-free political position make him of considerable continuing value." He was "willing to do whatever is required to advance the cause of liberating PBRUMEN [Cuba]," Alberto told them.

CIA breathed a collective sigh of relief. He is "slowly coming under our control," JMWAVE reported to Headquarters. Were he willing entirely to accept their authority, CIA would now provide him with "an operational expense fund."

Unbeknownst to Alberto, CIA had a new agenda with respect to his efforts. It planned to turn *Unidad* into a propaganda outlet "responsive to KUBARK direction and willing to turn over its clandestine assets and potential agents to JMWAVE for unilateral compartmentalized handling." *Unidad* would be utilized as CIA's corporate clients were: as cover for its assets and employees.

Albert was very scrupulous about asking Robert J. Kleberg, Jr. for funds unnecessarily. In August 1962, he sent a Western Union wire to Michael J. P. Malone to this effect. "Do not consult Uncle, for I consider he has helped in excess," Albert writes. "I will try to manage. Meanwhile evaluating situation trying to avoid paralyzing [sic] work." This meant a job that would remove him from anti-Castro activities on a daily basis.

In September 1962, Alberto was far from having given up on returning to Cuba as a sugar grower and cattleman. Michael J. P. Malone encouraged him, sending him a copy of *American Breed* magazine devoted to the raising of Charolais. He also sent a U.S. Department of Agriculture circular on the world meat trade, drawing Alberto's attention to "the tremendous possibilities that exist for Cuba, when she is back in the cattle business, for export to the U.S. and elsewhere."

A paper that Alberto authored around this time is titled: MINIMUM PROGRAM OF THE PROVISIONAL GOVERNMENT. It is prefaced by a quotation from the great Cuban poet and patriot, José Martí: "Before entering a war, the people should know what they will fight for, where it will lead them, and what will come after." It is a direct attack on the 26th of July Movement, which did not reveal its programs until after it took power, to the dismay of many.

What Alberto proposes is an "ideal of national reconstruction." He demands "adequate remuneration of teachers." He suggests that there be general elections within eighteen months of the overthrow of the "Communist tyranny," which had always been part of the program of *Unidad Revolucionaria*. He urges that the living standards of the people be raised, and lower-priced workers' dwellings be established.

He proposes agrarian reform with farmers to acquire small parcels of land with full ownership. He calls for the abolition of the "Latifundia," the class to which he himself had belonged. He calls for the stimulation and propitiation of farm cooperatives, with technical assistance and resources to be provided by the government. He asks that the laws annulling free unions be abolished along with the State control of labor. He calls for academic freedom: "full University autonomy."

He calls for a free national health service for all Cubans, "irrespective of their financial situation." He favors the disbanding of the militias. He calls for the "immediate liberation of all prisoners condemned for acts of resistance to the Communist tyranny."

And as if he were a socialist, although of course he was not, Alberto calls for the nationalization of public utilities, of light and power, telephone, aqueducts and railroads, entrusting the management to efficient autonomous institutions. Along the same lines, he urges the participation of workers in the earnings of the companies or enterprises. He demands equal opportunities of study, apprenticeship, and employment for youth. He calls for strengthening the social security institutions. Not surprisingly, he also favors private enterprise, to which by the year 2011 Cuba was to return anyway.

Alberto sent a copy of this program to Michael J. P. Malone, and it is to be found among Malone's papers. What Malone and Kleberg made of it is not indicated.

In August 1962, Alberto also authored a MEMORANDUM FOR THE RECORD. It contained his assessment of the struggle and, in particular, of the efforts of various Cuban exile groups. He expresses his sympathy for DRE, the revolutionary student directorate that had bombed a Havana theater out of frustration that "the U.S. was not proceeding in a definite manner to bring about the overthrow of Fidel."

"I believe most Cubans outside and inside Cuba share this belief," Alberto adds.

In this document, Alberto attacks CIA for its "lack of principles and propriety." He notes, with bitterness, that the *Directorio* (*DRE*) and the *MRR* had "been the pretty boys of the Company, [and] received more funds and more aid than practically all other movements combined." Not quite registering that the last thing CIA wanted was an overthrow of Castro if it were to lead to a government that the Agency could not control, Alberto suggests a new movement, one with "trustworthy" leaders.

He proposes a "Belic Department" (a term he invented, deriving from "bellicose," and signifying a war department). It would be led by "a person of rank and prestige."

He dares propose that CIA be "subservient to those willing to act." "This mess is your creation," he writes, "and you should be able to better it." He points out that there was no force available in the CRC set up "for infiltration and the waging of war against Castro." Yet he acknowledges that the CRC "cannot easily be eliminated for a face must be present to lead."

He suggests that a "cleansed and functioning" group take the place of the current Cuban Revolutionary Council. He wants the role of "personalities and movements" to be played down, to be subsumed before the task at hand. He proposes that "teams" be sent into all departments of the CRC, "checking its functions, its employees and its necessity and security."

His tone turns sharp as he writes, "No one in CRC could open his mouth without Belic Department consent." He grants that "both you and us know quite little of the CRC and all its bureaucratic pyramid or size."

Unwilling to acknowledge that this condition was precisely what CIA preferred, he adds, "Those willing are mostly idealistic and humble people who had spread out in quest of work, while awaiting the call to action and who prefer hardships than to be involved with CRC."

Alberto Fernández was so idealistic that he allowed himself not to register what the CIA's behavior revealed of its motives. He perceived the Agency's duplicity and longed to be rid of any connection to CIA. Yet he continued to believe that he and those with whom he worked could not succeed in liberating Cuba without its help, especially now that he'd spent what remained of his fortune. He saw no alternative but to continue a dialogue with this Agency that was proving to be increasingly recalcitrant and deaf to his pleas.

Once more demanding "facilities for training and maritime and air support for an infiltration of the whole island as simultaneously as possible," Alberto then proposes himself as the leader of the new "Belic Department." All that was required in the way of resources would be "a small office with a single strong personality present there with a secretary and a phone."

Recognizing that he could not operate without CIA, Alberto Fernández once more attempted to bring the Agency around to support the mission it had promised to pursue, the liberation of his homeland.

Yet despite CIA's having abandoned Alberto Fernández, the Agency had not abandoned its paramilitary intentions with respect to Cuba. An inadvertently released internal document, titled: "MEMORANDUM FOR: Director of Central Intelligence. SUBJECT: Final Report of Working Group on Organization and Activities," dated April 6, 1962, declares that the "Cuban operation" was not only not being abandoned, but in fact it demands "the creation of an organization from Agency-side assets."

The Working Group on Organization and Activities recommended the "creation of an office in the DD/P to be known as Paramilitary and Air Support Operations, under the direction of an Assistant DD/P, to develop the capability for covert and paramilitary and air support operations." This was a recommendation that was honored. The group proposed that the organization be headed by someone "drawn from military service and be a senior Colonel or a Brigadier General with wartime para-military experience" as once more, seamlessly, CIA and the military merged.

Indeed, an army general was appointed to head this new Special Operations Division for Paramilitary and Air Support Operations. The Air Proprietaries Branch was transferred to the Domestic Operations Division. War plans remained high on CIA's agenda, as this document reveals:

> Because of the vital importance of war plans to the Agency's relations to the Joint Chiefs of Staff, we recommend that the War Plans Group receive direct support from the DDCI, even though it should remain organizationally as a part of the Central Support Staff of the DD/P.

CIA had not abandoned its paramilitary arm; it was only that the Agency was not inclined to include Alberto Fernández in its operational strategies. AMDENIM-1 was not a person who would subsume his own goals to those of CIA, nor had he ever been.

CHAPTER 8

DIONISIO PASTRANA AND THE SOVIET MISSILES: HARD INTELLIGENCE

"He is now a fully accredited KUBARK agent in good standing."
CIA Memo, June 1963, referring to Alberto Fernández

One day in June 1962 Alberto received a telephone call from the sister of a sugar cane grower in Cuba named Victor Abreu Rodríguez, a member of *Unidad.* Having in the past worked for the United Fruit Company, Abreu had been trained by CIA in "secret writing." Unable to read the letter, his sister had sent it to Alberto. (In those days, CIA instructed its assets to read secret writing by spilling lemon juice on the page. You could also run a hot iron over the paper, and then the writing would emerge.)

Alberto turned the letter over to Bob Wall. One day Alberto arrived home to find a batch of messages from Wall. Abreu had reported that ice had been collected from the cities of Northern Oriente province. Victor Abreu Rodríguez, among others, had learned that offensive Soviet missiles had been placed in Cuba by discovering that ice, required for the storage of nuclear warheads, had been transported to the ten-acre cave system north of Banes, west of the Bay of Santiago. (Later Alberto would read in a biography of Nikita Khrushchev that the Russians had feared the discovery of the missiles due to the ice and coolants that had to be imported into the area because there wasn't enough power for the local refrigerant.)

Unidad now dispatched its militants, "simple, humble Cuban country people," Alberto called them, into the *Sierra Maestra* in search of the missiles. Simultaneously, as if he remained the director of Central Intelligence (which he officially was not), Allen Dulles assigned French clandestine services agent Philippe de Vosjoli, liaison with CIA, to investigate the missiles. De Vosjoli returned with photographs of MRBM missiles, offensive nuclear missiles, and SAM anti-aircraft rockets.

President Kennedy, by now CIA's bitterest enemy, was not informed of these discoveries, either by Dulles or by Ted Shackley, Chief of Station at JMWAVE. Shackley would later admit that "the station had by all its normal criteria what it termed 'hard intelligence' that there were missiles in Cuba long before the policy-makers would accept that fact."

De Vosjoli was not CIA's only source on the Soviet missiles and the Soviet military build-up in Cuba. The harbormaster of the port of Havana, who had served in the Cuban Navy, now worked for CIA. He reported to CIA on every ship entering Cuba just prior to the missile crisis.

A letter came to Allen Dulles, dated June 28, 1962, with the name of the author now redacted. It refers to a reliable source that "states positively that a multi-level concrete structure, partly under-ground, was being built in the town of El Naranjo in the Sierra de Nipe, with the assistance of Russian technicians."

Dulles kept his cards close to his vest. He already had "several reports of the general nature as that given in your letter," Dulles replied. CIA was well aware of the presence of large numbers of Soviet soldiers and armament in Cuba from the moment they arrived.

It wasn't that CIA's intelligence gathering was faulty or inadequate —it never was. Rather, CIA's first priority had become its own power and the Agency had begun to place its own institutional interests over those of the security of the country. This would categorize CIA's policy into the millennium. CIA withheld this information until it could determine how it might be utilized to the Agency's benefit. Embarassing John F. Kennedy might be motive enough.

For Alberto Fernández, the presence of Soviet missiles in Cuba was welcome news. Surely it meant that a second invasion of Cuba by the United States was inevitable. Infiltrating Cuba, Alberto's group discovered a second missile site in eastern Matanzas on the border of Santa Clara province. An *Unidad* operative saw an opportunity to poison the water supply of the main base under construction to house the Soviet missiles, and radioed Bob Wall. He requested that CIA supply poison. Wall turned him down.

Alberto informed Frank O'Brien of the two missile sites that had been located. But there was nothing the FBI could do. Then he trained for his own role, being airdropped into Cuba. He practiced how to fall from the roof of a house, and took a crash course in structural engineering, studying the vital points in the bridges he planned to blow up. One was a railroad bridge, the other a highway bridge. So Alberto Fernández readied himself for the down-and-dirty fighting in which he would soon participate now that a second invasion of Cuba seemed imminent.

Then what had seemed an opportunity for military action against Castro at last dissolved overnight. In his horror of an incendiary, indeed a nuclear war, Nikita Khrushchev yielded to John F. Kennedy. Khrushchev made his deal with Kennedy, who agreed to remove some obsolete missiles from Turkey. The Soviet missiles would depart from Cuba, and the U.S. promised again not to invade. Castro's belligerence, his seemingly impulsive and unilateral shooting down of an American spy plane, a U-2, killing the pilot, played no small role in Khrushchev's decision.

CIA continued to demonstrate that its overwhelming motivation was its own control over the Cubans and their operations. Charles Matt now reported to the Agency that "Fernández has dissociated himself from Hogan in recent months and has become a much more reasonable person to deal with." CIA had accused Hogan of trying to promote Alberto as the future President of Cuba or to persuade the U.S. government to promote him." This was not on CIA's agenda.

On July 1, 1962, Alberto's former *Tejana* captain, Lawrence Laborde, participated in a meeting at the office of William Baggs, editor of the *Miami Daily News*. Among the attendees were Theodore Racoosin, president of an entity called "International Broadcasting Company," obviously a CIA front, and William Hillman, the head of CIA's Radio Free Europe. Racoosin claimed that the White House had sent him to obtain a "true picture of Cuban matters." Also present were two *Tejana* veterans, Tony Cuesta and Eddie Bayo.

Laborde and Bayo reported that outboard motors had been used for water skiing by CIA agents, who were useless when enlisted in missions against Cuba. Revealing no loyalty to Alberto Fernández, Laborde then claimed that the *Tejana* had been purchased by Alberto Fernández for $8,000, although he submitted a bill for $40,000 for it to CIA, which was plainly false.

Laborde said he had "firsthand knowledge of the transaction and the present and previous owners of the boat." Diligently, Baggs took notes. In fact, Laborde had fabricated the story of CIA's paying $40,000 to Alberto Fernández for the *Tejana*. It would be more than fifty years before Alberto would learn of Laborde's traitorous accusation. Laborde was "a Bayou pirate," Alberto repeated. He was not surprised by Laborde's treachery, his attempt to ingratiate himself anew with the Agency at Alberto's expense.

Laborde had not been idle since leaving Alberto. A CIA document of April 30, 1962, claims he contacted a CIA representative in Key West, seeking permission to blow up a ship, the *S.S. Williams*, which was supposedly running machinery to Cuba. Laborde was told that he would receive $5,000 when the job was completed. At this time Laborde was working with American mercenaries Gerald Patrick Hemming, Edward Collins, and his old comrade from the *Tejana* days, Tony Cuesta.

Before long, the FBI learned that Laborde claimed to know the location of a CIA warehouse in Key West where arms were stored and that he planned to burglarize it. Yet, the Bureau feared, if Laborde were arrested and brought to trial, he might expose CIA operations.

In April 1962 as well, Alberto Fernández had advised Hemming that he should discontinue his association with Laborde, who was "irresponsible." As for Cuesta, an FBI informant related that during the time he was working for CIA, Alberto Fernández received "a certain quantity of money from CIA, to be used to buy food for the group operating a boat belonging to Fernández. However, Fernández kept the money." Cuesta has supposedly been the source.

Forty-Three Days Without a Bath

We left twenty-two-year-old old Dionisio Pastrana training on the *Tejana* preparatory to his infiltrating back into Cuba. Requiring further training, anxious to do whatever was necessary to advance the struggle, in September 1962 Dionisio volunteered for the U.S. Army. He would be part of a Cuban unit training in guerrilla warfare with the U.S. Special Forces. When he was ready to take part in operations into Cuba, the Army refused to release him. Bob Wall and CIA intervened. In keeping with the military's subservience to CIA, the Agency carried the day.

Among Dionisio's assignments for CIA was to infiltrate Cuba to confirm whether the offensive missiles remained in place, whether Castro and Khrushchev had been lying about the removal of Soviet nuclear missiles. Dionisio's experience with CIA was to mirror Alberto's. As Alberto had discovered, CIA's help was designed to fail. It was half-hearted, desultory, and even obstructive.

Dionisio's first insight into CIA's ambivalence came when he was told that CIA forbade the Cubans from carrying the most advanced U.S. automatic weapons into Cuba. Instead, they were compelled to rely on older models, or weapons CIA purchased from foreign countries. They did have the use of an M-3 sub-machine gun, but the ammunition was extremely heavy. The sixty-five-pound radio with which CIA supplied them was powered by a heavy, cumbersome generator.

One mission began disastrously. The objective was to establish a network, to find out what weapons the Cubans had and where they were stored, as well as to assess the political atmosphere in the mountains. Soon the mission began to unravel. Dionisio and his two comrades ran out of water. The river was dry and the only water they had was collected from the muddy tracks that had been left by passing automobiles. Having strayed from their target by two miles, climbing into the hills, they hid in the bushes.

A farmer leading a herd of thirty-five or forty cows sauntered by. He headed for the very bushes where they were hiding. He carried a copy of the newspaper, *Revolución,* making his purpose clear. Just as he pulled down his pants, Dionisio and his team emerged. They planted sub-machine guns with silencers at his head.

"We're going to *Santiago de Cuba,*" Dioniso said. He asked for directions to the thermo-electric refinery situated on the Bay of Santiago. "If you guide us," Dionisio said, "we'll pay you." The farmer agreed to help.

Then, knowing that the farmer would report whatever he said to the Army, Dionisio let the man go. In reality, they went not east, but crept steadily closer to the ocean. Out of the mud that remained as a vestige of Hurricane Flora, they built tunnels where they hid under a canopy of mud, living on a patch of sweet potatoes.

As Dionisio had predicted, believing their numbers were greater than they in fact were, Raúl Castro immediately sent his crack mechanized *División Cincuenta* in search of the invaders, so exposing his secret military capacity. From his cave in the middle of Oriente Province, surviving on those sweet potatoes, Dionisio was able to provide CIA with photographs of this highly mechanized division of Cuban soldiers, numbering between 10,000 and 15,000 men. They lacked an antenna, but still they managed to transmit information. Photographs were soon in the hands of CIA.

When Dionisio returned to Florida with his report, Bob Wall was not pleased.

"You are an idealistic person," Wall told Dionisio. "You should never have let that farmer go. You should have killed him and buried him."

Dionisio was not intimidated by his CIA handler.

"What the hell would you have wanted me to do with thirty-five cows?" Dionisio said, laughing. Wall apparently not only knew

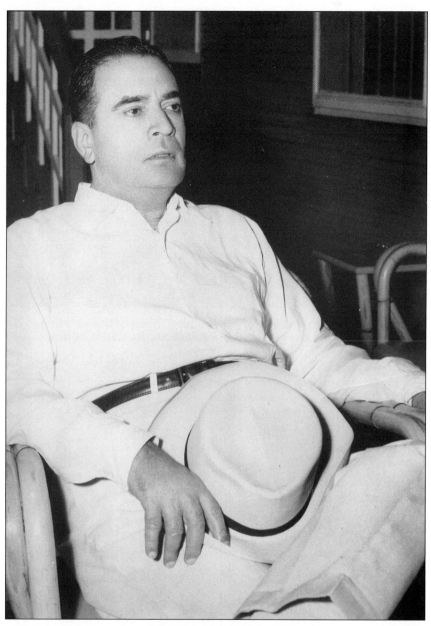

Federico Fernández Casas: Alberto appealed to his very rich father, who contributed most of the $300,000. *Courtesy of Gladys Smithies.*

Manuel Artime, left; Miró Cardona; President John F. Kennedy; Jacqueline Kennedy: Artime was advising CIA to land at a location that all but ensured defeat.

Allen Dulles, left, and General Edward Lansdale, second from left: "We're going to get clobbered!"

President Kennedy with Allen Dulles and John McCone: "It doesn't matter who takes Allen's place at CIA."

Allen Dulles, left; John F. Kennedy; and John McCone: "When you decide to become decent people, let me hear from you."

President John F. Kennedy reviewing the troops: The Agency had sought
to blackmail Kennedy.

John F. Kennedy with Allen Dulles: "The military thought the Bay of Pigs was better."
Courtesy of the Central Intelligence Agency.

Left: Richard Helms. What Helms neglected to tell Woodward was that Kendall had been an important CIA asset for years. Right: Allen Dulles. "If you don't put a stop to this, you'll end up in a Cuban jail—or a cemetery."

David Atlee Phillips: Jack Malone's "Chivas Regal Friend."

At left, Robert J. Kleberg, Jr.; center, Lyndon Baines Johnson; right, Kleberg's nephew, Belton Kleberg Johnson: "I agree with everything you're doing up to a point, and internationally 100 percent."

At Cedral: Bob, Juan Reynal, and John Armstrong: Their Venezuelan adventure began with a trip in a single-engine Cessna with John Armstrong. *Courtesy of Gustavo de los Reyes.*

Abbot, Gustavo, Louis, John, Bob, and Jack in Venezuela. *Courtesy of Gustavo de los Reyes.*

Robert J. Kleberg, Jr., Gus Wortham, chairman and chief executive of the American General Insurance Company, and Sterling C. Evans, at a Santa Gertrudis sale in 1966. Evans, president of the Houston Land Bank, was Wortham's ranching partner.

Robert J. Kleberg, Jr., center: "This man is a son-of-a-bitch." He is referring to Machiavelli.

The King Ranch chief landing with his entourage at San Felipe in Venezuela, his plane loaded with an ample supply of daiquiris. From left: Abbot Reynal, Alfie Fanjul, Louis Weaver, Jeanie Reynal, Tina and Etta, Jack Malone, Winnie Runnes, and Juan Reynal. *Courtesy of Gustavo de los Reyes.*

Robert J. Kleberg, Jr. introducing his men to President Rafael Caldera of Venezuela.

KING'S RANCH — President Rafael Caldera discusses several aspects of the "King's Ranch" with its proprietor Robert Kleberg at the Miraflores Palace. The King's Ranch which holds an investment of about Bs. 12 million in Venezuela, will step up its activities in the Venezuelan cattle industry. Accompanying Kleberg were Michael Malone, John Hines, John Armstrong, Joseph Kaykas and Gustavo de Los Reyes.

Beef rivaled oil and gas in importance.

Gustavo de los Reyes with the Shah of Iran and his wife, Farah. *Courtesy of Gustavo de los Reyes.*

Robert J. Kleberg, Jr. circling the globe: "You ever run away from anything?"

Robert J. Kleberg, Jr. with his grandchildren, the cheerful companions of his final years.

Robert J. Kleberg, Jr. at the races: "He was on the saddle—I was not." *Courtesy of Gustavo de los Reyes.*

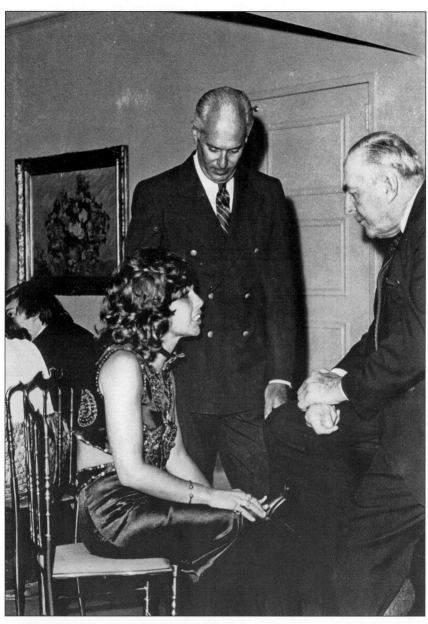

Robert J. Kleberg, Jr. hearing confession from Maruja Veracasa. Her former schoolmate, Princess Gabriela de Saboya, was Kleberg's guest. He was often in the company of very beautiful women.

An older Robert J. Kleberg, Jr.: He imagined himself returning in three weeks to work the
cattle on the Norias division of the ranch.

nothing about Cuba but, unlike the Cubans, he was not a man of feeling.

For CIA, Cuban operations were a game with no apparent objective, or at least no serious intention of unseating Fidel Castro. Not even Dionisio's confirmation that Soviet tactical nuclear devices remained in Cuba impressed Wall. CIA policy was increasingly to make a show of a struggle for Cuba, with greener pastures east of Suez awaiting Agency resources.

Another of Dionisio's missions involved his assessing whether the Russians had left behind nuclear missiles and, if so, how many. "Look for generators," CIA ordered Dionisio. The weakness of Castro's Soviet-engineered arsenal was that there was little solid fuel to launch a missile. Dionisio had been trained by CIA to recognize missiles by the amount of dry ice taken from a plant to freeze the fuel.

Following the lead of earlier operatives who had discovered the presence of Soviet missiles by the accumulation of ice, Dionisio confirmed the continued presence of Soviet nuclear devices in Cuba long after the deal made between Kennedy and Khrushchev. His suspicion was that Castro planned to use these weapons to destroy the Guantánamo base.

With Dionisio in Cuba, Alberto's hopes rose. He wrote to Kleberg, requesting a visit to King Ranch, only to receive a response from ranch manager Robert C. Wells. Kleberg was away, and so Wells recommended that he "keep in touch with Jack as to a convenient time and meeting place up there in that area." Wells, like Malone, believed that "there are more grounds for optimism than a short time ago, although 'patience' was required." Luckily, Wells said, flattering Alberto, "you have almost as much patience as you have fortitude."

In November 1962, idle, Alberto wrote a MEMORANDUM FOR THE RECORD commenting on a television address by Miró Cardona. "Absolute lies and nonsense," he thought. Miró "showed a lack of knowledge of Cuba's geography and utter ignorance of the missile emplacements." He used an interpreter except when he was asked whether he would be the provisional president of Cuba. This question Miró answered immediately, without waiting for the translation. Alberto signed this paper, "AMDENIM/1."

In March 1963, Alberto faced the dilemma of selling his wife's and her sister's shares in Czarnikow-Rionda at a fraction of "what they could be worth." He asked Malone for the option of drawing from an account for which Czarnikow would charge interest, and would be "covered by his shares in Czarnikow-Rionda," and two other companies.

"I would draw only the amounts necessary which would, as an average, be in the [range of] $750 to $1,250 per month," he said.

He also requested that Malone help him find work in New York. Alberto proposed an interview with Malone's friends at International Telephone & Telegraph, a company very close to CIA. He hoped to meet too with "Mr. Grace," Peter Grace, also a CIA asset. These employment possibilities did not materialize.

Malone remained sanguine. "I still believe that the clouds are going to clear away before Little Boy Blue stands for re-election," he wrote Alfonso Fanjul in May 1963. Malone and Fanjul understood each other. They preferred dictators "friendly" to the United States to Communists and socialists.

On May 20, 1963, Dionisio Pastrana headed for the former Freeport Sulphur Mine at Nipe Bay, west of Banes, in search of intelligence. His team arrived in a nineteen-foot aluminum canoe with two pontoons at the side. At Moa Bay they took the air out of the pontoons and sank the boat, planning to return and use it later to escape. Cane fields were burning. Dionisio walked twenty-five kilometers.

He was young and committed to a free Cuba, and it seemed there was no mission he could not accomplish. He ate Russian meat out of cans, and it tasted like greasy Spam; it was food the locals wouldn't touch. The Cuban people, friendly, supplied Dionisio and his men with week-old bread, which persuaded them that they would have the support of the Cuban population should the struggle develop.

Sympathetic to their effort, the Cubans they met indicated that they were afraid of the repression and that they hated the Castro government. Dionisio still had to be sure they would not talk, and reveal their presence. Cubans are "river loose," Dionisio told me. "They talk too much."

In Nicaro, he learned that Cuba had not only nickel, but uranium deposits as well. Dionisio wanted to blow up the Nicaro mine, but CIA refused. It was a three-month-long operation. A patrol of militia came by and Dionisio's group had no choice but to fire on them. The Castro forces then mobilized an entire company so that Dionisio's little team had to pack everything up and run. They moved south, traversing the roads from Mayarí into the Sierra Cristal.

Dionisio suspected that offensive nuclear weapons were being stored in the caves of the Sierra Cristal Mountains. These were weapons, CIA speculated, that the Soviets would have allowed Castro to use to destroy the Guantánamo base. In the area of Banes, Dionisio came upon a MIG-15 airplane without wings and no cabin, mounted on a ramp. This was a tactical nuclear weapon that would be used should Cuba be invaded by the U.S. at Banes.

The U.S. had counted the missiles Khrushchev had removed from Cuba, but didn't know about tactical missiles that remained under the discretion of local commanders. These could have been fired without Khrushchev's permission. Trained by CIA, Dionisio again learned that the Cubans lacked solid fuel. He searched for the radar "YAGI," the guidance system being used.

In the midst of this trip, three people belonging to the *Movimiento Democrático Cristiano* (*MDC*) suddenly appeared. They were led by Víctor Paneque, who had been a major in the rebel army in the early part of the revolution and a *comandante* at the Havana garrison. Armed with an obsolete M-1 rifle and some homemade grenades, Paneque was bent on engineering his own revolution.

"What are you doing here?" Dionisio said.

Its eye on Paneque, CIA had promised to stop him from landing in the area where Dionisio was operating. The incident epitomizes the carelessness with which CIA handled these dangerous Cuban operations, jeopardizing the safety of its operatives.

Twenty-four-year-old Dionisio summoned all his authority. He took the three marauders under his command. Then he sent a message to CIA: "I have them under control!"

On his most significant mission, Dionisio discovered fragments of the Soviet missile that had shot down the American U-2. He brought fragments of the skin of the Soviet missile back to the United States where it could be analyzed. From such evidence, Dionisio explained to me, one could learn the weight of the missile and the quality and level of the steel the Soviets were producing for their supersonic weapons.

Wall smiled, happy with the success of the mission. CIA shared the intelligence Dionisio had brought with the Israelis. In the 1967 war, Israel knew the quality of the missiles that the Soviet Union had provided to Egypt.

"You contributed to the seven days war!" Bob Wall told Dionisio later.

In March 1963, a conference took place at the Miami field office of the FBI. Present were representatives of a host of agencies: the Bureau of Customs; the Coast Guard; the Department of the Navy; the State Department; Central Intelligence Agency; Border Patrol; Immigration and Naturalization Service; and the FBI. Present as well was Assistant Attorney General J. Walter Yeagley, representing the Department of Justice. Revealing that government agencies functioned not as rivals, but with one common end, the group agreed to a united effort to "frustrate plans" for raids into Cuba. It was clearly policy now to allow Castro to survive, an after-effect of President Kennedy's agreement with Premier Khrushchev over the removal from Cuba of the Soviet missiles.

As years earlier Frank Wisner had decreed, so the FBI and CIA had continued to work together. Robert Hurwitch declared,

"Contrary to the opinion of some people in the [State] Department, I have found that the FBI and CIA are doing an excellent job of intelligence." Despite a demur from Ted Shackley, the FBI contended that it was providing CIA with "very voluminous" data.

The raids, all these groups agreed, were not "on balance" in the best interests of the U.S. Representing CIA out of Washington, Desmond Fitzgerald, joining Theodore Shackley, suggested that "undesirables" who violate this policy be prosecuted.

Where CIA had an "operational interest," that information would be shared with the FBI by CIA headquarters. It emerged that the FBI's Miami office regularly "telephoned urgent information to CIA." This communication procedure had been devised by the Internal Security Division of the Department of Justice. Liaison between the FBI and CIA proceeded, as it had from 1948 on, with the procedures over the years being refined and elaborated.

No matter what that conference of agencies concluded, missions in 1964 and 1965 took Dionisio again deep inside Cuba. It remained important fot the Agency perpetually to flex its operational muscles, if only to justify its incalculable budget. Never leaving behind a boat with which to escape, Dionisio searched for recruits for an effective political opposition that could collect information. Dionisio Pastrana set an operational record: forty-three days without a bath. He made the Cubans, he told me, "expend a lot of energy."

For its lack of commitment to removing Castro, Dionisio retained no bitterness toward CIA. He attributed the Agency's hesitation in liberating Cuba to its conviction that Castro would use the tactical nuclear weapons left behind by the Russians to destroy the Guantánamo base.

By 1965, when Dionisio left the clandestine services, a Johnson administration intelligence document permits CIA only "limited activities consisting of infiltration/exfiltration operations, intelligence collection, and economic measures against Cuba." CIA then objected. It wanted to "make Castro's life as difficult as possible at home as a deterrent to his mounting interference outside his own borders." Castro's assistance to revolutionary movements in Venezuela, Guatemala, and Colombia was a source of alarm to the Agency, as it had been to President Kennedy. But "higher-noise level operations" might only stimulate further Soviet aid. Cuban operations deteriorated even further.

Later Dioniso was troubled by what he feared might have been the consequences to the Cuban families in the countryside who had helped him and his teams. He learned that they were punished and sometimes murdered, in part because of their own indiscretion. He had been very well trained and disciplined, but those who helped him had not. "I have a lot of pain in my heart," he told me. "People were hurt because of missions I did."

Over the years, CIA remained in touch with Dionisio Pastrana. "Once you are a priest, you are always a priest," he smiled. "Once you're CIA, you're always CIA." His leadership qualities, as well as his humanitarian ideals, led to his becoming CEO of Goodwill Industries of South Florida where he was to fund training programs for people with physical and mental disabilities. Government contracts, including one for Goodwill to manufacture American flags, came his way.

He remembered that CIA refused to enlist the Underground led by former *Comandante* Humberto Sorí Marín that had been ready and waiting in Cuba at the time of the Bay of Pigs invasion. He concluded to me that those who were willing to act didn't get help, while the CIA people inside Cuba weren't "worth a damn."

Yet, as a man who lives in the moment, Dionisio Pastrana told me he held no grudge against the Agency. He retained his connection with CIA asset Félix Rodríguez, whom he remembered from the "good old days of CIA."

Politically sophisticated, he compared the fate of Camilo Cienfuegos, who fell by Castro's hand, to that of Leon Trotsky, murdered by Stalin's hired assassin.

Snookered

April 1963 found Alberto still determined to fight for Cuba's freedom and CIA still "attempting to assert a greater degree of control over subject." It again summarized its history with Alberto, enumerating "his attempts to assert his independence." The Agency accused him now, unfairly, of insisting upon independence from any "exile group he could not himself control." It also admitted that Alberto's files "portray a man dedicated to freeing Cuba—but on his own terms."

After the disaster at the Bay of Pigs, half of the crew of the *Tejana* refused to have anything to do with what Alberto called "our supposed friends." Tony Cuesta, once a member of the crew of the *Tejana,* started a group called COMMANDOS L. In full support, Alberto requested of his case officer Bob Wall that the Agency make use of COMMANDOS L, "since they had demonstrated their courage" and would "probably be more effective than any other group."

Cuesta's most flamboyant operation was the successful sinking of a Soviet ship, the *Baku*. Fearless, Cuesta placed the mines on the *Baku* himself as it stood in shallow water.

A terrified Andrew St. George had gone along, only to confront Alberto later. "How could you do that to me?" St. George demanded. "They're crazy. They put the mines on the Russian ship themselves! You told me it was safe!"

All the while, CIA attempted to manipulate COMMANDOS L into believing that they were not receiving CIA support, as CIA used Cuesta to destabilize the Castro regime.

In a JMWAVE report, CIA congratulated itself on manipulating Cuesta on an "unwitting" basis. CIA also attempted to use Alberto to inform against Cuesta.

"Can't you dissuade them?" Wall asked Alberto.

"No," Alberto said.

CIA gloated. How disappointed Alberto would be to learn that CIA had supported Cuesta on an "unwitting basis." The Agency had not revealed to Alberto that it had in fact utilized COMMANDOS L. Contradictory policies characterized this Agency that, after all, was accountable to no one and had always done what it pleased.

It was a favorite CIA tactic, one that it used more perniciously when performing drug experiments under the MKULTRA mind control program. Meanwhile Cuesta's group was on the list developed at the March 1963 conference of agencies of those whose raids into Cuba they planned to shut down.

In one operation in which Cuesta did not participate directly, with Russian P-T boats waiting, he lost an arm and also his eyesight.

Later, on a Florida radio program, when asked about his relations with the various exile groups, Cuesta revealed where his loyalty resided.

"My boss was Alberto," he said.

Other veterans of the *Tejana* fared even worse. William Pawley hired four or five Cubans to infiltrate a missile base and kidnap several Russians. They all embarked on Pawley's yacht heading for the north coast of Cuba where they were left in boats far from land. When they failed in their mission, Pawley ordered them killed. Among them was Eduardo (Eddie) Bayo, who didn't know how to swim yet dove into the sea attempting to rescue the baby who had fallen into the water on that fateful day when Humberto Sorí Marín had returned to Cuba for the last time.

Alberto continued to refuse to accept a salary from CIA. Taking money from them would be "a symbol of the loss of his independence." In 1963, he was still puzzled at how CIA "increasingly moved in the direction of using the Cubans for ends which are often clouded." Yet he continued to believe that "without KUBARK aid, he could do nothing."

When Alberto made an unauthorized trip to Washington, D.C., in February 1963, CIA wrote, "The incident had lowered considerably the degree to which the Case Officer was willing to accept his word." He had been betrayed by many, including Don Hogan, who told CIA, "Out of fear Alberto would come to him." "Perhaps, keeping him apart from the others, I can also push him into action," Hogan wrote Robert Hurwitch. Hogan would later be murdered in Mexico while writing an account of his anti-Castro exploits.

"I don't know if the Company killed him, or the Mexicans," Alberto would tell me.

Alberto did what he could, discovering further arenas for action to help the Cuban people. He recruited female radio operators. He organized a fishing fleet, the fishermen to be kept "unwitting" of his continuing CIA involvement. CIA and the FBI both generated documents suggesting that Alberto discussed with them former Cuban senator Rolando Masferrer Rojas' plans to invade Haiti, there to set up a base for the purpose of invading Cuba. Masferrer's goal was to replace Fidel Castro with himself. Alberto denied that he did so.

It was only now that Alberto arranged a final settlement from CIA for the widow of *Unidad* leader Rafael Díaz Hanscomb. JMWAVE noted with approval "the absence of any kickback." JMWAVE documents the settlement at $1.25 million; Alberto remembered that it was between $15,000 and $25,000.

Some in CIA sympathized as Alberto struggled to "keep up his own morale" in the absence of progress toward his dream of returning to a free Cuba. He cashed in his last $10,000 worth of stock. "He is basically a very soft-hearted guy," one CIA operative notes, "and has given away enough money to those of his former sugar institute and ranch employees . . . to have otherwise postponed his financial problems considerably." Alberto was "basically a sentimentalist," they conclude. CIA advised Michael J. P. Malone to inform Alberto's father of his son's precarious financial situation.

In July 1963, NBC invited Alberto to participate in a documentary, *White Paper*, about Cuba. His role would be to comment on the Bay of Pigs operation and the missile crisis. Dutifully, Alberto reported the contact to Bob Wall. Alberto added that the NBC representative seemed to hold an "unfavorable attitude" toward CIA. Loyal to a fault, Alberto accepted CIA's advice and expressed so disdainful an attitude toward the project that NBC dropped him, which was how Alberto rejected their offer.

CIA affected surprise. Alberto is "operating to his own personal disadvantage in following our instructions," Bob Wall noted. "Prominence in an NBC documentary would have enhanced his prestige considerably in Cuban exile circles." CIA did not understand Alberto yet. From the struggle against Fidel Castro, Alberto had never asked anything for himself.

The harsh South Texas country was hard on women. Debilitating bronchitis led to Helen Kleberg's hospitalization at Harkness Pavilion in New York. Tuberculosis followed. Then she developed a brain tumor.

She asked Bob if they might return to some places that they had visited together. Among them was Alberto Fernández's *Guanabo* ranch located an hour from Havana with its house perched high on a cliff overlooking the sea.

By May 10, 1963, Helen Kleberg was hospitalized in New York. As Michael J. P. Malone wrote to Alfonso Fanjul, "There is absolutely no hope for her."

Helen Kleberg died on June 12, 1963. She was sixty-two years old.

The Kennedy assassination came and went. Only one article on the subject appears in the copious files of Michael J. P. Malone, a clipping describing the Communist Party's denial that Lee Harvey Oswald was a leftist. "Reds Try to Disown Oswald," the headline read. Oswald was "more 'right wing than left,'" the story said.

October and November 1963 comprise one not very full file in Michael J. P. Malone's papers.

In early 1964, Alberto continued to monitor the fate of the sugar industry in Cuba. He learned that there was "a de-emphasis on Nuevitas as a sugar shipping port, and that sugars from Senado and Lugareño in Camgüey" that were normally shipped through

Nuevitas were being sent over to Guayabal, that Guayabal was "being pushed as the principal sugar port in that general zone." To have his pulse on the economy of Cuba meant keeping his dream alive.

In May 1964, Alberto was informed by the Agency that if he wanted to meet with people at CIA headquarters, he was to enlist Michael J. P. Malone as his intermediary. Alberto sent a message through Malone that he wished to revive the *Tejana* for operations.

CIA was not happy about the idea. If CIA helped Alberto refurbish the *Tejana*, he might "try to enlist support for further independent efforts against AMTHUG-1, Fidel Castro." Alberto now had time to regret his decision to sideline the *Tejana*.

CIA wielded the greater power. From CIA headquarters, Special Affairs Staff (SAS) Chief Desmond Fitzgerald found time to request confidential information from the IRS. Had Michael J. P. Malone's "principals," by which he meant Robert J. Kleberg, Jr., taken a "tax write-off" when they provided Alberto Fernández with funds? Although Kleberg's name would be redacted from CIA documents as late as March 1998, the time of the Assassination Records Review Board, CIA searched for any means possible to control Alberto Fernández, even if it meant harassment of Kleberg.

Malone encouraged both his boss, George A. Braga, and Alberto. "There appears to be increasing dissension within the country," Malone wrote Braga on June 12, 1964, "and in certain areas the food shortages are extreme to the point of hunger." It was wishful thinking, as Malone noted "increasing troubles within" and advocated "more harassment from the outside."

Kleberg's satellite King Ranches in Latin America continued to flourish. The annual sale at King Ranch in Argentina in June 1964 was "most successful" with the top selling bull going for $11,000. That June, Kleberg traveled to New York to attend the races at Aqueduct.

(King Ranch was to average $825,000 a year in purse money from its racetrack winners.) He then planned to go to Washington, D.C., for a meeting with David Rockefeller and to conduct, as well, "some political business."

In June 1964, Alberto wrote a fifteen-page memorandum to Bob Kleberg, offering a new set of suggestions about what might be done to liberate Cuba. He bypassed CIA. "Am I going to fold up my arms and not do anything?" he pleaded with Kleberg, who had never refused him anything.

When Alberto passed the memorandum to Michael J. P. Malone so that he could deliver it to Kleberg, Malone first sent a copy over to JMWAVE. Malone also sent a copy to Al Rodemeyer at CIA headquarters. On June 19th, Malone, in fact, sent several "letters that I have received from Alberto Fernández for transmission to Mr. Kleberg" over to Rodemeyer. (Rodemeyer's real name was Al Rodríguez.)

In his covering letter, Malone writes Rodemeyer that he wanted to "review this matter with you." Malone wrote to Rodemeyer at Box 1104, MPO, in Washington, D.C., a CIA address to which Malone had been granted access.

Malone was not about to operate outside the purview of the Agency, nor did he inform Alberto that he was sharing his letters with CIA. The chief of station at JMWAVE was in possession of Alberto's document before Kleberg saw it. JMWAVE notes that Alberto was "just as fired up as ever to do something."

"I've been snookered!" Alberto would say forty-five years later, learning that his letters to Kleberg, letters he had entrusted to Malone, went first to CIA.

"For Uncles," the document opens. Alberto argues that "the battle of South America is still in Cuba," and that "unless Fidel & Co. go, we are in trouble everywhere." He writes, "Fidel's situation is on the decline." Morale in Castro's army is low, while the Cuban economy is faltering, information he had, in part, from Dionisio Pastrana's experiences infiltrating Cuba when so many Cubans had welcomed and assisted him and his teams, jeopardizing their own safety.

Alberto knew that the Russians had not taken all of their offensive missiles out of Cuba, even as Lyndon Johnson's agenda now looked to Vietnam. "Just let me get elected, and then you can have your war," a newly elected President Johnson had told the joint chiefs of staff at a 1963 Christmas Eve White House reception. Further evidence that CIA planned to concentrate its efforts in Vietnam appears in JMWAVE Station Chief Ted Shackley's being transferred to Laos and being assigned to direct covert action programs in Vietnam.

Alberto proposed to Kleberg that he sponsor further infiltrations into Cuba. He hoped to disrupt Castro's shipping. With a budget of a quarter of a million dollars, Alberto argued, he would be able to return to the operations at which he excelled: maritime action with his own task force.

There is no available record of Kleberg's response. JMWAVE's reply was to "handle" Alberto, while ignoring his pleas for renewed operations and maritime sabotage. CIA requested that he provide "analyses of developments in Cuba." In August 1964, Alberto was not included in a CIA-sponsored infiltration into Oriente Province, his home territory.

Alberto was livid. People he himself had recruited were entering Cuba, while the team leader of the project, AMSEED-3, had requested that Alberto be cut out because he was "primarily interested in his own welfare and not Cuba." This was so grotesque a distortion of the reality that even Bob Wall protested. Exile politics were ugly and self-serving, and defeating of what efforts against Castro remained. CIA's obsession with Alberto's "strong stand of not being subordinate to KUBARK or any individual" had a deleterious effect on the objectives CIA professed to embrace.

In a letter to Jeff Allott, Managing Director of the United Molasses Co. Lt. in London, Alberto Fernández makes clear his political position with respect to American businesses operating in Cuba. He tells Allott that his company, and its U.S. subsidiary, would have to "face the rancor of an incensed people" should they return to Cuba.

"Erroneously you may be led to believe that a new Cuba will find the same pre-1959 sugar leaders in power or those of base qualities as those that have now destroyed our sugar riches," he writes. Alberto is acerbic as he charges this molasses company with having operated in Cuba with no regard for the needs of the Cuban people. "We know that ideals and principles are not a factor in your interests," Alberto tells Allott. In the same letter, he requests a financial contribution to his Fund for the Relief of Cuban Exiles.

Of course it was only after the Castro revolution that the issue of agrarian reform became a priority. In a letter to Alberto Fernández on July 10, 1964, Malone talks about Cuban exile farm specialists "working on a program of agrarian reform to be put into effect if Fidel Castro is overthrown. The purpose is to give Cuban peasants hope for a better future and thus a reason to join the movement to oust Castro." Included in the proposal are redistribution of the land and "the use of modern methods for getting maximum production."

In July 1964, William Pawley remained a close acquaintance of Bob Kleberg, and Kleberg accompanied Pawley to a meeting with Richard Nixon. Having spent an hour with Paley and Nixon, Kleberg came away believing that "the three of us saw eye to eye." He was pleased that Pawley and Nixon would work for Goldwater. "We must all work very hard on this matter as it is our best chance," Kleberg thought.

As he attempted to continue his efforts, Alberto had to cover his own gas mileage. He reported to CIA that an American molasses company was "beating the blockade of Cuba by working through its British subsidiary." After his report, some of this molasses company's customers canceled their orders.

Michael J. P. Malone was not entirely pleased. He thought that Alberto in his efforts for his Fund for the Relief of Cuban Exiles should not assess the various people on a fee basis, but should make an appeal on general terms asking for their contribution, with "some sort of a dollar figure" as "a minimum for the cause." Most, he was not pleased that Alberto had spoken of him "as a coordinator."

Malone was not appeased by Alberto's decision not to ask either himself or Czarnikow to contribute. "For many reasons I think it would be best not to have my name appear," Malone said, in response to Alberto's sentence, "I am asking Malone of Czarnikow, who is in close contact with me often, to be a sort of coordinator, for I am absent and away a great deal." This was far too public an exposure for Malone, who preferred several degrees of separation from any kind of notoriety.

Still, Malone raised funds for Alberto from Joe Rubenstone and Joss Edwards; another contributor was J. Y. Edwards of Cargill, Incorporated, who sent $500, "which I hope in a small way will assist you in your important work." Malone checked out contributors with Frank O'Brien at the FBI.

As always, Malone was a dubious ally. There was talk of Alberto visiting Spain and Portugal in October 1964 for fundraising, but that did not materialize either.

In September 1964, Malone approached David Atlee Phillips ("our friend Chivas Regal") with a request from George Braga. The Bragas were concerned about an uprising in Bolivia. Phillips reassured his assets "that this situation will be alright since it appears that the uprising was not a spontaneous affair but has all the elements of having been rigged."

Malone added "Relative to Domingo they are watching this area closely and feel there may be some changes. However, they see no danger from the Left." American corporations not only in Cuba, but in all of Latin America, proceeded with the close advice and consent of the Central Intelligence Agency.

The Agency continued a close watch on Cuba. "The situation," Phillips told Malone, who reported the contact to George A. Braga "continues to deteriorate, economically, politically and psychologically. The ruling group now consists of Fidel, Raúl [his brother], Dorticós and Guevara, in that order . . . estimates of the sugar crop appear to be roughly the same as last year, from the opinion that we get from the Company . . . the opinion was expressed that if our government does no more or less in the months to come there is a good chance that the regime will fall in a year." Hardly an idealist like Alberto Fernández, Malone was, rather, indulging himself and his boss, Braga, in wishful thinking.

"Andrew K. Reuteman," an alias for Ted Shackley, summed up Alberto's situation at this time coldly. "The road of the exile is a hard one at best and for those with pride it is even harder."

Shackley ordered that Alberto now devote himself exclusively to "the intellectual side of the operation."

In 1964, CIA was taking a hard, unfriendly look at Alberto Fernández in terms of its own needs and priorities. His value to KUBARK, it decided, was his knowledge and ability to develop action of various kinds in Oriente Province. It granted his "uncontested integrity." For these reasons, the Agency was willing to keep him "on the string provided he is not too expensive in any one of several ways."

From JMWAVE's cynical point of view, CIA wrote, "he costs very little other than an occasional surge of adrenaline due to some minor act of spite on his part due to some unrealized slight to his pride. Another consideration in making plans for Subject is his financial status. It is now pretty well determined that he is going to have to establish another source of income. How long he will continue to stretch his family's resources cannot be determined . . ." There is little compassion or gratitude in this assessment.

Yet the Agency had to grant that Alberto Fernández, his pride not-withstanding, "provides an otherwise unavailable and unmatchable source of operational knowledge." No less, Alberto was an "astute analyst," and invaluable to them.

CIA's faulty understanding of his history indicates how little it knew of Alberto Fernández. "Formerly of ministerial rank," is how one CIA document describes him. This was never the case.

By September 1964, Alberto himself had concluded that there were "deep divisions within the ranks of the Agency." Clarence had been one thing; Bob Wall, another. One faction battled another for power, on ideological grounds, and there was "no responsible leadership." "As of today," he had concluded, the U.S. has no potential to do anything in Cuba if it so wished, unless through direct action of the U.S. armed forces."

He believed that CIA had "wasted the years 1961, 1962, and 1963 learning modes of operation into Cuba that we already knew but that in their Oedipus complex had to be done their way. And learned all over again. While we fiddle, Fidel protected his coast with radar and picket boats, so that no infiltration can go long undetected."

He analyzed the Cuban population, living as it was in "an efficient police state": "5% will fight for Fidel; 15% is entrapped in its militia and bureaucratic system and probably at first will have to give some semblance of support to the regime; 40% against but fence sitters or too weak to fight until the result is obvious; 20% who will fight violently against." It was now September 1964, and he concluded, "There will be no internal upheavals." He had long known that "there is no internal or external leadership to guide or lead."

Based in part on Dionisio Pastrana's missions into Cuba, Alberto also concluded that "in the countryside, the lower the level of farmers economically, the more violent is their desire to fight and cooperate." He thought, "The country as a whole is fully ripe for Civil War of a violence not known in modern times—even worse than the Spanish Civil War."

Alberto Fernández was disgusted that "one hundred Russians in Cuba are enough to paralyze the U.S.," and concluded, "The U.S. might step in if no Russians are around." Demonstrating the shrewdness for which CIA had always given him credit, Alberto writes, "The fear of Cubans attacking Russians is the biggest worry of the U.S. apparatus." Of "Fidel's economic bungling," he was not alone in being convinced.

Of CIA's penetration of Castro's Cuba, he was persuaded. "I must say that I do believe that through direct penetration of the Cuban armed forces and spheres of government, the Co. does know probably more than we suppose of what goes on inside the Cuban government. To this must be added what the U.S. finds out through allied and neutral diplomats." His experience had taught him not to underestimate KUBARK.

Still, he had learned from his Washington contacts that in the first eight months of 1964, a total of 255 English and another 280 Greek and Lebanese merchantmen had gone to Cuba. "These are what we want to hit," he writes, flashing his customary militancy.

"The U.S. through the Co. [CIA] cannot be a party to this *matter,*" [italics in the original], he was certain. "Hence we must do it on our own, not even confiding in the Co. for example: attacks on maritime shipping. . . . Those who think as we do *must participate* in the final process to have a voice in the future Cuba."

Alberto Fernández was nothing if not if a Quixotic figure, as his references to Cervantes in our interviews suggest. "Cuba will be free on its own in from one to two years hence," he writes in 1964, even as, all his life, he would remember his friend Dan Taylor's words: "I want you to know, you'll never go back to Cuba."

Meanwhile he requested of "Uncle" through Malone support "up to August of next year. As I must move about and activate myself further," he writes, "I may need up to one third additional support of what I have requested per month for personal use." He was utilizing off September and October of 1964 "for work in gathering funds from Cuban sources."

By now, all CIA factions agreed that Alberto Fernández could not be trusted to place the interests of CIA above his determination to unseat Fidel Castro. Persistently, Alberto refused, as late as October 1963, to accept funds from CIA. He told Wall that he would no longer accept his operational expenses fund "because the presence of the money was actually costing him more in the long run than if he didn't receive any."

Malone wrote to Alberto Fernández on November 23, 1964, about a "newspaper" called *Ramparts* which is "Catholic" but "ultra-liberal."

Alberto Fernández's final meeting with Bob Wall took place in February 1965. They met in Wall's automobile. Wall instructed Alberto to respect the security of KUBARK's activities and to remain silent about everything. It was as if the struggle to liberate Cuba had been all along about CIA.

Alberto would now be utilized by CIA only "at the statesman level." Since Alberto had not obeyed its wishes voluntarily, CIA had taken steps. Polite as always, offering no rebuttal, Alberto said he would call the next day. Then he got out of the car and walked off.

Only now did CIA "reimburse" Alberto Fernández for its previous uses of the *Tejana*. Payment took the form of a $20,000 paper liquidation of his debts, rather than cash. For the record, CIA denied any liability for damages to the boat or "the validity of any claims." Malone's name appears on this final document.

Alberto had planned to go to Spain to see his father after taking one of his daughters to school in New York on September 15th. Instead, he returned to Miami to meet his new handler.

KUBARK now offered Alberto $100 a month for use of his automobile and an oral commitment of $750 a month to him as a "field agent." Information from and about him would be distributed by CIA "within a narrow field." Acknowledging "the patriotic manner in which you serve this struggle," as well as "the personal sacrifices, including heavy financial contributions, that the fight has cost you," CIA demanded that Alberto sign a statement releasing CIA "from all claims arising out of or in conjunction with the use of the *Tejana.*" A man of honor, he complied.

So CIA claimed victory over Alberto Fernández, who emerged with the hard-earned wisdom that KUBARK had scant interest in the liberation of Cuba. The Agency was confident that Alberto had "accepted the fact that KUBARK and ODYOKE represent the sole means by which Cuba can be liberated."

Alberto Fernández de Hechavarría was now forty-seven years old, with more than four decades of life in exile before him.

CHAPTER 9

ENDGAME: CUBA

"We promise nothing. The world
promises us nothing."
                                    Robert J. Kleberg, Jr.

Michael J. P. Malone had kept watch over Gustavo de los Reyes as he languished during his four-year ordeal of, as he put it, "enduring hunger," at Fidel Castro's Isle of Pines prison. The building had been wired to blow up should there be another "Yankee" invasion, the inmates had been informed. High-power explosives had been placed all around the prison foundation.

The atmosphere was suffused with terror. "We fear, therefore we exist," the prisoners joked among themselves. Emaciated, Gustavo de los Reyes hung on, editing a prison newsletter.

One of his cellmates was a philosophy professor. On the walls of the cell they had written a passage from Lord Byron's *The Prisoner of Chillon*. Byron's words, as de los Reyes remembered them, served to reinforce their courage: "My hair is gray but not with years/Nor grew it white in a single night . . . Eternal Spirit of the Chainless Mind!/Brightest in dungeons, Liberty! Thou art."

De los Reyes would conclude that there was no "better anti-Communist text than a Communist book," even as he feared that he might be "subjected to a new trial for subversion of prisoners and that this would end my life, [being] shot against the wall."

Alfonso Fanjul approached former Ambassador Earl E. T. Smith and Prince Stanislaus Radziwill, John F. Kennedy's brother-in-law. Smith in turn wrote to Bobby Kennedy on behalf of de los Reyes. No help materialized.

Malone had not been idle with regard to Gustavo's plight. In June 1962, Malone had requested of Charles Matt that CIA use its influence to have de los Reyes transferred to the farm outside the main prison area. "We know of no such mechanism," Matt said, unmoved. "If we get any information as to how this might be done, we'll let him know." CIA offered no assistance.

Early in 1964, Swiss Ambassador Emil Stadelhofer, still representing U.S. interests in Cuba, devised a plan. "I have a way of getting Gustavo out of prison if he's willing to do what we want him to do," Stadelhofer told Gustavo's sister, Sylvia Weaver. The plan was for Gustavo to serve as an intermediary for Fidel Castro and travel to Washington, D.C., with a message from the "Maximum Leader."

The message to be delivered to the U.S. government was that Castro would reimburse the American owners of the confiscated properties on the island and release a number of political prisoners in exchange for a restoration of the pre-Castro sugar quota. Stadelhofer had convinced Castro that the emissary should not be someone who was part of his government. Gustavo's American education at Georgetown, his connections, and his seemingly "timid character" made him the ideal messenger.

Pretending to go along with the scheme, de los Reyes was released. He carried with him the "grub bowl" that he had used in prison and had to spend a month in a hospital just to be presentable enough to appear in public. Then he was invited to a party at the Mexican embassy in Havana where he was scrutinized (subtly, he told me) by Russians who spoke better Castilian Spanish than he did. He was assisted not only by Stadelhofer, but by Mexican Ambassador Gilberto Bosques and, to a lesser extent, as Richard Helms put it, "by the Brazilian Ambassador Bastian Pinto." Annie Boissevain, the wife of the former Dutch ambassador, was also involved.

On February 14th, another cattleman who had been a leader in the cattlemen's conspiracy, Armando Caíñas Milanés, was also released from prison.

De los Reyes agreed to everything. He accepted that death might "accidentally" befall him should he betray his mission. On February 25th, Stadelhofer put him on a *Cubana de Aviación* plane bound for Mexico City. There, at the U.S. embassy, he was given an American residency card.

CIA officers swarmed around him. He ran into that ubiquitous CIA officer David Atlee Phillips.

"Do you know me?" Phillips said slyly. All de los Reyes remembered about Phillips was that he "worked for the Company." He did not betray the details of his mission to these CIA operatives.

Gustavo's trust in CIA had evaporated in 1959 and was never restored. Gustavo de los Reyes had not forgotten the chilly reception of Allen Dulles' meeting with the cattlemen. Nor had he forgotten Dulles' betrayal of their confidence, his reporting on the meeting when he had promised not to do so.

De los Reyes told a CIA officer whom he met in Mexico City on February 24th that he had been chosen by Fidel Castro "to serve as a messenger to the United States government to offer release of all political prisoners in Cuba and their families in return for a U.S. pledge of no invasion of Cuba by either U.S. forces or Cuban exiles." There were 20,000 people in jail at the time; they were to be allowed to go to a country of their choice. De los Reyes did not reveal the terms of his actual mission.

When he arrived at the fourth floor of the State Department in Washington, D.C., de los Reyes met with George White at the

Cuban desk and delivered Castro's message. Then he added, "I would rather go back and die in that jail than see this proposal accepted by the U.S. government. The great majority of the political prisoners feel exactly the same way."

White colored with anger when de los Reyes would say no more.

"Do you know what you're exposing yourself to?" White said.

"I'm willing to talk only to Mr. Robert Kleberg, Jr., owner of the King Ranch," de los Reyes said. Only after Kleberg granted his permission would de los Reyes talk to the CIA representative.

When Malone arrived, de los Reyes informed him of Castro's proposition. Only now did de los Reyes produce the eleven-page document outlining the sugar trade agreements Cuba had signed with Communist countries that he had brought with him. It contained dates of delivery and prices of sugar per pound, and revealed Cuba's five-year agreement to deliver sugar to the Soviet Union, China, Czechoslovakia, East Germany, and Poland. It outlined how the molasses trade worked. An agreement with Czechoslovakia sent Cuban tobacco, manganese, and nickel in exchange for textiles, power plant equipment machinery, and vehicles. In the hope that Castro might yet be unseated, all intelligence regarding the Cuban economy was welcome. For de los Reyes, courage was by now second nature.

Reader's Digest

In the United States for good, de los Reyes, now fifty years old, decided to write an article describing his prison ordeal. He would expose the visits of Castro's "indoctrinator" to the Isle of Pines, and the brutal conditions of his imprisonment. He had a title: "Communism: High Crime in Cuba." De los Reyes was also bitter at the "compliance, the forgetfulness and the lack of understanding" of the "free world" regarding his plight.

Malone suggested as a venue the CIA-connected *Reader's Digest*. They had also considered *Look* magazine as a venue to which Malone had access, but settled on *Reader's Digest*. Two years earlier, George Braga had enlisted Malone to ask Jim Monahan at *Reader's Digest* to publish one of "Nate White's" articles; the relationship between Malone, CIA, and this magazine was long-standing.

The process of de los Reyes' article finding its way to publication revealed CIA to have infiltrated *Reader's Digest* at the highest levels. De los Reyes' experience with the magazine was fraught with conflict, with Malone in constant touch with CIA officers, and censorship the rule rather than the exception.

When de los Reyes agreed to submit his article to *Reader's Digest,* he was entirely unaware of CIA's influence at the magazine. He couldn't have imagined that he would be writing his article under CIA scrutiny, with Malone acquiescing, hovering nearby, all things to all people.

On April 6, 1964, Kleberg wrote to Hoover, sending him a report by Gustavo de los Reyes about his prison stay in Cuba. "I thought you would find it of interest," Kleberg added. He closed his letter with "Sincerely, your friend, Robert J. Kleberg, Jr."

For years, among his many favors to CIA was that Malone acted as an agent for *Reader's Digest.* In June 1962, when the Cuban government confiscated the color printing press belonging to the magazine, and was about to sell and ship it to a buyer in a "friendly" nation, Malone had enlisted Alberto Fernández to find out the name of the consignee, destination, name of the ship, and date of shipment of the dismantled "extremely valuable" press.

Behind de los Reyes' back, Malone first approached CIA's Al Rodemeyer. Rodemeyer then put Malone in touch with Ken Gilmore, the *Reader's Digest* editor based in Washington, D.C., who was known to be closest to the Agency. Gilmore's sister had worked for CIA and his brother was a USIA (United States Information Agency) official in New Delhi. Gilmore's taste ran to "cloak-and-dagger" spy stories.

Reader's Digest had operated under the sway of CIA from the early days of the Agency when it printed disinformation on behalf of CIA's Operation GLADIO in Italy.

In 1947, through its Office of Policy Coordination, an early name for CIA's clandestine services, the Agency recruited from the Marseilles docks a Corsican criminal named Pierre Ferri-Pisani to assist in influencing the coming general election in Italy. In this earliest of CIA's murder operations, CIA unleashed both a paramilitary operation and psychological warfare to ensure that in the 1948 elections the Christian Democrats would defeat the left-wing coalition of the Italian Communist and Socialist parties.

Assisting CIA were veterans of Mussolini's secret police and a variety of Mafia reliables. The terrorist attacks that ensued under Operation GLADIO were attributed to the left. When the Director of Central Intelligence, Admiral Roscoe H. Hillenkoeter, was dubious of the methods employed under GLADIO, he turned to CIA's Chief Counsel Lawrence Houston, who acknowledged that GLADIO was illegal. "You do not have the authority," Houston told Hillenkoeter, after the fact.

From then on, *Reader's Digest* enjoyed "most favored status" with CIA. By the time he met Gustavo de los Reyes, Gilmore had, according to author Peter Canning, "participated in dozens of CIA-connected *Reader's Digest* projects." (Canning does not write about de los Reyes' experience.) With *Reader's Digest*'s capability of listening in on telephone calls, one editor remarked, "You might as well be working for the CIA."

Malone arranged for de los Reyes to fly to Washington. In June 1964, Rodemeyer sent him a typewriter so that he could write the article in his hotel room. In charge of the project at *Reader's Digest* would be Gilmore and Senior Editor James Monahan, who had edited CIA asset Dr. Tom Dooley's memoir, *Deliver Us From Evil*, which had been condensed in the magazine. Together, Gilmore and Monahan had authored *The Great Deception: The Inside Story of How the Kremlin Took Cuba*. Both were blatant CIA assets.

Knowing he required CIA guidance for such a sensitive subject, Monahan requested that Malone solicit advice about the editing of the de los Reyes article from someone with significant authority at the Agency. Malone chose Charles Matt. When Malone reported to Matt about de los Reyes' effort for *Reader's Digest,* Malone admitted that he was acting as an intermediary for *Reader's Digest's* senior editor James Monahan. If Malone "could furnish us an advanced copy of the article, we would be willing to make informal, unofficial comments for their information," Matt said.

In July 1964, Malone reported to Al Rodemeyer that Ken Gilmore would have the article ready for November publication. Then, in August, to the dismay of de los Reyes, Gilmore suddenly dropped out of communication. De los Reyes contacted Malone, who was baffled.

"Can you give me any direction on this?" Malone wrote Ken Gilmore on September 3rd. De los Reyes suspected that "Kenneth wants to write the article himself," which was but half the story. Puzzled, de los Reyes tried at least to ensure "that they will not publish anything without our previous consent." All of this resembles the Stalinist government in the late 1930s affixing the poet Boris Pasternak's name to manifestos he never signed.

As de los Reyes sat in his Washington hotel room, negotiations with *Reader's Digest* abruptly resumed and he received an edited manuscript. Armed with the blue pencil of CIA censorship, Gilmore had cut a passage describing how the U.S. government (and the U.N.) had known that the prison on the Isle of Pines had been mined to blow up should there be another armed invasion of Cuba. Gone was a reference to the "ingenuity of the American people" in not facing up to what was happening in Cuba. Gone was de los Reyes' astonishment at how little his American friends knew of what was going on inside Cuba.

Gone as well was the contrast between the "superior classes" who fled Cuba and the "humble classes without the means to escape," who "had to remain in Cuba and fight." These cuts suggested that CIA was reacting to the implied criticism of its betrayal of people like Alberto Fernández, and all those who saw through CIA's pretense that it planned to liberate Cuba.

Gone were such lines as: "The prison was the only free territory that was left in my country" and "There is not a better anti-Communist text than a Communist book." Gone were ironic anecdotes like one about the arrival at the prison of survivors of the fight in the Escambray: "It was as if these mountain peasants after going through Russia had arrived again to a free Cuba." Gone too was a passage about an "abnormal American called Herman":

> To create even among us hatred against Americans, the chief of the shooting squads was an abnormal American called Herman. This guy was to come frequently to the grated door of those condemned to die to behold with a smile what he called in his bad Spanish "the fresh meat" that he had prepared for that night.

And gone was the passionate outcry of the Cuban Underground betrayed by their supposed CIA allies. They all had the same story:

> We did not receive from abroad the arms and ammunition that they promised us . . . if we had not been betrayed we would have been able to resist . . . Will not the free world understand that we are all fighting for the same cause? But the free world remained insensible because consciousness of the meaning of the word "liberty" had been lost.

Deleted by CIA as well were all the references to de los Reyes' unsatisfactory meeting with Allen Dulles, an event that he had described in full in the original version of the article.

Alarmed, de los Reyes requested an assurance from *Reader's Digest* that they "will not publish anything without our previous consent." Then he telephoned Kleberg.

"Remain in Washington," Kleberg said. "Hold firm. Don't leave anything out."

One morning, de los Reyes received a call from the hotel lobby. Two gentlemen wished to talk with him in his room. De los Reyes refused to see them.

"But, sir, they're FBI agents," the hotel employee said.

When the men arrived at de los Reyes' room, they identified themselves as former United States Army officers, another surfacing of how CIA and the military operated in tandem, and how CIA's rise to power rested on the support of the military.

"We've read your article. Although we know you are telling the truth, we're asking you to cut some things because they're detrimental to the prestige of the United States," one of the men said. It was CIA-speak: "United States" was, again, a euphemism for CIA.

"The detrimental thing is not to tell the truth," de los Reyes said. "I'm in a free country."

It was a stalemate. De los Reyes returned home to Palm Beach. Three months passed. Then Kleberg telephoned. It was at once clear. When it came to CIA's control of the media, even Robert J. Kleberg, Jr. was powerless.

"Let them do what they want because it's better to tell the public something of what is happening on the island than to tell them nothing," Kleberg said. "Isn't it better to get something published?"

Kleberg left it to Malone further to spell out his message. "*Reader's Digest* is the best medium to get your story across since it is also being published in Spanish and Portuguese," Malone told de los Reyes. Later the article would appear in other languages as well.

Before long, *Reader's Digest* sent a representative to Palm Beach with the final CIA-edited manuscript in hand. De los Reyes was instructed to sign his name. Under oath, he was to swear that nothing had been removed or changed from the original.

"It's against my honor to accept this," he said. "Everything in there is a lie. Critical facts have been distorted." Then he capitulated out of his passionate need that at least a portion of his experience reach the public. Compromise is not pleasant, but in Cuban as in other arenas it is, alas, the rule rather than the exception. Let de los Reyes be forgiven for taking the seasoned advice of Robert J. Kleberg, Jr.

CIA controlled the time of publication, as Malone conveyed to de los Reyes: "From certain information that I have had from what we call the 'Company,'" Malone wrote, "it seems as though publication in the January [1965] issue will be most timely." The article, "Imprisoned by Castro," appeared in May 1965.

Malone copied this letter to Al Rodemeyer at CIA; to Alfonso Fanjul; to George A. Braga; and to RJK, Robert Kleberg, Jr. Malone continued to collaborate with CIA on articles to be published in *Reader's Digest*. One about Brazil was passed from Malone to Kleberg—prior to publication.

In 1964 as well, Kleberg happened upon an article by the despised Herbert Matthews, published in Stanford University's *Hispanic American Report*. Still hoping to silence Matthews, who had been so instrumental in granting Fidel Castro credibility with the U.S. public, Kleberg forwarded it to J. Edgar Hoover. "I would be very glad to discuss these matters with you at your convenience," Kleberg wrote Hoover.

Hoover passed the Matthews article to Special Agent M. A. Jones, who reported to the FBI's third-in-command, Cartha DeLoach. Jones summarized the article grimly. Matthews was, indeed, "very laudatory of Castro." Matthews was still attempting "to alibi away Castro's Communist affiliations" with the argument that prior to the revolution, Cuba was "an economic colony of the United States." The purpose of the revolution had been "to break this domination."

Noting that Kleberg was not only "a wealthy and influential businessman," but also "very friendly to the Bureau," Jones recommended that Hoover send Kleberg a short, cordial letter. Hoover complied. "I found the article most illuminating," Hoover wrote as he extended an invitation for Kleberg to visit with him when next he traveled to Washington. It was Hoover hedging his bets, holding his cards close to his vest, and thinking first of protecting the Bureau from unnecessary exposure, as showing open favoritism

to Kleberg might have done. Then Hoover had the entire correspondence placed in Herbert Matthews' hefty FBI file.

Cedral

Having arrived in the United States without a penny in his pocket,
as he put it, Gustavo de los Reyes found employment for a year
managing a Florida breeding ranch that was owned by Gulf & Western. One day he received a call from Alfonso Fanjul, whose son,
Alfie, was married to de los Reyes' daughter, Tina. Robert J. Kleberg,
Jr. was visiting Palm Beach and wished to meet with him.

"Do you want to work with me?" Kleberg said. If Bob liked you,
Gustavo concluded, you were friends for life.

"Why didn't you ask me earlier?" de los Reyes said.

"I was watching you to see if you could fend for yourself,"
Kleberg said. He paused. "Where do you want to go?"

De los Reyes chose Venezuela, where he had friends. Kleberg
demurred. "Venezuela is no good," he said. "The people are not
honest." He preferred Colombia, the most politically conservative
country in all of Latin America.

"Venezuela is where we're needed," Gustavo said. "We can be an
exception."

By November 1964, de los Reyes was in Venezuela touring
the ranch of that "good friend" of Kleberg's, Nelson Rockefeller. Santa Gertrudis cattle grazed peacefully on the land. Not
that Kleberg ever exhibited any reverence for a Rockefeller. Once
at a conference, Kleberg listened to a long, windy discourse by
Nelson Rockefeller. Finally, Rockefeller arrived at the subject of
agriculture. From the respectful silence, Robert J. Kleberg's voice
boomed out.

"Nelson, you don't know anything about agriculture!" Kleberg
said.

Their Venezuelan adventure began with a trip in a single-
engine Cessna with John Armstrong. They slept in hammocks in

a dilapidated house and subsisted on *arepas* and coffee. The next morning they rode out onto the savannah in silence.

"I like it," Kleberg said. There were no wasted words.

De los Reyes named King Ranch Venezuela "*Cedral.*" He placed the running "W" brand at the top of the entrance gate, along with a favorite Kleberg motto: "*Operibus Credite et Non Verbis*" (Credit deeds and not words). As his manager, de los Reyes hired John Barclay Armstrong, the son of Tobin and Anne Armstrong, and nephew of John Armstrong. Barclay would resign when his mother was appointed ambassador to the Court of St. James's, and he was required to return to Texas to manage the family ranch.

They began near San Felipe, in the state of Yaracuy, surrounded by a dense jungle filled with snakes, jaguars, and insects; they cleared the wooded valleys and planted grass. Then came the white Brahma and cherry-red Santa Gertrudis cattle.

When de los Reyes requested more Brahma bulls because in that climate they alone possessed the sweat glands needed to refresh the animal, Kleberg was surprised. Kleberg believed he had created in the Santa Gertrudis a breed that could withstand anything. It was not quite so.

On one visit to *Cedral*, he inspected a herd of cows.

"What have you done with the cattle?" Kleberg demanded.

"Nothing," de los Reyes said.

"Well, then, don't touch them," Kleberg said. He deferred to others, but only when he had examined a situation firsthand. Control, trusting first himself, had been the habit of Robert K. Kleberg, Jr. since he had taken over King Ranch when he was in his early twenties.

When de los Reyes revealed his accomplishments in the *llanos*, which had the largest flood plain in the world, Kleberg was impressed. He may have been taciturn, but he was never short of praise for those who fulfilled his expectations of them.

"I did it with your help," de los Reyes said. "Without you, nothing would have been accomplished."

During these years, Kleberg's customary reading was cowboy novels. One day, de los Reyes presented him with a copy of Machiavelli's *The Prince*.

"This man is a son-of-a-bitch," Kleberg said when he was done.

"I gave it to you to defend yourself," de los Reyes said. "To warn you to be cautious with man."

"I already know that," Kleberg said. "I thought you wanted me to imitate him!"

Over the years, de los Reyes came to enjoy Kleberg's bluntness, his rapid coming to a point, his impatience with self-censorship. At a manager's reunion, at which de los Reyes was present, Kleberg listened impatiently as his nephew Bobby Shelton rattled on and on.

"Bobby, sit down!" Kleberg called out. "You're talking too much!"

To *Cedral*, the King Ranch in Venezuela, managed by Gustavo de los Reyes for twenty years, Kleberg invited friends like the president of the Metropolitan Museum of Art and writers Arthur Miller, William Styron, and John Updike, along with such CIA favorites as the Shah of Iran and his wife, Farah Diba. Kleberg and Malone were likely to fly to Venezuela at any time in a plane loaded with daiquiris.

The guerrilla movement led by Douglas Bravo took hold in Venezuela.

"You ever run from anything?" Kleberg said when he heard.

"Nothing that I can remember," de los Reyes replied.

"Neither have I," Kleberg said, picking up his battered old hat. "I'll need this when I come back to San Felipe." And that was that.

Later Kleberg gave de los Reyes a plaque that read: "To the immensely honest and trustworthy Gustavo de los Reyes." It suggests the credo of both men.

Kleberg's reliance on CIA, his belief in its efficacy and its capacity for good, had retreated into disenchantment. He still continued quietly to provide money to anti-Castro exiles, at times using labor columnist Victor Riesel as his intermediary. Riesel spoke out in his newspaper column against Castro and thereby earned a financial contribution from Kleberg. Kleberg employed Cuban refugees at King Ranch until they could return to the struggle.

Near Lake Okeechobee and Belle Glade, in Florida, he bought a ranch called the "Big B" and arranged that it be run entirely by anti-Castro refugees. The land was swampy and flat, and Santa Gertrudis cattle did not thrive there. Jack Malone was a director of that enterprise, too. Exiled Cubans also were given an opportunity to work at King Ranch in Australia. Worldwide, King Ranch was operating on 13 million acres. What mattered was that Kleberg kept always in mind those who had been displaced from their lives in Cuba.

Unlike entrepreneurs of a later time, Kleberg did whatever he could to alleviate the suffering of those whose plights came to his attention. In his later years he lived well, but his compassion and generosity, under the radar of public notice as they remained, were legion. Without sentimentality, he appreciated other human beings, and their needs mattered to him.

The oil revenues that flowed unendingly to King Ranch were channeled to Kleberg's overwhelming purpose, which was to feed the hungry with beef. Grandiose as it seems, his goal was to feed the world. He saw this purpose as exciting, worth the day's effort. It was the right thing to do, and he expected nothing in return. He was too worldly to wish to be noticed for his achievements and efforts.

Robert J. Kleberg, Jr. would never have spoken such words, but they represented his credo. Privilege in itself meant little to him. All his life he had served as the caretaker of the legacy of his grandfather, Captain Richard King, and he took that responsibility seriously. He was a man whose life belongs to the history of this republic.

By now, Robert J. Kleberg, Jr. was a man accustomed to meeting the head of state of every country he visited. Outwardly, he was not a social reformer; he seemed not to have concerned himself with developing a social program that might serve the needs of the Cuban people should Fidel Castro leave office. Rather, at times he behaved in his last years even recklessly, as when on safari with Major Tom Armstrong he spent an evening shooting out lanterns swinging from the trees.

He enjoyed his racing stables, even as the horses and stables were owned not by himself, but by the King Ranch Corporation. King Ranch had long owned a thoroughbred farm in Kentucky. Kleberg took his own form of risks, paying a million dollars for *Canonero*, a horse with no pedigree. Having criticized the jockey during the 1972 Belmont, Kleberg admitted, after *Canonero* had won, that he had been wrong.

"He was on the saddle—I was not," Kleberg said. "That often happens with managers." He was a seasoned man, and a worldly one. His guest that day was the president of Citibank. Through the lens of that outing, Kleberg might be seen as just another member of the corporate elite whose office walls were adorned by photographs of the horses who had won for him.

Kleberg had bet $10 on *Canonero*. He won $25,000. Then he handed his winnings over to Gustavo de los Reyes to distribute among Venezuelan charities. A third went to Jack Malone's Knights of Malta.

On a collective farm in Georgia, Union of the Soviet Socialist Republics, a businessman on tour spotted a herd of lusty red cows grazing. Some were branded with an upside down "W" with a bar drawn under it. This was the *Becerra* brand, denoting Santa Gertrudis cattle born in Cuba. Others bore the running "W" of Santa Gertrudis cattle native to King Ranch in Texas. The Soviet Union had enforced its Faustian bargain with Fidel Castro. Soviet aid had not come cheap.

So the Soviets seized what had been Kleberg's prized Santa Gertrudis animals as payment in part for the oil and the arms they had sent to Cuba, and the red cattle made the long journey to the USSR. It was a portion of the price Cuba paid for what was something less than Soviet beneficence. By 1975, half of the income from the Cuban sugar crop was going to the Soviet Union to settle Cuba's debt.

Marabou reclaimed the land that had once been *Compañía Ganadera Becerra.*

Farewell to Robert J. Kleberg, Jr., Farewell to "the Company"

No sentimentalist, Bob Kleberg perceived that Alberto's struggle had been lost. He had deserved better from "the Company." Now it was time to move on. Kleberg instructed Malone to call Alberto.

"Uncle wants to talk to you," Malone said. Kleberg was flying from Texas to Florida especially to see Alberto. Accompanying Kleberg in his private plane were the grandchildren who, after Helen Kleberg's early death, had become the cheerful companions of his final years. Kleberg put up at the Kenilworth in Bal Harbour. He arranged a private dinner at a restaurant frequented by racing aficionados like himself.

In the middle of dinner, Kleberg rose from his seat. He tapped his glass with a spoon.

"If any of you repeat anything you hear today," he said, "you will incur my wrath forever.

"I'm going to address myself to Alberto," Kleberg went on. He wished first to honor the many sacrifices Alberto had made for a struggle that Kleberg had embraced as his own. Now Kleberg had a proposal.

"I appreciate Alberto's commitment to rid Cuba of Fidel Castro," he continued. But clearly it was not meant to be. Kleberg had long known that neither the U.S. government nor CIA had a serious commitment to removing Castro from power.

"There's a large jungle area in Brazil on the Amazon, the *Mato Grosso,*" Kleberg continued. In partnership with Swift Meat Packing, King Ranch already was a formidable presence in Brazil where it operated as "King Ranch *do Brasil.*" Now Kleberg proposed to buy a chunk of land and create a steer-feeding operation in that country. Alberto would run it.

"I'll buy this forest only if Alberto agrees to be in charge," Kleberg added. It didn't sit right with Robert J. Kleberg, Jr. to leave

Alberto Fernández empty-handed after all he had committed to the struggle, how much he had lost.

Alberto did not hesitate before rendering his decision.

"I can't give this up, I can't leave this," he said. He declined Kleberg's offer, one that would have restored him to financial solvency, as a similar proposal had rescued Gustavo de los Reyes.

Some time later, Alberto phoned Kleberg.

"It would have been a failure, you know," he said. The *Mato Grosso* receives 125 inches of rainfall a year, washing out the minerals from the soil. You couldn't grow grass. Plus, no white man could survive there. One amoeba goes to the heart, the other to the groin.

Alberto Fernández de Hechavarría and Robert J. Kleberg, Jr. were never to meet again.

Alberto labored on. He despaired of Cuba now. Having lost all faith in CIA, he wrote a paper on the subject of land reform programs in Latin America that he urged the U.S. to oppose. On December 22, 1965, he sent his recommendations to Michael J. P. Malone with instructions that Malone forward the document to J. Edgar Hoover.

Hoover was a master at knowing when not to cross the boundary between his agency and CIA. Hoover told Malone himself to "communicate with appropriate governmental agencies."

In a despairing letter of 1966, Alberto once again voiced his disenchantment with CIA. "There is no longer any trust," he writes in a memorandum. "The best trained and experienced men have dispersed to look after their survival." He is, of course, referring to himself.

"The 'friends' with whom we have collaborated for five long years have expressed their wish for no further semi-joint work and for many months our relations have been very superficial," he relates. Quixotically, he hopes that some U.S. "citizens of means" would unite with "some Cubans" to accomplish the goal. "There is nothing else," he concludes.

At the turn of the New Year 1966, Kleberg had Michael J. P. Malone write to J. Edgar Hoover regarding his own views on the

subject of land reform in Latin America. He also requested that
Hoover bring the matter "to the attention of the proper officials in
the State Department, AID, and members of Congress, so that a full
review might be made of the land reform problems to date."

Kleberg sought Hoover's help in persuading our government not to
"undertake continued support of 'land reform' programs unless such a
study indicates that they in fact accomplish the objectives claimed for
them at a cost commensurate with the results." He had lost his ranch
in Cuba and feared that his other King Ranch properties in Latin
America, Brazil, Argentina, and Venezuela might meet a similar fate.

"It is simply not consistent with human nature to assume that
large numbers of inexperienced people can be transformed into successful operators of agricultural properties simply by being given a
tract of land," Kleberg writes. Even government grants and government directions of their efforts would not be enough.

Yet as sympathetic as Hoover was to Kleberg, and as appreciative
of his position as a man of wealth and influence, Hoover stepped
back. The matter was "not within the investigative jurisdiction of the
FBI," Hoover replied, as he had done to Malone when he had presented Alberto's memo. "I can only suggest that you communicate
with appropriate governmental agencies regarding these matters."

Investigating the Kennedy assassination in New Orleans,
Orleans Parish District Attorney Jim Garrison wondered about the
CIA connections of the Louisiana-born *Tejana* captain, Lawrence
Laborde. Laborde was sufficiently troubled to contact the local CIA
field office and request direction.

Garrison was casting a wide net. Whoever had a connection with
both CIA and Cuban operations might have some connection to the
Kennedy assassination, even as Lee Harvey Oswald was spotted at
an anti-Castro training camp north of Lake Pontchartrain in the
company of David Ferrie, Garrison's chief suspect. CIA's David
Atlee Phillips, Chivas Regal himself, had been present there as well.
Garrison hoped to learn some things from Lawrence Laborde and
he called him in. Laborde at once made himself scarce.

Before long, Laborde's son Michael appeared at Garrison's office at Tulane and Broad on a fishing expedition. Inevitably, Alberto Fernández's name came up.

Michael Laborde then rushed off to report on the meeting to the FBI. Soon David Atlee Phillips, now CIA's Chief of the Western Hemisphere, Cuban Operations Group, knew everything that had been said. Laborde was to make four visits to Tulane and Broad.

In October 1967, Phillips ordered that JMWAVE terminate all contact with Alberto Fernández.

At the turn of the New Year 1968, Phillips articulated his concerns. There were "potential security hazards" in CIA's dealing in any manner now with Alberto Fernández. It was not, of course, the security of the country that was at stake—not then, and not later, when CIA would regularly invoke this pretext as a means of keeping its operations secret.

What was at stake, rather, was the secrecy of CIA's illegal operations. A document of the period notes that CIA assets Robert K. Brown, later editor of *Soldier of Fortune* magazine, and Martin Xavier Casey, who was involved in two CIA-financed invasions of Haiti, had been spotted on board the *Tejana.*

CIA officers at JMWAVE, considering that Alberto was so well connected and articulate, decided, "An abrupt break in contact might offend Fernández and result in his complaining to several high-level friends in Washington." Alberto's termination would have to arrive "in a friendly manner." Should Alberto wish again to contact CIA, however, he would have to use a Washington, D.C., post office box. This he should utilize "only in event necessary to transmit important info and not to be used for trivial correspondence."

Alberto now went to work using his training as an engineer. His employer was a Canadian construction company. Alberto worked for them for ten years.

In 1994, in Washington on the occasion of a grandson's graduation from Georgetown University, Alberto called on his old Princeton classmate, William Colby, long having been a "retired" (actually fired) Director of Central Intelligence. They descended to Colby's office, which was in his basement, where they discussed whether a Phoenix program like the one Colby had run in Vietnam might have been enlisted to protect the Cuban Underground.

They met four times, twice at Colby's house, twice outside. Colby was driving around Washington, D.C., in a British MG with the top down, as if he were a college student. His wife had been an Under Secretary of State for the Antilles, and Alberto eyed her warily. She did not make a good impression on him, and he wondered about her loyalty to his old friend.

He would have liked to help, Colby said, but there was nothing more to be done. "Never come back to this town," Colby said during their final encounter, reinforcing Alberto's suspicion that there were deep divisions within CIA. The opposing faction would not have approved of Colby's even talking to Alberto Fernández. When Colby, a master sailor, perished in a canoeing accident soon after their final meeting, Alberto wondered whether "CIA bumped him off." It was not inconceivable.

Further Endgames

During the final years of his life, Robert J. Kleberg, Jr. drank heavily, while holding together his empire of King Ranches. Still he brandished his particular competence. He carried a leather case stitched with King Ranch insignia, custom-made by the King Ranch saddlery, that he dubbed his "mobile drinks cabinet." Ever greedy for dividends from the King Ranch oil revenues, his relatives continued to oppose his "overseas empire."

As always, Kleberg held them at bay. Money remained a taboo subject. Even as he had criticized those around him if they gained weight, he now grew paunchy. To some, it seemed that he had lost his customary discipline.

Lyndon Johnson had not vanished entirely from his life. On the rare occasions that Kleberg telephoned the White House, "Lyndon," always obsequious before this man, dropped everything to take his call. On one occasion, Johnson called Kleberg for advice on stocking the LBJ ranch outside Austin with exotic wildlife. Johnson admitted to the purpose of amusing visiting "drugstore cowboys" from Congress.

Kleberg laughed and offered to send Johnson a herd of Nilgai antelopes, "perfectly delicious eating" if "hard to catch." Lyndon might enjoy them because "nobody will know what the hell they are."

"They're native to Indo-China and Cambodia," Kleberg said, tongue-in-cheek. Johnson laughed nervously, sensing with his practiced deviousness that the joke was on him. Every mention of "Vietnam" was fraught with irony for Johnson as he fulfilled his own Faustian bargain with CIA and the military.

The Nilgai had thrived on King Ranch since the 1930s when surplus animals had made their home there, courtesy of the San Diego Zoo. They were native not to Vietnam, as Kleberg needled "Lyndon," but to India and eastern Pakistan. His cousin Caesar Kleberg's foundation for the protection of wildlife could finance the transfer, Kleberg added. He was well aware of Lyndon Johnson's stinginess.

"We have the money and we don't know what to do with it," Kleberg said.

Kleberg had backed Barry Goldwater in the 1964 general election, but that was not reason enough to prevent him from asking Lyndon Johnson for a favor. On September 10, 1966, Kleberg phoned the White House to request an ambassadorship to the Argentine for their mutual friend Earl Rudder, President of the Texas A&M universities.

Abruptly, Johnson asked Kleberg where he was.

"I'm in Corpus Christi," Kleberg said, "an environment you'd like to be in!"

"I think everything's going all right in South America and the Argentine," Kleberg remarked casually. "And I agree with everything you're doing up to a point, and internationally 100 percent." If the Vietnam War suited Robert J. Kleberg, Jr., that wasn't the case with Lyndon Johnson's "Great Society" legislation. (Johnson's legislative ambitions included a "War on Poverty," through the Economic Opportunity Act of 1964; environmental protection laws; funding for Medicare and Medicaid; a Civil Rights Act (1964); and a Voting Rights Act (1965), among other progressive initiatives. The financial exigencies of the protracted Vietnam War soon diminished dramatically what Johnson hoped would be the legacy of his presidency.)

Revealing no great respect for a mere president—he had known several—let alone for this one, Kleberg invited Johnson to visit King Ranch Australia "when you get out of this damn job." Rudder never became the ambassador to Argentina, or anywhere else, although in 1967 Lyndon Johnson did award him a Distinguished Service Medal. Johnson never visited King Ranch Australia.

When he involved himself in local politics, Kleberg was interested in such issues as having pari-mutuel betting legalized in Texas. The Texas Racing Association supported the idea, but it failed in Bob Kleberg's lifetime.

In these years, when Kleberg wasn't in his cups chewing the fat with Corpus Christi cronies, he was in the company of very beautiful women invariably a third of his age. Sometimes they were close to royalty. Kleberg enjoyed mixing with high Caracas society, la crème de la crème of that culture.

His favorite Caracas restaurant was called *La Belle Epoque*, a place not known for its food but for its piano music and highly refined atmosphere. One night he hosted a dinner for two European women, both highly cultured graduates of European finishing schools. Completing the group was Gustavo de los Reyes. Those schools, de los Reyes believed, were places were young women were taught how to pour tea and to charm gentlemen, making them feel superior.

One of the young women, a brunette, was Maruja Veracasa, and she was the sister of the bride at a wedding they were scheduled to attend.

Maruja needed only a Spanish mantilla and comb in her hair to look like an Andalusian woman and favored very scanty attire. The other woman, a tall blonde, was Princess Gabriela de Saboya, the youngest daughter of the deposed putative King Humberto of Italy. With her blue eyes, she looked like a northern Catira.

After dinner, when the women excused themselves to leave for another function, Bob, now quite tipsy, grabbed the arm of Gustavo de los Reyes.

"Gustavo," Bob Kleberg said, "I want you know that there are few fine moments in life, and this has been one of them."

It was at that wedding, to which Kleberg escorted Princess Gabriela de Saboya, that de los Reyes introduced him to a young Caracas socialite named Diana Marturet Brillembourg, with whom, at the age of seventy, Kleberg fell in love. Of all the women Robert J. Kleberg, Jr. knew in his last years, Diana never took his money. Other women felt no such restraint.

Diana was as skinny as the British model Twiggy, rail-thin, and chattered constantly, sounding like a cricket. Her hair stood up in spikes. Over a two-year period, Kleberg fancied her.

One day at Kleberg's Pierre Hotel apartment in New York City, Michael J. P. Malone confided a problem to Gustavo de los Reyes.

"Bob wants to marry Diana."

"No way!" de los Reyes said.

"It would cause problems in the family," Malone said. Now de los Reyes and Malone took it upon themselves to prevent the marriage. Half-disapproving, half-envious, de los Reyes noted that Kleberg had never assumed the spirit of a man of his age. He always thought of himself as young. But there would be no wedding.

Robert J. Kleberg, Jr. remained bawdy, unaffected, and natural, more Kingsville than New York. With de los Reyes, he was riding up Park Avenue when suddenly Kleberg said, "Stop the car! I've got to take a piss!"

A proper Cuban gentleman, Gustavo demurred. There were ladies present.

"Don't worry, Gustavo," Kleberg said. "It ain't that big!"

Michael John Patrick Malone died on March 12, 1971, at the age of fifty-six. He was mourned by his wife, four children, a sister, and a brother who was a Monsignor at the Maryknoll Seminary in

Glen Ellyn, Illinois. His *New York Times* obituary does not mention King Ranch or his having worked for Robert J. Kleberg, Jr. Nor does it mention the cause of death, only that he died "after a short illness."

In 1973, Kleberg was still extolling beef as a source of energy "to keep people healthy." Beef rivaled oil and gas in importance, he believed. When Federico Fernández Casas died in 1974 in Madrid, his children flew to Spain and buried him in San Sebastían.

In September 1974, Bob Kleberg fell ill; he made plans to go to Australia in November, but submitted to surgery at St. Luke's Hospital in Houston to remove a large tumor affecting his liver.

Robert Justus Kleberg, Jr., third of the name, died of pancreatic cancer on October 13, 1974. He was seventy-eight years old. With him were his daughter Helenita, his grandson John Deaver Alexander, and five granddaughters. Hovering at his deathbed as well was his nephew Belton Kleberg Johnson, who hoped, in vain, that in his last hours his uncle would pass the leadership of King Ranch over to him.

Despite Belton's imprecations, Bob Kleberg never wholly trusted him since that day he had quit his job at King Ranch. Kleberg had been running King Ranch for fifty-six years. Even on his deathbed, he imagined himself returning in three weeks to work the cattle on the Norias division of the ranch. Kleberg did not designate Belton as the person to take over King Ranch after he was gone.

Bob Kleberg's will protected Gustavo de los Reyes, offering him *Pozo Azul* Ranch in exchange for shares worth $1.5 million. Kleberg's heirs attempted to strip de los Reyes of his stock options and the property Kleberg had willed to him, even invoking a "land grant by King Charles of Spain." But Kleberg had seen to it that his will was airtight.

Kleberg's instructions for his funeral, to be held at King Ranch, were that his friends take it as their sacred duty to drink his wine cellar dry. They did. Former Texas governor John Connally was there, along with current governor Dolph Briscoe and a slew of executives from EXXON. His factotum Holland McCombs said of Robert J. Kleberg, Jr., borrowing from Jonathan Swift's *Gulliver's Travels*, that he "made two blades of grass grow where one had grown before."

This, of course, was literally true. Kleberg had told McCombs, "Perhaps my best service to mankind would be to spread human energy where it was most needed, in underdeveloped countries and regions." So he saw himself.

"He had balls!" Alberto Fernández remembered for me, with a knowing smile. Kleberg was buried not in the family plot in Kingsville, but beside his wife on a small island in a lake on the Norias division of King Ranch. On Kleberg's gravestone, a simple marble slab, was engraved his credo: "Your life is an expression of what you are."

King Ranch as it had been died with Robert J. Kleberg, Jr. With the dividends that Bob had denied to them now in sight, his King/Kleberg heirs quickly sold off King Ranch's foreign enterprises. They undersold their interest in the flourishing Australian operation on several million acres, where "business was booming," for a mere $100 million. Then they sued EXXON for unpaid oil royalties.

Bob Kleberg had long known that EXXON was underpaying on the oil and gas royalties. Once he remarked, "There existed an undecided issue between us to be resolved at a later date." It turned out that Humble/EXXON cheated King Ranch out of $158 million—just for the years 1973–1976. In 1977, Humble oil and gas royalties on King Ranch amounted to $680 million.

Kleberg had been operating as a world leader without portfolio, putting King Ranch resources at the service of the liberation of Cuba. His overriding purpose was that those gleaming, cherry-red Santa Gertrudis animals would feed the world's hungry, rendering famine an anachronism. Kleberg's values had been his calling card.

His personal frailties; his impatience with incompetence; his refusal to suffer fools gladly; his irritation with federal authority; the consolations of bourbon; and, at the end, his weakness for younger women—all pale in significance before his formidable achievements.

"They dealt me the hand and I played it," he once said with humility. "They" referred to his father, his older brother Richard, and his cousin Caesar Kleberg. No one else had really mattered.

As for his relationship with CIA, it was always about what the Agency could do to further the causes he held dear, never the other way around. Despite his global outreach, Robert J. Kleberg, Jr. was no poster boy for American imperialism. When CIA disappointed him, and proved to be hypocritical in its commitment to remove Castro and restore *Becerra* to him, he does not seem to have been surprised. Bob Kleberg knew all about hired hands, whether they were named "Lyndon Johnson," "Allen Dulles," or "J. Edgar Hoover," and he kept their malfeasances in perspective.

Robert J. Kleberg, Jr. emerges free of the taint of any Faustian bargain with CIA. The Agency could not appeal to his rapacity, as it would to its lifelong partners Herman and George Brown of Brown & Root, because for Kleberg it was never about money or profits. Kleberg expanded the King Ranch empire, but he was no spiritual descendant of Mirabeau Buonaparte Lamar, the expansionist second president of the Republic of Texas.

George A. Braga, no hero in this saga, died laden with debt. Having lived extravagantly, he had run out of money. If Robert J. Kleberg, Jr. had been mindful of what King Ranch might contribute to better the lives of ordinary Cubans, Braga and Czarnikow had been about their own profit. Unlike Kleberg with his sensitive approach to the needs of Cuba, Czarnikow had been a prime example of what Fidel Castro had opposed as imperialist exploitation.

Alberto Fernández lived on into his nineties, impoverished and still passionate in his love for his homeland. "My country has gone down the drain forever," he despaired. "I don't know how it can get going. Where will the money come to get the country going again? The misery has no limit; the people are walking around like hungry zombies."

He remained bitter about the "friends," the "Company," as he still called CIA. He had long ago concluded that CIA never intended to unseat Fidel Castro, something he suspected from the day of his first Agency-sponsored operation when he opened that box of rusty Springfield rifles. He wished CIA had not allowed Batista to escape so easily. It had been difficult for him to register that CIA's quarrel was not with Castro so much as it was with John F. Kennedy.

Alberto was a casualty of the Castro takeover. No less was he a victim of the self-serving puppet show of exile politics. He was, most, a victim of KUBARK. Of CIA, he concluded, "I think they're capable of anything." Into his nineties, he remained appalled by the "treason of the Company."

In 2008 he spoke to someone inside Cuba for the first time since he had left. It was the daughter of the man who was in charge of his big ranch, *Vega Beaaca*, and it was to give her the assignment of taking care of the family graves. He knew of the deprivations suffered by the people left behind in Cuba. In the town where his big ranch was located, a woman, unable to feed her children, had hanged herself; a decade later, her husband hanged himself, too.

Alberto's very character, his independent spirit and his selflessness, rendered him a liability for CIA. He was "too effective" for the Agency ever to be comfortable with him. "Too Cuban!" he added. He retained "the highest regard" for Malone and Kleberg, "for their deeds." Yet he had to conclude that neither Kleberg nor Malone was "up to snuff" when it came to completing the job of restoring Cuba to the people, even if it meant defying CIA. Among Malone's limitations was that he was dependent on the Bragas. In all their time together, Alberto had had no political conversations with either Kleberg or Malone.

As for Cuban allies, after Sorí's death, he told me, "I was alone." Rich Miami Cubans like the Fanjuls and the Bragas were interested only in re-establishing their wealth. Others, like Miró Cardona, dreamed of power in a post-Castro Cuba that would never arrive in their lifetimes.

For years, Alberto Fernández lived alone in a small, una-dorned apartment in Key Biscayne, crowded with files, maps, and photographs. Prominent was a pamphlet of the Constitution of 1940. He existed among his beliefs. Only his nephew, Eduardo Sánchez, would appreciate what he had sacrificed for the struggle, leaving himself with no safety net. His own children, who had gone to good schools, continued to resent that there had not been more for them.

In a further demonstration of his resilience, when he was past ninety, Alberto Fernández married again, fashioning a new life with Josefina García, a fellow worker at the Sugar Institute. They had remained close friends over the years. Now at last they were together. Proud as ever, Albert spoke of his plan "to survive with her." They were married in 2009.

At an annual mass for Humberto Sorí Marín, the surviving comrades of *Unidad Revolucionaria* were reunited, brothers in the struggle still. Only in 2012 was Alberto Fernández overtaken by illness, the trouble to which even the most stalwart, alas, are not immune.

In November 2012, Gustavo de los Reyes celebrated his ninety-ninth birthday.

Alberto Fernández de Hechavarria died on Sunday, October 14, 2012, at two in the afternoon, at the age of ninety-four. He was survived by his wife, Josefina García de Fernández, and his sister Gladys Smithies, and by his nephews and niece and his children. The heir to his archive was his nephew, Eduardo Sánchez Rionda. He was buried with his mother, Dolores de Hechavarría de Fernández.

NOTES

CHAPTER 1: MR. BOB IN HIS ASCENDANCY

1: "Who is to give Texas character?" Quoted in Marshall De Bruhl, *Sword of San Jacinto: A Life of Sam Houston* (New York: Random House 1993), 258.

1: "Gone To Texas": Stanley Siegel, *A Political History of the Texas Republic, 1836–1845* (Austin: University of Texas Press, 1956), viii.

2: "a country filled with habitual liars, drunkards, blasphemers . . . ": Joseph William Schmitz, *Texas Culture In the Days of the Republic, 1836–1846.* (San Antonio: The Naylor Company, 1960), 7.

2: "the avarice of selfish and dishonest men": Brown, *History of Texas,* 1:131.

3: Texas, a state whose history "is unique and unlike that of any other member of the Union": John Henry Brown, *History of Texas, from 1685 to 1892* (Austin and New York: Jenkins

Publishing Company and the Pemberton Press, 1970), 1:4.

6-7:" five hundred agents were using corporate covers": Kirkpatrick Sale, "Spies With and Without Daggers," in *Uncloaking the CIA,* ed. Howard Frazier (New York: The Free Press, 1978), 156–157.

7: "Bechtel opens its doors to CIA: Laton McCartney, *Friends in High Places: The Bechtel Story: The Most Secret Corporation and How It Engineered the World* (New York: Simon & Schuster, 1988), 115.

7: "Nowhere but in Texas is the relationship between government and business . . . ": Terry Leonard, "Power Brokers: Who Are the Ones Who Run Texas?" *The San Francisco Chronicle* (November 1982): 1A, 18A.

7: Herman and George Brown were assets of CIA's clandestine services. The following extraordinary document generated by CIA and outlining the dates of Herman and George's service to the Agency was released under the JFK Act and is available at the National Archives: CIA. 104-10117-10202. TO: CHIEF, LEOB/SRS. FROM: HALL, SARAH K. TITLE: DECEMBER 1967 "RAM-PARTS" ARTICLE TITLED "THE CIA'S BROWN AND ROOT DIMEN-SIONS." DATE: December 20, 1967. PAGES: 8. SUBJECTS: "RAMPARTS," BROWN AND ROOT. JFK42.F12 1994.03.21.14:46:56:680028. NARA.

7: robber barons: See Matthew Josephson, *The Robber Barons: The Great American Capitalists, 1861-1901* (New York: Harcourt, Brace & World, Inc., 1962). This book was originally published in 1934.

8: "Don't do that!" Telephone conversation: Lyndon Johnson to Robert J. Kleberg, Jr., April 9, 1966. Miller Center for Public Affairs, Johnson Presidential Recordings.

10: Biographical material on the King and Kleberg families is available in the Holland McCombs Papers at the University of Tennessee at Martin. McCombs, a *Time-Life* journalist, was the researcher for Tom Lea's two-volume authorized biography: Tom Lea, *King Ranch* (Boston: Little Brown & Co., 1957).

12: "coarse-looking": Interview with Walter Billingsly. Box 361, File 1. Papers of Holland McCombs.

13: Dulles flew to King Ranch after speaking at the Dallas Council on World Affairs: Allen W. Dulles to H. N. Mallon, October 26, 1953. Papers of Allen Dulles. Selwyn Mudd Library, Princeton University.

13: Robert Justus Kleberg represents both Helen Chapman and Richard King: Don Graham, *Kings of Texas: The 150-Year Saga of an American Ranching Empire* (Hoboken: John Wiley and Sons, Inc, 2003), 184.

15: "You know best": CHAPTER TWO. Box 355, File 15. Papers of Holland McCombs.

16: "a better cactus for Texas": Luther Burbank to R. J. Kleberg, March 9, 1918. Box 358, File 10. Papers of Holland McCombs.

16: artesian wells: Robert Kleberg II wept when he discovered his first artesian well: Interview with Mr. Matthew John Kivlin. Box 361, File 1. Papers of Holland McCombs.

17: "the good of humanity": From the speech by Robert J. Kleberg, Jr. at the King Ranch centennial conference. Box 358, File 19. Papers of Holland McCombs.

17: Bob Kleberg shoots coyotes: Frank Goodwyn, *Life on the King Ranch* (College Station, Texas: Texas A&M University Press, 1993), 278–279.

17: "Robert, the liveliest of all": Kleberg family poem. Box 355, File 16. Papers of Holland McCombs.

18: Henrietta King gives Bob a Packard for his birthday: Lea, *King Ranch*, 1:563.

18: "pungent thinking": Holland McCombs to Selma Wolff, July 13, 1959. Box 66, File 4. Papers of Holland McCombs.

19: electrical engineering: Lea, *King Ranch*, 1:574–575.

19: Eight days after his twenty-first birthday: Lea, *King Ranch*, 1:593.

19-20: bandits turn King Ranch into an armed camp: See "Greatest Ranch

in Texas Is Turned into Armed Camp," *Houston Express*, August 26. Box 355, File 11. Holland McCombs Papers. It reads, in part, "A number of the more timid women are said to have left there and others have been sent away by their husbands to Corpus Christi, San Antonio, and other places. . . . Not until the Kleberg's erected the big searchlight and hauled to the roof the old Civil War cannon, and in the mouth of one a lark had built is nest, did the situation take on a terrorizing aspect. And when the Kleberg's armed their men with modern high power weapons others in the community begun [sic] to follow their lead."

20: "the King Ranch is his life": Frank Goodwyn, *Life on the King Ranch* (New York, 1921), 278–279.

CHAPTER 2: EL PATRÓN

21: J. Edgar Hoover sends Tommy guns to Robert J. Kleberg, Jr.: Martin Booth, *The Life of Belton Kleberg Johnson*. Limited Private Edition. (Published by Belton Kleberg Johnson, 2001), 68.

21: "don't ever sell mothers!" Booth, *The Life of Belton Kleberg Johnson*, 23–24.

22: "it's like a chess game . . . they'll starve": Holland McCombs conversation with Robert J. Kleberg, Jr.: September 1952. Box 355, File 16. Papers of Holland McCombs.

22: "No excuses": John Cypher, *Bob Kleberg and the King Ranch: A*

Worldwide Sea of Grass (Austin: University of Texas Press, 1995), 41.

22: wide grin: Lea, *King Ranch*, 1:554.

23: head thrown back: Goodwyn, *Life on the King Ranch*, 278–279.

23: a "whirlwind of a man": Quoted in *Fortune* magazine article about Robert J. Kleberg, Jr. Box 363, File 1. Papers of Holland McCombs.

23: "someone I will never interrupt": Helen Kleberg Groves, *Bob and Helen Kleberg of King Ranch* (Albany, Texas: Bright Sky Press, 2004), 65.

"Helenita" is the only child of Bob and Helen Kleberg.

23: "I wish you hadn't said that": Quoted in Booth, *The Life of Belton Kleberg Johnson*, 30. Belton Kleberg Johnson's suggestion that the Klebergs were less than loving—"They were simply not people for whom love was a criterion" (30) and "for Bob to have displayed affection would have meant a sign of weakness" (75)—should be viewed in the light of Belton's competitive attitude toward his uncle and his bitterness at Bob Kleberg's refusal to designate him as heir apparent to run King Ranch after Kleberg's death.

24: "cold, distant and dispassionate": Martin Booth, *The Life of Belton Kleberg Johnson*, 75.

26: dinner at King Ranch: Lea, *King Ranch*, 2:520.

26: the cottage that had belonged to a ranch foreman: Booth, *The Life of Belton Kleberg Johnson*, 21.

28: Humble Oil, a longtime Brown & Root ally: David Welsh, "Building Lyndon Johnson," *Ramparts* magazine, vol. 6, no. 5 (December 1967), 59.

28-29: "biggest single individual oil and gas lease": Interview with Mr. Theodore Koch, Jr. November 19, 1954. Box 355, File 10. Papers of Holland McCombs.

29-30: Richard Kleberg, "encouraged by his friends," runs for Congress: LYNDON BAINES JOHNSON LIBRARY. Interview I. DATE: July 9, 1969. INTERVIEWEE: ROBERT KLEBERG, JR. PLACE: King Ranch Offices, 2nd floor, Kleberg National Bank, Kingsville, Texas.

30: Richard Kleberg dies one million dollars in debt to King Ranch: Booth, *The Life of Belton Kleberg Johnson*, 49.

30: Lyndon Johnson collects $4,000 and goes to Washington as Richard Kleberg's secretary: J. Evetts Haley, *A Texan Looks at Lyndon: A Study in Illegitimate Power* (Canyon, Texas: Palo Duro Press, 1964), 21.

30-32: Doris Kearns Goodwin offers a far more benign picture of how Lyndon Baines Johnson went to work for Richard Kleberg: Doris Kearns Goodwin, *Lyndon Johnson and the American Dream* (New York: St. Martin's Press, 1991), 69–71.

31: "Kleberg didn't do anything": Ronnie Dugger, *The Politician: The Life and Times of Lyndon Johnson* (New York: W. W. Norton & Company, 1982), 170. In his multi-volume biography of Lyndon Johnson, Robert A. Caro does not explore the relationship between the Klebergs and Lyndon Johnson otherwise than to mention it.

31: It was Congressman Richard Kleberg who was responsible for the U.S.

government certifying Santa Gertrudis: Cypher, *Bob Kleberg and the King Ranch*, 14.

32: Richard Kleberg "actively collaborated" to ensure that Brown & Root were awarded the contract for the Corpus Christi Naval Station: Joseph A. Pratt & Christopher J. Castaneda, *Builders: Herman and George Brown* (College Station, Texas: Texas A&M University Press, 1999), 69.

32: Sam Houston Johnson wreaks havoc on the office of Congressman Richard Kleberg: Robert A. Caro: *The Years of Lyndon Johnson: Master of the Senate* (New York: Vintage Books: Random House, 2003), 433–434.

32-35: Archer and George Parr, Highway 77, and the defeat of Congressman Richard Kleberg: Memorandum for Holland McCombs. Subject: John Emmett Lyle, Jr., et. al. 4 pages. Box 148, File 25. Papers of Holland McCombs.

32: "You vote as your conscience dictates": Addition to Chapter IV of Lea history of King Ranch. Box 355, File 9. Papers of Holland McCombs.

33: "I don't want a road through my pasture": Memorandum for Holland McCombs. Subject: John Emmett Lyle, Jr., et. al. 4 pages. Box 148, File 25. Papers of Holland McCombs.

34: Lyndon Johnson did nothing to help Dick Kleberg: James Rowe to

Holland McCombs. April 9, 1964. Box 148, File 25. Papers of Holland McCombs.

35: Billie Sol Estes: "if Lyndon Johnson didn't want you elected, you weren't elected": Telephone conversation with Billie Sol Estes. June 15, 2010.

35: "It is a matter of record": Kleberg on highway rights of way and King Ranch: Box 355, File 11. Papers of Holland McCombs.

36: Alice Kleberg's letter to the board of directors: Box 355, File 7. Holland McCombs Papers. "TO THE SANTA GERTRUDIS BOARD OF DIRECTORS" from Mrs. R. J. Kleberg. Along with letter addressed to "BOB" and signed "Mother." Undated.

36: "you do things with and through people": Unidentified narrative. Box 359, File 30. Papers of Holland McCombs.

36-37: "colloidal film": Memorandum to: Tom Lea. From: Holland McCombs. December 28, 1954. Box 355, File 17. Papers of Holland McCombs.

37: "inert, barren, like cement": To: Tom Lea. From: Holland McCombs. December 28, 1954. Box 355, File 17. Papers of Holland McCombs.

37: "Santa Gertrudis": Monkey was bred to his own daughters and granddaughters while his best sons were bred to his best daughters, their sisters. In the thirties, to cite one detail of Kleberg's genetic experiment, he sent a lone Santa Gertrudis bull to Australia as a gift to cattlemen who were buying a shipment of his Brahma bulls. Cattle-raising in Australia was at once transformed.

37: "in the medium of heredity with the steady hand and eye . . .": Alden Whitman, "Robert Kleberg Jr. Dies; Owner of Huge King Ranch," *New York Times*. October 15, 1974.

38: "new creature": Handwritten notes of Holland McCombs. Box 359, File 30. Papers of Holland McCombs.

38: "outlasting the country": Robert J. Kleberg, Jr., speech before the American Meat Institute, meeting held at King Ranch, April 6, 1952. Series 29. Box 358, File 2. Papers of Holland McCombs.

38: you could cut it with a fork: SANTA GERTRUDIS—Smith (Paine). March 5, 1952. Box 359, File 21. Papers of Holland McCombs.

39: "*Está habiéndose su ropa*": Box 355, File 10: Papers of Holland McCombs.

39: "When it runs, it loses money": Box 355, File 10. Papers of Holland McCombs.

39: cattle-raising as a branch of agriculture: So contends Cuban rancher

Gustavo de los Reyes, speaking for himself and Kleberg: See: Gustavo de los Reyes, "Cuba's Agricultural Future," *La Herencia* magazine, vol. 13, no. 1 (2007). Courtesy of Gustavo de los Reyes.

39: "I never wanted to do anything else": Lea, *King Ranch*, 1:563.

39-40: breakfast of Robert Kleberg, Jr.: Cypher, *Bob Kleberg and the King Ranch*, 44.

40: rest is "hard physical exercise": Robert J. Kleberg, Jr. to Holland McCombs. January 26, 1953. Box 361, File 10. Papers of Holland McCombs.

40: "horseback decisions": Box 355, File 10. Papers of Holland McCombs.

40: "Cow punching is baseball": Holland McCombs notes. Box 355, File 21. Papers of Holland McCombs.

40: didn't stop for a drink of water: For this depiction of a typical Kleberg day, see Booth, *The Life of Belton Kleberg Johnson,* 104, 152.

41: 920,000 acres and 85,000 head of cattle: Box 359, File 21. Papers of Holland McCombs.

41: "Any damned fool can fire somebody": Unidentified narrative. Box 272, File 1. Holland McCombs Papers. Also quoted in Cypher, *Bob Kleberg and the King Ranch*, 37.

42: the King Ranch carpenter was Matthew John Kivlin. His remarks are in Box 361, File 1. Papers of Holland McCombs.

42: "You'll be back": Booth, *The Life of Belton Kleberg Johnson*, 159.

42: "petulant, opinionated, short-tempered, charismatic, domineering . . .": Belton Kleberg Johnson biography, 152.

43: "he fought it tooth and claw": Ibid., 53.

43: "they work for the King Ranch too": Interview with Kleberg. Box 355, File 10. Papers of Holland McCombs.

43: "I live here": Interview with Robert J. Kleberg, Jr., November 12, 1953. Box 361, File 5. Papers of Holland McCombs.

43: "high-hat," "exclusive": Statement of Carleton W. Adams. Two pages. Box 355, File 7. Papers of Holland McCombs.

43: Kleberg urges that President Eisenhower make beef surpluses available to countries with shortages: *The Presidential Papers of Dwight David Eisenhower, vol. XIV—The Presidency: The Middle Way.* Document #470; October 20, 1953. Available online.

43: "I really believe he is going to win": Robert J. Kleberg, Jr. to Holland McCombs. July 15, 1952. Papers of Holland McCombs.

44: "dictatorial": "Bob was a dictator," Gustavo de los Reyes says. Interview with Gustavo de los Reyes. September 21, 2008.

44: "meat store": Handwritten notes of Holland McCombs. Box 359, File 30. Papers of Holland McCombs.

45: "not only me": Scenes of the life at King Ranch are derived from "THE BIG THING." Box 358, File 7. Papers of Holland McCombs.

45: Kleberg on "tradition": Interview with Robert J. Kleberg, Jr., March 1952. Box 355, File 10. Papers of Holland McCombs.

45: "the BEST way": Box 355, File 1. Papers of Holland McCombs.

45: "failures which have been corrected": Box 355, File 16. Papers of Holland McCombs.

45: "I don't agree with ANYTHING": Holland McCombs notes. Box 363, File 1. Papers of Holland McCombs.

45: "You should goddamn well know": John Cypher, *Bob Kleberg and the King Ranch*, 8.

46: "We operated the ranch for eighty-five years without oil": Booth, *The Life of Belton Kleberg Johnson*, 92.

46: seven Humble chairmen: Booth, *The Life of Belton Kleberg Johnson*, 108.

47: Bing Crosby solicits an invitation to King Ranch: Booth, *The Life of Belton Kleberg Johnson,* 108.

47: "You can't sing with that in your mouth!": Groves, *Bob and Helen Kleberg of King Ranch*, 113.

47-48: Kleberg's remarks at the King Ranch centennial conference: Papers of Holland McCombs notes. Box 358, File 16. Papers of Holland McCombs.

47: "civilization came and remained because of a ranch": Robert J. Kleberg, Jr., address at the King Ranch centennial conference. Box 358, File 19. Papers of Holland McCombs.

48: Tom Slick shows the text of his speech to be delivered at the King Ranch centenary to Neil Mallon: Holland McCombs to Helen and Bob [Kleberg]. September 15, 1953. Box 361, File 10. Papers of Holland McCombs.

49: "we should stay out of print": Robert J. Kleberg, Jr. to Holland McCombs. February 13, 1958. Box 21, File 5. Papers of Holland McCombs.

50: Bob Kleberg supports Barry Goldwater: "Robert Kleberg, Jr. Dies; Owner of Huge King Ranch," *New York Times*. October 15, 1974.

50: Kleberg had already supported Eisenhower: "I have devoted a lot of last-minute attention to it," Kleberg said of Eisenhower's 1952 campaign, "hoping something I do will be helpful. I really believe he is going to win." Kleberg agreed to serve on Eisenhower's "Committee for Economic Development" and on a "National Conference Board," which dealt with agricultural policy: Robert J. Kleberg, Jr. to Holland McCombs. July 15, 1952. Box 361, File 10. Papers of Holland McCombs. For Kleberg's positions with the Eisenhower administration, see Martin Booth, *The Life of Belton Kleberg Johnson*. Belton Kleberg Johnson was a nephew of Robert J. Kleberg, Jr. This is an authorized biography, written in the third person voice of Belton Kleberg Johnson.

50: Kleberg's meetings with Lyndon Johnson: See interview with Robert Kleberg, Jr. for the Lyndon Johnson library.

50: "Mr. President": Tapes of Lyndon Johnson's presidential recordings can be heard on the website of the Miller Center of Public Affairs. Another person who choked at having to utter the words "Mr. President" when speaking to Lyndon Johnson was Edward M. Kennedy. On occasion, however, Kennedy managed it.

50: "my opinion of Mr. Johnson": Ronnie Dugger, "Notes and Sources" for *The Politician*, 432.

50: "In a Republican district, I was a Republican": Josephson, *The Robber Barons*, 132.

51: "No politics of any kind": Josephson, *The Robber Barons*, 350.

51: "It matters not one iota what political party is in power": Ibid., 352.

51-55: Edna Ferber and King Ranch: Booth, *The Life of Belton Kleberg Johnson*, 119; Holland McCombs to "Mary," February 25, 1940; Holland McCombs to Edna Ferber, September 14, 1948, Ibid.; Edna Ferber to Holland McCombs, September 23, 1948; Lee Gillette to Holland McCombs, November 15, 1948. All in Box 15, File 17, Papers of Holland McCombs. See also: Groves, *Bob and Helen Kleberg of King Ranch*, 158. The final product was Edna Ferber, *Giant* (New York: Doubleday & Company, Inc., 1952).

51-52: "to write a book about Texas would be an impertinence": *Houston Chronicle*, March 1, 1940, 1.

51: "put officers in both the Republican and Democratic campaign committees": AGENCY: SSCIA. RECORD NUMBER: 157-10005-10224. AGENCY FILE NUMBER: R174. TITLE: TESTIMONY OF LAWRENCE HOUSTON. DATE: 06/02/75. PAGES: 111. BOX 248-1. NARA.

52: "really new rich Houston oil boys and girls": Edna Ferber to Holland McCombs. September 23, 1948. Box 15, File 17. Papers of Holland McCombs.

54: "a couple of good bites of ranch stuff": Edna Ferber to Holland McCombs. October 28, 1948. Papers of Holland McCombs.

55: the Klebergs attended the opening of Glenn McCarthy's hotel: Booth, *The Life of Belton Kleberg Johnson*, 118.

55: "the only woman I ever called a son-of-a-bitch": Interview with Gustavo de los Reyes. September 21, 2008.

55: "truth, rather than fiction": *Corpus Christi Caller-Times*, July 12, 1953.

55: "I don't give a damn what you write": Robert J. Kleberg to Holland McCombs. July 18, 1957; To: Robert J. Kleberg, Jr. From: Holland McCombs. September 13, 1955. Box 361, File 10. Papers of Holland McCombs.

55: "very close to the truth": Robert J. Kleberg, Jr. to Holland McCombs. July 18, 1957. Box 361, File 10. Papers of Holland McCombs.

55: "bare knuckles": From: Holland McCombs. To: Robert J. Kleberg, Jr. September 13, 1955. Box 361, File 10. Holland McCombs Papers. McCombs is quoting Kleberg back to him.

CHAPTER 3: KING RANCH GOES GLOBAL

57: "I'll take care of the cattle": John Cypher, *Bob Kleberg and the King Ranch*, 76.

58: "Cuba has some of the best grazing land on earth": Robert J. Kleberg, Jr., speech at the King Ranch centennial conference. Box 358, File 19. Papers of Holland McCombs.

58: "Find some place in the world where it rains?": Ed Erard, quoted in the *Corpus Christi Caller-Times*, July 12, 1953. Box 355, File 23. Papers of Holland McCombs.

59: Tom Slick at the centennial conference, October 20, 1953: Box 359, File 8. Papers of Holland McCombs.

59: the Bragas exploit both cane workers and laborers: Interview with Alberto Fernández: Alberto's story is drawn from interviews conducted in Florida in September and December 2008, December 2009, and from dozens of telephone conversations between 2008 and 2011.

59-60: squatters on the Braga land in Cuba: James Cypher, "A Rancher's Paradise: The King Ranch, Peasant Insurgency and the Cuban Revolution of 1959." Unpublished paper. July 31, 2002. Courtesy of Mr. Cypher. See also: Interviews with Alberto Fernández de Hechavarría, September 19 and 21, 2008.

61: "One thing is Kleberg": The story of the Bragas' treatment of Salvador Rionda and the squatters on the Braga fallow land comes from interviews with Alberto Fernández, 2008–2010.

62: Knights of Malta and CIA: e-mail from former CIA employee John Quirk, August 5, 2010. See also: Françoise Hervet, "Knights of Darkness: The Sovereign Military Order of Malta," *CovertAction Information Bulletin*. Number 25 (Winter 1986), 27–38.

62: you won't find Malone's name: John Cooney, *The American Pope: The Life and Times of Francis, Cardinal Spellman* (New York, 1984).

62: both Malone and George A. Braga had worked with Allen Dulles during the war: Interview with Gustavo de los Reyes. September 21, 2008.

62: "an agent of the United States Government": Cooney, *The American Pope*, 231–235.

63: "his Holiness' bag-man": Booth, *The Life of Belton Kleberg Johnson*, 132.

63: a wonderful fellow: Interview with Joseph F. Dryer, Jr., Palm Beach, January 8, 2010.

63: Dated March 12, 1951, the joint venture agreement between King Ranch and Czarnikow-Rionda is printed as an Appendix in Lea's history of King Ranch, I: 770. See also: Holland McCombs to Jack Malone. July 10, 1969. Box 66, File 4. Papers of Holland McCombs.

63: *Compañía Ganadera Becerra*: For a summary of King Ranch in Cuba, see Holland McCombs to Jack Malone. July 10, 1969. Box 66, File 4. Papers of Holland McCombs.

63: "the least desirable land": James Cypher, "A Rancher's Paradise: The King Ranch, Peasant Insurgency and the Cuban Revolution of 1959." Manuscript. July 31, 2002. Courtesy of James Cypher.

64: "I know nothing about cattle": John Cypher, *Bob Kleberg and the King Ranch*, 76.

64: Malone as an FBI informant: FBI. TO: DIRECTOR, FBI. FROM: SAC, NEW YORK. DATE: January 23, 1964. SUBJECT: ALEXANDER IRWIN RORKE, JR. IS-CUBA. 97-4623. NARA.

65: CIA keeps two 201 files on Malone: CIA. 104-10168-10386. TITLE: LIST OF NAMES WITH 201 NUMBERS. 04/04/67. SUBJECTS: LANZ, DÍAZ. NARA.

65: CIA keeps 201 files on individuals and 301 files on corporations: The source is an internal Historical Review Group document. Since it was created for CIA's own purposes, this document was accompanied by no riff, no TO: and FROM: The heading is particularly opaque: "CL BY: CL REASON: 1. b(c)/DECL ON: X1/DRV FROM: MIS 2-82. The document begins: "An extract is used when an individual/ company in a document has a 201/301 file, but the length of the document may be too long to 'B' code (B code: to cross-file an entire copy of a document onto a 201/301) . . ." If this seems impenetrable to an outsider, obviously it was meant to be.

65: CIA refers to Malone as AMPATRIN: See, for example, CIA. 104-10172-10088. TO: SAO PAOLO. FROM: DIRECTOR. TITLE: REQUEST COB CABLE DETAILED ACCOUNT BACKGROUND DEALING WITH AMPATRIN. DATE: June 4, 1964. PAGES: 2. NARA.

65: "Chivas Regal friend": Not surprisingly, there is only a fragmentary record elaborating Malone's many CIA connections and his contacts with them. Two memoranda in particular are striking. One, dated March 16, 1962, refers to "Conversation with my luncheon friend." This was Raford Herbert. "Conversation with my Chivas Regal friend" refers to a meeting between Malone and David Atlee Phillips. Both memoranda, designed for Robert J. Kleberg, Jr., were copied by Malone to the FBI.

65: David Atlee Phillips refers to Kleberg as "Bob": Michael J. P. Malone to David Atlee Phillips. November 7, 1960. Papers of Michael J. P. Malone.

65-66: "James S. Pekich" instructs agents prior to their infiltration into Cuba: CIA. 104-10103-10120. MEMORANDUM FOR THE RECORD. FROM: LEADER, JOHN L.TO: MFR. DATE: August 10, 1977. PAGES: 1.SUBJECT: Interview with Mr. James S. Pekich. NARA.

66: "not a CIA employee": FBI MEMORANDUM. TO: D. J. BRENNAN. FROM: S. J. PAPICH. DATE: June 27, 1962. PAGES: 2. SUBJECT: FRANK ANTHONY STURGIS a.k.a. Frank Fiorini. NEUTRALITY MATTERS. 62-149-96. NARA. Papich functioned as CIA's liaison to the FBI.

66: "You will do what I ask you to do!": Cypher, *Bob Kleberg and the King Ranch*, 41.

66: little brass buttons to fasten Kleberg's collar: Ibid., 160–161.

67: King Ranch Cuba: See: TO: Mary Johnston—FORTUNE. FROM: Holland McCombs. DATE: June 3, 1959. Box 66, File 4. Holland McCombs Papers. See also: TO: Isabel Benney. FORTUNE. From: Holland McCombs. DATE: March 19, 1952. Box 359, File 8. Papers of Holland McCombs.

67: "*Qué hombre!*" Notes on Robert J. Kleberg, Jr. Box 272, File 1. Papers of Holland McCombs.

67: "One of the Texans liked your horse": Interview with Gustavo de los Reyes.

68: "acquisition and possession of land by foreign persons": "The Hemisphere: Cuba: Confiscation!" *Time* magazine, June 1, 1959, 34.

68: "grass is the forgiveness of nature": "A Bundle of Relations," Memoir of George A. Braga, unpublished. Papers of Michael J. P. Malone.

68: grade up the herds: Robert J. Kleberg, Jr., speech at the 1953 King Ranch centennial conference. Box 358, File 19. Papers of Holland McCombs.

68: "I'm going to be bull-headed": Interview with R. J. Kleberg, Jr., No date. Box 355, File 23. Papers of Holland McCombs.

69: first mechanical brush-clearing equipment: Holland McCombs notes. Box 359, File 15. Papers of Holland McCombs.

69: "Mr. Kleberg's idea of converting cane into meat": Quoted by James Cypher.

70: *Becerra* treated its Cuban workers fairly: e-mail from Professor James Cypher, York University, Canada.

August 17, 2008. Cypher's father, John Cypher, worked for Robert J. Kleberg, Jr. at King Ranch for years and was the author of *Bob Kleberg and the King Ranch: A Worldwide Sea of Grass*.

70: only Cuban cowboys: Cypher, "A Rancher's Paradise," 15–16.

70: Freeport Sulphur receives tax concessions from Batista: The Batista government granted favorable tax concessions to Freeport Sulphur: Earl E. T. Smith, *The Fourth Floor: An Account of the Castro Communist Revolution* (New York: Random House, 1962), 206–207.

Smith was U.S. Ambassador to Cuba in the last days of Batista. Freeport was building a $75 million nickel and cobalt plant at the time Castro took over: Thomas G. Paterson, *Contesting Castro: The United States and the Triumph of the Cuban Revolution* (Oxford: Oxford University Press, 1994), 36.

70: a 7 percent raise to all the labour on their contracting jobs: MEMORANDUM. TO: Mr. George A. Braga. FROM: Michael J. P. Malone. DATE: March 26, 1959. Papers of Michael J. P. Malone. This raise came only after 26th of July took power.

70: the Fanjuls are not sympathetic to the workers: Jane Mayer and José de Córdoba, "First Family of Sugar Is Tough on Workers, Generous to Politicians," *The Wall Street Journal*, July 29, 1991, A1.

70: "*El agua es la semilla*": Interview with Robert J. Kleberg, Jr., September 1953. Box 361, File 5. Papers of Holland McCombs.

71: "these are elephants": Box 356, File 1. Papers of Holland McCombs.

71: "produced and created things": Holland McCombs to Tom Lea. August 29, 1952. Box 359, File 8. Papers of Holland McCombs.

71: King Ranch did not extract any money from Cuba: See: TO: Mary Johnston—FORTUNE. FROM: Holland McCombs. DATE: June 3, 1959: "The King Ranch also sent money, and kept on sending it and spending it in Cuba—never taking out a dollar. The money-yield from any cattle and horse calls in Cuba went back into the Cuban operation per se."

73: "a verbal agreement was usually binding": Cypher, *Bob Kleberg and the King Ranch*, 36.

79: "growing winter vegetables": Michael J. P. Malone Memorandum to Mr. George A. Braga. DATE: January 22, 1958. Papers of Michael J. P. Malone.

80: "an attractive climate for private United States investment": Michael J. P. Malone to Messrs. G. A. Braga—B. R. Braga. May 1, 1958, and April 23, 1958. Papers of Michael J. P. Malone.

81: "Jack Malone is to handle everything": George A. Braga Memorandum. May 14, 1958. Papers of Michael J. P. Malone.

81: Kleberg buys property in Argentina: Michael J. P. Malone to George A. Braga. September 4, 1958. Papers of Michael J. P. Malone.

81: "another Korea": Michael J. P. Malone to Mr. George A. Braga. July 22, 1958. Papers of Michael J. P. Malone.

81: "which flushed the rebels out": Michael J. P. Malone to George A. Braga. August 25, 1958. Papers of Michael J. P. Malone.

82: "The liquidation of the armed revolt": Alfonso Fanjul to George A. Braga. August 7, 1958. Papers of Michael J. P. Malone.

82: By the fall of 1958, foreman Lowell Tash: TO: Mr. Lowell H. Tash. FROM: Michael J. P. Malone. Re: Subjects discussed during my visit to *Becerra*—Augs. 1958. Papers of Michael J. P. Malone.

82: $370 million from sugar: "The Hemisphere: Cuba: Confiscation!" *Time* magazine, June 1, 1959, 37.

83: "looking for financial backing for the other people": Ibid. Michael J. P. Malone to George A. Braga. September 4, 1958.

84: "stop all operations of these mills": FBI. DATE: December 16, 1958.

Interview with J. S. Levene by Special Agent Thomas G. Spencer. File # 97-1531. (Levene was Vice President and Treasurer of the Francisco Sugar Company; its offices were located at 106 Wall Street, where Michael J. P. Malone also was based.)

84: Freeport Sulphur offered to help: Interview with Jorge Navarro Custín. August 17, 1999.

84: García Beltrán, co-endorsing the checks: Information Report. Central Intelligence Agency. December 17, 1958. Payment of Funds to Castro: 77-36 [remaining numbers illegible]. 97-3602. Report No. B-3, 119,380. TO: Director, Federal Bureau of Investigation. Attention: Mr. S. J. Papich. FROM: Deputy Director, Plans. SUBJECT: U.S. Banking Transactions by Marcelino García Beltrán, friend of former President Batista of Cuba. DATE: February 25, 1959. 109-480-1718.

85: Alberto was the "contact man": Department of State. Memorandum of Conversation. October 25, 1958. Subject: Activities of Cuban Rebels. Participants: ARA—Mr. Rubottom, Mr. Braga, President of the Francisco Sugar Company, New York. NARA.

85-86: George Braga visited the State Department on October 25, 1958. The State Department memorandum of Braga's conversation with Rubottom was forwarded by James P. McDonnell at the Bureau of Security and Consular Affairs, Department of State,

to William S. Kenny at the Internal
Security Division, Department of Jus-
tice. Subject: Attempt by Cuban Rebel
movement to extort "Tax" from the
Francisco Sugar Company. DATE:
November 6, 1958. PAGES: 1. NARA.

86: "Mr. Braga's report is much appreci-
ated": Department of State. TO: William
S. Kenny, Internal Security Division,
Department of Justice. FROM: James
P. McDonnell, Bureau of Security and
Consular Affairs, Department of State.
DATE: November 6, 1958.

86: Kleberg and Malone visit the State
Department in October 1958 to discuss
the situation in Cuba. Memorandum of
a Conversation, Department of State,
Washington, D.C., October 31, 1958.
Available at http://www.latinamerican-
studies.org/cable/cable-10-31.htm.

86: Lone Star Cement: Their Uruguayan subsidiary "provided cover for
CIA operations officer in Montevideo": Philip Agee, *Inside the Company:
CIA Diary* (Harmondsworth, Middlesex: Penguin Books, 1975), 614.

87: an FBI document reveals
how deeply American business
had penetrated Cuba: FBI. Title
of Case: ALBERTO FERNÁN-
DEZ HECHAVARRÍA. Report of:
THOMAS G. SPENCER. DATE:
December 22, 1958. CHARACTER
OF CASE: REGISTRATION ACT-
CUBA. FBI file of Alberto Fernández.

87: Jorge Navarro Custín, a Cuban living in Miami, believed that CIA was

ready to act against Fidel Castro at
this point, but the State Department
was not. Interview with Jorge Navarro
Custín. August 17, 1999.

88: "joined up with Fidel Castro":
R. Rionda Braga's report to the
FBI: UNITED STATES DEPART-
MENT OF JUSTICE, FEDERAL
BUREAU OF INVESTIGATION.
Report of: THOMAS G. SPENCER.
DATE: December 22, 1958. Office:
NEW YORK. FBI file of Alberto
Fernández.

88: a stinging personal letter to his
friend, Allen Dulles: FBI Office
Memorandum. TO: Mr. A. H. Bel-
mont. FROM: Mr. S. B. Donahoe.
DATE: January 12, 1959. SUBJECT:
ALBERTO FERNÁNDEZ CASSAS
[sic]. [The Bureau here has confused
Alberto with his father]. INTER-
NAL SECURITY—CUBA. See also:
FBI 124-10200-10158. HQ. Agency
file number: 97-3602-6, 7. FROM:
DONAHOE, S. B. TO: BELMONT,
A. H. DATE: January 12, 1959. PAGES:
4. SUBJECTS: AHH, MONEY, PRO-
CASTRO ACT, KLEBERG, BOB,
RELATIONS, U.S. AND CASTRO
GOVERNMENT. NARA.

89: "expedited": FBI Office Memoran-
dum. TO: A. H. Belmont. FROM: S.
B. Donahoe. DATE: January 21, 1959.
SUBJECT: ALBERTO FERNÁN-
DEZ HECHAVARRÍA REGISTRA-
TION ACT—CUBA. PAGES: 1.
NARA. Donahoe quotes "the Direc-
tor," Hoover, at length.

CHAPTER 4: ALBERTO FERNÁNDEZ RETURNS TO CUBA

91: Land reform would be the "fundamental law" of the revolution: "Castro Dooms Land Reform Opponents," *The Dallas Morning News*, July 8, 1959.

92: at the office, Alberto is grouchy: Conversation with Joséfina García, December 2008. Joséfina worked for the Sugar Institute in 1959.

95: Bonsal is investigated by the Castro government in February 1959: FBI document. URGENT. To: Director, From: SAC, NEW YORK. DATE: February 9, 1959. NARA.

98: Earl E. T. Smith handles the Cuban investments of Senator George Smathers and Bebe Rebozo: FBI. TO: A.H. Belmont. FROM: S. B. Donahoe. DATE: February 10, 1959. SUBJECT: CUBAN REVOLUTIONARY ACTIVITIES. INTERNAL SECURITY—CUBA. 109-480. NARA.

99: "maintain our attitude of understanding": Bonsal added that this was important as "furthering of American interests": Memorandum from the Ambassador to Cuba (Bonsal) to the Assistant Secretary of State for Inter-American Affairs (Rubottom). Washington, September 1959. SUBJECT: Cuban-American Relations. "Foreign Relations of the United States," 1958–1960. vol. VI, 611.

99: "The *Dallas Morning News* ran an article": Robert E. Baskin, "Cuba threatening King Ranch Land," May 28, 1959.

99: "vulgar, obscene telephone calls": FBI. TO: DIRECTOR, FBI. FROM: SAC, HOUSTON. DATE: May 30, 1959. SUBJECT: ROBERT KLEBERG, MISCELLANEOUS—INFORMATION CONCERNING. 62-105517-1. FBI file of Kleberg, Robert Justus, Mr. FOIPA No. 1091903-000. U.S. Department of Justice, Federal Bureau of Investigation. The FBI discovered who was making the calls, but redacted her name from Kleberg's file.

100: no attempt made to "admonish the caller": FBI. TO: The Director. From: A. Rosen. DATE: June 3, 1959. SUBJECT: ROBERT KLEBERG, MISCELLANEOUS—INFORMATION CONCERNING. 62-105517-2. The woman's telephone toll records were examined and the FBI did a credit check on her as well. See: TO: DIRECTOR. FROM: SAC, WFO (62-8113). DATE: June 2, 1959. 62-105517-3.

100: "dear" and "darling": FBI AIRTEL. TO: DIRECTOR, FBI. FROM: SAC, HOUSTON. RE: ROBERT KLEBERG—MISCELLANEOUS INFORMATION CONCERNING. DATE: June 16, 1969. 62-105517-6.

100: "two disasters": FBI. TO: DIRECTOR, FBI. FROM: SAC, WFO. DATE: July 1, 1959. 62-105517-7.

100: "You used my money to buy this land in Cuba": FBI. TO: DIRECTOR, FBI. FROM: SAC, HOUSTON. RE: ROBERT KLEBERG. DATE: July 1, 1959.

101: Kleberg expresses his appreciation to Hoover: Robert J. Kleberg, Jr. to Mr. J. Edgar Hoover. July 15, 1959. 62-105517-9.

101-102: Robert Kleberg and Michael J. P. Malone visit Herbert Matthews at the *New York Times*. Belton Kleberg Johnson claims that his Uncl e Bob blamed his Cuba problems on Matthews: Booth, *The Life of Belton Kleberg Johnson*, 214.

102: CIA had access to the *New York Times* computer: 37: MEMORANDUM FOR THE RECORD. SUBJECT: CI Staff Responsibility for CIA publicity. DATE: July 7, 1975. PAGES: 3. Signed: Theodore C. Poling. CI/R & A/0. NARA.

103: Using Malone as his intermediary, Kleberg enlists J. Edgar Hoover to silence Herbert Matthews: See Robert J. Kleberg, Jr. to Mr. J. Edgar Hoover. July 15, 1959. 62-105517-9; MEMORANDUM FOR MR. TOLSON, MR. BELMONT, MR. DELOACH. October 14, 1959. Signed: John Edgar Hoover, Director; LHMEMORANDUM TO: Mr. DeLoach. FROM: M. A. Jones. SUBJECT: ROBERT J. KLEBERG, JR., PRESIDENT KING RANCH, INC. KINGSVILLE, TEXAS. April 13, 1964. 62-105517-10. NARA.

Kleberg had known Hoover for years, and had toured Bureau headquarters in 1940: J. Edgar Hoover to Michael J. P. Malone. January 19, 1966. 62-105517-14. FBI file of Robert J. Kleberg, Jr.

103: Matthews "in favor of the Abraham Lincoln Brigade": FBI. MEMORANDUM FOR MR. TOLSON, MR. BELMONT, MR. DELOACH. October 14, 1959. From: John Edgar Hoover. FBI file of Robert J. Kleberg, Jr.

103: "very pro-Castro in tone": MEMORANDUM FOR MR. TOLSON, MR. BELMONT, MR. DELOACH. October 14, 1959.

103: Holland McCombs attempts to interest the media in stories about King Ranch in Cuba: Box 66, File 4. Papers of Holland McCombs.

105: let Cuba's sugar quota be slashed: Meeting of June 24, 1959. "Foreign Relations of the United States," 1958–1970. Vol. VI, 539-541.

105: Kleberg favored a total blockade of Cuba: Holland McCombs explained it this way: Holland McCombs to Lee (Gillette). November 10, 1959: "All this could be cured if the United States would just quit buying the sugar. I think we are treating Cuba too much like a spoiled brat. The Castros in this world do not respond properly to that sort of treatment." Series 3, Box 65, File 7. Papers of Holland McCombs.

CHAPTER 5: AWAY ALL BOATS: THE LION AND CIA

107: "Without the Company": The "Company" is a euphemism for CIA among its employees and assets. Agee, *Inside the Company*.

107: Jack Malone introduced Gustavo de los Reyes to David Atlee Phillips: James Cypher, "Interview with Gustavo de los Reyes," November 14, 1999. Courtesy of Mr. Cypher.

108: Freapane: In his later years, living in Florida, Freapane/Groves would devote himself to stamp collecting.

109: "Castro" calls Allen Dulles "the first gringo to seem conciliatory": Norberto Fuentes, *The Autobiography of Fidel Castro,* trans. Anna Kushner (New York: W. W. Norton & Company, 2010), 410. Now living outside Cuba, Fuentes includes the following note: "The Author has avoided mention of any event of which confirmation, besides his own testimony, is inaccessible."

110: Ambassador Bonsal sends a telegram to Cuban Foreign Minister Raúl Roa: "Foreign Relations of the United States, 1958–1960, vol. VI, 348, Editorial Note, 349. Airgram From the Embassy in Cuba to the Department of State. August 2, 1959, 579–580.

110: Caíñas: "establish a Communist regime in Cuba . . .": "U.S. Note Questions Castro's Land Reforms," *The Dallas Morning News*, June 12, 1959.

111: a sub-machine gun pressed to the back of his neck: Gustavo de los Reyes is arrested: Interview with Gustavo de los Reyes by Joan Mellen, September 19, 2008.

111: CIA sends Edward Browder to rescue William Morgan: HSCA 180-10077-10040. RECORD SERIES: NUMBERED FILES: AGENCY FILE NUMBER: 005081. FROM: BROWDER, EDWARD, FEDERAL PENITENTIARY. DATE: January 12, 1978. PAGES: 13. BOX 105. NARA.

111: Gustavo de los Reyes is placed against the wall of *La Cabaña* prison and told that he was going to be shot: CIA. DISPATCH. TO: Chief, WHD. FROM: Chief of Station, Habana. DATE: September 18, 1959. SUBJECT: Operational Treatment of Gustavo de los Reyes. ACTION REQUIRED: None; for information only. Signed: Nelson L. Raynock. NARA.

113: Castro decides to remove Gustavo de los Reyes from the list of those scheduled to be executed: John D. Alexander, Jr. to Gustavo de los Reyes. June 14, 2011. Courtesy of Gustavo de los Reyes. John Alexander is a grandson of Robert J. Kleberg, Jr.

113: "He almost joined me on the Isle of Pines": Interview with Gustavo de los Reyes, September 21, 2008.

113: CIA (KUBARK) knows that Alberto Fernández is in the leadership of a "counterrevolutionary movement against Fidel Castro": CIA. 104-10264-10006. TO: COS [Chief of Station], HABANA. FROM: CHIEF, WHD [Western Hemisphere Division]. TITLE: DISPATCH SUBJECT—ODENVY [FBI] REPORT CONCERNING STATEMENT ALLEGEDLY MADE BY A MEMBER OF STATION HABANA. DATE: August 7, 1959. PAGES: 1. SUBJECTS: DON HOGAN. JFK64-8:F19 1998.07.16.21:29:40:530115. NARA. CIA subsequently denied the story as "completely false and illogical." It was, in fact, true: CIA. 104-10128-10338. TO: DIRECTOR. FROM: HAVANA. TITLE: RE ACTIVITIES IN CUBA. DATE: August 18, 1959. PAGES: 2. SUBJECTS: CABLE, ACTIVITIES CUBA. JFK45:F3C 1997.09.13.12:01:20:216031.

113-114: Alberto Fernández's private conversation with Fidel Castro: Cable August 7, 1959. Marked "Private and Confidential." Papers of Michael J. P. Malone.

114: "its nefarious imperialistic practices": Quoted in an article by Reeve Waring and sent to the editor, Kingsville Record, Kingsville, Texas. August 31, 1959. Papers of Michael J. P. Malone.

114: Castro wants a bigger share of the profits of Nicaro and the Moa Bay Mining Company. See The Wall Street Journal, September 30, 1959. See also Corpus Christi Caller-Times, September 29, 1959, and R. Hart Phillips, "Castro Says Cuba Can Build Alone," New York Times, September 30, 1959.

116: For this account of the murder of Camilo Cienfuegos, the source is Alberto Fernández, reporting on the account given to him by Humberto Sorí Marín. In his biography of Cienfuegos, Carlos Franqui leaves the manner of the death of his subject a mystery. Carlos Franqui, Camilo Cienfuegos (Los Tres Munos: Seix Barral, 2001). This book is presently available only in Spanish.

Castro's penchant for violence has been described by one of his biographers, Robert E. Quirk, who traces Fidel's fascination with guns to when he was nine years old and habitually fired at his mother's chickens with a shotgun. Quirk depicts Castro with his pistol ever-ready, even at a meeting of artists and writers where, before he addressed the audience, he "removed his pistol from its holster and laid it on the table in front of him. The significance of that menacing gesture was not lost on those who feared the worst": Robert E. Quirk, Fidel Castro (New York: W. W. Norton & Company, 1993), x, 383.

116: The King Ranch pilot is accused of complicity in the death of Camilo Cienfuegos: "Cuba Detains King Ranch Pilot," The Dallas Morning News, November 9, 1959.

117: "Cuba confiscated the ranch!" Groves, *Bob and Helen Kleberg of King Ranch*, 241.

118: a detachment of soldiers drove up: "Castro To Take Over King Ranch In Cuba," *The Dallas Morning News*, November 9, 1959; "King Ranch Chief Detained In Cuba," *The Dallas Morning News*, November 8, 1959.

118: Lowell Tash escapes from Cuba with the assistance of Michael J. P. Malone: Cypher, *Bob Kleberg and the King Ranch*, 78–79. See also, "King Ranch Chief Detained In Cuba," *The Dallas Morning News*, November 8, 1959.

119: two freighters belonging to the United Fruit Company are enlisted to participate in the Bay of Pigs invasion: Jonathan Kwitny, *Endless Enemies: The Making of an Unfriendly World* (New York: Congdon and Weed, Inc., 1984), 219.

119: Kleberg and Malone visit Washington, D.C., on November 24, 1959: "Memorandum of a Conversation, Department of State, November 24, 1959, "Revised U.S. Policy Toward Cuba." Number 397. "Foreign Relations of the United States," 1958–1960, vol. VI, 677.

119: Castro "a dictator": From Bob Kleberg. May 29, 1959. Box 66, File 4. Holland McCombs Papers.

119-120: By October 1960, Kleberg had sent Santa Gertrudis cattle to Jamaica: SAVOY HOTEL LONDON. Memo from Michael J. P. Malone to George Braga. October 3, 1960. Papers of Michael J. P. Malone, University of Florida, Gainesville.

120: "where American ventures are concerned—Cuban administrations honor the obligations of their predecessors": Langbourne M. Williams to Mr. Robert J. Kleberg, Jr., October 7, 1958. Papers of Michael J. P. Malone. Kleberg requested of Malone that the letter be "treated confidentially." Kleberg had, in turn, promised Williams that his correspondence would be "treated with discretion." Robert J. Kleberg, Jr. to Mr. Langbourne Williams, September 25, 1958.

122: "I told you this was a good place": Memo from Bob Kleberg to Jack. July 27, 1960. Papers of Michael J. P. Malone.

122: not yet taken over the business office in Camagüey: Michael J. P. Malone to Mr. Richard M. Kleberg, Jr., August 19, 1960. Papers of Michael J. P. Malone. This was Dick Kleberg's son, who worked at King Ranch.

122: Alberto is granted Covert Approval under PROJECT JHNRC: CIA. 104-10237-10036. TO: CHIEF, WESTERN HEMISPHERE DIVISION. FROM: DEPUTY DIRECTOR OF SECURITY. TITLE:

MEMORANDUM: REFERENCE IS MADE TO YOUR REQUEST. DATE: May 1, 1960. PAGES: 1. SUBJECTS: PROJECT JHNRC. JFK64-2:F13 1998.05.05.07:58:20:200124. FILE ORIGINAL IS PREVIOUSLY SANITIZED DOCUMENT. NARA.

122: Don Hogan reports on everything Alberto Fernández does to the FBI field office in New Haven: FBI. OFFICE MEMORANDUM. TO: DIRECTOR, FBI. FROM: SAC, NEW YORK. DATE: March 31, 1960. SUBJECT: CATHERINE TAAFFE. REGISTRATION ACT—CUBA. 65-59364-36. NARA.

123: "of extremely doubtful reliability" (Taaffe): FBI. Assistant Attorney General J. Walter Yeagley. Director, FBI. DATE: June 30, 1961. PAGES: 2. NARA. Assaulted in Miami in February 1960 supposedly by supporters of Fidel Castro, Taaffe blamed the State Department, CIA, and the Bureau. Taaffe listed her occupation as "engineer."

124: Fernández is a member of the cabinet: FBI. Assistant Attorney General, Internal Security Division, Director, FBI. DATE: January 19, 1959. 97-3602. PAGES: 2. Cover memo S. J. Papich to R. R. Roach re Alberto Fernández Cases [sic], prepared 1-13-59 by SJP:bjt. Alberto Fernández FBI file.

124: Alberto Fernández's name is not redacted in one place on FBI

Memorandum. TO: A. H. Belmont. FROM: S. B. Donahoe. DATE: February 10, 1959. Subject: CUBAN REVOLUTIONARY ACTIVITIES. INTERNAL SECURITY-CUBA.

125: Malone is happy to arrange an interview with Alberto for CIA: CIA. 104-10172-10083. TO: MFR. FROM: WITHHELD. TITLE: MEMO TELEPHONE CALL FROM JACK MALONE. DATE: July 26, 1960. PAGES: 1. SUBJECTS: MALONE, JACK. JFK64-8:F19 1998.02.16.11:18:32:936108. NARA. Alberto went on to request CIA's assistance in rescuing his friends and colleagues from Cuba.

125: cash delivered to DRE in brown paper grocery bags: Interviews with DRE leaders by Joan Mellen: Dr. Luis Fernández Rocha, January 7, 2004; and Isidro Borja, January 5, 2004. Miami.

125: Malone serves as the intermediary for Kleberg, requesting CIA's guidance before contributing Kleberg's money to the anti-Castro cause: CIA. 104-10172-10078. TO: DIRECTOR. FROM: MASH. TITLE: CABLE, AMPATRIN-1 NOW IN MASH AREA MET MANSON. DATE: September 13, 1960. PAGES: 1. SUBJECT: AMPATRIN-1. JFK64-8:F19 1998.02.16.10:53:40:013108. NARA.

125: Malone meets with Salvador Ferrer and offers Phillips the opportunity to meet him: CIA. 104-10265-10064. TO: REDACTED. FROM: MALONE, MICHAEL J. P. TITLE: LETTER: "I WAS IN MIAMI BRIEFLY ON SUNDAY, FEBRUARY 5TH AND HAD A MEETING WITH SALVADOR FERRER." DATE: January 3, 1961. PAGES: 1. The letter opens, "Dear Dave," and the address at the bottom left corner of the document is "Mr. David Phillips, 6209 Dahlonega Road, Washington, D.C."

125-126: half of the Agency's budget is being spent on covert action: William E. Colby Oral History. Interview II. Lyndon Baines Johnson Oral History Collection. LBJ Library, Austin, Texas.

126: "no prominent features": CIA's portrait of Alberto Fernández: MEMORANDUM FOR: C/TFW/PA-PROP. SUBJECT: Alberto Fernández Echevarría [sic]. (AMDENIM-1). This is an attachment to CIA. 104-10172-10150. June 27, 62. NARA.

126: A summary of the history of Alberto Fernández's relationship with CIA may be gleaned from the following: CIA. 104-10404-10442. RUSS HOLMES WORK FILE. TITLE: MEMO NO. 5—GARRISON AND THE KENNEDY ASSASSINATION. DATE: August 7, 1967. PAGES: 42. NARA. See also: CIA. 104-10435-10030. RUSS HOLMES WORK FILE. MEMO. NO. 6. TITLE: GARRISON AND THE KENNEDY ASSASSINATION. September 7, 1967. PAGES: 7. JFK-RHO2:F050-1

1998.11.17.06:10:09:140129. CIA's Memorandum No. 6 examines some of the people named in the Garrison case and describes their possible CIA connections. Alberto appears as a "DDP contact starting in December 1960 and continuing at least through 31 January 1966." The later date, CIA adds, is that of UGFA-24373, which reported that by then "our financial assistance to FERNÁNDEZ had stopped but that contact was continuing." CIA notes that Garrison had not been in touch with Fernández, which was true. Nor had Lawrence Laborde, another DDP contact who worked with Fernández, although Laborde's son Michael did visit Garrison's office in quest of information. One document describes Alberto as "well-connected with KUBARK": CIA. 104-10172-10080. TO: DIRECTOR. FROM: HAVAN. TITLE: CABLE AMPALM-4 WHO RECENTLY RETURNED FROM MIAMI. REPORTED FOLL TO STATIN CUT-OUR GORDON M. BINIARIS 24 AUGUST. DATE: August 26, 1960. PAGES: 2. SUBJECTS: AMPALM-4. JFK64-8:F19 1998.02.16.11:06:03:606108. NARA.

126: The Constitution of 1940: See: *La Constitución de 1940: Ciclo de Conferencias*. (Miami, Centro de Artes Gráficas: Colegio Nacional de Abogados de Cuba, Inc., 1991.)

128: CIA has the names of the individuals and their groups, "their true names and war names," who signed the articles of *UNIDAD REVOLUCIONARIA*:

CIA. 104-1-226-10285. TO: CHIEF, WHD. FROM: ACTING CHIEF OF STATION, HABANA. TITLE: COMPOSITION OF THE *UNIDAD REVOLUCIONARIA*. DATE: December 28, 1960. PAGES: 1. SUBJECTS: COMPOSITION *UNIDAD REVOLUCIONARIA*. JFK64-61:F4 1998.09.30.19:49:08:326031. NARA.

129: Delio Gómez Ochoa: CIA. 104-10172-10073. TO: DIRECTOR. FROM: MASH. TITLE: CABLE, FERNÁNDEZ TELEPHONED MASH FROM NEW YORK INFORM RELEASE FOR DELIO GÓMEZ OCHOA. DATE: November 15, 1960. PAGES: 1. SUBJECTS: OCHOA, GÓMEZ D. JFK64-8:F19 1998.02.16.10:41:15:060108. NARA.

129: Alberto Fernández also alerted CIA about suspected Cuban G-2 agents entering the United States: CIA. 104-10163-10388. TO: DIRECTOR. FROM: MASH. TITLE: CABLE: AMCLATTER-1 SAID THAT AMRASP COURIER ARRIVING FROM HAVANA INFORMED AMCIGAR VIA ALBERTO FERNÁNDEZ HECHAVARRÍA. DATE: November 18, 1960. PAGES: 1. SUBJECTS: AMCLATTER-1. JFK64-2:F13 1998.04.29.08;10:10:326124. GREENBAND. NARA.

129: "free from foreign influences": CIA. 104-10264-10008. TO: JMGOLD, HAVANA. FROM: DIRECTOR. TITLE: CABLE: SEND BIOGRAPHIC INFO ALBERTO FERNÁNDEZ. DATE: December 3, 1960. PAGES: 1. SUBJECTS: HOGAN, FERNÁNDEZ. JFK64-8:F19 1998.07.16.21:35:50:373115. NARA.

129: AMDENIM-1's "shrewdness": CIA. 104-10264-10054. TO: DIRECTOR. FROM: JMBAR. TITLE: CABLE: ON 11 JULY RAÚL ACOSTA WHO HAS WORKED WITH BILL MURRAY . . . DATE: August 12, 1961. PAGES: 1. SUBJECTS: AMDENIM-1. JFK64-8:F20 1998.07.17.12:43:59:653128. NARA.

130: "four hundred of his ex-employees": CIA. 104-10172-10081. FROM: WITHHELD. TITLE: THE CUBAN ANTI-CASTRO GUERILLA [sic] ORGANIZATION OF ALBERTO FERNÁNDEZ. DATE: December 12, 1960. PAGES: 3. SUBJECTS: FERNÁNDEZ, A. JFK64-8:f19 1998.02.16.11:13:52:576108. NARA.

130: "any precipitous steps": CIA. 104-10172-10079. TO: HAVANA, MEXICO, JMASH. FROM: DIRECTOR. TITLE: CABLE, HOGAN'S REPUTATION KNOWN TO YOU. DATE: August 29, 1960. PAGES: 2. SUBJECTS: HOGAN'S REPUTATION. JFK64-8:F19 1998.02.16.10:55:35:043108. NARA.

130: twenty-three charter signatory organizations join *UNIDAD*: CIA. 104-10166-10226. TITLE: *UNIDAD REVOLUCIONARIA*. DATE: April

16, 1963. SUBJECTS: *UNIDAD REVOLUCIONARIA.* JFK64-5:F10 1998.01.26.09:58:24:560082. NARA.

132: CIA contracts with General Dynamics for a high-speed boat: Sale, "Spies With and Without Daggers," 153.

132: four hours and forty-five minutes: CIA clocks the speed of *El Real* and is ready to send explosives into Cuba: CIA. 104-10172-10077. TO: DIRECTOR. FROM: MASH. TITLE: AMRASP COORDINATOR MADE REQUEST 21 SEP FOR ARMS. DATE: September 22, 1960. PAGES: 2. SUBJECTS: AMRASP, ARMS. JFK64-8:F19 1998.02.16.10:51:23:106108. NARA.

132: By 2010 nickel would be Cuba's largest export: Jorge Castañeda, "Cuba's Endgame?" *Newsweek*, April 26, 2010, 9.

132-133: *"Fidelismo sin Fidel"* was not a tendency with which Alberto Fernández, Michael J. P. Malone, or Robert J. Kleberg, Jr. had any sympathy: See: Alfred W. Webre to Mr. M. J. P. Malone, March 3, 1961. Malone Collection. Czarnikow-Rionda Papers. University of Florida at Gainesville.

134: to at least 31 January 1966: CIA. MEMORANDUM NO. 8. PREPARED BY CI/R & A. DATE: January 11, 1968. SUBJECT: Garrison and the Kennedy Assassination. NARA. See also: CIA. 104-10404-10442. RUSS HOLMES WORK FILE. TITLE:

MEMO NO. 5. GARRISON AND THE KENNEDY ASSASSINATION. DATE: August 7, 1967. PAGES: 42. NARA. See also: CIA. 104-10435-10035. MEMO. NO. 6. RUSS HOLMES WORK FILE. TITLE: MEMO: GARRISON AND THE KENNEDY ASSASSINATION. DATE: September 7, 1967. PAGES: 7. JFK-RHO2:F050-1 1998.11.17.06:10:09:140129. ALSO: FC 1345-1057.

In Memo No. 6, CIA examines people in the Garrison case in terms of their CIA links. Alberto appears once more as having been "a DDP contact starting in December 1960 and continuing at least through 31 January 1966." The latter date, CIA adds, is that of UFGA-24373, which reported that by then "our financial assistance to FERNÁNDEZ had stopped, but that contact was continuing." CIA noted that Garrison had not been in touch with FERNÁNDEZ, which was true.

134: This account of the operations of the *Tejana* derives from interviews with Alberto Fernández between September 2008 and February 2011.

134-135: CIA pays Laborde $700 a month: See: CIA. 104-10172-10383. TO: DEPUTY DIRECTOR FOR PLANS. FROM: WHD. TITLE: MEMORANDUM: INTERLOCKING RELATIONSHIP BETWEEN BROWN/SLAFTER AND GARRISON. DATE: 00/ 17, 1967. PAGES: 5. SUBJECTS: GARRISON, HEMMING, G. NARA. In April 1963,

CIA decided that Laborde was "a poor security risk" and dropped him. He had been "indiscreet, drank too much, and had an unsavory reputation": CIA. 104-10189-10089. TITLE: LAWRENCE LABORDE. DATE: May 12, 1967. PAGES: 3. Laborde had earlier been fired by the U.S. Department of Agriculture for whom he worked from 1947 to 1949 for "excessive drinking, discharging unauthorized firearms, and non-support of dependent children."

135-136: CIA requests cryptonyms for the crew of the *Tejana*: CIA. 104-10172-10067. TO: BELL. FROM: WAVE. TITLE: CABLE REQUESTS CRYPTS BE ASSIGNED FOR ALL INDIVIDUALS WHO CREW AND MAINTAIN THE *TEJANA.* DATE: February 22, 1961. PAGES: 2. SUBJECTS: *TEJANA.* JFK64-8:F19 1998.02.16.10:15:04:950108. NARA.

137: The *Tejana* would arrive and drop anchor: Conversation with Alberto Fernández, January 31, 2010.

138: ABC Manufacturing: Interview with the late Martin Xavier Casey, January 14, 2009.

140: Cesario Diosdado helps Alberto Fernández: CIA. 104-10167-10399. DISPATCH: TO: Chief of Station, JMWAVE. FROM: Chief, W/4. TITLE: U. S. customs agent JMBAR. NARA.

141: 19,000 pounds of ammunition into Cuba: See: Lyman B. Kirkpatrick, INSPECTOR GENERAL'S SURVEY OF THE CUBAN OPERATION AND ASSOCIATED DOCUMENTS. MEMORANDUM FOR: Director of Central Intelligence. SUBJECT: Inspector General Survey of the Cuban Operation, dated October 1961, p. 112.

141: "putting out the C. Wright Mills book": MEMORANDUM. TO: Mr. Frank O'Brien. FROM: Michael J. P. Malone. DATE: January 23, 1961. Papers of Michael J. P. Malone.

CHAPTER 6: THE AGONY OF HUMBERTO SORÍ MARÍN

143: "It was common street knowledge": Interview with Edward Browder before the HSCA. RECORD NUMBER: 180-10077-10040. AGENCY FILE NUMBER: 00581. DATE: January 12, 1978. PAGES: 13. Box 105. NARA. This testimony was released and made public only in 1996 at the initiative of the Assassination Records Review Board (ARRB).

143: CIA notes that on March 1, 1961, Sorí was exfiltrated by the *Tejana* along with four other individuals and that they plan to debrief him: CIA. 104-10172-10064. TO: BELL. FROM: WAVE. TITLE; CABLE: *TEJANA* RETURNED KEY WEST 01140Z REPORTED OPERATION JEAN COMPLETE SUCCESS. DATE: March 1,1961. PAGES:

1. SUBJECTS: *TEJANA.* JFK64-8F19 1998.02.16.10:07:59:106108. NARA.

143: "safe house...black visit": CIA. 104-10166-10226. TITLE: *UNIDAD REVOLUCIONARIA.* DATE: April 16, 1963. PAGES: 148. SUBJECTS: *UNIDAD REVOLUCIONARIA.* JFK64-5:F10 1998.01.26.09:58:24:560082. NARA.

144: Artime had the personal support at CIA of E. Howard Hunt: MEMORANDUM. TO: G. Robert Blakey. FROM: Fonzi & Gonzales. Re: Interview with MANOLO RAY RIVERO. DATE: June 28, 1978. Courtesy of Gaeton Fonzi.

145-147: Sorí's "Plan": "Plan URM." Three pages. Courtesy of Alberto Fernández.

148: "a paid CIA source named Bernard Barker": See: FBI. MEMORANDUM. TO: D. J. BRENNAN. FROM: S. J. PAPICH. SUBJECT: FRANK ANTHONY STURGIS, a.k.a. Frank Fiorini. DATE: JUNE 27, 1962. NEUTRALITY MATTERS. NARA.

149: a *"junta executiva"* is selected in Washington, D.C.: CIA. 104-10172-10049. FROM: INFORMATION REPORT. TITLE: TOP-LEVEL SECRET CONFERENCE AMONG EXILED CUBAN LEADERS FAILS TO RESOLVE DIFFERENCES. DATE: March 16, 1961. SUBJECTS: CUBAN LEADERS. JFK64-8:F19 1998.02.16.08:58:46:373108. NARA.

150: Edward Lansdale was considered a "military detailee": CIA. MEMORANDUM FOR: Inspector General. ATTENTION: Mr. John Leader. VIA: Deputy Director for Administration. DATE: June 5, 1975. PAGES: 3. SUBJECT: Senate Select Committee on Intelligence Operations (Edward Geary Lansdale). Signed Charles W. Kane. Director of Security. This was a 1998 CIA release. CIA. 104-10309-10018. RECORD SERIES; JFK. AGENCY FILE NUMBER: OFF. OF SEC WORK FILES. TO: INSPECTOR GENERAL. FROM: KANE, CHARLES W. DIRECTOR OF SECURITY. TITLE: MEMO: SENATE SELECT COMMITTEE ON INTELLIGENCE OPERATIONS. (EDWARD GEARY LANSDALE). DATE: June 5, 1975. PAGES: 3. SUBJECTS: LANSDALE. JFK-WF04:F1 1998.09.17.14:10:44:466128. NARA. A 1950 report ranked Lansdale "superior in moral conduct . . .": REPORT OF OFFICER EFFECTIVENESS. 10 MARCH 50. Grade: LtCol. Component: USAF. Signed George A. Chester, Colonel. Agency: Department of Defense. An AARB release.

151: "We're going to get clobbered": Cecil B. Currey, *Edward Lansdale: The Unquiet American* (Boston: Houghton Mifflin Company, 1988), 211–212.

151: "It doesn't matter who takes Allen's place": Andrew Tully, *CIA: The*

Inside Story (New York: William Morrow and Company, 1962), 34.

152: The *Tejana* infiltrated Humberto Sorí Marín back into Cuba on March 12: CIA. 104-10264-10126. TITLE: BOAT OPERATIONS USING *TEJANA*. PAGES: 2. SUBJECT: BOAT OPERATIONS. (The March 6, 1961, date on this document is apparently incorrect since the document lists operations that took place as late at April 7.) JFK64-8:F19 1998.12.27.08:14:52:780107. NARA.

153: CIA had been following Rafael Díaz Hanscomb. They discovered that his control over the *UNIDAD* groups was "quite loose": CIA.104-10226-10283. TO: MEMO FOR THE RECORD. FROM: DC/WH/4. TITLE: DISCUSSION OF SABOTAGE AGAINST THE CUBAN PETROLEUM INDUSTRY. DATE: January 13, 1961. PAGES: 2. SUBJECTS: SABOTAGE, PETROLEUM, *UNIDAD REVOLUCIONARIA*. JFK64-61:F4 1998.09.30.19:46:54:763031. NARA.

153-154: The arrest of Humberto Sorí Marín: Fabián Escalante, the former head of Cuban state security, offers a different account of the arrest of Humberto Sorí Marín in *The Secret War: CIA Covert Operations Against Cuba, 1959–62* (Melbourne, Australia: Ocean Press, 1995), 82–83. Escalante has Aldo Vera present in Cuba after Alberto had already exfiltrated him and brought him to the United States.

Escalante also had Alberto making contact with E. Howard Hunt (71), an event that never took place.

Alberto doubts that *UNIDAD* had been penetrated, as Escalante insists, with G-2 monitoring Sorí Marín's movements for several months prior to his arrests. (Escalante appears not to know of Sorí's trip to the United States.) Escalante writes of Sorí and "the infiltrators": "They were unaware that the G-2 knew about the conclave and that for several months the counter revolutionary groups that the conspirators thought they could rely on had already been penetrated. Thus a 'rebellion' was staged by Captain Alcibiades Bermúdez and a group of his comrades in order to infiltrate Sorí Marín's group and give the impression that a large band of outlaws operated in the *Sierra de los Organos* . . . the G-2 gate-crashed the party and confiscated the plans, maps, outline and, of course, the weapons and explosives designed to terrorize the population." (80).

According to Alberto Fernández, Castro's G-2 did not close in on Sorí nor did they have any idea of his whereabouts. Sorí was captured when that patrol in search of a neighborhood thief inadvertently entered the home of the engineer where Sorí was meeting with fellow members of the Underground.

It should be noted, however, that Escalante's version of Sorí's arrest was confirmed by a *UNIDAD* member named Bonifacio Herrera Fernández, nicknamed "Bony." According to "Bony," as reported by the CIA at

JMWAVE where he was debriefed in May 1961, upon his arrival from Cuba: "In March 1961, SORÍ, Rafael [Díaz Hanscomb] and Francisco were arrested as the result of information furnished to G-2 by one Captain BERMÚDEZ, who was working under SORÍ and supposedly in command of a group of guerrillas in Pinar del Rio": CIA. 104-10308-10034. AGENCY FILE NUMBER: LA DIV WORK FILE. TO: CHIEF, WESTERN HEMISPHERE DIVISION. FROM: CHIEF OF BASE, JMWAVE. TITLE: DISPATCH: DEBRIEFING OF BONIFACIO HERRERA FERNÁNDEZ AKA "BONY" AND "EL GUAJIRO." PAGES: 4. SUBJECTS: CASTRO. JFK-WF02:F3 1998.09.17.10:50:04:030128. ATTACHED ROUTING AND RECORD SHEET. NARA.

153-154: Fabián Escalante claims that Castro's G-2 had infiltrated Sorí's group: See Escalante, *The Secret War*, 80. It was apparently to discredit Alberto Fernández that Escalante writes that he made contact with E. Howard Hunt (ibid., 71), which was not so. Nor are the stories of the plan to rescue Sorí Marín accurate (ibid., 82–83). Aldo Vera, whom Escalante names, was not even present in Cuba at the time; he had been exfiltrated to the United States on the *Tejana*.

154-155: Nixon tells Helms that Donald Kendall did not want Allende to take power: Bob Woodward, *Veil: The Secret Wars of the CIA 1981–1987.*

(New York: Simon & Schuster, 1987.) 24–25. Paperback edition: 2005

155: "few pennies": the Cubans contributed 50,000 Cuban pesos: CIA. 104-10520-10106. TITLE: REPORT: *UNIDAD REVOLUCIONARIA* (REVOLUTIONARY UNITY). DATE: November 24, 1962. PAGES: 4. SUBJECT: UNIDAD. JFK64-61:F5 1999.08.27.09:17:14:310128. NARA.

155: Geddes in *La Cabaña* prison: CIA. 104-10166-10226. TITLE: *UNIDAD REVOLUCIONARIA.* The information that Geddes was rescued by Field Marshal Montgomery comes from Alberto Fernández.

155: "we do not know at this stage of the game whether or how much GEDDES has talked": CIA. 104-10226-10844. TO: CHIEF, WH/4/ PM. FROM: WH/4/CI. DATE: June 14, 1961. JFK64-61:F3 1998.05.02.09:09:57:390107. NARA.

156: "A portion of the *UR* has been blown by the events in this case": CIA. MEMO TO: CHIEF/WH/4/ PM. FROM: WH/4/CI. TITLE: ROBERT M. GEDDES AND THE *UNIDAD REVOLUCION-ARIA*. Reference WAVE 6678 (IM 3091) 12 June 1961. DATE: June 14, 1961. PAGES: 3. JFK64-61:F3 1998.05.02.09.09:57:390107. NARA.

156: Hobbling on a crutch: This account of Humberto Sorí Marín at

La Cabaña prison comes from John Martino, *I Was Castro's Prisoner: An American Tells His Story* (Southlake, Texas: JFK Lancer Publications & Productions, 2008), 147–150. Originally published in 1963.

156: a "*barbudo*" without a beard: Martino, *I Was Castro's Prisoner*, 147.

157: On the *Santa Ana*: Interviews with Alberto Fernández. Yet another suicidal scheme had CIA asset William Pawley recruit four members of the *Tejana* to help him capture some Russians out of Cuba and transport them to the United States. After several attempts, all of which failed, Pawley betrayed the group to save himself, and all were murdered in Cuba. Telephone conversation with Albert Fernández, February 19, 2009.

158: Nixon orders Dulles not to debrief candidate Kennedy: Peter Wyden, *Bay of Pigs: The Untold Story* (New York: Simon & Schuster: New York, 1979), 67n. See also: Quirk, *Fidel Castro*, 347.

159: "one of the worst parts of Cuba to make a beachhead": FBI. 4/27/61. TO: DIRECTOR, FBI. FROM: SAC, NEW YORK. 105-89923-192. PAGES: 4. NARA.

159: Dulles explains why the Cuban Underground was not contacted to participate in the Bay of Pigs operation: See: Quirk, *Fidel Castro*, 362n. See also letter to Dulles, June 28,

1960, and Dulles' reply of July 10, available in the Dulles Papers, Princeton University.

160: "In the *Sierra* I learned to love your brother": Interview with Mariano Sorí Marín by Fidel Castro is described in Humberto Fontova, "Monster," FrontPageMagazine.com, July 15, 2005.

160: Mariano collapsed in shock: See Humberto Fontova, "Bay of Pigs, 40 Years After" conference, Fidel Castro and the lying Media," BrookesNews.com, April 25, 2005. Available online.

161: "we were at war with Cuba": quoted in Anne Karalekas, *History of the Central Intelligence Agency* (Laguna Hills, California: Aegean Park Press, 1977), 68.

161: Kim Philby on Dulles and the Bay of Pigs: Leonard Mosley, *Dulles: A Biography of Eleanor, Allen, and John Foster Dulles and their Family Network* (New York: The Dial Press/James Wade, 1978), 282.

161: People to People program: MEMORANDUM FROM: Michael J. P. Malone. TO: Mr. George A. Braga. Ref: The People to People Program. DATE: April 21, 1961. Papers of Michael J. P. Malone.

164: Alberto begins to put quotation marks around the word "friends" when referring to CIA: See, for example, Alberto Fernández to Michael J. P.

Malone, May 9, 1962. Czarnikow-Rionda Collection. University of Florida at Gainesville.

165: "a traitor to his country": Quoted in John Loftus and Mark Aarons, *The Secret History of the Jews: How Western Espionage Betrayed the Jewish People* (New York: St. Martin's Press–Griffin, 1994), 71.

165: "procurement and evaluation of information": David K. E. Bruce, "The National Intelligence Authority," *Virginia Quarterly Review*, Summer 1946, 355–369.

165: Eisenhower suggests that David Bruce, assisted by Robert Lovett, report on CIA's covert activities. The passages quoted are from Arthur M. Schlesinger, Jr., *Robert Kennedy and His Times* (New York: Ballantine, 1978).

165: Doolittle, a friend of Wisner: Karalekas, *History of the Central Intelligence Agency*, 52. Doolittle a friend of D. H. Byrd, see D. H. Byrd, *I'm an Endangered Species: The Autobiography of a Free Enterpriser* (Houston, Texas: Pacesetter Press, 1978), 40–41. Byrd calls Doolittle "my esteemed friend and hunting and fishing partner." There is a photograph in the book of General "Jim" Doolittle, as Byrd calls him, with Byrd on safari in Africa.

165: Doolittle wrote his report with "the very active support and cooperation of Allen Dulles": John Ranelagh, *The Agency: The Rise and Decline of the CIA* (New York: A Touchstone Book: Simon & Schuster, 1987), 276.

166: "mingling in the internal affairs of other nations . . . where will we be tomorrow?": Schlesinger, *Robert Kennedy and His Times*, 490–491.

166: For the complete text of 10/2, see: "Foreign Relations of the United States, 1945–1950. Emergence of the Intelligence Establishment," (Washington, D.C.: U.S. Printing Office), XXXI-XXXV.

166: "the greatest mistake I ever made": Wilson D. Miscamble, *George F. Kennan and the Making of American Foreign Policy, 1947–1950* (Princeton: Princeton University Press, 1992), 109.

Kennan expressed his regret over having written 10/2 on another occasion: "I regret to say . . . it did not work out at all the way I had conceived it": 94th Congress 2nd Session Senate Report No. 94-755 Supplementary Detailed Staff Reports on Foreign and Military Intelligence, Book IV, Final Report of the Select Committee to Study Governmental Operations with Respect to Intelligence Activities, United States Senate. U.S. Government Printing Office: Washington, D.C., 1976. See also: George Kennan, "Morality and Foreign Policy," *Foreign Affairs,* Winter 1985–1986, 214.

167: "authority to conduct operations": Schlesinger, *Robert Kennedy and His Times*, 493.

167: "a total reassessment": Ibid., 492.

168: "an old DDP operator": Ray S. Cline, *Secrets, Spies and Scholars: The Essential CIA* (Washington, D.C.: Acropolis Books, Ltd., 2009), 194.

168: "the sound of a single CIA spade digging": Nelson D. Lankford, *The Last American Aristocrat: The Biography of David K. E. Bruce, 1898–1977* (Boston: Little, Brown and Company, 1996), 282.

CHAPTER 7: LITTLE BOY BLUE AND OUR CHIVAS REGAL FRIEND, 1962–1967

170: the tangled CIA operation in the Congo: An excellent account of CIA machinations in the Congo can be found in Kwitny, *Endless Enemies*.

170-171: Alberto meets with Bebe Rebozo: Interviews with Alberto Fernández. See also: CIA. 104-10264-10047. TO: DIRECTOR. FROM: JMWAVE. TITLE: CABLE: ADAMS KEY, DUE EAST OF HOMESTEAD FLORIDA IS IDEAL BASE. DATE: November 22, 1961. PAGES: 1. SUBJECTS: AMDENIM-1. JFK64-8:F20 1998.07.17.11.08:27:326128. NARA.

171: Alberto Fernández, Michael J. P. Malone, and Donald Hogan meet with Bernard E. Reichhardt: CIA. 104-10172-10052. TO: MFR. FROM: BERNARD E. REICH-HARDT, ACTING CHIEF, WH/4/ OPS. TITLE: MFR: MEETING WITH ALBERTO FERNÁNDEZ, DONALD HOGAN, AND JACK MALONE ON 16 MAY 1961. DATE: May 16, 1961. PAGES: 10. SUBJECTS: *UNIDAD REVOLUCION-ARIA*, HOGAN, DON. JFK64-8:F19 1998.02.16.09:13:06:873108. NARA.

171: CIA considers Hogan an "undesirable hanger-on": CIA. 104-10172-10425. TO: BELL. FROM: WAVE. TITLE: CABLE. PARA 1 OF REF A MENTIONS INCLUSION OF DON HOGAN IN TALKS. DATE: May 19, 1961. PAGES: 1. SUBJECTS: AMDENIM. JFK64-8:F19 1998.7.16.19:20:45:576115. NARA.

173: Kappas and Stevens are hired by CIA and refuse to talk to Don Hogan: Don Hogan to Dear Bob. November 11, 1962. NARA.

174: Alberto must formalize his understanding with KUBARK: CIA. 104-10172-10047. TO: AVE. FROM: BELL. TITLE: CABLE APPROVE REF AN ON BASIS AGREEMENT OBTAINED AS GENERALLY OUT-LINE IN PARA 2 REF B. DATE: June 13, 1961. PAGES: 1. SUBJECT: BASIS AGREEMENT. JFK64-8:F19. 1998.02.16.08:47:26:250108. NARA.

174: Tony Varona's disillusionment: Tony Varona tells Hurwitch that the

U.S. is abandoning Cuba: July 7, 1961. Memorandum of Conversation. Washington. Subject: Cuban Revolutionary Council. "Foreign Relations of the United States," 1961–63." Vol. X, 1961-1962, 242.

174: "It is a fallacy to suppose that clandestine activity": "Foreign Relations of the United States, 1961–1963," vol. X. Cuba, 1961–1962. July 8, 1961. Kennedy Library. Papers of Arthur Schlesinger. Cuba 1961. Box 31. Secret.

175: his "plans or whereabouts," his wife "evasive": CIA. 10264-10052. TO: DIRECTOR. FROM: JMWAVE. TITLE: CABLE: IN ACCORDANCE PARA 2 REF B. DATE: July 15, 1961. PAGES: 2. SUBJECTS: AMDENIM. JFK64-8:F 20 1998.07.17:11:33:17:513128. NARA. After the *Tejana* "blew all seals on one engine during sea trials on August 15, 1961," Headquarters agreed to "provide limited support AMDENIM/1 for one op": CIA. 104-10264-10051. TO: DIRECTOR. FROM: JMBAR. TITLE: CABLE: AMDENIM-4 ADVISES C/BAR THAT TEJANA III BLEW SEALS ON ONE. DATE: August 16, 1961. PAGES: 1. SUBJECTS: AMDENIM-4. JFK64-8:F20 1998.07.17:11:31:21:950128. NARA. By August 1961, Raford W. Herbert (AC/WHD) was in charge of monitoring Alberto and the operations of the *Tejana*.

175: "coordinate my family necessities with my other activities": Alberto Fernández de Hechavarría to Michael

J. P. Malone, March 15, 1963. Papers of Michael J. P. Malone.

175: The *Tejana* is refurbished and operates out of Key Largo: CIA. 104-10264-10050. TO: DIRECTOR. FROM: JMWAVE. TITLE: CABLE: AMDENIM-1'S *TEJANA* CAN BE MADE OPERATIONAL FOR TEN THOUSAND. DATE: September 29, 1961. PAGES: 2. SUBJECTS: AMDENIM-1. JFK64-8:F20 1998.07.17.11:28:45090128. NARA.

175: "reluctant to again place supervision and monetary control of these matters in AMDENIM-1's hand": CIA. MEMORANDUM FOR: C/TPW/PA-PROP. SUBJECT: Alberto Fernández Echevarría [sic] (AMDENIM-1). 27 June 1962. Signed Martha Tharpe. TFW/PA-PROP. NARA.

175: CIA requests a "political profile" of Alberto Fernández . . ." no substantive derogatory information . . .": CIA. 104-10172-10150. TO: C/TFW/PA-PROP. FROM: THARPE, MARTHA TFW/PA-PROP. TITLE: MEMORANDUM: ALBERTO FERNÁNDEZ ECHEVARRÍA [sic]. (AMDENIM-1. DATE: June 27, 1962. PAGES: 4. SUBJECTS: ECHEVARRÍA, A.F. AMDENIM/1. JFK64-8F20:1998.02.20.15:02:41:950109: OFFICIAL ROUTING SLIP ATTACHED. NARA.

175: "bringing certain Army and Navy personnel out of Cuba": CIA. May 1, 1962. TO: Director, Central Intelligence

Agency. Attention: Deputy Director, Plans. FROM: John Edgar Hoover, Director. SUBJECT: ALBERTO FERNÁN-DEZ, INTERNAL SECURITY-CUBA. HSCA SUBJECT: Alberto Hechevarría [sic], Main File 97-3602. FEDERAL BUREAU OF INVESTIGATION, INVESTIGATIVE AND ADMINIS-TRATIVE FILES.

176: "rocky and will continue so": CIA. 104-10172-10150. TO: C/TFW/PA-PROP. FROM: THARPE, MAR-THA TFW/PA-PROP. TITLE: MEMORANDUM: ALBERTO FERNÁNDEZ ECHEVARRÍA [sic]. (AMDENIM-1. DATE: June 27, 1962. PAGES: 4. SUBJECTS: ECHE-VARRÍA, A.F. AMDENIM/1. JFK64-8F20:1998.02.20.15:02:41:950109: OFFICIAL ROUTING SLIP ATTACHED. NARA.

176: Alberto continues to cir-cumvent JMWAVE control: CIA. 10264-10053. TO: DIRECTOR. FROM: JMWAVE. TITLE: CABLE: AMDENIM-1 CALLED JOBES 11 JUNE AND ASKED STATUS PAYMENT MONEY. DATE: July 12, 1961. PAGES: 2. SUBJECTS: AMDENIM-1.   JFK64-8:F20 1998.07.17.11:35:10:810128. NARA.

176: CIA hired informants to find out what *UNIDAD* was up to: CIA. 104-10189-10048. TO: CHIEF OF STATION, JMWAVE. FROM: CHIEF, TASK FORCE W. TITLE: DISPATCH—JOSÉ MANUEL MARTÍNEZ SIERRA. DATE: August

14, 1962. PAGES: 1. JFK64-24:F13 1998.08.23.10:50:05:590107. NARA.

177: "was inclined to do": Malone telephoned CIA on December 15, 1961. CIA. 104-10521-10087. TO: REDACTED. FROM: CHIEF, WH/4/PM. TITLE: MFR: TELECOM BETWEEN MICHAEL J. MALONE AND CHARLES W. MATT, 15 DECEMBER 1961. DATE: Decem-ber 19, 1961. PAGES: 2. SUBJECTS: MALONE, MICHAEL. NARA. "Malone must evaluate the worth and reliability": Ibid. CIA. 104-10520-10087. FROM: CHIEF, WH/4/PM. Malone first tried to reach "Mr. Pekich" (James S. Pekich) and Kudzu, and when they were not available, Charles W. Matt took the call. By 1968, Pekich would be in Venezuela. Walter P. Kudzu worked alongside E. Howard Hunt and would become notorious for providing Hunt with an alibi for his whereabouts on November 22, 1963, the day of the Kennedy assassination.

177-178: Matt trusts neither Alberto nor Malone and wants to insure [sic] at least tacit agreement that he is not acting contrary to U.S. interests: Ibid., CIA. 104-10520-10087.

177-178: For evidence that CIA was aware that Kleberg would be provid-ing the remaining $6,000: CIA. 104-10172-10175. TO: DIRECTOR. FROM: WAVE. TITLE: CABLE AN ACTION PROBABLY HIS EFFORT OBTAIN PART OF MONEY FOR ADAMS KEY OF REF B AND

PREVIOUS AS BASE FOR *TEJANA* AND *UR* TRAINING. DATE: December 28, 1961. PAGES: 1. SUBJECTS: AMDENIM-1. JFK64-8:F20 1998.02.2107:51:37:373108. NARA.

177-178: CIA created a furor over the $6,000 that Alberto was seeking. It appears as if Malone was also asking Charles Matt for the $6,000 to help Alberto purchase a farm as a "safe site": Ibid., CIA. 104-10520-10087. TO: REDACTED. FROM: CHIEF, WH/4/PM. TITLE: TELECOM BETWEEN MICHAEL J. MALONE AND CHARLES W. MATT. DATE: DECEMBER 15, 1961. See also on this subject: CIA. 104-10172-10176. TO: JMWAVE. FROM: DIRECTOR. TITLE: CABLE O/A 15 DEC 1961 REQUESTED $6, 000 FROM HQS. CONTACT KNOWN TO INGHURST. DATE: December 19, 1961. PAGES: 1. SUBJECTS: AMDENIM-1. JFK64-8:F20 1998.02.21.07:57:40:076108. NARA.

178: "classes in man-to-man combat; explosives . . .": CIA. 104-10226-10148. TO: DIRECTOR, FBI. FROM: DD, PLANS. TITLE: SUBJECT: ACTIVITIES OF THE *UNIDAD REVOLUCIONARIA*, ANTI-CASTRO GROUP. DATE: September 6, 1961. PAGES: 4. SUBJECTS: ANTI-CASTRO, UFGA-1830; AMCHEER-1. JFK64-61:F3 1998.09.21.19:10:04:090102. NARA.

179: "Little Boy Blue": MEMORANDUM of Michael J. P. Malone. Re: Conversation with my Chivas Regal friend." March 16, 1962. NARA. Note: In the film, *State of the Union* (1948), Van Johnson calls the presidential hopeful played by Spencer Tracy "Little Boy Blue" in an attack on Tracy's naïveté. President Eisenhower may have borrowed the locution that he applied to John F. Kennedy from this film.

179: Radio Swan: Interview with Howard K. Davis.

179: CIA infiltrates the Peace Corps: John F. Kennedy Memorial Library, Dictabelt 17A, Item 17A4. April 2, 1963.

180: Malone meets with CIA asset Dr. Alton Ochsner: Michael J. P. Malone to Dr. Alton Ochsner, February 20, 1962. NARA. The record from CIA's files of Ochsner's service to the Agency is copious. See, for example: CIA. 104-10170-10221. TO: CHIEF, CI/R & A. TITLE: GARRISON INVESTIGATION— DR. ALTON OCHSNER. DATE: May 23, 1968. PAGES: 2. JFK64-25:F8 1998.08.27.05:45:29:186129. ROUTING AND RECORD SHEET ATTACHED. NARA: "Dr. Edward William Ochsner was a cleared source (Approved Caution since 13 May 1955). He was used infrequently as a contact of our New Orleans Office in the collection of intelligence information. Last official contact with Dr. Ochsner was 8 January 1962."

See also: CIA.104-10170-10242. TITLE: OCHSNER, EDWARD WILLIAM ALTON AKA OCHSNER, ALTON. DATE: May 31, 1968. JFK64-25:F9 1998.08.27.06:33:39:856129. NARA: "On 12 April he was security approved (caution) for contact use through a SECRET level. Subject at that time was to attend the 16th Congress of the International Society of Surgery, Copenhagen, Denmark. He was asked to furnish copies of advance circulars, provisional programs and registration data on Soviet-bloc countries in particular attending the conference. ..."

On May 17, 1968, the Chief Security Research Staff of the Office of Security headed by Paul F. Gaynor denied that the Office of Security had files on Alton Ochsner. Given that the Office of Security had its own entirely separate set of indices, the Office of Security may have been telling the truth. See: MEMORANDUM FOR: CHIEF, CI/R& A. ATTENTION: Mr. Kesler. SUBJECT: OCHSNER, Alton. Signed Paul F. Gaynor, Chief, Security Research Staff/OS. 17 May 1968. PAGES: 1. NARA.

The above-cited documents exploring CIA's connections with Dr. Ochsner date from Jim Garrison's 1966–1969 investigation during which Dr. Ochsner's name surfaced. Lloyd Ray, running the New Orleans CIA field office, and Hunter Leake, his second-in-command, had to convey to Washington that they were indeed social friends of Ochsner:

CIA. 104-10189-10231. FROM: CONTACTS/NEW ORLEANS TO: CONTACTS/WASHINGTON. TITLE: TWX: CASE 49364. OUR LAST OFFICAL REPEAT OFFICIAL CONTACT WITH DR. ALTON OCHSNER. DATE: May 22, 1968. PAGES: 1. JFK64-24:F15 1999.02.18.14:26:52:450120. NARA: "Both [Hunter] Leake and I," Lloyd Ray writes, "are acquainted socially with Alton Ochsner and see him occasionally at social gatherings." CIA's emphasis on the word "officially" to indicate Ochsner's end date of service suggests that the conclusion of their relationship was otherwise.

CIA Counter Intelligence wrote memoranda quoting the FBI as saying that Jim Garrison believed that Ochsner was one of the principals involved in the conspiracy to assassinate President Kennedy. This was false. Garrison believed no such thing. But see: MEMORANDUM FOR: George S. Musulin, DCS/Operational Support Staff. SUBJECT: Dr. Alton OCHSNER. DATE: May 20, 1968. Signed James W. Kesler, CI/R & A. NARA.

180: "study ranching conditions": See: "International Bank Official to Give Talk Here Monday," *Dallas News*, October 16, 1952; "Prosperity To Stay, World Banker Says," *The Dallas Times Herald*, October 20, 1952.

180-181: Robert Wells tries to organize a meeting for anti-Castro exiles at the

Dallas Council for World Affairs: Luis V. Manrara to Mr. Robert C. Wells, October 11, 1961, written on the letterhead of "The Truth about Cuba Committee, Inc." See also: Robert C. Wells to General Philip Bethune, Dallas Council on World Affairs," October 13, 1961. Wells copied his letter to Bethune to both Robert J. Kleberg, Jr. and Michael J. P. Malone.

181: "Romualdi, Serafino. AFL representative for Latin America and principal CIA agent for labour operations in Latin America": Agee, *Inside the Company*, 620.

181: Romualdi's wartime acquaintance with Allen Dulles in Switzerland is discussed in Bruce Adamson, "Oswald's Closest Friend: The George de Mohrenschildt Story: Wolfen Communism Without Trotsky," vol. VIII, 38.

181-183: Romualdi's conversation with Michael J. P. Malone is summarized in: FBI. DIRECTOR, FBI. SAC, NEW YORK. April 5, 1962. ANTI-FIDEL CASTRO ACTIVITIES. IS-CUBA. 105-35353-991[remaining numbers illegible]. PAGES: 5. NARA.

183: King Ranch contributes to the AIFLD: FBI. INSIDE LABOR, "Fight Against Mao-ists and Castroites Hurt When CIA Ignored Specific Warning Not to Use Unions As Cover" by Victor Riesel. April 6, 1967. 62-80750. NARA.

183: Michael J. P. Malone meets with Raford Herbert: Their conversation is reported in FBI. TO: SAC, New York. FROM: Director, FBI. SUBJECT: Anti-Fidel Castro Activities. IS-Cuba. DATE: April 5, 1962. (105-35353). NARA. See also: MEMORANDUM: Re: Conversation with my luncheon friend. TO: Robert J. Kleberg, Jr. FROM: Michael J. P. Malone. DATE: March 16,1962. This memo also describes Malone's meeting with Romualdi.

185: Malone meets with David Atlee Phillips: See: FBI. DIRECTOR, FBI. SAC, NEW YORK. ANTI-FIDEL CASTRO ACTIVITIES. IS-CUBA. APRIL 5, 1962, NARA. Malone reports on his meetings with Raford Herbert, David Phillips, and Serafino Romualdi in this report. See also: MEMORANDUM. Re: Conversation with my Chivas Regal friend. From: Michael J. P. Malone. To: Robert J. Kleberg, Jr. DATE: March 30, 1962. NARA.

187: "CIA would fully utilize his abilities and equipment": This quotation may be found in "Conversation with my Chivas Regal friend," March 16, 1962.

187: 1948 Agreement between CIA and FBI: Frank Wisner requests the cooperation of the FBI to forge an alliance with CIA: CIA. 104-10213-10146. AGENCY: CIA. ORIGINATOR: FBI. TITLE:

CORRESPONDENCE WITH FBI ON CIA/FBI LIAISON AGREEMENT IN 1948. PAGES: 18. JFK64-48:F26 1998.10.22.14:10:26:590108. NARA. Later CIA would deny that this agreement existed: See: CIA. 104-10213-10181. TO: OFFICE OF LEGISLATIVE COUNSEL. FROM: SHEPANEK, NORBERT. TITLE: MEMO: PARA 2 REQUEST OF REF. DATE: July 31, 1978. PAGES: 1. JFK64-48:F6 1999.03.01.10:44:15:686129. NARA.

187-188: Malone reports on Frank Fiorini, Alexander Rorke, and Pedro Díaz Lanz: CIA. 104-10221-10285. TO: MFR. FROM: CHARLES MATT TFW/PM. TITLE: MEMORANDUM: FRANK FIORINI. DATE: July 3, 1962. PAGES: 3. SUBJECTS: FIORINI, FRANK. NARA. Malone reported again to Matt after meeting with Rorke: CIA. 104-101700-10046. TO: MEMORANDUM FOR THE RECORD. FROM: MATT, C. W. TFW/PM. TITLE: 17 OCTOBER 62. MEETING WITH MICHAEL MALONE, CZARNIKOV [sic]-RIONDA COMPANY. DATE: October 19, 1962. PAGES: 1. NARA.

Rorke told Malone that he needed money for a boat, and Malone conveyed this message to Charles Matt: CIA. 104-10180-10054. TO: DIRECTOR, FBI. FROM: DEPUTY DIRECTOR (PLANS). ATTN: MR. S. J. PAPICH. TITLE; MEMORANDUM: SUBJECT MICHAEL J. P. MALONE.

DATE: September 11, 1962. PAGES: 2. SUBJECTS: RORKE. NARA.

Rorke informs to the Bureau about CIA and Fiorini, and the Bureau in turn informed CIA of Rorke's report: TO: DIRECTOR, FBI. FROM: SAC, NEW YORK. SUBJECT: FRANK ANTHONY STURGIS a.k.a. Frank Fiorini. NEUTRALITY MATTERS. DATE: June 22, 1962. 67-45909. 62-1474-94 [remaining numbers illegible] This FBI document was released by CIA. See also: TO: D. J. BRENNAN. FROM: S. J. PAPICH. DATE: June 27, 1962. SUBJECT: FRANK ANTHONY STURGIS a.k.a. Frank Fiorini. NEUTRALITY MATTERS.

188: Díaz Lanz's defection, the "first major break in Castro's revolutionary command": Editorial Note. Document #327. "Foreign Relations of the United States, 1958–1960," vol. VI.

188-189: Matt wants Malone to persuade Alberto Fernández to join CRC, and participate in this "united front": CIA. C. W. Matt: 1-251853. Reviewed by S. Bolten and Charles Ford. June 5, 1962. Available on maryferrell.org.

188-189: Alberto Fernández writes to Michael J. P. Malone. May 9, 1962. NARA. No identifying riff attached.

189: Alberto Fernández and Miró Cardona. On November 3, 1961, Alberto had told Miró Cardona that he would not join the Cuban

Revolutionary Council or reveal *UR*'s operational details to anyone belonging to that organization: CIA. 104-10264-10049. TO: DIRECTOR. FROM: JMWAVE. TITLE: CABLE: FOR HQS INFORMATION AFTER MEETINGS HURWITCH. DATE: November 6, 1961. PAGES: 3. SUBJECTS: AMCLATTER-1, HURWITCH. JFK64-8:F20 1998.07.17.10:29:05:170128. NARA. Alberto was accused of "complicating life for AMBUD-1 (Cardona)": Ibid., CIA. 104-10172-10127. DATE: March 15, 1963.

189: Alberto telephones Hurwitch and talks about Miró Cardona's joining *UR:* CIA. 104-10264-10037. TO: JMWAVE. FROM: DIRECTOR. TITLE: CABLE: AMDENIM-1 PHONED STATE DEPT OFFICER FROM NY 5 JUNE. DATE: June 7, 1962. PAGES: 1. SUBJECTS: AMDENIM-1. JFK64-8:F20 1998. 07.17.10:08:57:466128. NARA. Robert A. Hurwitch was Special Assistant for Cuban Affairs, June 1962–January 1963, then Deputy Coordinator for Cuban Affairs, Department of State, January 1963 to August 1963.

189: "agitate" the relationship between ODACID and KUBARK: CIA. 104-10172-10178. TO: WAVE. FROM: DIRECTOR. TITLE: CABLE HQS RECOGNIZES VALIDITY STATION DESIRE CONTROL. DATE: November 24, 1961. PAGES: 1. SUBJECTS: AMDENIM-1. JFK64-8:F20 1998.02.21.08:05:55:950108. NARA.

190: Alberto Fernández follows the direction of his case officer, Robert Wall: CIA. 104-10172-10141. TO: CHIEF TASK FORCE W. FROM: COS WAVE. TITLE: PROGRESS REPORT 30 SEPTEMBER 1962. DATE: September 17, 1962. SUBJECTS: AMDENIM-1. JFK64-8:F20 1998.02.20.14:36:24:153108. NARA.

190: CIA uses Malone to persuade Alberto Fernández that *UNIDAD* should join the CRC: CIA. 104-10172-10165. TO: WAVE. FROM: DIRECTOR. TITLE: CABLE TELECON WITH MICHAEL MALONE, KUBARK CONTACT CZARNIKOW-RIONDA. MALONE PUT AMDENIM-1 ON LINE. DATE: June 5, 1962. SUBJECTS: AMDENIM-1. JFK64-8:F20 1998.02.20.16:02:40:780108. NARA.

190-191: news of Alberto Fernández talking on the telephone to Matt about *UR* joining the CRC is conveyed to JMWAVE and beyond: CIA. 104-10226-10097. TO: JMWAVE. FROM: DIRECTOR. TITLE: CABLE RE: ON 4 JUNE 1962 TELECOM WITH MICHAEL MALONE, KUBARK CONTACT. DATE: June 6, 1962. PAGES: 1. SUBJECTS: ANTI-CASTRO. JFK64-61:F5 1998.05.15.20:31:00:403115. NARA.

191: "corroborating reassurances": Malone puts Alberto Fernández on the line to talk with Charles W. Matt:

CIA. 104-10520-10110. FROM: CHIEF, TFW/PM. TITLE: MFR. 4 JUNE 1962 TELECON WITH MICHAEL J. MALONE. DATE: June 5, 1962. PAGES: 2. SUBJECTS: FERNÁNDEZ. JFK64-61:F5 1998.08.27.09:25:54:670128. NARA.

191: The Western Hemisphere leadership up to William K. Harvey watches to see whether Alberto Fernández will bring *UNIDAD* into the Cuban Revolutionary Council: CIA. 104-10226-10413. TO: JMWAVE. FROM: DIRECTOR. TITLE: AMDENIM-1'S CONTACT WITH STATE DEPARTMENT. DATE: June 7, 1962. PAGES: 1. SUBJECTS: AMDENIM-1. JFK64-61:F5 1998.10.06.18:19:33:590031. NARA.

191-192: "a rather tricky person . . . the Inspector General": CIA. 104-10172-10143. TITLE: PERSONAL RECORD QUESTIONNAIRE, PART II–OPERATIONAL INFORMATION. DATE: October 10, 1962. PAGES: 8. SUBJECTS: JFK DOCUMENT. JFK64-8:F20 1998.02.20.14:43:00:483108.

192: CIA wants to subject Alberto Fernández to a lie detector test: Ibid., CIA. 104-10172-10163. Alberto's "clearance" was canceled temporarily for failure to provide PRQ: PART II. CIA. 104-10172-10144. TO: COS JMWAVE. FROM: CHIEF, TASK FORCE W. TITLE: WITHHELD. DATE: October 3, 1962. PAGES: 2. SUBJECTS: JFK DOCUMENT. JFK64-8:F20 1998.02.20.14:45:23:216108. NARA.

192: "provided somewhat more of a workout for the flutter operator": CIA. DISPATCH. TO: Special Affairs Staff. FROM: Chief of Station, JMWAVE. SUBJECT: Progress Report 31 May 1963. NARA.

192: "of considerable continuing value": CIA. 104-10172-10164. TO: DIRECTOR. FROM: WAVE. TITLE: CABLE: UPON HIS RETURN WAVE AREA AMDENIM-1 ADVISED HE HAD TELECON WITH HQS REP. DATE: June 12, 1962. PAGES: 2. SUBJECTS: AMDENIM-1. JFK64-8:F20 1998.02.2015:55:11:340108. NARA.

192: "whatever is required to advance the cause": CIA. 104-10172-10163. TO: CHIEF, TASK FORCE W. FROM: COS JMWAVE. TITLE: DISPATCH: AMDENIM-1 PROGRESS REPORT FOR THE PERIOD 1 MAY TO 16 JUNE. DATE: June 19, 1962. PAGES: 2. SUBJECTS: AMDENIM-1. JFK64-8:F20 1998.02.20.15:53:25:640108. NARA.

193: KUBARK wants the *UR* to "turn over its clandestine assets and potential agents to JMWAVE for unilateral compartmentalized handling": CIA. 104-10226-10110. TO: CHIEF, TASK FORCE W. FROM: COS JMWAVE. TITLE: DISPATCH, *UNIDAD REVOLUCIONARIA*: DEVELOPMENT

AS PROPAGANDA MECHANISM AND COVER FOR UNILATERAL OPERATIONS. DATE: January 16, 1963. PAGES: 5. SUBJECTS: *UNIDAD REVOL*, ESPADA, JOSÉ. JFK64-61:F6   1998.05.16.09:15:30:216108. NARA.

193: Western Union wire from Alberto Fernández to Michael J. P. Malone. August 25, 1962. Papers of Michael J. P. Malone.

193: Michael J. P. Malone encouraged him: Michael J. P. Malone to Alberto Fernández, September 27, 1962. Papers of Michael J. P. Malone.

195: Alberto Fernández authors a MEMORANDUM FOR THE RECORD: CIA. 104-10235-10243. ORGINATOR: CIA.   TITLE: MFR—DIRECTORIO RAID AND RECOMMENDATION RE CRC. DATE: August 30, 1962. PAGES: 4: SUBJECTS: MDC, CRC. JFK64-69:F7   1998.10.18.12:39:30:250108. NARA.

197: "Because of the vital importance": Memorandum for: Director of Central Intelligence. Subject: Final Report of Working Group on Organization and Activities. DATE: April 6, 1962. PAGES: 35. NARA.

CHAPTER 8: DIONISIO PASTRANA AND THE SOVIET MISSILES

Chapter note: Dionisio Pastrana: All references to Dionisio Pastrana and his CIA-sponsored operations derive from: Interview with Dionisio Pastrana. December 14, 2009. Miami, Florida.

199: "He is now a fully accredited KUBARK agent in good standing": CIA. 104-10172-10096. TO: CHIEF, SPECIAL AFFAIRS STAFF. FROM: COS   JMWAVE.   TITLE: DISPATCH: AMDENIM-1. PROGRESS REPORT 31 MAY 1963. DATE: June 25, 1963. PAGES: 6. SUBJECTS: DOGGO,   AMDENIM-1.   JFK64-8:F20   1998.02.16.15:54:25:310102. NARA. It was only in April 1963, when the cause was lost, and ODYOKE's

support a long-gone dream, that Alberto Fernández was granted its approval by CIA as an OA (Operational Asset).

199: lemon juice to read the secret writing: Taylor Branch and George Crile III, "The Kennedy Vendetta: How the CIA waged a silent war against Cuba," *Harper's Magazine*, August 1975, 52.

200: Ted Shackley: "the station had by all its normal criteria . . . hard intelligence that there were missiles in Cuba": MEMORANDUM. TO: G. Robert Blakey. FROM: Gaeton Fonzi. SUBJECT: Interview with Ted Shackley. Courtesy of Gaeton Fonzi.

200: the letter to Allen Dulles informing CIA of the Soviet missiles in Cuba is available in the Dulles Papers.

201: airdropped into Cuba: Conversation with Alberto Fernández, January 31, 2010.

201-202: Lawrence Laborde tells the people assembled at the office of William Baggs that Alberto cheated: CIA: FBI. 124-10325-10308. RECORDS SERIES: HQ. AGENCY FILE NUMBER: 62-80750-NR. TO: DOJ. FROM: HQ. DATE: July 6, 1962. PAGES: 4. SUBJECTS: CIA LIAISON FILE. NARA.

202: CIA burns out one of the motors on the *Tejana* and will not commit itself to repairing or replacing it: FBI. DIRECTOR, FBI. SAC, NEW YORK. DATE: April 19, 1962. ANTI-FIDEL CASTRO ACTIVITIES. 109-584-5131. NARA.

202: Alberto Fernández denies Laborde's charge that CIA paid him $40,000 for the *Tejana*: Conversation with Alberto Fernández, September 30, 2011.

203: "a certain quantity of money from CIA": FBI. TO: DIRECTOR, FBI. FROM: SAC, MIAMI. SUBJECT: LARRY J. LABORDE; GERALD PATRICK HEMMING; EDWARD COLLINS; ANTONIO CUESTA. DATE: April 30, 1962. 105-110398-3. FBI FILE OF ALBERTO HECHAVARRÍA.

205: "you have as much patience as you have fortitude": Robert C. Wells to Alberto Fernández: January 29, 1963. Papers of Michael J. P. Malone. Wells sent Malone a blind copy of this letter.

205-206: Alberto reports on Miró Cardona's television address: CIA. MEMORANDUM FOR THE RECORD. DATE: November 14, 1962. SUBJECT: Comment on MIRÓ's TV address. FROM: AMDENIM/1. PAGES: 1.

206: a fraction "of what they could be worth": Ibid., Albert Fernández de Hechavarría to Michael J. P. Malone, March 15, 1963.

206: "Little Boy Blue stands for re-election": Michael J. P. Malone to Alfonso Fanjul, May 27, 1963. Papers of Michael J. P. Malone.

206: dictators "friendly" to the U.S.: Alfonso Fanjul to Michael J. P. Malone, May 17, 1963. Papers of Michael J. P. Malone.

208-209: Conference in 1963 attended by FBI, CIA, and other agencies: "frustrate plans": FBI. RECORD NUMBER: 124-90139-10146. RECORDS SERIES: HQ. AGENCY FILE NUMBER: CR 109-584-3502. TO: SULLIVAN. FROM: WANNALL. DATE: March 31, 1963. PAGES: 15. SUBJECTS: CIA LIAISON MATERIAL; ANTI-CASTRO ACTIVITIES IN THE UNITED STATES. NARA.

Desmond Fitzgerald represented CIA. See also: FBI. RECORD NUMBER: 124-90139-10145. RECORDS SERIES: HQ. AGENCY FILE NUMBER: CR 109-584-3502. TO: CIA. FROM: HQ. DATE: April 5, 1963. PAGES: 2. SUBJECTS: CIA LIAISON MATERIAL. ANTI-CASTRO ACTIVITIES IN THE UNITED STATES.

209: Dionisio Pastrana leaves the clandestine services in 1965: "limited activities" are all the government is prepared to endorse: June 11, 1965. MEMORANDUM FOR: ARA—Mr. Vaughn. FROM: INR/DOC—Murat W. Williams. SUBJECT: Minutes of the 303 Committee Meeting, June 10, 1965.

211: "they had demonstrated their courage": CIA. DISPATCH. TO: Deputy Chief, WH/SA. FROM: Chief of Station, JMWAVE. SUBJECT: Period October 1, 1963–May 31, 1964. NARA.

211: CIA attempted to manipulate COMMANDOS L into believing that they were not receiving CIA support: CIA. 10172-10096. TO: CHIEF, SPECIAL AFFAIRS STAFF. FROM: COS JMWAVE. TITLE: DISPATCH: AMDENIM-1. PROGRESS REPORT 31 MAY 1963. DATE: June 25, 1963. PAGES: 6. SUBJECTS: DOGGO, AMDENIM-1. JFK64-8:F20 1998.02.16.15:54:25:310102. NARA.

211: "unwitting basis": CIA frequently used unwitting subjects, for example, in its MKULTRA program. See: H. P. Albarelli, Jr., *A Terrible Mistake: The Murder of Frank Olson and the CIA's Secret War Experiments* (Walterville, Oregon: Trine Day, 2009).

211: a JMWAVE report insists that Alberto reported to them about Tony Cuesta's COMMANDOS L activities, "in advance": CIA. 104-10172-10096. TO: CHIEF SPECIAL AFFAIRS STAFF. FROM: COS JMWAVE. TITLE: DISPATCH: AMDENIM-1. PROGRESS REPORT 31 MAY 1963. DATE: June 25, 1963. PAGES: 6. SUBJECTS: DOGGO, AMDENIM-1. JFK64-8:F20 1998.02.16.15:54:25:310102. NARA.

211: Alberto Fernández would be disappointed to learn that CIA was secretly sponsoring Tony Cuesta on an "unwitting" basis: CIA. 104-10172-10121. TO: CHIEF, SPECIAL AFFAIRS STAFF. FROM: COS JMWAVE. TITLE: DISPATCH, PROGRESS REPORT 30 SEPTEMBER 1963. DATE: October 14, 1963. PAGES: 6. SUBJECTS: AMDENIM-1. JFK64-8:F20 1998.02.20.13:16:22:700108. ROUTING AND RECORD SHEET ATTACHED. NARA.

212: Alberto Fernández goes to Washington to "see a few people he hadn't seen for a long time. ..." The incident "lowered considerably the degree to which the Case Officer was willing to accept his word": CIA. 104-`0`72-10127. TO: CHIEF SPECIAL AFFAIRS STAFF. FROM: COS JMWAVE. TITLE: PROGRESS REPORT 28 FEBRUARY 1963. DATE: March 15, 1963. PAGES: 5. SUBJECTS: AMDENIM-1. JFK64-8:F20 1998.02.20.13:39:27:530108. ROUTING AND RECORD SHEET ATTACHED. NARA.

212: Alberto Fernández is betrayed by Don Hogan: "cut off completely by the CIA . . . he will come to me": Donald Hogan to Robert Hurwitch, November 11, 1962. 4 pages. Letterhead is Hogan & Company, Inc. NARA. See also: to Dear Bob. November 8, 1962. 4 pages. NARA. Don Hogan presented himself to Robert Hurwitch as an "independent activist." Hurwitch realized that there is "a divorce between the people who daily or minute by minute had access to information" and others. See: John Franklin Campbell, *The Foreign Affairs Fudge Factory* (New York: Basic Books, 1971).

213: Alberto Fernández reports to CIA on Masferrer's efforts in the Miami area: CIA. 104-10172-10095. TO CHIEF, SPECIAL AFFAIRS STAFF. FROM: COS JMWAVE. TITLE: PROGRESS REPORT—30 SEPTEMBER 1963. DATE: October 8, 1963. PAGES: 6. SUBJECTS: TONY CUESTA. JFK64-8:F20 1998.02.16.15:43:15:606102. NARA.

213: FBI debriefs Alberto Fernández on Masferrer: CIA.104-10172-10101. TO: DEPUTY CHIEF, WH/SA. FROM: COS JMWAVE. TITLE: DISPATCH: PROGRESS REPORT ON AMDENIM-1 PERIOD 1 OCT 63-31 MAY 64. PAGES: 6. SUBJECTS: AMSPARK TEAM. JFK64-8:F20 1998.02.16.16:07:42:483102. ROUTNG AND RECORD SHEET ATTACHED. NARA.

213: "the absence of any kickback": CIA. 104-10172-10096. TO: CHIEF, SPECIAL AFFAIRS STAFF. FROM: COS JMWAVE. DATE: June 25, 1963. SUBJECTS: DOGGO, AMDENIM-1. JFK64-8:F20 1998.02.16.15:54:25:310102.

213: "a very soft-hearted guy": Ibid., CIA. 104-10172-10096. 06/26/63.

213: "basically a sentimentalist": CIA. 104-101720-10121. TO: CHIEF, SPECIAL AFFAIRS STAFF. FROM: COS JMWAVE. TITLE: DISPATCH, PROGRESS REPORT 30 SEPTEMBER 1963. DATE: October 14, 1963. PAGES: 6. SUBJECTS: AMDENIM-1. JFK64-8:F20 1998.02.20.13:16:22:700108. ROUTING AND RECORD SHEET ATTACHED. NARA.

213: Michael J. P. Malone enlisted to speak with Federico Fernández Casas about his son's financial situation: CIA.104-10172-10095. TO: CHIEF, SPECIAL AFFAIRS STAFF. FROM: COS JMWAVE. TITLE: PROGRESS

REPORT 30 SEPTEMBER 1963.
DATE: October 8, 1963. PAGES: 6.
SUBJECTS: TONY CUESTA. JFK64-
8:F20   1998.02.16.15:43:15:606102.
NARA.

213-214: Alberto Fernández per-
ceived an "unfavorable attitude"
toward CIA on the part of the NBC
White Paper representative, and so
sacrificed the opportunity to appear
in their documentary about Cuba:
CIA.104-10172-10095. TO: CHIEF,
SPECIAL AFFAIRS STAFF. FROM:
COS JMWAVE. TITLE: PROGRESS
REPORT 30 SEPTEMBER 1963.
DATE: October 8, 1963.

214: "absolutely no hope for her":
Michael J. P. Malone to Alfonso Fan-
jul, May 10, 1963. Papers of Michael
J. P. Malone.

215: Alberto Fernández tells Malone that
he wants permission to speak to Head-
quarters about damages to the *TEJANA*:
CIA. 104-10172-10090. TO: JMWAVE.
FROM: DIRECTOR. TITLE: ON
23 MAY AMPATRIN-1 ADVISED
THAT. DATE: May 26, 1964. PAGES:
1. SUBJECTS: AMDENIM-1. JFK64-
8:F20   1998.0216.15:20:05:170102.
NARA. JMWAVE has written reports
of every meeting "Manson" has had with
AMPATRIN (Michael J. P. Malone)
regarding Agency use of the *TEJANA*:
CIA. 104-10172-10102. TO: DIREC-
TOR. FROM: SAO PAULO. TITLE:
CABLE: REPLIES TO ALL THREE
QUESTIONS RAISED. DATE: June
12, 1964. PAGES: 1. SUBJECTS:

AMPATRIN, MANSON. JFK64-
8:F20   1998.02.16.16:09:29:733102.
NARA.

215: CIA fears that should they honor
Alberto Fernández's claims for money
owing to him from CIA's use of the
TEJANA he will use the money "to try
to enlist support for further independent
efforts" against Castro: CIA. 104-10173-
10207. TO: DEPUTY CHIEF/WH/
SA. FROM: CHIEF OF STATION,
JMWAVE. TITLE: DISPATCH:
OPERATIONAL/AMDENIM-1. PRO-
GRESS REPORT: 1-30-JUNE 1964.
DATE: July 13, 1964. PAGES: 4. SUB-
JECTS: HERNÁNDEZ [sic]. Jfk64-9:f2
1998.07.17.05:23:01:590129. NARA.

215: sale at Argentina King Ranch
"most   successful":   MEMORAN-
DUM. From: Michael J. P. Malone.
To: Mr. George A. Braga. June 16,
1964. Papers of Michael J. P. Malone.

216: $825,000 a year in purse money:
"The Handbook of Texas Online."
KLEBERG, ROBERT JUSTUS, JR.
Available online.

216: Alberto Fernández writes a memorandum to Robert J. Kleberg, Jr. on
what is to be done: CIA.104-10173-
10197. TO: CHIEF OF STATION,
JMWAVE. FROM: DEPUTY CHIEF,
WH (SPECIAL AFFAIRS). TITLE:
DISPATCH: TYPIC/AMDENIM.
07/14.64. PAGES:15. NARA.

216: Malone shows Alberto Fernández's
letters to CIA before passing them on to

Kleberg: Michael J. P. Malone to "Dear Al" (Rodemeyer). June 19, 1964. NARA. Available at http://www.maryferrell.org/mffweb/archive/viewer/showDoc.do?mode=searchResult&absPageId=807543. See also: CIA. 104-10173-10196. TO: DEPUTY CHIEF/WH/SA. FROM: CHIEF OF STATION, JMWAVE. TITLE: DISPATCH: OPERATIONAL/AMDENIM-1. PROGRESS REPORT 1-31-JULY 1964. DATE: August 17, 1964. PAGES: 4. SUBJECTS: HERNÁNDEZ [sic]. JFK64-9:f2 1998.07.16.12:40:29:090129. NARA.

216: "just as fired up as ever to do something": CIA. 104-10173-10207. TO: DEPUTY CHIEF, WH/SA. FROM: CHIEF OF STATION, JMWAVE. TITLE: DISPATCH: OPERATIONAL/AMDENIM-1. PROGRESS REPORT: 1-30 JUNE 1964. DATE: July 13, 1964. SUBJECTS: HERNÁNDEZ [sic]. JFK64-9:F2 1998.07.17.05:23:01:590129. NARA.

216: "I've been snookered": Interviews with Alberto Fernández.

217: "you can have your war": Quoted in Stanley Karnow, *Vietnam: A History* (New York: Penguin Books, 1991), 342. A new book, by James G. Hershberg, *Marigold: The Lost Chance for Peace in Vietnam* (Stanford University Press/Wilson Center Press, 2012), makes much of a Polish-Italian peace initiative of 1966, with a supposed agreement for peace talks having been scheduled for late 1966. This "breakthrough" was thwarted by the U.S. bombing of Hanoi. The point of the Vietnam

War, of course, was duration, as George Orwell noted about imperial wars in general: "The war is not meant to be won. It is meant to be continuous." There was no chance that Johnson would leave Vietnam so early, no "lost chance" for peace at all.

217: Alberto Fernández is not included in an infiltration of Oriente Province for fear that his association with JMWAVE would come to light: CIA. 104-10173-10195. TO: DEPUTY CHIEF, WH/SA. FROM: CHIEF OF STATION, JMWAVE. TITLE: OPERATIONAL/AMDENIM-1.PROGRESS REPORT THROUGH 15 SEPTEMBER 1964. DATE: September 24, 1964. PAGES: 4. SUBJECTS: HERNÁNDEZ [sic]. JFK64-9:F1 1998.07.16.12:35:48:060129. NARA.

217: Alberto Fernández's "strong stand of not being subordinate to KUBARK, or any individual": CIA. 104-10173-10195. TO: DEPUTY CHIEF, WH/SA. FROM: CHIEF OF STATION, JMWAVE. TITLE: DISPATCH: OPERATIONAL/AMDENIM-1. PROGRESS REPORT THROUGH 15 SEPTEMBER 1964. DATE: September 24, 1964. PAGES: 4. SUBJECTS: HERNÁNDEZ [sic]. JFK64-9F1 1998.07.16:12:35:48:060129. NARA.

218: "face the rancor of an incensed people": Alberto Fernández to Mr. Jeff Allott, November 12, 1964. Papers of Michael J. P. Malone.

218: Kleberg and William Douglas Pawley visit Richard Nixon: William

Pawley to Alfonso Fanjul, July 28, 1964. Papers of Michael J. P. Malone. See also: Robert J. Kleberg, Jr. to Alfonso Fanjul, July 22, 1964. Papers of Michael J. P. Malone.

218: "it is our best chance": Robert J. Kleberg, Jr. to Alfonso Fanjul. July 22, 1964. Papers of Michael J. P. Malone.

218: an American company is "beating the blockade of Cuba by working through its British subsidiary": CIA. 104-10172-10101. TO: DEPUTY CHIEF, WH/SA. FROM: COS JMWAVE. TITLE: DISPATCH: PROGRESS REPORT ON AMDENIM-1. PERIOD 1 OCT 63-31 MAY 64. PAGES: 6. SUBJECTS: AMSPARK TEAM. JFK64-8:F20 1998.02.16.16:07:42:483102. ROUTING AND RECORD SHEET ATTACHED. NARA.

219: "it would be best not to have my name appear": Michael J. P. Malone to Alberto Fernández, July 2, 1964. Papers of Michael J. P. Malone.

219: "the uprising was not a spontaneous affair": MEMORANDUM. From: Michael J. P. Malone. To: Mr. George A. Braga. September 23, 1964. Papers of Michael J. P. Malone.

220: "continues to deteriorate": MEMORANDUM. From: Michael J. P. Malone. To: Mr. George A. Braga. Date: September 15, 1964. Papers of Michael J. P. Malone.

220: "Andrew Reuteman's" assessment of Alberto Fernández's situation in 1964: "The road of the exile is a hard one at best": Ibid., CIA. 104-10172-10101.

221: "Formerly of ministerial rank": CIA. TO: DIRECTOR. FROM: JMWAVE. DATE: February 11, 1964. NARA.

221-222: By September 1964: Document, Situation of the Cuban problem as of September 1, 1964 with regard to: "1. U.S. directed and controlled activity against Cuba . . . " Papers of Michael J. P. Malone.

223: "costing him more in the long run": CIA. DISPATCH. TO: Deputy Chief, WH/SA. FROM: Chief of Station, JMWAVE. SUBJECT: Progress Report on [redacted]. Period: October 1963–May 31, 1964. NARA.

223: "paper liquidation of his debts": CIA. 104-10173-10193. TO: DEPUTY CHIEF, WH/SA. FROM: CHIEF OF STATION, JMWAVE. TITLE: DISPATCH: SETTLEMENT OF TEJANA CLAIM. DATE: December 21, 1964. PAGES: 4. SUBJECTS: HERNÁNDEZ [sic]. JFK64-9:F2 1998.07.16.12:27:03:920129. NARA.

223: Alberto had planned to go to Spain to see his father: CIA. 104-10173-10195. TO: DEPUTY CHIEF, WH/SA. FROM: CHIEF OF STATION, JMWAVE. TITLE:

DISPATCH: OPERATIONAL/ AMDENIM-1 PROGRESS REPORT THROUGH 15 SEPTEMBER 1964. DATE: September 24, 1964. JFK64-9:F2 1998.07.16.12:35:48:060129. NARA.

223: as a "field agent": CIA. 104-10173-10156. TO: DEPUTY CHIEF, WH/ SA. FROM: COS JMWAVE. TITLE: TRANSMITTAL OF MOC FOR IDENTITY A. PAGES: 4. SUBJECTS: ORAL COMMITMENT, FERNÁN-DEZ, ALBERTO. JFK64-9:F2 1998.02.24.17:41:38:500102. NARA.

224: Alberto is asked to sign a statement releasing CIA from all claims arising out of its use of the *Tejana*: CIA. 104-10173-10193. TO: DEPUTY

CHIEF WH/SA. FROM: CHIEF OF STATION, JMWAVE. TITLE: DISPATCH: SETTLEMENT OF *TEJANA* CLAIM. DATE: December 21, 1964. PAGES: 4. JFK64-9:F2 1998.07.16.12:27:03:920129: NARA.

224: "accepted the fact that KUBARK and ODYOKE represent the sole means by which Cuba can be liberated": CIA. 104-10173-10190. TO: DEPUTY CHIEF, WH/SA. FROM: CHIEF OF STATION, JMWAVE. TITLE: DISPATCH: OPERA-TIONAL TRANSMITTAL OF EVALUATION OF FIELD AGENT AMDENIM-1. DATE: March 16, 1965. PAGES: 4. SUBJECTS: HERNÁNDEZ [sic]. JFK64-9:F2 1998.07.16.12:19:21:140129. NARA.

CHAPTER 9: ENDGAME: CUBA

226: Michael J. P. Malone asks Charles Matt at CIA to get Gustavo de los Reyes transferred to a prison farm: CIA. MEMORANDUM FOR THE RECORD. 5 June 1962. SUBJECT: 4 June 1962. Telecon with Michael J. Malone. NARA.

227: "Do you know me?": de los Reyes meets David Atlee Phillips in Mexico City: Gustavo de los Reyes to Joan Mellen, September 7, 2009.

227: Gustavo de los Reyes tells the CIA representative in Mexico City that his mission involves the release of political

prisoners: CIA. MEMORANDUM FOR: The Director of Central Intelligence. SUBJECT: Cuban Proposal for Release of Political Prisoners in Exchange for Pledge of No Invasion of Cuba. DATE: February 27, 1964. Signed Richard Helms. Deputy Director for Plans. NARA.

227-228: Gustavo de los Reyes pretends to make a deal with Castro: CIA. 202-10002-10031. TO: DIREC-TOR, CENTRAL INTELLIGENCE. FROM: RICHARD HELMS. TITLE: CUBAN PROPOSAL FOR RELEASE OF POLITICAL PRISONERS.

DATE: Januart 27, 1964. PAGES: 3. Taylor Papers. Box 7. Memorandum for DCI regarding political prisoners in Cuba and U.S. pledge not to invade Cuba. NARA.

228: "I would rather go back and die in that jail": MEMORANDUM FOR: The Director of Central Intelligence. FROM: Richard Helms, Deputy Director for Plans. February 27, 1964. SUBJECT: Cuban Proposal for Release of Political Prisoners in exchange for Pledge of No Invasion of Cuba. NARA.

228: "I'm willing to talk only to Mr. Robert Kleberg, Jr.": AGENCY: JCS. 202-10020-10031.   RECORDS SERIES: TAYLOR PAPERS. TO: DIRECTOR CENTRAL INTELLIGENCE. FROM: RICHARD HELMS. TITLE: CUBAN PROPOSAL FOR RELEASE OF POLITICAL PRISONERS. DATE: February 27, 1963. PAGES: 3. NARA.

228: Only when Kleberg granted his permission would de los Reyes talk to the CIA's representative: Ibid. CIA. MEMORANDUM. February 27, 1964.

228: an eleven-page document of Cuba's trade agreements: TO: DISTRIBUTION LIST. RE: Sugar Trade Agreements with Communist countries. FROM: Research. REF: MRR#23. DATE: March 5, 1964. There is a cover letter: Michael J. P. Malone to Dear Gustavo, March 25, 1964. Papers of Michael J. P. Malone. Czarnikow-Rionda Collection. University of Florida at Gainesville.

228: For the saga of Malone's attempting to get de los Reyes' article about his prison experiences published in *Reader's Digest*: See: Michael J. P. Malone to Dear Al, July 17, 1964; Gustavo de los Reyes to Dear Jack, August 20, 1964; Michael J. P. Malone to Dear Ken, September 3, 1964; Michael J. P. Malone to Dear Gustavo, September 15, 1964; Michael J. P. Malone to Mr. John Armstrong, September 22, 1964; Gustavo de los Reyes to Dear Jack, September 23, 1964; Gustavo de los Reyes to Dear Jack, October 17, 1964—all from the Papers of Michael J. P. Malone. See also: Interview with Gustavo de los Reyes by Joan Mellen.

229: "I thought you would find it of interest": Robert J. Kleberg, Jr. to Mr. J. Edgar Hoover, April 13, 1964. 62-105517-12. FBI file of Robert J. Kleberg, Jr.

229: Malone acts as an agent for *Reader's Digest* in Cuba: Michael J. P. Malone to Alberto Fernández, June 6, 1962. Papers of Michael J. P. Malone.

229: "cloak-and-dagger": John Heidenry, *Theirs Was the Kingdom: Lila and DeWitt Wallace: The Story of the Reader's Digest* (New York: W. W. Norton & Company, 1993), 454.

229: *Reader's Digest* and Operation GLADIO: Peter Canning, *American Dreamers: The Wallaces and Reader's Digest: An Insider's Story* (New York: Simon & Schuster, 1996), 95.

230: "most favored status": Ibid., 244.

230: dozens of CIA-connected *Reader's Digest* projects: Ibid., 255.

230: "listening in": Ibid., 320.

230: For a full discussion of Tom Dooley's relationship with CIA, see Hugh Wilford, *The Mighty Wurlitzer: How The CIA Played America* (Cambridge: Harvard University Press, 2008), 178–182.

230: James Monahan and Kenneth O. Gilmore, *The Great Deception: The Inside Story of How the Kremlin Took Over Cuba*": Heidenry, *Theirs Was the Kingdom*, 454.

231: "we would be willing to make informal, unofficial comments": CIA. 104-10520-10110. MEMORANDUM FOR THE RECORD. TO: REDACTED. FROM: CHIEF, TFW/ PM. DATE: June 5, 2962. SUBJECTS: FERNÁNDEZ. NARA.

234: Kleberg sends an article by Herbert Matthews to J. Edgar Hoover: Robert J. Kleberg to Mr. J. Edgar Hoover, April 6, 1964. FBI file of Robert J. Kleberg, Jr.

234: Jones reported to Cartha DeLoach: Memorandum. TO: Mr. DeLoach.

FROM: M.A. Jones. SUBJECT: Robert J. Kleberg, Jr., President, King Ranch, Inc. Kingsville, Texas. DATE: April 13, 1964. PAGES: 2. 62-105517-10.

234: "most illuminating": J. Edgar Hoover to Mr. Robert Kleberg, Jr. April 22, 1964.

235: de los Reyes visited the Rockefeller ranch: Oscar M. Ruebhausen to Ivan B. Maldonado, November 10, 1964. Czarnikow-Rionda Papers.

235: "Nelson, you don't know anything about agriculture": Cypher, *Bob Kleberg and the King Ranch*, 160.

237: Gustavo de los Reyes presents Kleberg with a copy of The Prince: Interview with Gustavo de los Reyes by Guillermo Cowley, Palm Beach Journal, 2008. Courtesy of Gustavo de los Reyes.

237: "You ever run away from anything?" Gustavo de los Reyes, "The Last American Empire," essay on King Ranch Venezuela. Courtesy of Gustavo de los Reyes.

238: Kleberg buys a ranch near Lake Okeechobee: Booth, *The Life of Belton Kleberg Johnson*, 217–218.

239: a herd of Santa Gertrudis cattle is spotted on a collective farm in the Soviet Union: Cypher, *Bob Kleberg and the King Ranch*, 79. Cypher reports that later the Russians sent several missions to the United States to purchase more Santa Gertrudis cattle. Ibid., 80.

240: Alberto Fernández receives a telephone call from Jack Malone. Interviews with Alberto Fernández.

241: "There is no longer any trust. . . .": CIA. 104-10173-10323. TITLE: MEMORANDUM AS TO CONDITIONS IN CUBA OAS OF MARCH 1, 1966. DATE: March 1, 1966. PAGES: 8. SUBJECTS: TAYLOR, GEN. JFK64-9:F1   1998.12.27.08:00:35:793108. NARA.

241-242: Kleberg solicits the support of J. Edgar Hoover in opposing land reform movements in Latin America: Michael J. P. Malone to Mr. J. Edgar Hoover, January 10, 1966 (62-105517-14). FBI file of Robert J. Kleberg, Jr. See also: J. Edgar Hoover to Michael J. P. Malone, January 19, 1966: MEMORANDUM DATE: December 22, 1965. 62-105517-14. PAGES: 2. From: Robert J. Kleberg, Jr. Unsigned.

242: Malone asks Hoover to disseminate Alberto Fernández's suggestions about land reform to the "proper officials": Michael J. P. Malone to J. Edgar Hoover, January 10, 1966. 62-105517-14. The reply from Hoover is J. Edgar Hoover to Michael J. P. Malone, January 19, 1966. 62-105517. NARA.

243: Laborde's son visited Jim Garrison's office four times in the space of three weeks, informing the FBI field office of what transpired during these visits. The FBI duly informed CIA: CIA.   104-10189-10287.   TITLE: LABORDE, MICHAEL. PAGES: 2. NARA. When someone in Garrison's office asked young Laborde the name of the Cuban with whom his father worked, Laborde said it was "Alberto Fernández."

243: When Alberto Fernández's name surfaced in the Garrison investigation, CIA, at the instruction of David Atlee Phillips, severed all contact with him: CIA. 104-10173-10179. TITLE: SUMMARY OF AMDENIM/1 CONTACT. SUBJECTS: FERNÁNDEZ. See also: CIA. 104-10173-10178. TO: JMWAVE. FROM: DIRECTOR. TITLE: CABLE: HQS CONCURS REF A PROPOSAL TERMINATE LOCAL CONTACT WITH AMDENIM/1. DATE: January 29, 1968. PAGES: 1. SUBJECTS: HERNÁNDEZ [sic]; AMDENM-1. NARA.

Neither Garrison nor any of his staff were ever in contact with Alberto Fernández. See: CIA. MEMORANDUM NO. 6. DATE: September 7, 1967. SUBJECT: Garrison and the Kennedy Assassination. REFERENCE: A. CI/R & A. Memorandum of 7 August 1967, subject as above. NARA.

243: Robert K. Brown and Martin Xavier Casey are seen on board the *TEJANA*: CIA. 104-10172-10383. TO: DEPUTY DIRECTOR FOR PLANS. FROM: CHIEF, WHD.

TITLE: INTERLOCKING RELA-
TIONSHIPS BETWEEN BROWN/
SLAFTER AND GARRISON.
00/17/67. SUBJECTS: GARRISON,
HEMMING, G. NARA.

243: "An abrupt break in contact
might offend": CIA suggests that
Alberto use a Washington, D.C.,
post office box: CIA. 104-10173-
10179. TITLE: SUMMARY OF
AMDENIM/1 CONTACT. SUB-
JECTS: FERNÁNDEZ. JFK64-9:F1
1998. 07.16.11:41:37983129. NARA.

245: Kleberg offers to send Lyndon
Johnson Nilgai antelope to amuse
"drug store cowboys": April 9, 1966.
Recordings of Robert J. Kleberg's tel-
ephone conversations with Lyndon
Johnson are available at the Miller
Center of Public Affairs presidential
tapes project online.

246: An evening at *La Belle Epoque* :
Unpublished memoir of Gustavo de
los Reyes.

247: skinny as Twiggy: Cypher, *Bob
Kleberg and the King Ranch*, 81.

247: "Bob wants to marry Diana":
Interview with Gustavo de los Reyes.

247-248: Michael J. P. Malone died:
"Michael Malone, Industrialist
Who Served King Ranch Dead,"

New York Times, March 14, 1971.
ProQuest Historical Newspapers,
New York Times, 75.

248: pass the leadership of King Ranch
over to him: Booth, *The Life of Belton
Kleberg Johnson*, 240.

248: drink his liquor and wine cellar dry: For the best account of the
last days of Robert J. Kleberg, Jr.,
see Cypher, *Bob Kleberg and the King
Ranch*, 223–228.

249: "Your life is an expression of what
you are": These words are engraved on
Robert J. Kleberg's grave, a simple
marble slab; they represent his credo:
Cypher, *Bob Kleberg and the King
Ranch*, 228.

249: on Humble Oil and EXXON
royalties: Ibid., 262–263.

249: "business was booming": Booth,
The Life of Belton Kleberg Johnson, 258.

250: George A. Braga dies laden with
debt: Interview with Gustavo de los
Reyes.

250: Alberto Fernández's survival:
Interviews with Alberto Fernández.

252: Alberto Fernández's final illness:
Conversations with Gladys Smithies,
Josefina García de Fernández.

BIBLIOGRAPHY

Agee, Philip. *Inside the Company: CIA Diary*. Harmondsworth, Middlesex: Penguin Books, 1975.

Bancroft, Mary. *Autobiography of a Spy: Debutante, Writer, Confidante, Secret Agent: The True Story of Her Extraordinary Life*. New York: William Morrow and Company, Inc., 1983.

Binkley, William C. *The Expansionist Movement in Texas, 1836–1850*. New York: Da Capo Press, 1970. Originally published in 1925.

Booth, Martin. *The Life of Belton Kleberg Johnson*. Limited Private Edition. Published by Belton Kleberg Johnson, 2001.

Brands, H. W. *Lone Star Nation: How a Ragged Army of Volunteers Won the Battle for Texas Independence—and Changed America*. New York: Doubleday, 2004.

Briody, Dan. *The Halliburton Agenda: The Politics of Oil and Money*. Hoboken: John Wiley & Sons, Inc., 2004.

Bryce, Robert. *Cronies: How Texas Business Became American Policy—and Brought Bush to Power*. New York: Public Affairs, 2004.

Burrough, Bryan. *The Big Rich: The Rise and Fall of the Greatest Texas Oil Fortunes*. New York: The Penguin Press, 2009.

Byrd, David Harold ("Dry Hole"). *I'm an Endangered Species: The Autobiography of a Free Enterpriser*. Houston: Pacesetter Press, 1978.

Campbell, Randolph B. *Gone to Texas: A History of the Lone Star State*. New York: Oxford University Press, 2003.

------------------------------. *"Sam Houston and the American Southwest*. New York: Longman, 2001.

Canning, Peter. *American Dreamers: The Wallaces and Reader's Digest: An Insider's Story*. New York: Simon & Schuster, 1996.

Cantrell, Gregg. *Stephen F. Austin: Empresario of Texas*. New Haven and London: Yale University Press, 1999.

Caro, Robert A. *The Years of Lyndon Johnson: The Passage of Power*. New York: Alfred A. Knopf, 2012.

------------------------. *Master of the Senate*. New York: Alfred A. Knopf, 2002.

------------------------. *Means of Ascent*. New York: Alfred A. Knopf, 1990.

------------------------. *The Path to Power*. New York: Alfred A. Knopf, 1982.

Chang, Laurence and Peter Kornbluh, eds. *The Cuban Missile Crisis, 1962: A National Security Archive Documents Reader*. New York: The New Press, 1992.

Cline, Ray S. *Secrets, Spies and Scholars: The Essential CIA*. Washington, D.C.: Acropolis Books, Ltd., 2009. Originally published in 1976.

(La) Constitución de 1940. Ciclo de Conferencias. Miami, Centro de Artes Graficas: Colegio Nacional de Abogados de Cuba. Inc., 1991.

Cooney, John. *The American Pope: The Life and Times of Francis, Cardinal Spellman*. New York: Times Books, 1984.

Currey, Cecil B. *Edward Lansdale: The Unquiet American*. Boston: Houghton Mifflin Company, 1988.

Cypher, John. *Bob Kleberg and the King Ranch: A Worldwide Sea of Grass*. Austin: University of Texas Press, 1995.

Davis, William C. *Lone Star Rising: The Revolutionary Birth of the Texas Republic*. New York: Free Press, 2004.

De Bruhl, Marshall. *Sword of San Jacinto: A Life of Sam Houston*. New York: Random House, 1993.

De Vosjoli, P. L. Thyraud. *Lamia*, Boston: Little, Brown and Company, 1970.

Dobbs, Michael. *One Minute to Midnight: Kennedy, Khrushchev, and Castro on the Brink of Nuclear War*. New York: Alfred A. Knopf, 2008.

Dugger, Ronnie. *The Politician: The Life and Times of Lyndon Johnson*. New York: W. W. Norton & Company, 1982.

Escalante, Fabián. *The Secret War: CIA Covert Operations Against Cuba 1959–62*. Melbourne, Australia: Ocean Press, 1995.

Estes, Billie Sol. *Billie Sol Estes: A Texas Legend*. Granbury, Texas: BS Productions, 2005.

Estes, Pam. *Billie Sol: King of Texas Wheeler-Dealers*. Granbury, Texas: Pemelaco Productions, 1983.

Fehrenbach, T. R. *Lone Star: A History of Texas and the Texans*. New York: American Legacy Press, 1983.

Ferber, Edna. *Giant*. New York: Doubleday & Company, Inc., 1952.

Franqui, Carlos. *Camilo Cienfuegos*. Los Tres Mundos: Seix Barral, 2001. (In Spanish)

Frazier, Howard, ed. *Uncloaking the CIA*. New York: The Free Press, 1978.

Fuentes, Norberto. *The Autobiography of Fidel Castro*. Translated by Anna Kushner. New York: W. W. Norton & Company, 2010.

Goodwin, Doris Kearns. *Lyndon Johnson and the American Dream*. New York: St. Martin's Press, 1991.

Graham, Don. *Kings of Texas: The 150-Year Saga of an American Ranching Empire*. Hoboken: John Wiley & Sons, Inc., 2003.

Grose, Peter. *Gentleman Spy: The Life of Allen Dulles*. Amherst: The University of Massachusetts Press, 1994.

Groves, Helen Kleberg. *Bob and Helen Kleberg of King Ranch*. Albany, Texas: Bright Sky Press, 2004.

Hale, Edward Everett. *How to Conquer Texas Before Texas Conquers Us*. Boston: Redding & Co., 1846.

Haley, J. Evetts. *A Texan Looks At Lyndon: A Study in Illegitimate Power*. Canyon, Texas: Palo Duro Press,1964.

Hardin, Stephen L. *Texian Iliad: A Military History of the Texas Revolution, 1835–1836*. Austin: University of Texas Press, 1994.

Heidenry, John. *Theirs Was the Kingdom: Lila and DeWitt Wallace: The Story of the Reader's Digest*. New York: W. W. Norton & Company, 1993.

Hersh, Burton. *The Old Boys: The American Elite and the Origins of the CIA*. New York: Charles Scribner's Sons, 1992.

Higgins, Trumbull. *The Perfect Failure: Kennedy, Eisenhower and the CIA at the Bay of Pigs*. New York: W. W. Norton & Company, 1987.

Hinckle, Warren and William Turner. *Deadly Secrets: The CIA-MAFIA War Against Castro and the Assassination of J.F.K.* New York: Thunder's Mouth Press, 1992.

Jack, Charles, J. "Re-Annexation of Texas to the United States." Philadelphia, 1844. Speech.

James, Marquis. *The Raven: A Biography of Sam Houston*. New York: Paperback Library, Inc., 1996. Originally published in 1929.

Jones, Anson. *Memoranda and Official Correspondence Relating to the Republic of Texas, Its History and Annexation*. Chicago: The Rio Grande Press, Inc., 1966. Originally published in 1859.

Josephson, Matthew. *The Robber Barons: The Great American Capitalists, 1861–1901*. New York: A Harvest Book: Harcourt, Brace & World, Inc. 1963. First published, 1934.

Karalekas, Anne. *History of the Central Intelligence Agency*. Laguna Hills, California: Aegean Park Press, 1977.

Karnow, Stanley. *Vietnam: A History*. New York: Penguin Books, 1991.

Kornbluh, Peter, ed. *Bay of Pigs Declassified: The Secret CIA Report on the Invasion of Cuba*. New York: The New Press, 1998.

Kwitny, Jonathan. *Endless Enemies: The Making of an Unfriendly World*. New York: Congdon & Weed, Inc.,1984.

Lack, Paul D. *The Texas Revolutionary Experience: A Political and Social History, 1835–1836*. College Station, Texas: Texas A&M University Press, 1992.

Lankford, Nelson D. *The Last American Aristocrat: The Biography of David K. E. Bruce, 1898–1977*. Boston: Little, Brown and Company, 1996.

Latell, Brian. *Castro's Secrets: The CIA and Cuba's Intelligence Machine*. New York: Palgrave Macmillan, 2012.

Lea, Tom. *King Ranch*. (Boxed Set). Two Volumes. Boston: Little, Brown and Company, 1957.

Loftus, John and Mark Aarons. *The Secret War Against the Jews: How Western Espionage Betrayed the Jewish People*. New York: St. Martin's Press, 1994. See also: Mark Aarons and John Loftus, *Unholy Trinity: How the Vatican's Nazi Networks Betrayed Western Intelligence to the Soviets*. New York: St. Martin's Press, 1991.

Loftus, John J. *America's Nazi Secret: An Insider's History*. Waterville, Oregon: Trine Day, 2010.

Long, Jeff. *Duel of Eagles: The Mexican and U.S. Fight for the Alamo*. New York: William Morrow and Company, 1990.

Lynch, Grayston L. *Decision for Disaster: Betrayal at the Bay of Pigs: A CIA Participant Challenges the Historical Record*. Washington, D.C.: Brassey's, 2000.

Martino, John. *I Was Castro's Prisoner: An American Tells His Story*. Southlake, Texas: JFK Lancer Productions & Publications, 2008. First published in 1963.

McCartney, Laton. *Friends in High Places: The Bechtel Story: The Most Secret Corporation and How It Engineered the World*. New York: Simon & Schuster, 1988.

Mellen, Joan. *A Farewell to Justice: Jim Garrison, JFK's Assassination and the Case That Should Have Changed History*. Dulles, Virginia: Potomac Books, 2005.

Miller, Merle. *Plain Speaking: An Oral Biography of Harry S. Truman.* New York: Berkley Publishing Corporation, 1973.

Miscamble, Wilson D. *George F. Kennan and the Making of American Foreign Policy, 1947–1950.* Princeton: Princeton University Press, 1992.

Mosley, Leonard. *Dulles: A Biography of Eleanor, Allen, and John Foster Dulles and their Family Network.* New York: The Dial Press/James Wade, 1978.

Paterson, Thomas G. *Contesting Castro: The United States and the Triumph of the Cuban Revolution.* Oxford: Oxford University Press, 1994.

Prados, John. *William Colby and the CIA: The Secret Wars of a Controversial Spymaster.* Lawrence, Kansas: University Press of Kansas, 2009.

Pratt, Joseph A., and Christopher J. Castaneda. *Builders: Herman and George Brown.* College Station, Texas: Texas A&M University Press, 1999.

Prouty, L. Fletcher. *The Secret Team: The CIA and Its Allies in Control of the United States and the World.* New York: Skyhorse Publishing, 2008.

Quirk, Robert E. *Fidel Castro.* New York: W. W. Norton & Company, 1993.

Rasenberger, Jim: *The Brilliant Disaster: JFK, Castro, and America's Doomed Invasion of Cuba's Bay of Pigs.* New York: Scribner, 2011.

Ranelagh, John. *The Agency: The Rise and Decline of the CIA.* New York: A Touchstone Book: Simon & Schuster, 1987.

Reeves, Richard. *President Kennedy: Profile of Power.* New York: Simon & Schuster, 1993.

Schmitz, Joseph William. *Texas Culture: In the Days of the Republic, 1836–1846*. San Antonio: The Naylor Company, 1960.

Siegel, Stanley. *A Political History of the Texas Republic, 1836–1845*. Austin: University of Texas Press, 1956.

Sizer, Mona D. *The King Ranch Story: Truth and Myth*. Plano, Texas: Republic of Texas Press, 1999.

Smith, Earl E. T. *The Fourth Floor: An Account of the Castro Communist Revolution*. New York: Random House, 1962.

Weiner, Tim. *Legacy of Ashes: The History of the CIA*. New York: Doubleday, 2007.

Wilford, Hugh. *The Mighty Wurlitzer: How the CIA Played America*. Cambridge: Harvard University Press. 2008.

Woodward, Bob. *Veil: The Secret Wars of the CIA, 1981–1987*. New York: Simon & Schuster, 1987. Paperback edition: 2005.

Wyden, Peter. *Bay of Pigs: The Untold Story*. New York: Simon & Schuster, 1979.

INDEX

Throughout this index, the abbreviation "dc" indicates "document copy"; the abbreviation "ins" indicates a photograph in the photographic insert; the abbreviation "n" indicates an endnote.

first meeting of, 67
gift of "Babar" (Santa Gertrudis bull) by, 68, *ins*
gift of Machiavelli's "*The Prince*" to, 237
at *La Belle Epoque*, 246–247
lawyer of (Yturria) pleads for life of, 112–113, *ins*
on manner of, 258n
powerless to CIA censorship of article by, 232, 233
in Venezuela, 235–237
Cedral's manager, in Venezuela, 236–237, 239, *ins*
Cuban Cattlemen's Association
  Dulles betrays plot of, 110, 112, 227
  involvement in, 107
  meets with Allen Dulles on behalf of, 108–109
escape plan
  castro's sugar trade agreements with Communist countries, revealed to CIA by de los Reyes, 227
  deliver's Castro's message to George White, in Washington, 227–228
  devised by Stadelhofer, 226–227
  explains part of mission to CIA operative in Mexico City, 227
  special mission for Castro, xxiii
with horse, *ins*
imprisonment of
  at Isle of Pines, xliv, 113, 225
  at *La Cabaña*, xliv, 111
  and psychological torture endured by, 111–112
La Caridad ranch owner, 67
November 2012 ninety-ninth birthday, 252
Reader's Digest, dealings with, xli, 228–235
with the Shah of Iran and wife Farah, *ins*
de Sosa, Eugenio, 83
de Vosjoli, Phillipe, 200
Dean, James, xxxi, 55
defense contractors ("robber barons"), 3–4, 7–8
Delgado, Efigenio Almeiras, 111
Deliver Us From Evil (Dooley), 230
DeLoach, Cartha, 234
Denman, Leroy, 44, 66
Deputy Director of Plans
  . *see* clandestine services of CIA (DD/P); DD/P
Díaz, Eugenio de Sosa, xxix
Díaz Lanz, Marcos, xxix
Díaz Lanz, Pedro, xxix, 188

Diba, Farah (wife of the Shah of Iran), 237, *ins*
Dillon, Douglas, 119
Dillon Read, 7
Diosdado, Cesario, li, 140
Directorate for Plans
  . *see* clandestine services of CIA (DD/P)
Directorio Revolucionaria Estudantil
  . *see* DRE (*Directorio Revolucionario Estudiantil)*
División Cincuenta (Raúl Castro's secret army), 204
Dobie, J. Frank, 52
Dodd, Thomas J., xxix, 182
Dooley, Tom, 230
Doolittle, James, 165, 282n
Dorticós Torrado, Osvalado, xxx, 110, 220
Dostoevsky, Fyodor, 112
DRE (*Directorio Revolucionario Estudiantil)*, xlvii, lii, 125, 195
Dresser Industries, xl, xlvi, 48
Dugger, Ronnie, 31, 50
Duke of Duval
  . *see* Parr, George B.
Dulles, Allen
  and Alberto Fernández, xxi, 89
  associates of, 7
  Bay of Pigs
    assumes no responsibility for disaster at, 150–151, 159, 161
    in Nixon's debt, is ordered not to brief Kennedy about, 158
  biographical overview of, xxx
  and Bob Kleberg
    allies himself with, 8
    friendship with, xv, 9
    visits King Ranch, 13, 58
  and Braga, xxvi, 62
  consulted by Wrightsman on holding Texan oil properties, 4–5
  corrupt view of a central intelligence agency, 165
  Cuban Cattlemen's Association
    betrayal of, 110, 112, 227
    meets with de los Reyes to aid, 108–109
  director of CIA
    appointment as, xxi, xxxix
    fired by President Kennedy, xxii
    replaced by McCone, xli
  files in Dulles collection, xi
  and George Kennan, xxxvi, 166
  hires de Vosjoli to investigate Soviet missiles in Cuba, 200
  influence on Doolittle Report, 165

  with Kennedy and McCone, *ins*
  Nazi alliances, xxx, xxxi, 158, 165
  on policy planning and CIA, 133
  relationship with Mary Bancroft, xxv, 110
  on U.S. embargo of Cuba, 132

E

Earman, Jack, 89
East, Alice Kleberg
  kidnapping of, 19
  marriage of, to Tom East, 17
  son of, avoids military service, 20
East, Tom, 17
Eisenhower, Dwight David
  Adlai Stevenson defeated by, xlvii
  appoints "President's Intelligence Advisory Board," 165
  assistance to Hungarian freedom fighters, denied by, xlix
  biographical overview of, xxx
  and Bragas, 85–86
  Bruce-Lovett Report commissioned by, xii, xxvii, xxxvii, xl, 165
  CIA role in destroying presidency of, xxx
  denied entry to King Ranch centennial, 49
  and Edward Lansdale as secretary of defense, xxxix
  Khrushchev refuses to meet, xxxvii
  and Kleberg Jr., 43, 50, 260n
  replaces Truman as president, xlviii
  "Special Group" of, 132
  on Texan business' influence on domestic policy, 6
El Diario de la Marina (anti-Batista newspaper), 83
El Paso Natural Gas, 5
El Patrón
  . *see* Kleberg, Robert J., Jr. ("Bob")
El Real, 131–132, 134
"El Tigres," xliv
Electronic Data Systems (Ross Perot), 5
Elkins, James, xlix
Ellender, Allen J., xxx, 182
Elliott, Dean, 26
Erie Railroad, xxxii
Escalante, Fabián, xxx, 153–154, 279
Estes, Billie Sol
  biographical overview of, xxx
  on Kleberg's information, 66
  on Lyndon Johnson, 35
EXXON, 7, 29, 46, 249